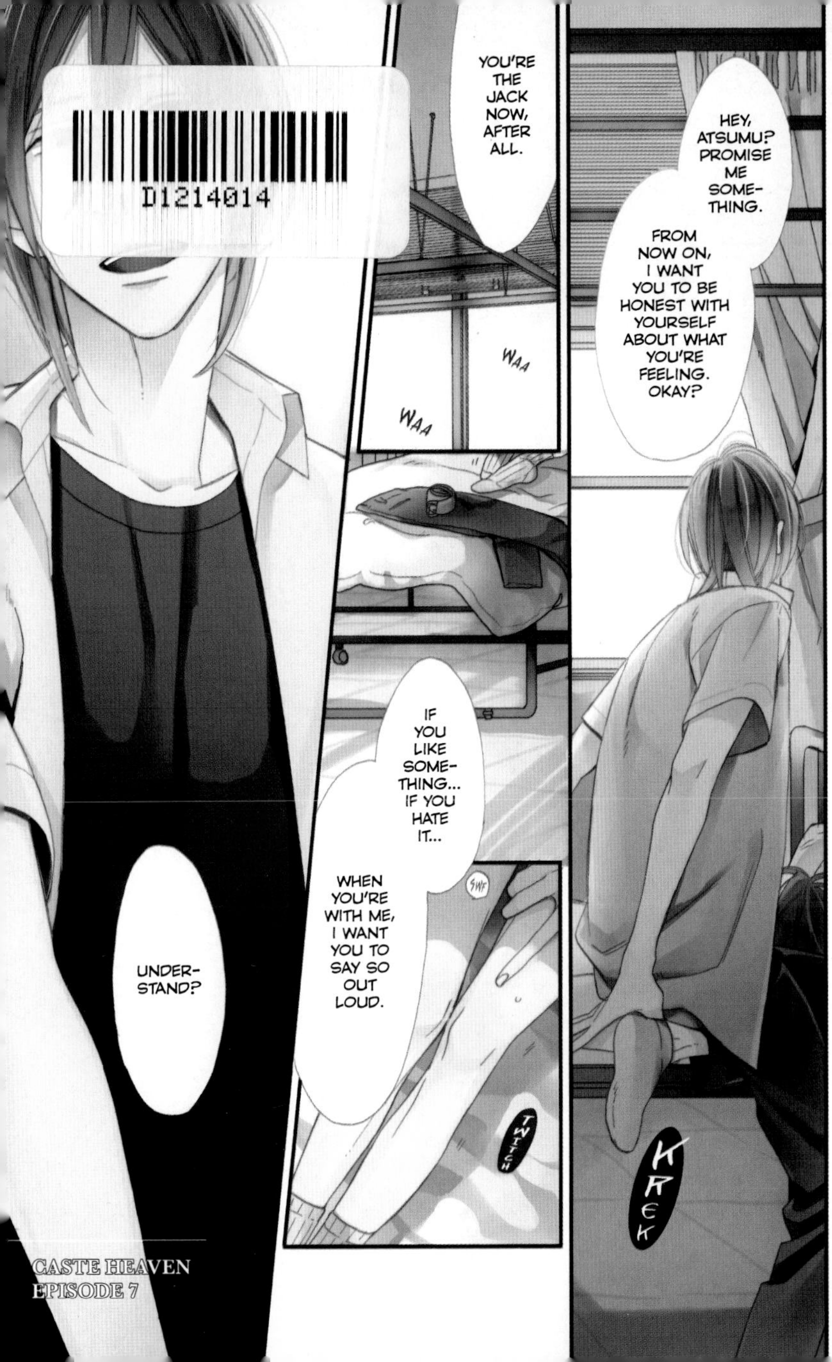
HEY, ATSUMU? PROMISE ME SOME-THING.
FROM NOW ON, I WANT YOU TO BE HONEST WITH YOURSELF ABOUT WHAT YOU'RE FEELING. OKAY?
KREK
YOU'RE THE JACK NOW, AFTER ALL.
WAA
WAA
IF YOU LIKE SOME-THING... IF YOU HATE IT...
WHEN YOU'RE WITH ME, I WANT YOU TO SAY SO OUT LOUD.
SWF
TWITCH
D1214014
UNDER-STAND?

CASTE HEAVEN
EPISODE 7

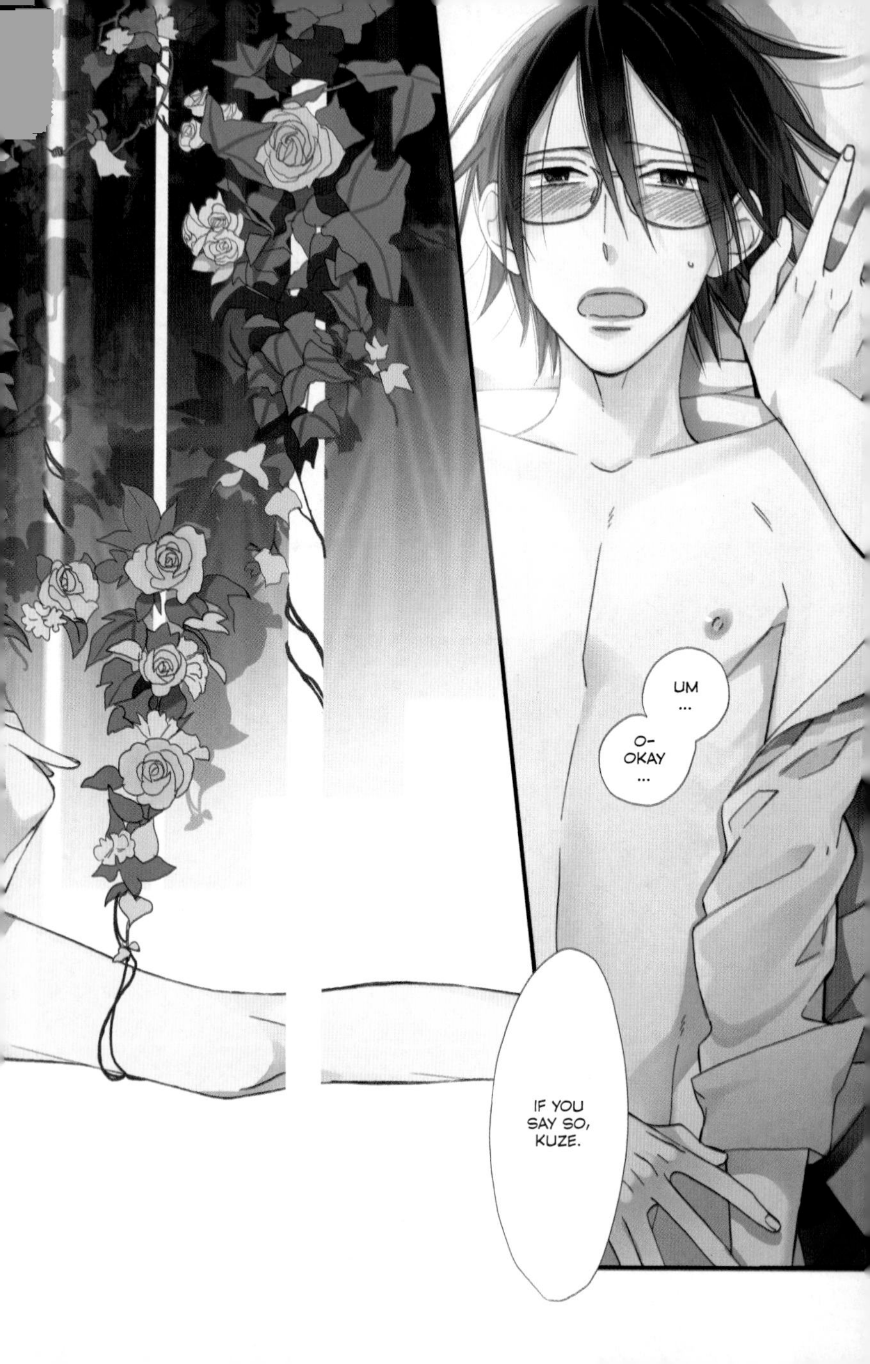
UM... O-OKAY...
IF YOU SAY SO, KUZE.

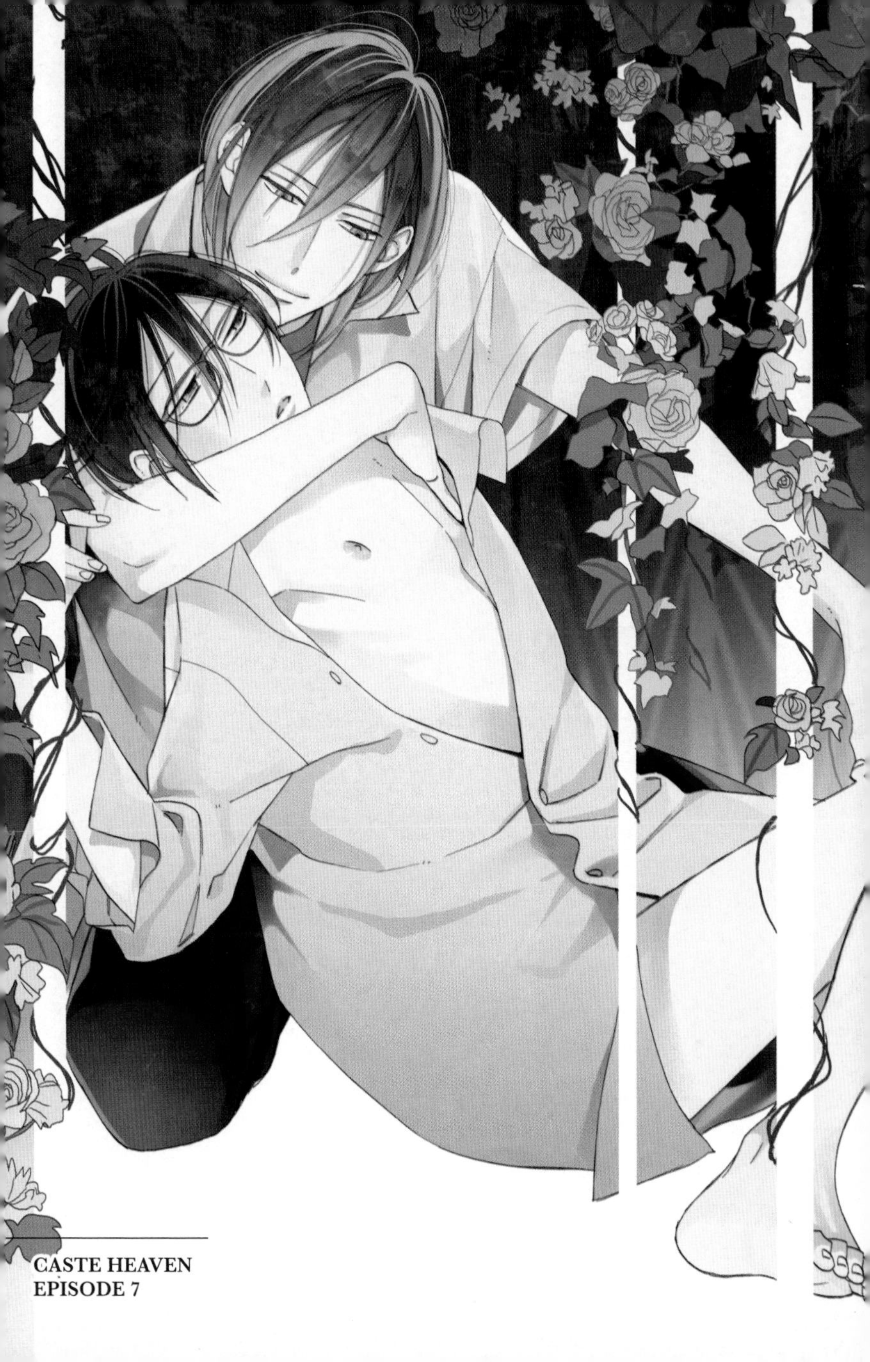

CASTE HEAVEN
EPISODE 7

CONTENTS

Episode 7 — 1

Episode 8 — 41

Episode 9 — 83

Episode 10 — 121

Episode 11 — 161

Behind the Game — 199

Afterword — 205

Caste Heaven

2

CHISE OGAWA

CASTE GAME

RULES

◆ CASTES ARE DETERMINED BY PLAYING CARDS.

THE GAME BEGINS WHEN AN EMPTY BOX OF CARDS IS PLACED ON THE TEACHER'S PODIUM. THAT'S THE SIGNAL TO THAT PARTICULAR CLASS THAT THE CASTE GAME WILL BE PLAYED THAT AFTERNOON AFTER CLASS. STUDENTS MUST FIND ONE OF THE PLAYING CARDS HIDDEN THROUGHOUT THE SCHOOL AND BRING IT BACK. THAT CARD DETERMINES THEIR CASTE.

◆ THOSE IN A LOWER CASTE MUST OBEY THOSE IN A HIGHER ONE.

CASTES ARE ABSOLUTE. ALL STUDENTS ARE REQUIRED TO SUBMIT TO THE RULES OF THEIR CASTE UNTIL THE NEXT TIME THE GAME IS PLAYED.

◆ THOSE WHO CHOOSE NOT TO PARTICIPATE IN THE GAME OR SEEK TO DISRUPT IT WILL BE ASSIGNED THE CASTE OF TARGET BY DEFAULT.

HIERARCHY

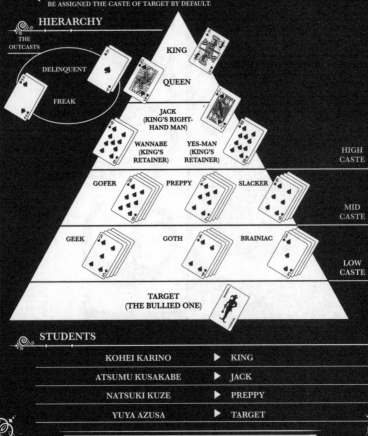

THE OUTCASTS

DELINQUENT

FREAK

KING

QUEEN

JACK (KING'S RIGHT-HAND MAN)

WANNABE (KING'S RETAINER)

YES-MAN (KING'S RETAINER)

HIGH CASTE

GOFER

PREPPY

SLACKER

MID CASTE

GEEK

GOTH

BRAINIAC

LOW CASTE

TARGET (THE BULLIED ONE)

STUDENTS

KOHEI KARINO	▶	KING
ATSUMU KUSAKABE	▶	JACK
NATSUKI KUZE	▶	PREPPY
YUYA AZUSA	▶	TARGET

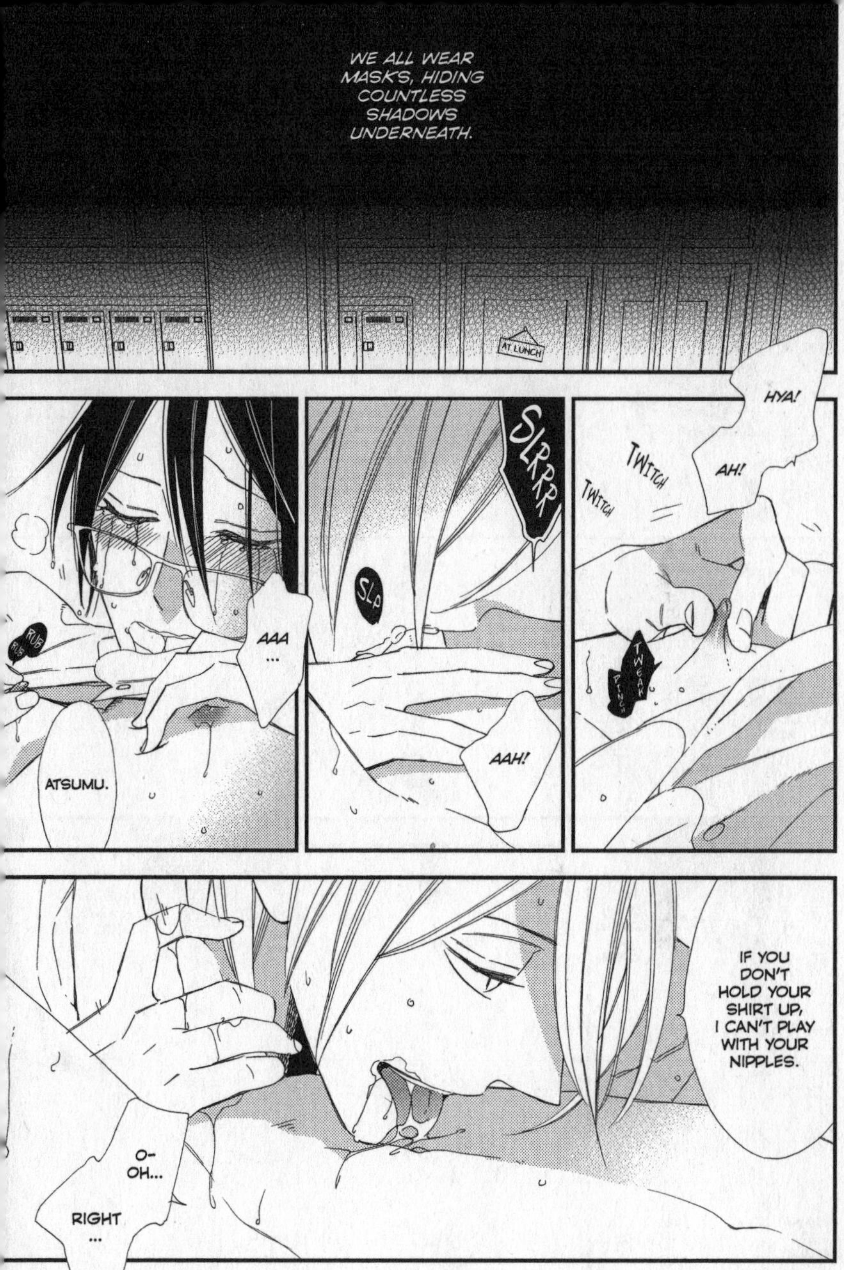
WE ALL WEAR MASKS, HIDING COUNTLESS SHADOWS UNDERNEATH.
AT LUNCH
HYA!
AH!
TWITCH
TWITCH
TWEAK
PINCH
SLRRR
SLP
AAH!
AAA ...
RUB
RUB
ATSUMU.
IF YOU DON'T HOLD YOUR SHIRT UP, I CAN'T PLAY WITH YOUR NIPPLES.
O- OH... RIGHT ...

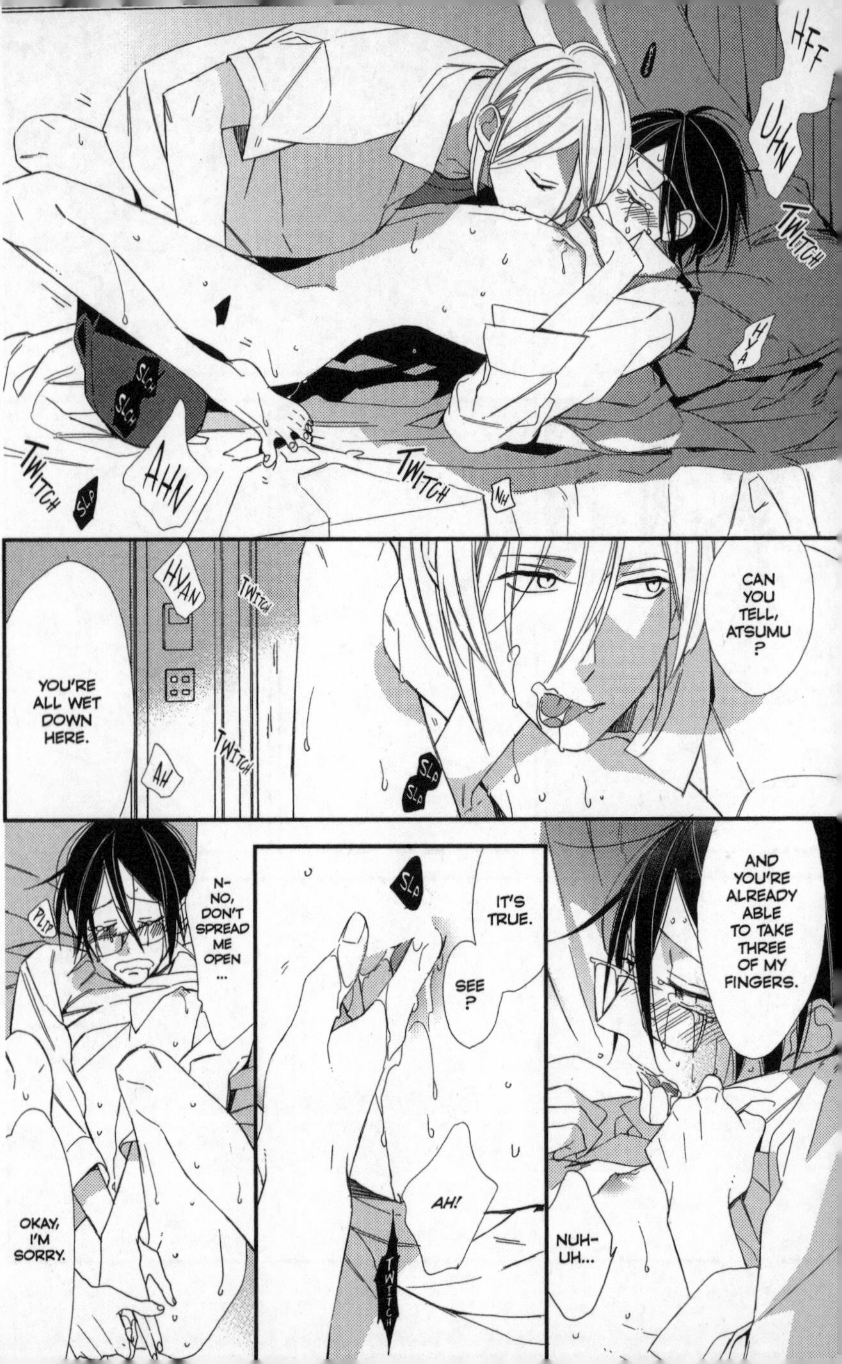
HFF
UHN
TWITCH
!
HYA
SLCH SLCH
TWITCH
NH
AHN
SLP
TWITCH
CAN YOU TELL, ATSUMU?
SLP SLP
TWITCH
HYAN
YOU'RE ALL WET DOWN HERE.
TWITCH
AH
AND YOU'RE ALREADY ABLE TO TAKE THREE OF MY FINGERS.
NUH-UH...
SLP
IT'S TRUE.
SEE?
AH!
TWITCH
N-NO, DON'T SPREAD ME OPEN...
PLIP
OKAY, I'M SORRY.

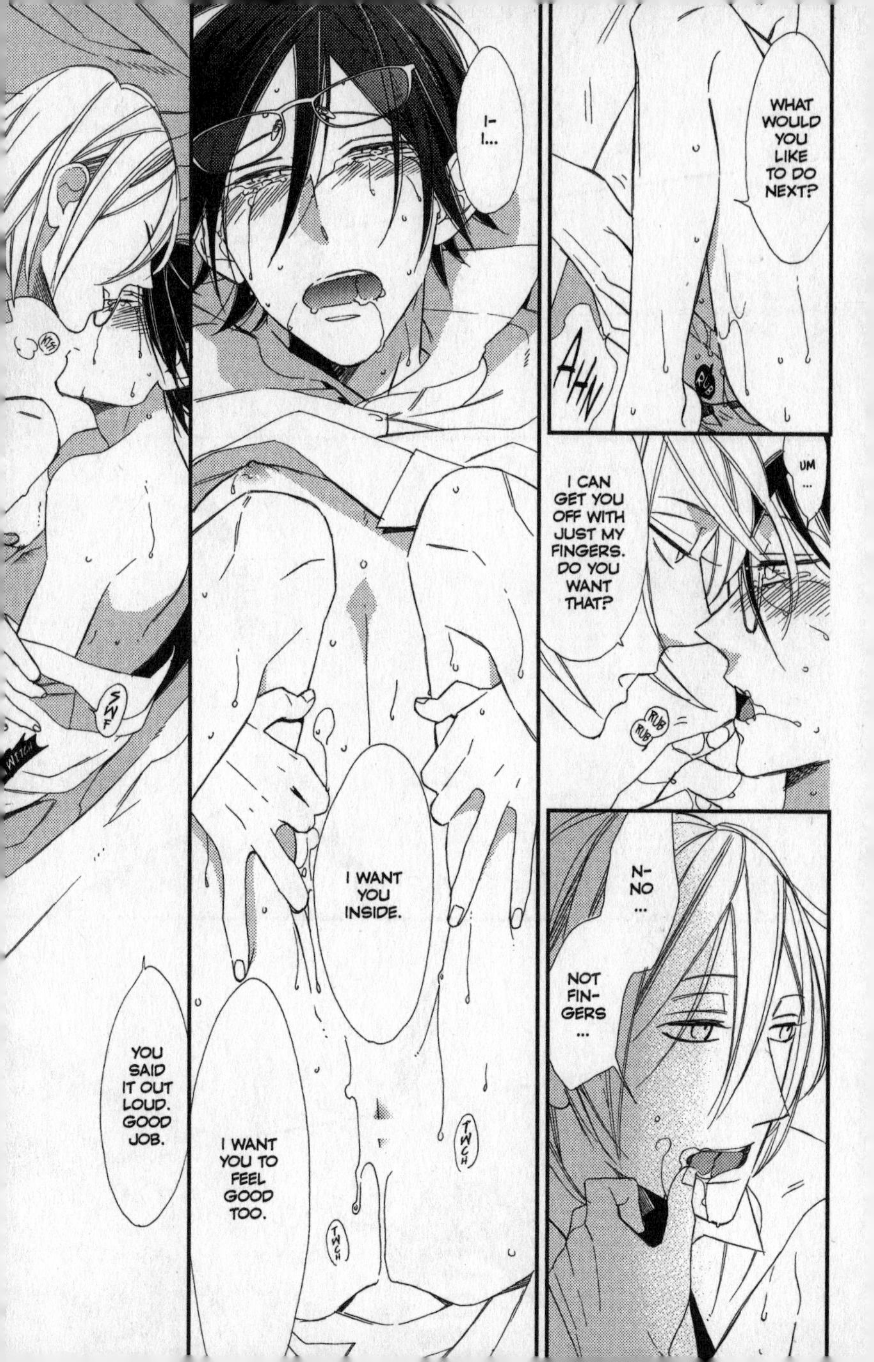

WHAT WOULD YOU LIKE TO DO NEXT?
AHN
RUB
UM ...
I CAN GET YOU OFF WITH JUST MY FINGERS. DO YOU WANT THAT?
RUB RUB
N-NO ...
NOT FIN-GERS ...
I- I...
I WANT YOU INSIDE.
TWCH
I WANT YOU TO FEEL GOOD TOO.
TWCH
SWF
YOU SAID IT OUT LOUD. GOOD JOB.

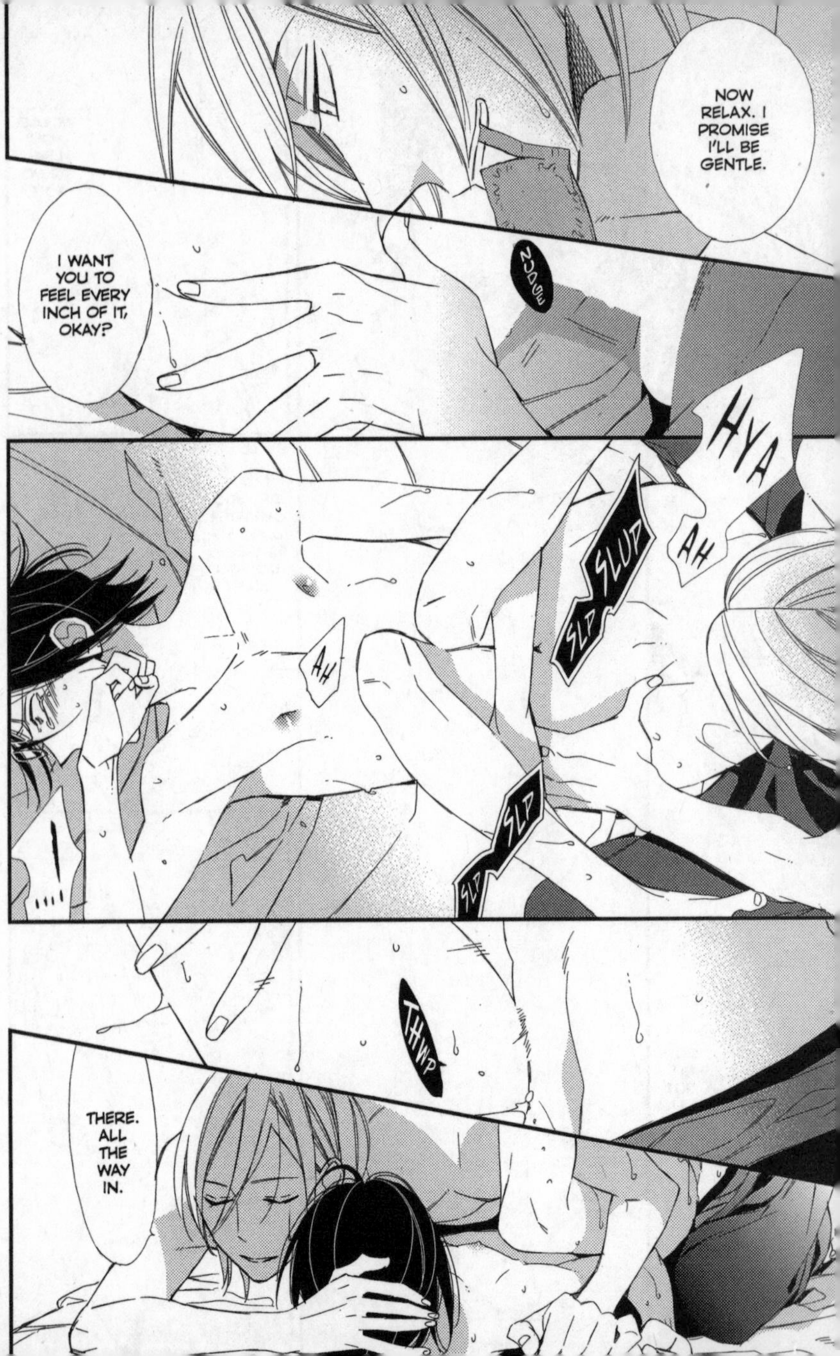
NOW RELAX. I PROMISE I'LL BE GENTLE.
NUDGE
I WANT YOU TO FEEL EVERY INCH OF IT, OKAY?
HYA
AH
SLUP
SLP
AH
SLP
SLP
SLP
THWP
THERE. ALL THE WAY IN.

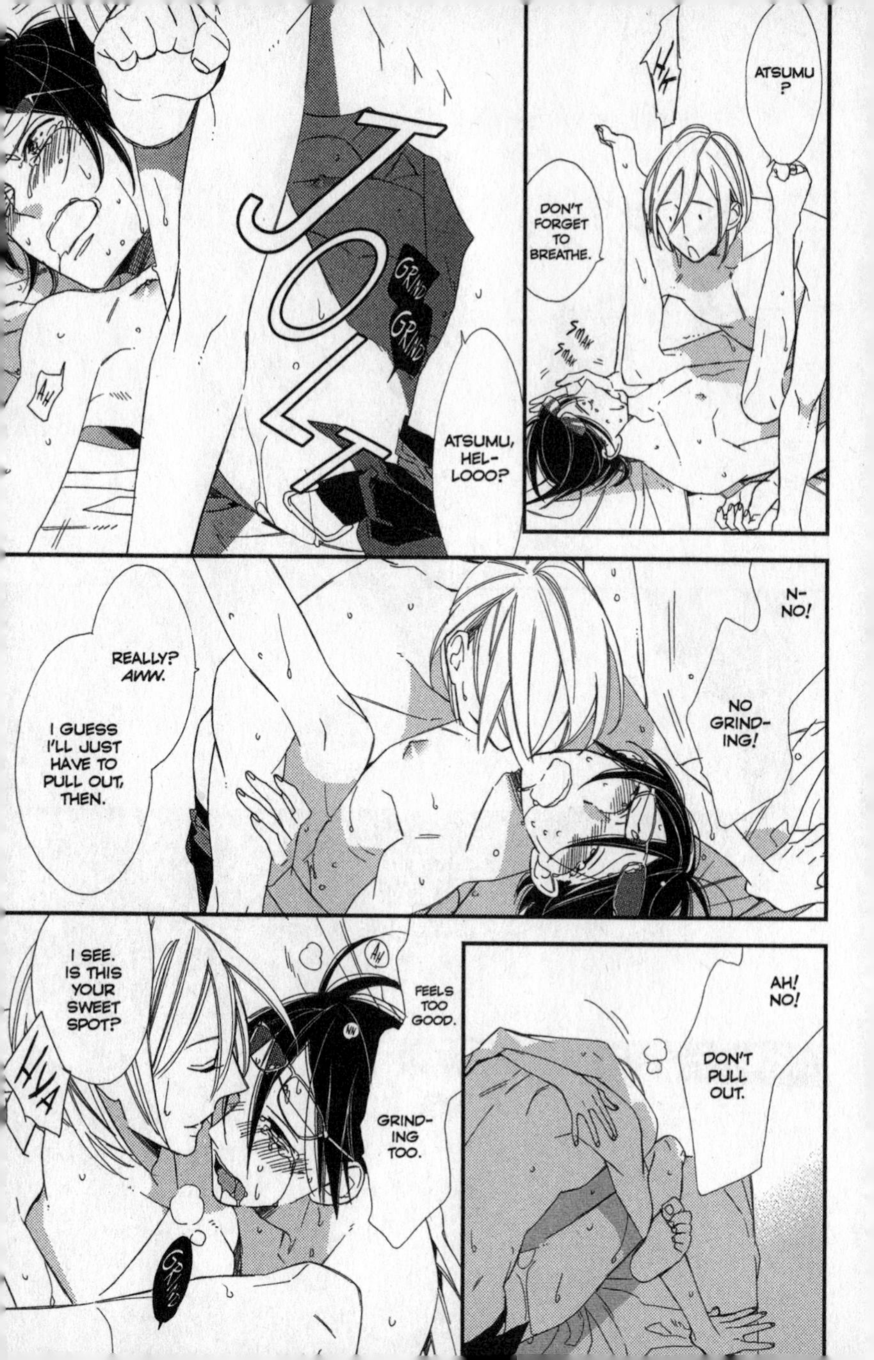
ATSUMU?
HK
DON'T FORGET TO BREATHE.
SMAK SMAK
ATSUMU, HEL-LOOO?
JOLT
GRIND GRIND
AH
N-NO!
NO GRIND-ING!
REALLY? AWW.
I GUESS I'LL JUST HAVE TO PULL OUT, THEN.
AH! NO!
DON'T PULL OUT.
AH
FEELS TOO GOOD.
NN
GRIND-ING TOO.
I SEE. IS THIS YOUR SWEET SPOT?
HYA
GRIND

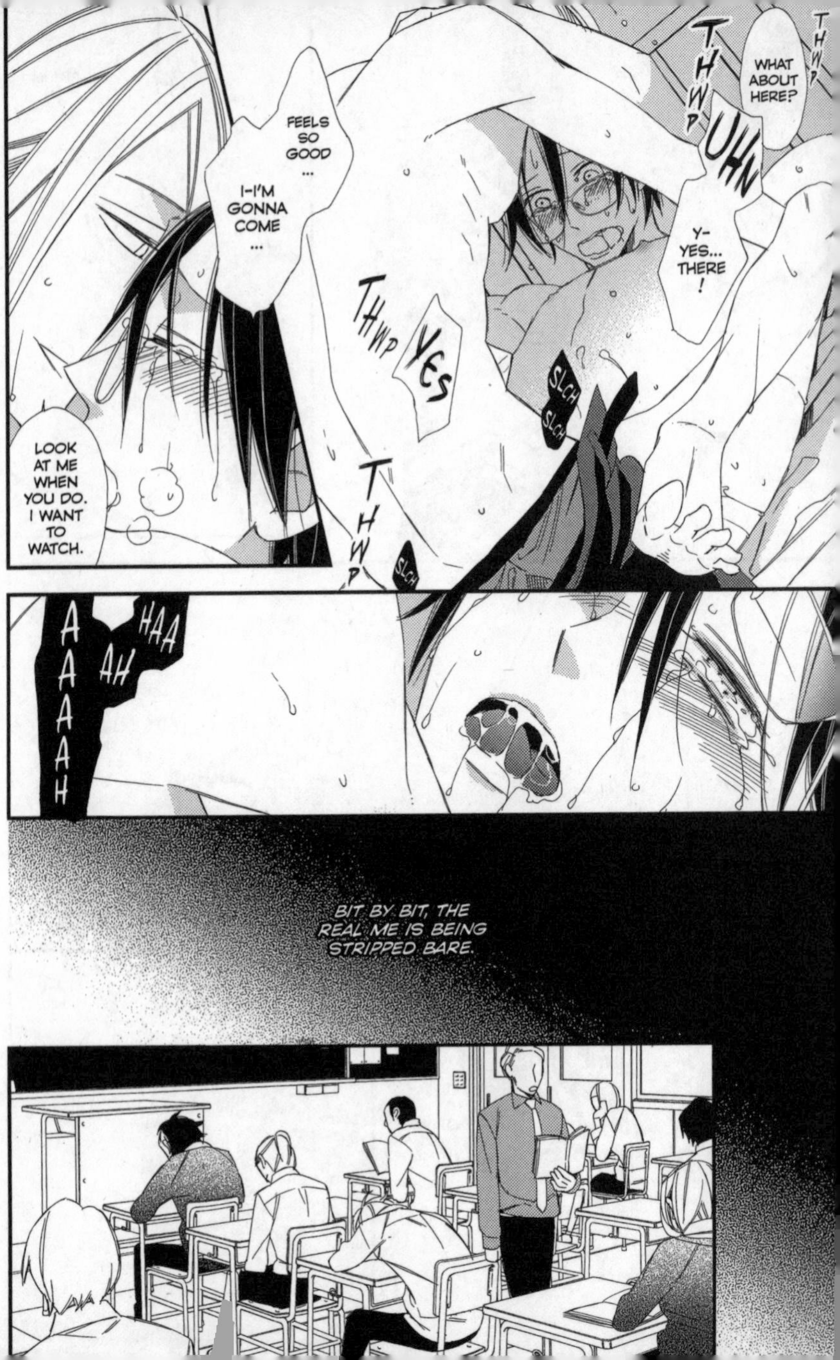
THWP
WHAT ABOUT HERE?
THWP
UHN
Y-YES... THERE!
FEELS SO GOOD...
I-I'M GONNA COME...
THWP
YES
SLCH SLCH
THWP
SLCH
LOOK AT ME WHEN YOU DO. I WANT TO WATCH.
HAA
AH
AAAAAAH
BIT BY BIT, THE REAL ME IS BEING STRIPPED BARE.

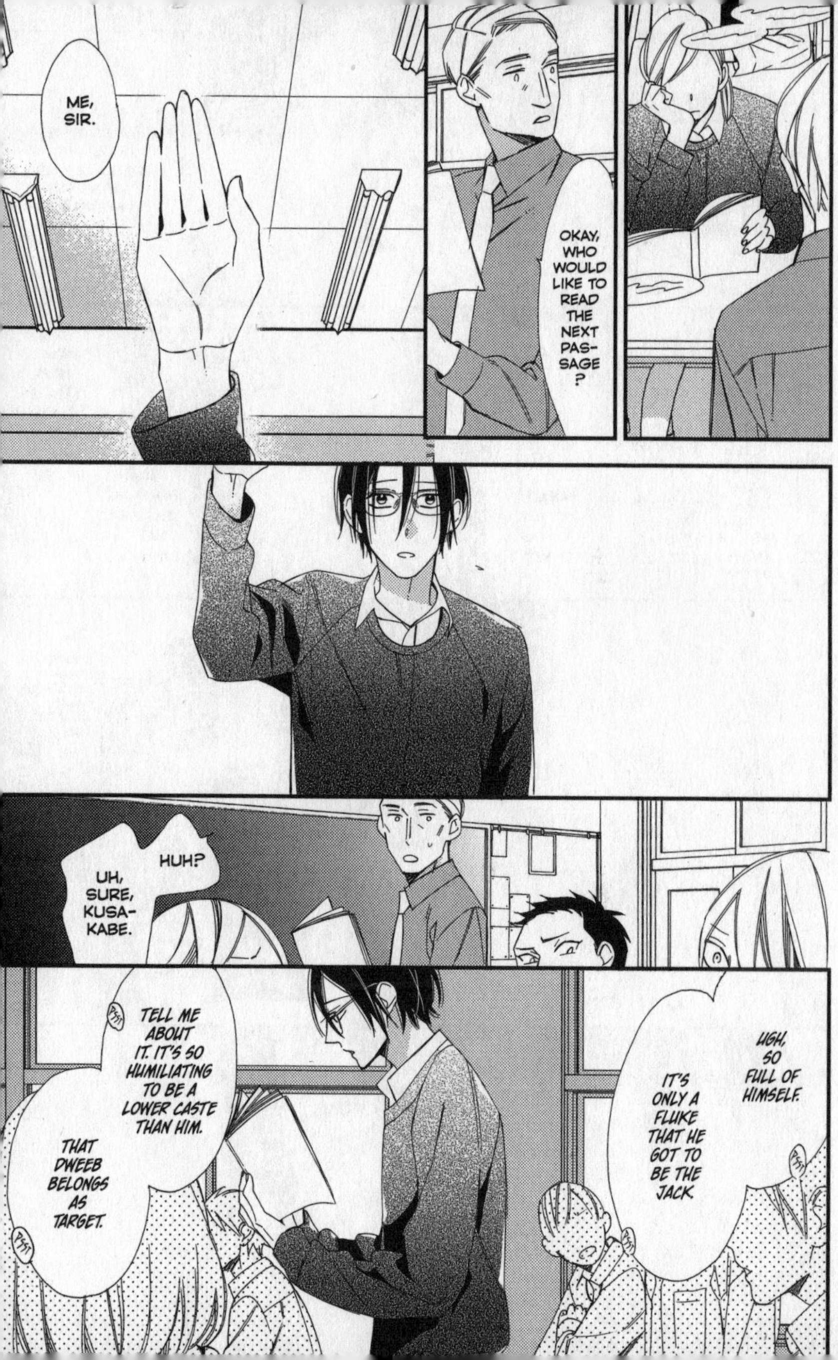
OKAY, WHO WOULD LIKE TO READ THE NEXT PAS-SAGE?
ME, SIR.
HUH?
UH, SURE, KUSA-KABE.
UGH, SO FULL OF HIMSELF.
IT'S ONLY A FLUKE THAT HE GOT TO BE THE JACK.
TELL ME ABOUT IT. IT'S SO HUMILIATING TO BE A LOWER CASTE THAN HIM.
THAT DWEEB BELONGS AS TARGET.

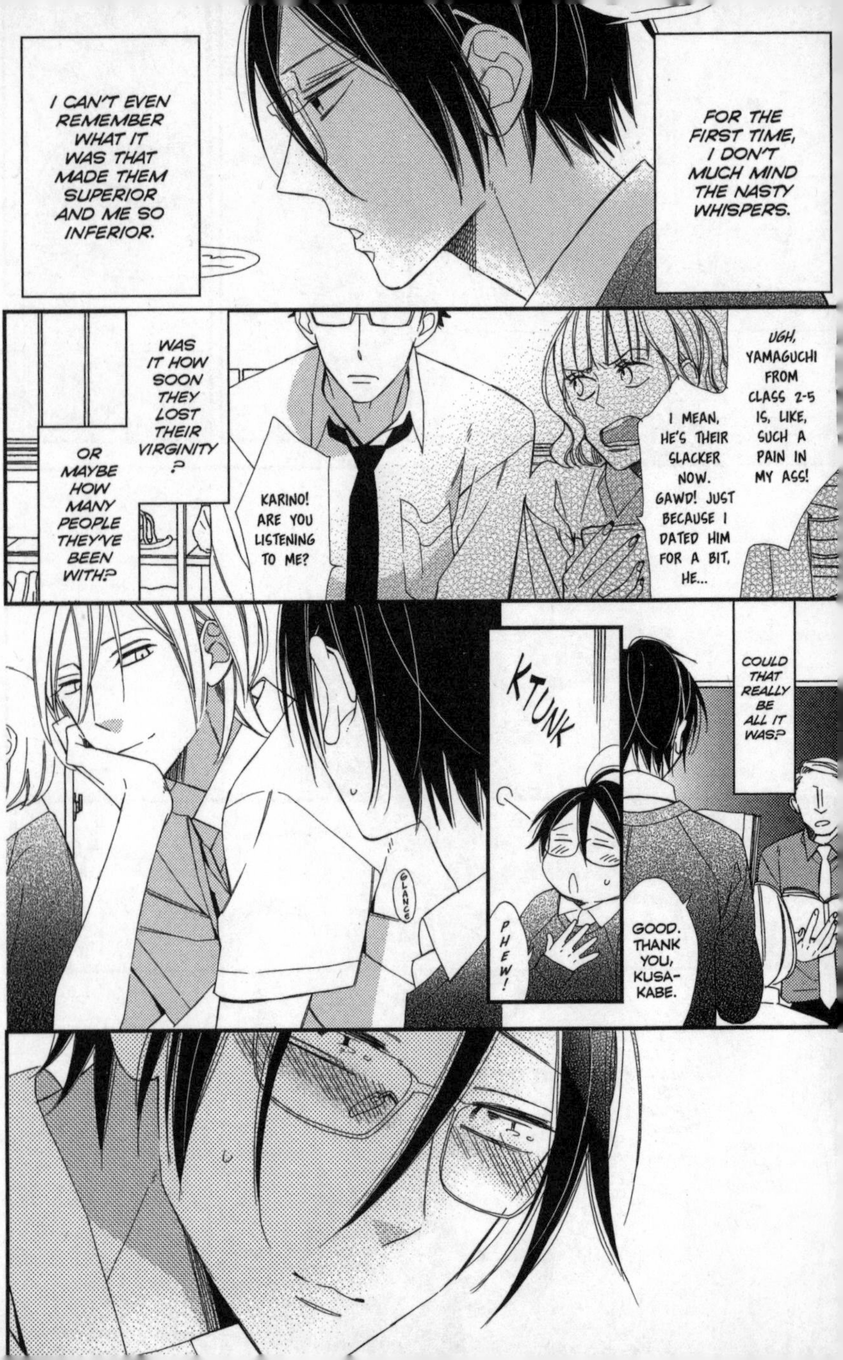
FOR THE FIRST TIME, I DON'T MUCH MIND THE NASTY WHISPERS.
I CAN'T EVEN REMEMBER WHAT IT WAS THAT MADE THEM SUPERIOR AND ME SO INFERIOR.
UGH, YAMAGUCHI FROM CLASS 2-5 IS, LIKE, SUCH A PAIN IN MY ASS!
I MEAN, HE'S THEIR SLACKER NOW. GAWD! JUST BECAUSE I DATED HIM FOR A BIT, HE...
KARINO! ARE YOU LISTENING TO ME?
WAS IT HOW SOON THEY LOST THEIR VIRGINITY?
OR MAYBE HOW MANY PEOPLE THEY'VE BEEN WITH?
COULD THAT REALLY BE ALL IT WAS?
KTUNK
GOOD. THANK YOU, KUSA-KABE.
PHEW!
GLANCE

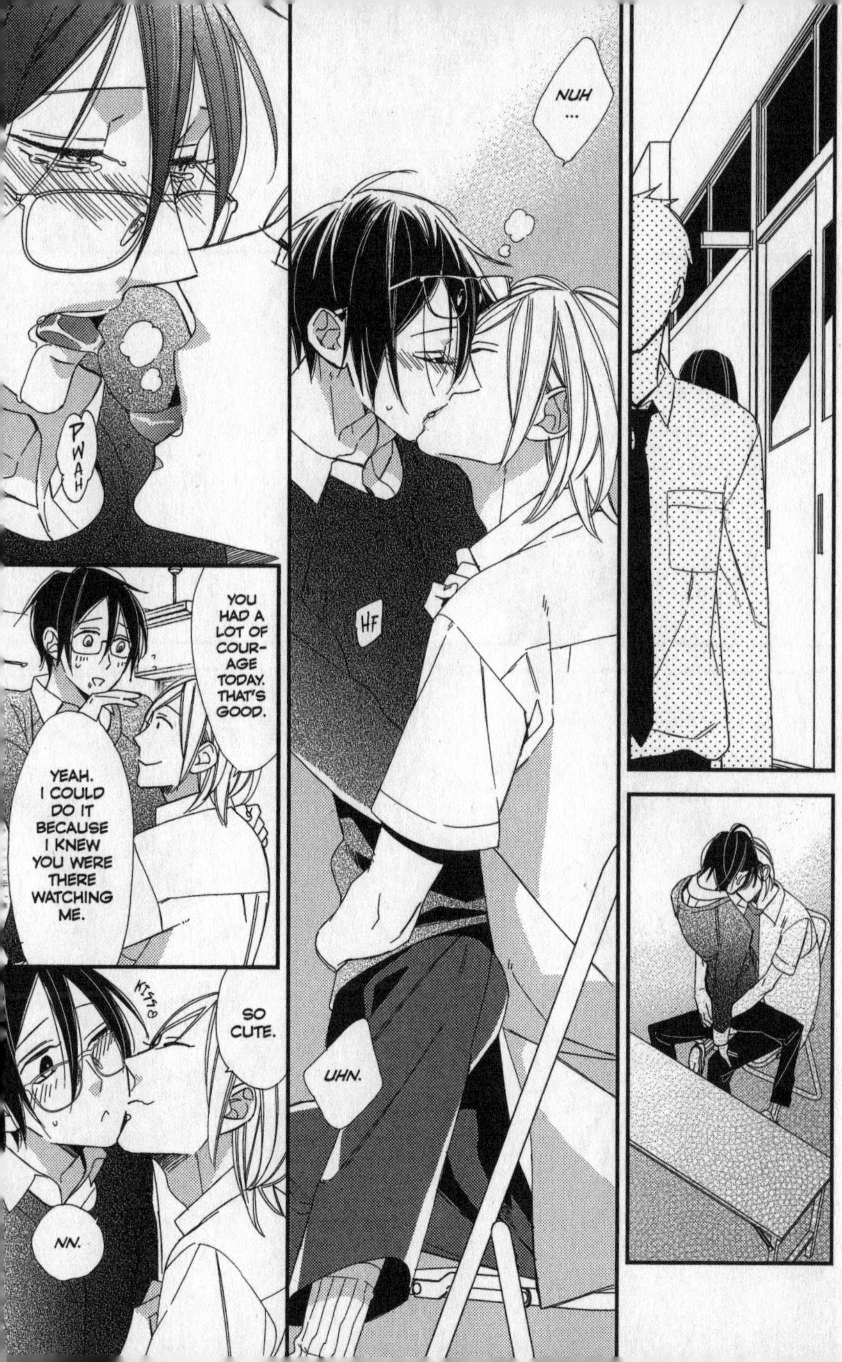
NUH ...
HF
UHN.
PWAH
YOU HAD A LOT OF COURAGE TODAY. THAT'S GOOD.
YEAH. I COULD DO IT BECAUSE I KNEW YOU WERE THERE WATCHING ME.
KISS
SO CUTE.
NN.

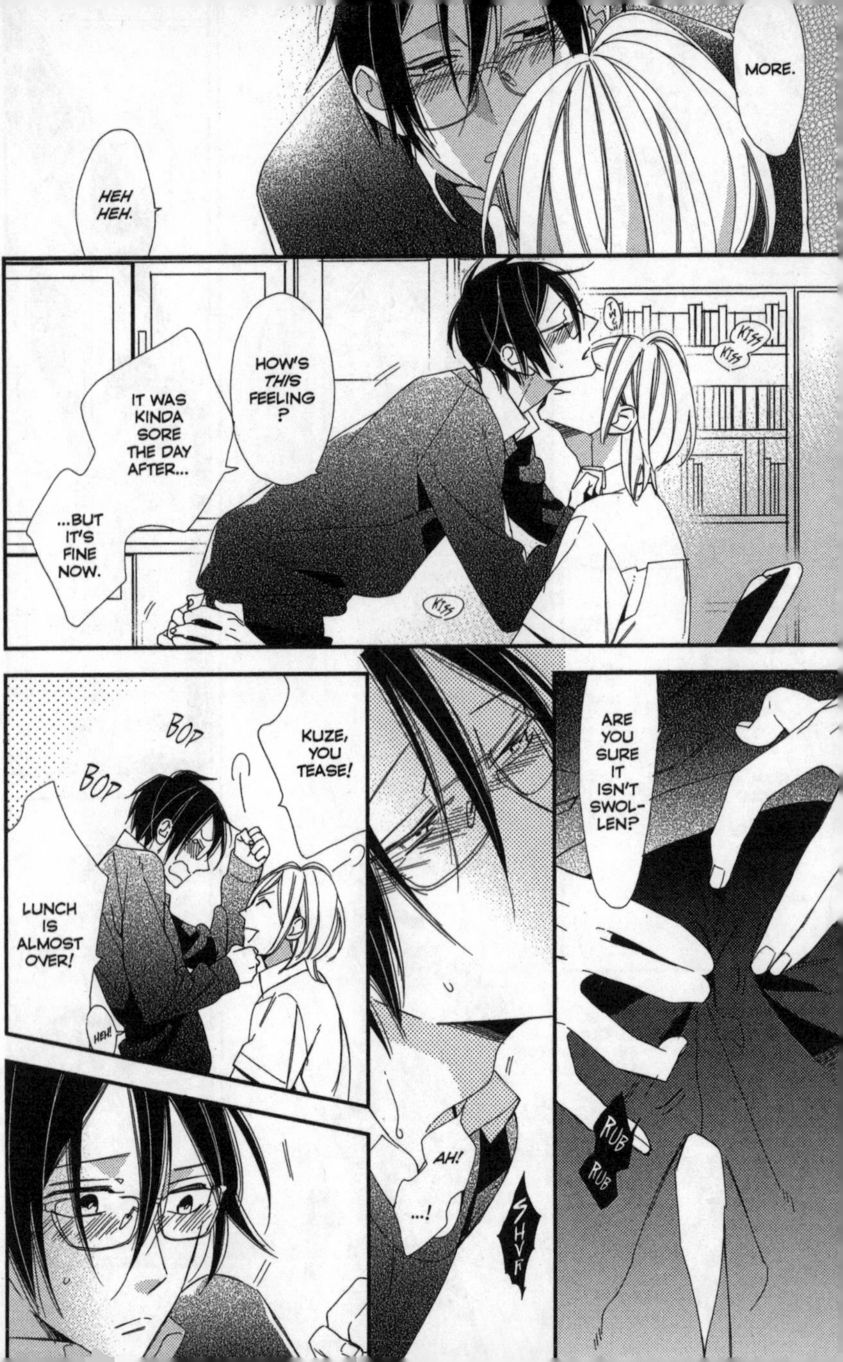
MORE.
HEH HEH.
KISS KISS
HOW'S THIS FEELING?
IT WAS KINDA SORE THE DAY AFTER...
...BUT IT'S FINE NOW.
KISS
ARE YOU SURE IT ISN'T SWOL-LEN?
RUB RUB
SHVF
AH!
...!
KUZE, YOU TEASE!
BOP BOP
LUNCH IS ALMOST OVER!
HEH!

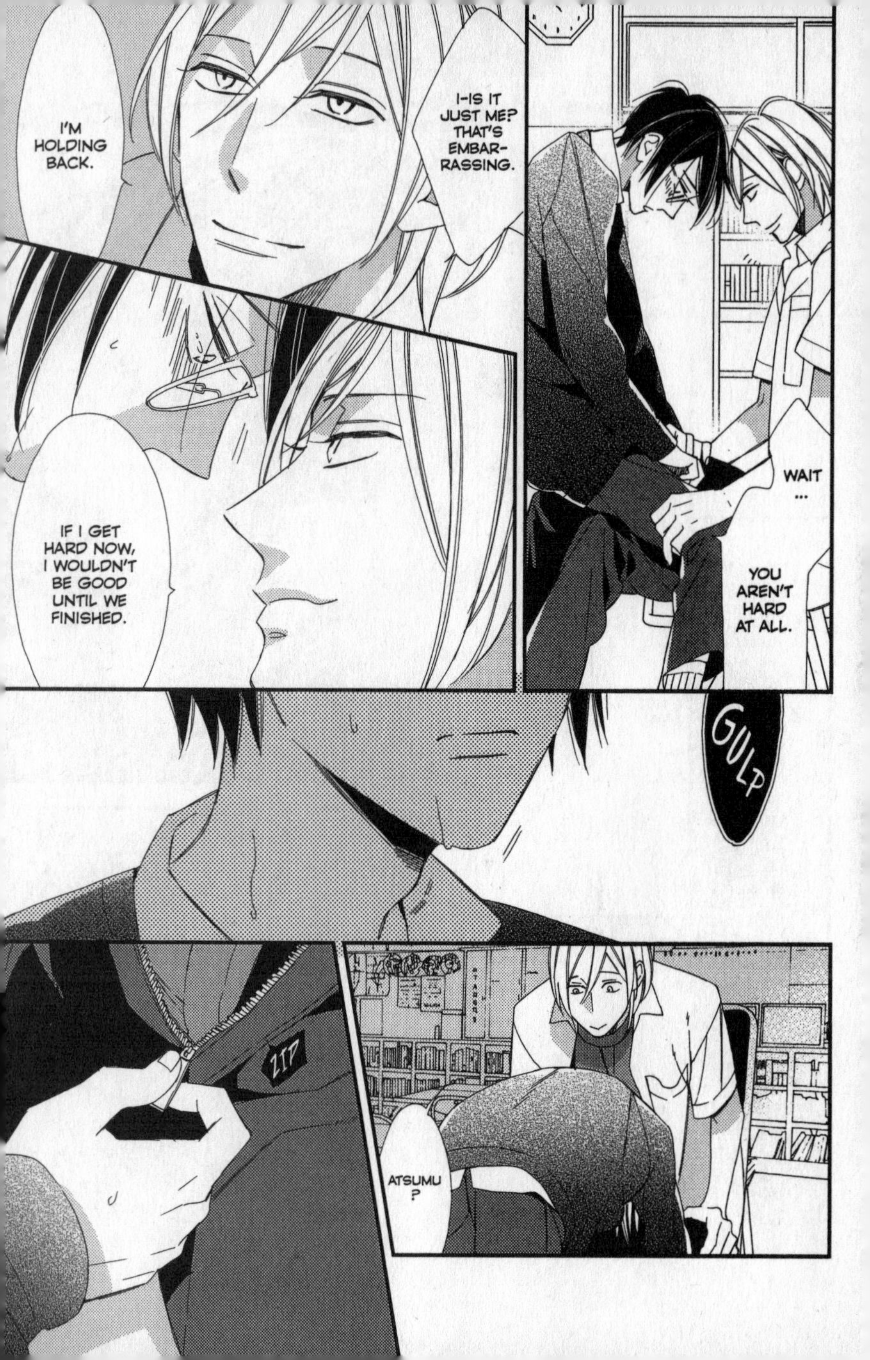
WAIT ...
YOU AREN'T HARD AT ALL.
I-IS IT JUST ME? THAT'S EMBAR-RASSING.
I'M HOLDING BACK.
IF I GET HARD NOW, I WOULDN'T BE GOOD UNTIL WE FINISHED.
GULP
ATSUMU ?
ZIP

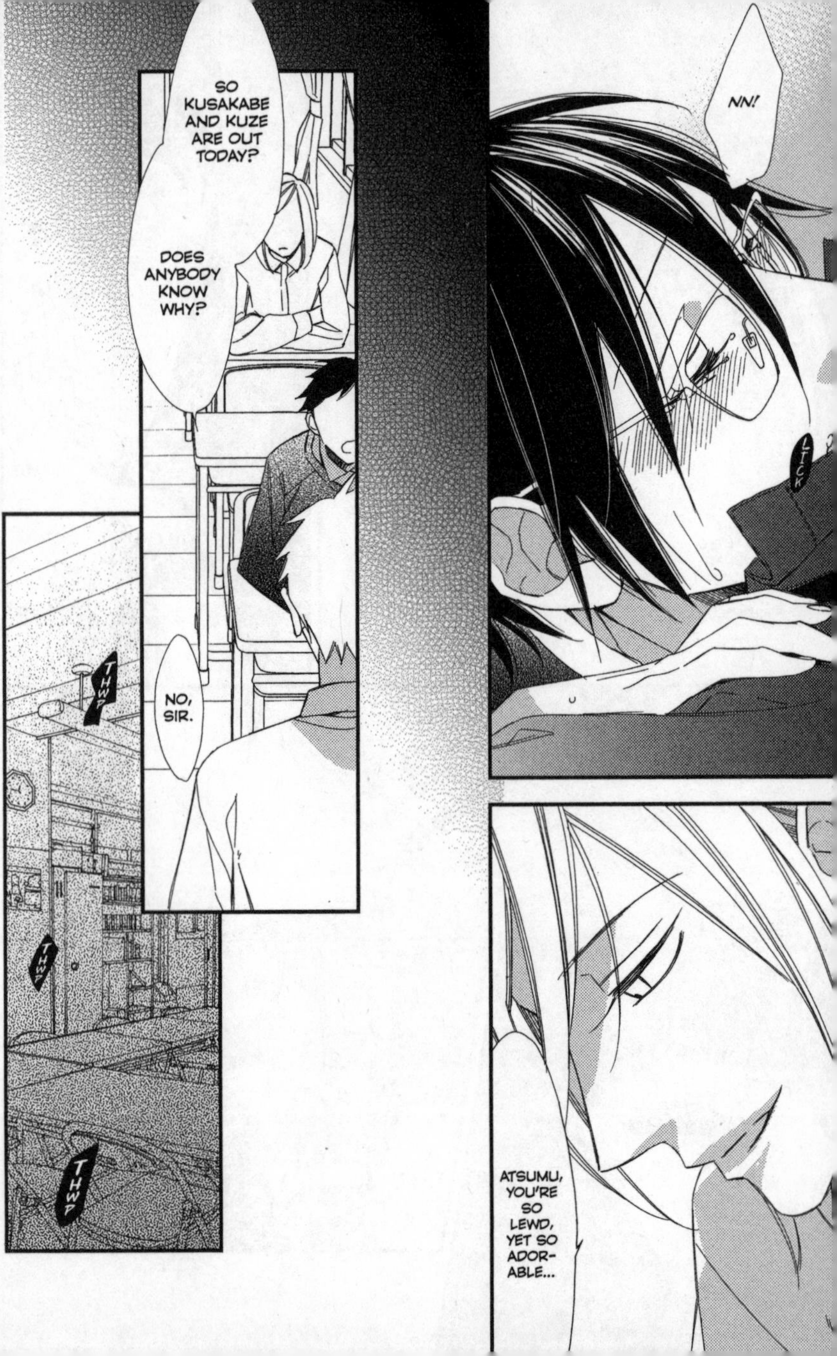
NN!
LICK
ATSUMU, YOU'RE SO LEWD, YET SO ADOR-ABLE...
SO KUSAKABE AND KUZE ARE OUT TODAY?
DOES ANYBODY KNOW WHY?
NO, SIR.
THWP
THWP
THWP

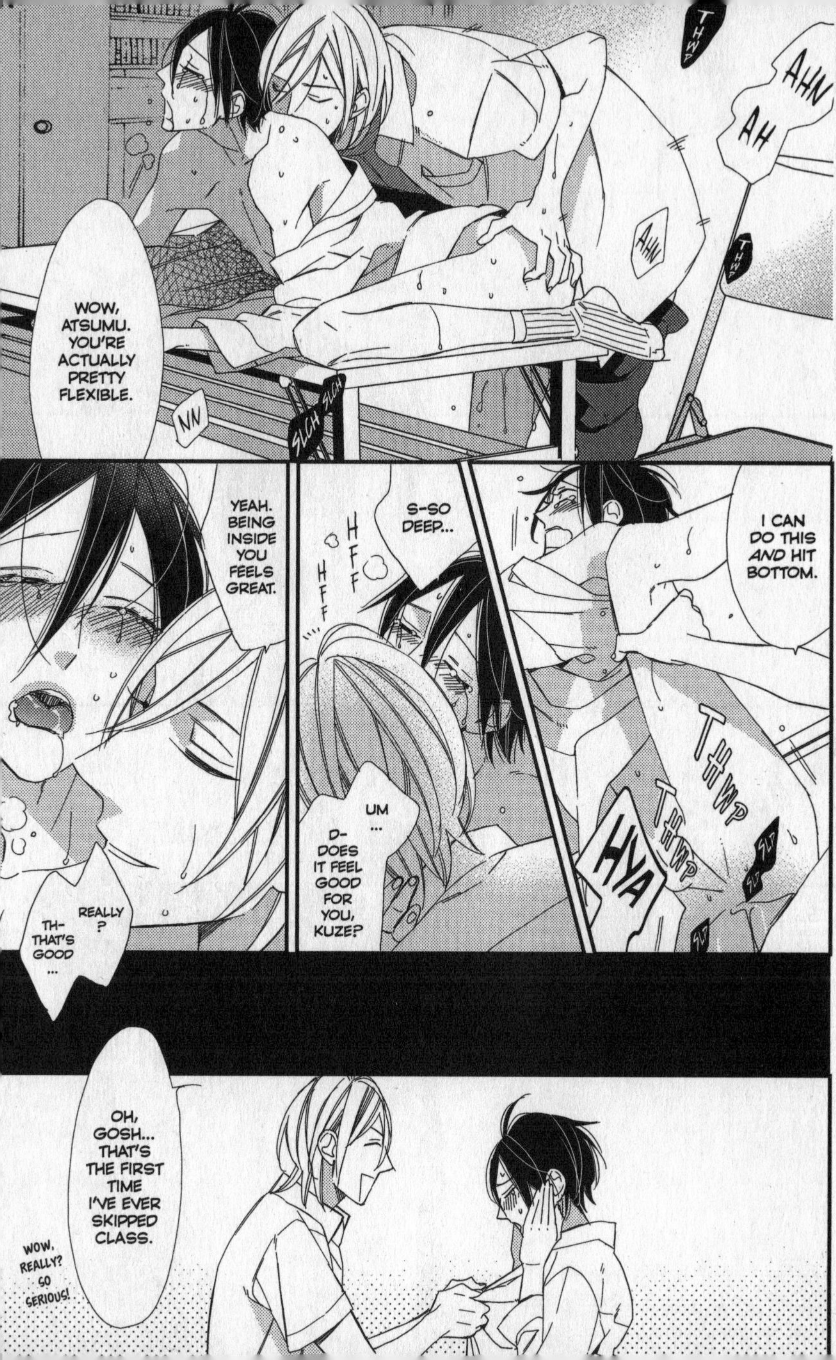
THWP
AHN AH
AHN
THWP
WOW, ATSUMU. YOU'RE ACTUALLY PRETTY FLEXIBLE.
NN
SLCH SLCH
I CAN DO THIS *AND* HIT BOTTOM.
THWP THWP THWP
HYA
SLP SLP SLP
S-SO DEEP...
HFF HFF
UM... D-DOES IT FEEL GOOD FOR YOU, KUZE?
YEAH. BEING INSIDE YOU FEELS GREAT.
REALLY? TH-THAT'S GOOD...
OH, GOSH... THAT'S THE FIRST TIME I'VE EVER SKIPPED CLASS.
WOW, REALLY? SO SERIOUS!

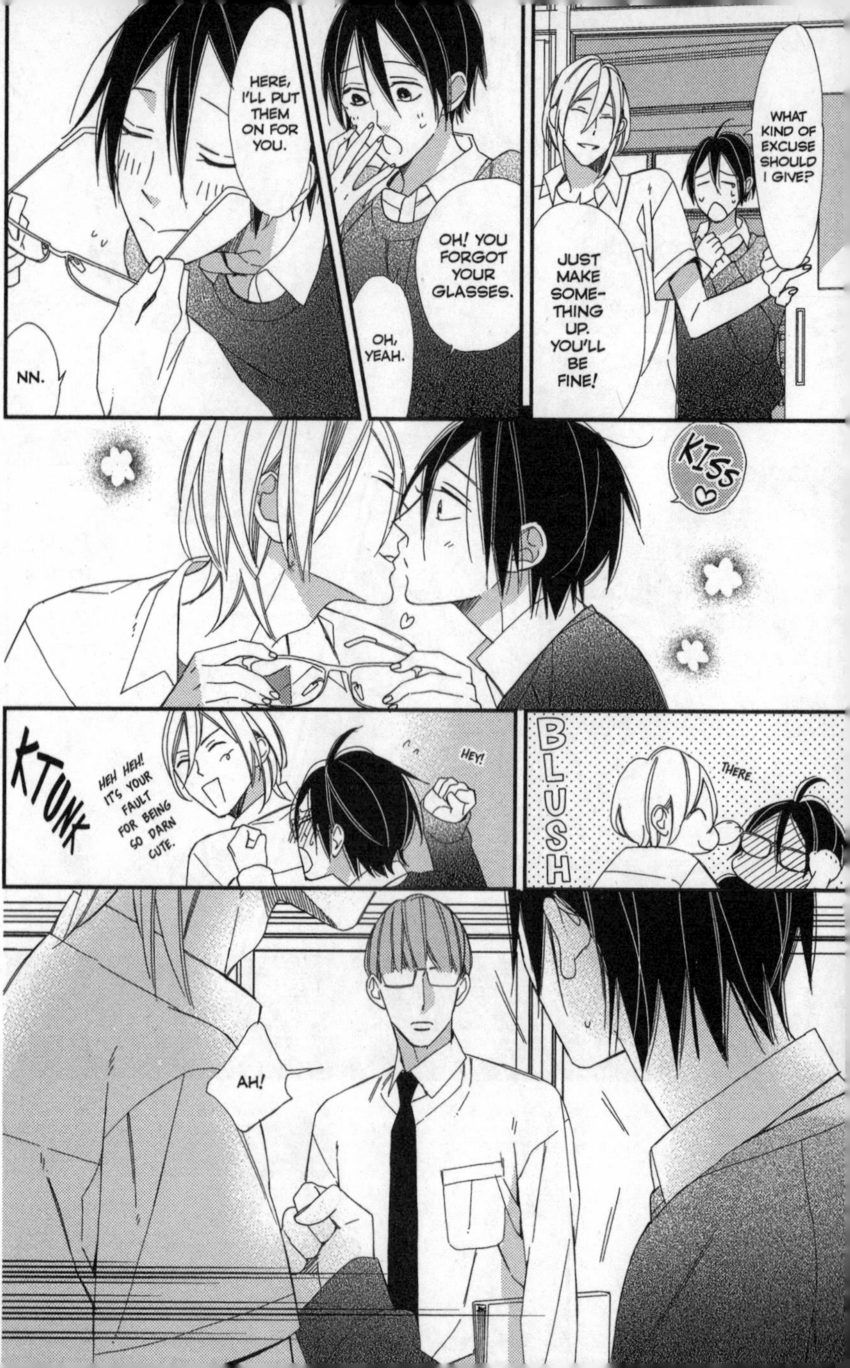
WHAT KIND OF EXCUSE SHOULD I GIVE?
JUST MAKE SOME-THING UP. YOU'LL BE FINE!
OH! YOU FORGOT YOUR GLASSES.
OH, YEAH.
HERE, I'LL PUT THEM ON FOR YOU.
NN.
KISS
BLUSH
THERE.
HEY!
HEH HEH! IT'S YOUR FAULT FOR BEING SO DARN CUTE.
KTONK
AH!

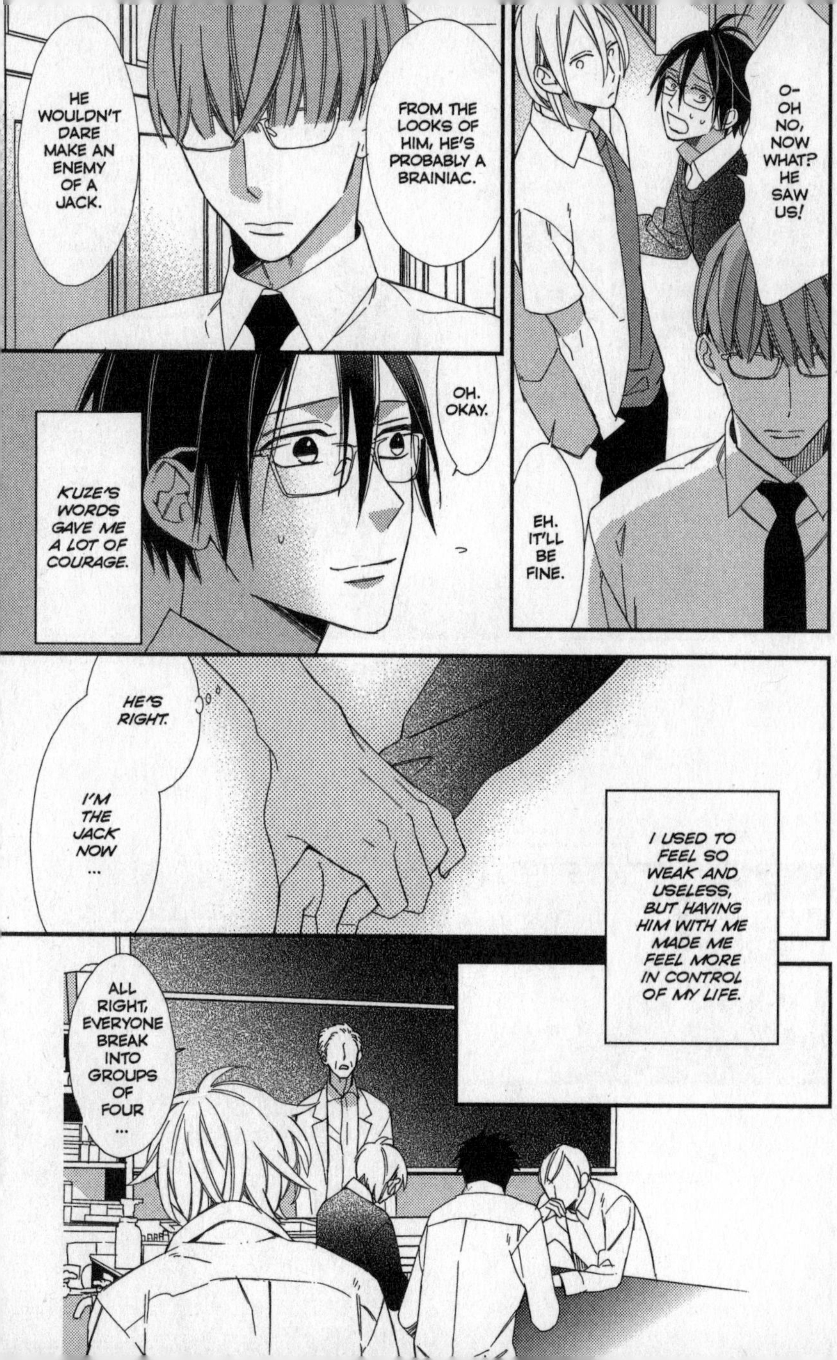
O-OH NO, NOW WHAT? HE SAW US!
EH. IT'LL BE FINE.
FROM THE LOOKS OF HIM, HE'S PROBABLY A BRAINIAC.
HE WOULDN'T DARE MAKE AN ENEMY OF A JACK.
OH. OKAY.
KUZE'S WORDS GAVE ME A LOT OF COURAGE.
I USED TO FEEL SO WEAK AND USELESS, BUT HAVING HIM WITH ME MADE ME FEEL MORE IN CONTROL OF MY LIFE.
HE'S RIGHT.
I'M THE JACK NOW ...
ALL RIGHT, EVERYONE BREAK INTO GROUPS OF FOUR ...

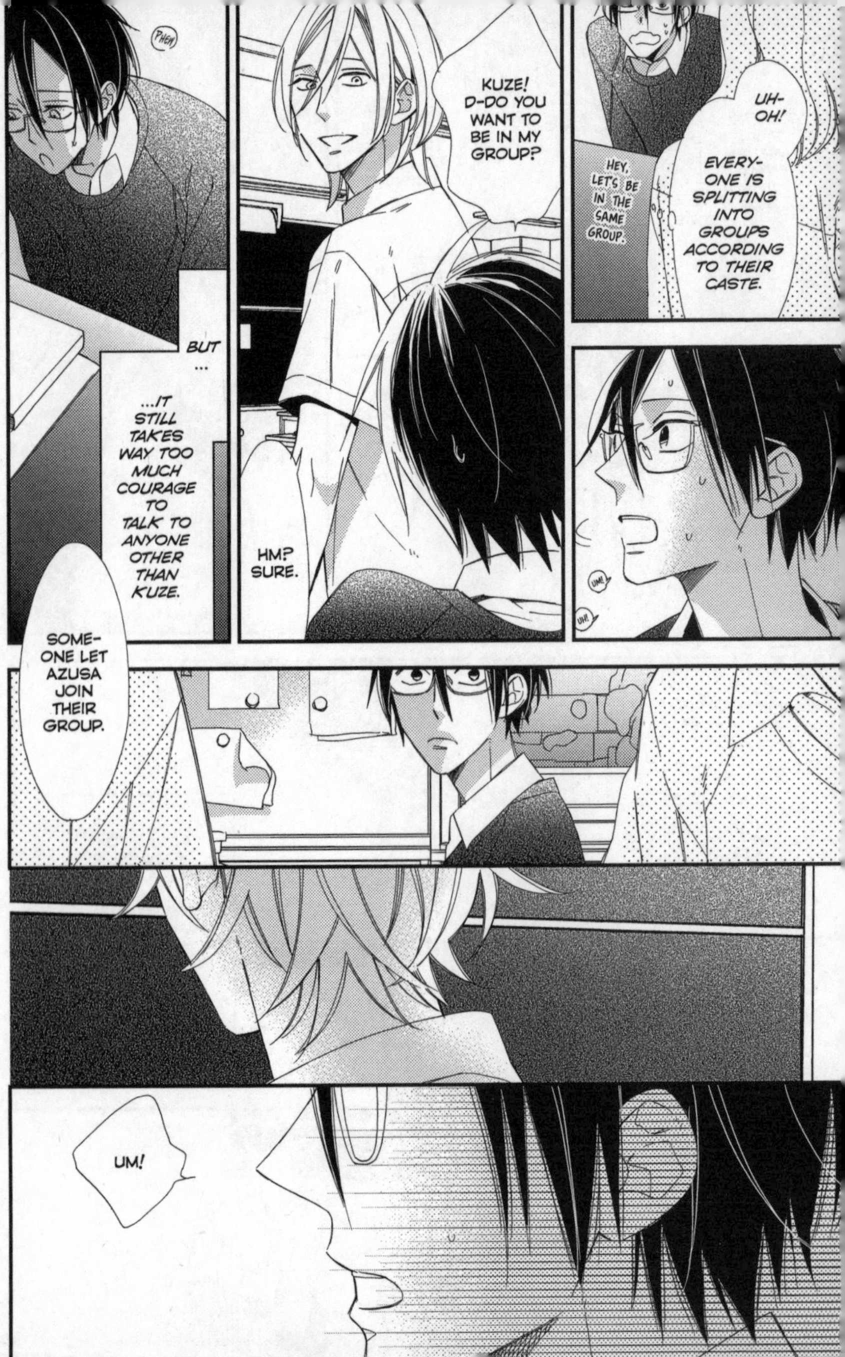
UH-OH!
EVERY-ONE IS SPLITTING INTO GROUPS ACCORDING TO THEIR CASTE.
HEY, LET'S BE IN THE SAME GROUP.
UM!
UH!
KUZE! D-DO YOU WANT TO BE IN MY GROUP?
HM? SURE.
PHEW
BUT ...
...IT STILL TAKES WAY TOO MUCH COURAGE TO TALK TO ANYONE OTHER THAN KUZE.
SOME-ONE LET AZUSA JOIN THEIR GROUP.
UM!

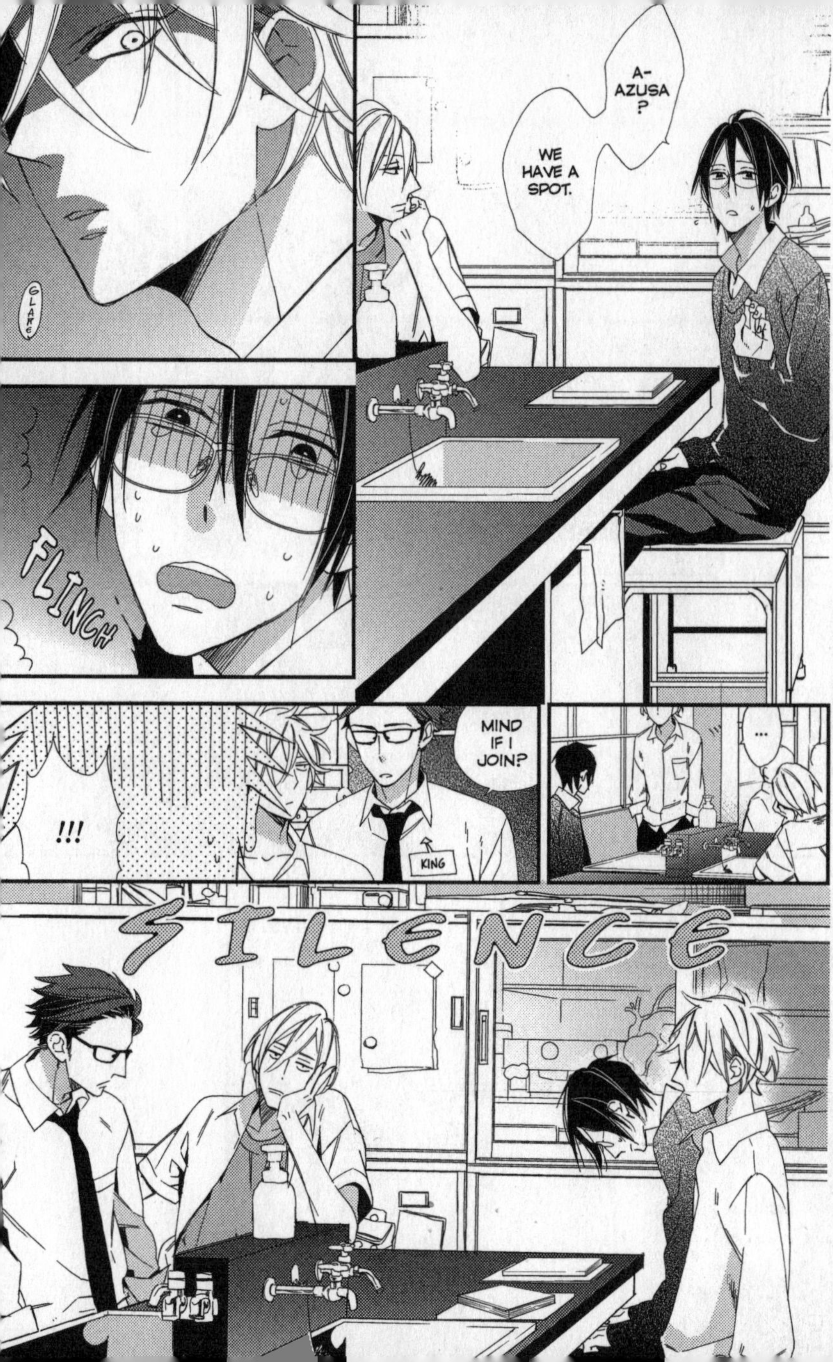
A-AZUSA?
WE HAVE A SPOT.
GLARE
FLINCH
...
MIND IF I JOIN?
KING
!!!
SILENCE

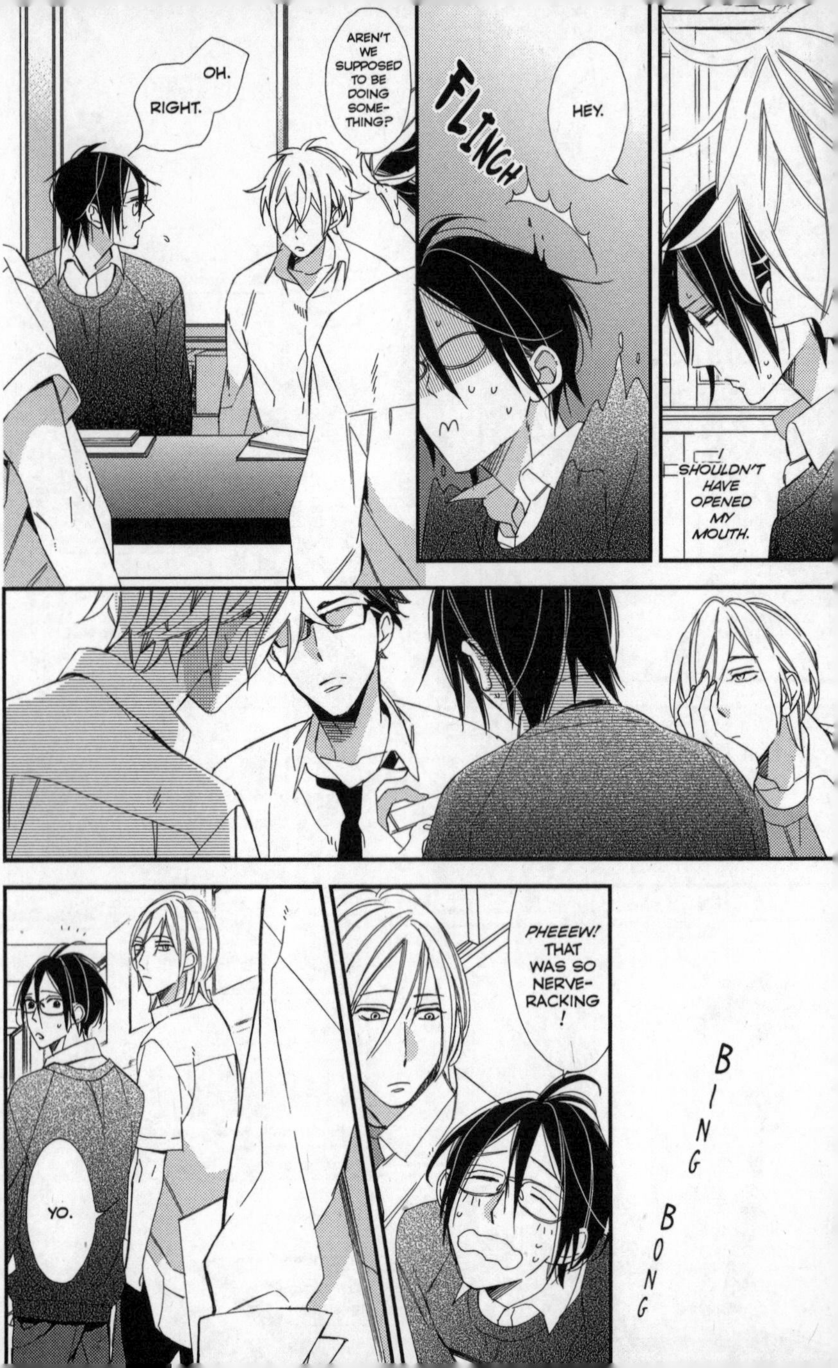
I SHOULDN'T HAVE OPENED MY MOUTH.
HEY.
FLINCH
AREN'T WE SUPPOSED TO BE DOING SOME-THING?
OH.
RIGHT.
PHEEEW! THAT WAS SO NERVE-RACKING!
BING BONG
YO.

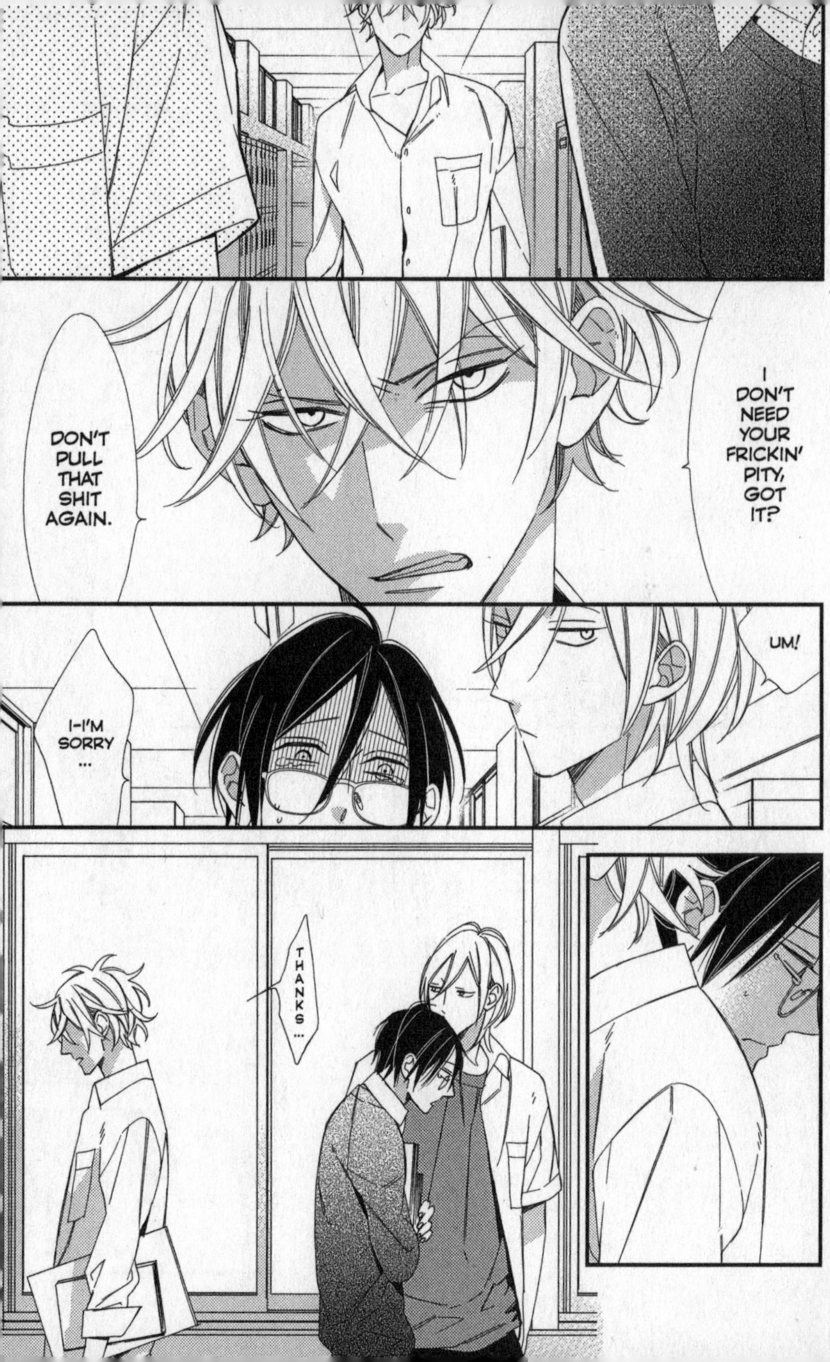
I DON'T NEED YOUR FRICKIN' PITY, GOT IT?
DON'T PULL THAT SHIT AGAIN.
UM!
I-I'M SORRY ...
THANKS ...

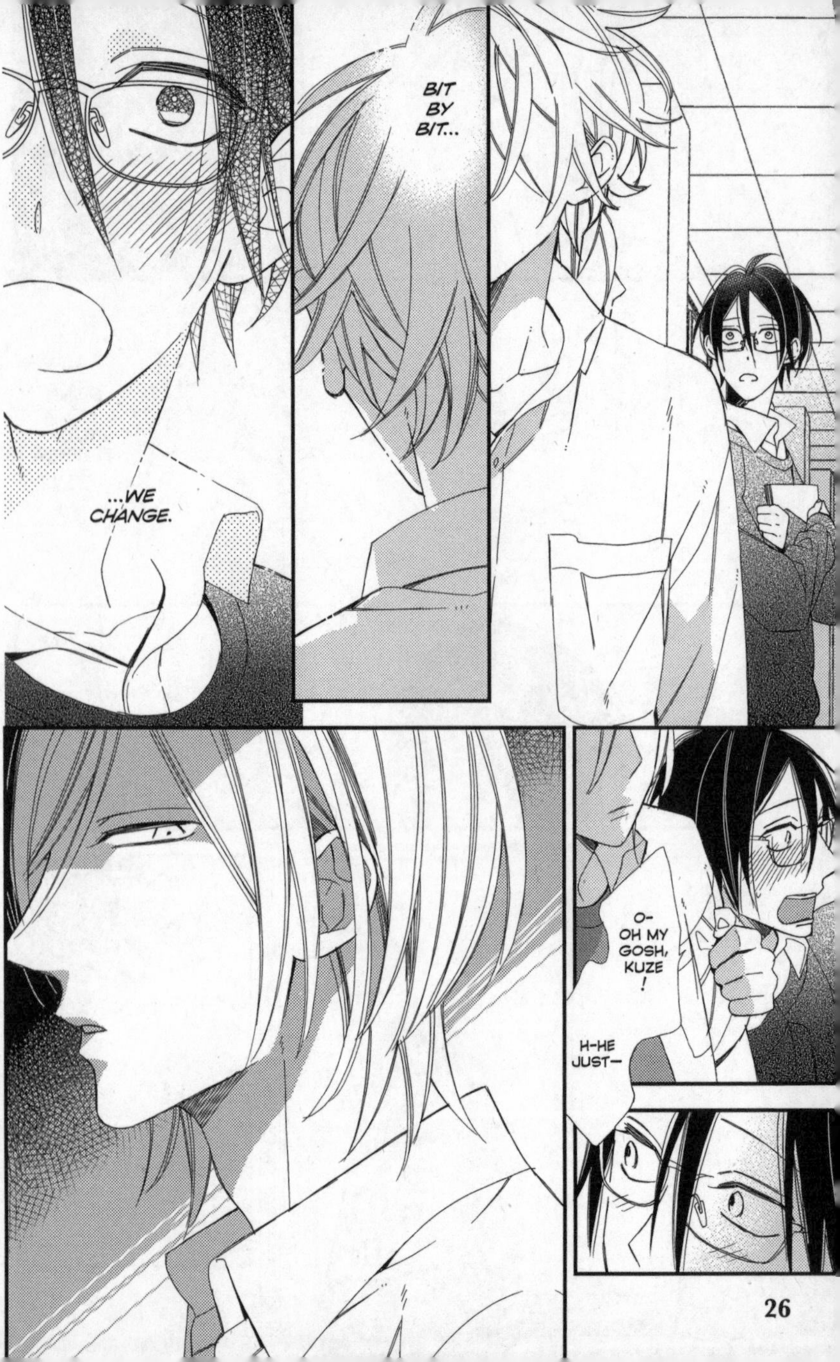

BIT BY BIT...
...WE CHANGE.
O- OH MY GOSH, KUZE!
H-HE JUST—

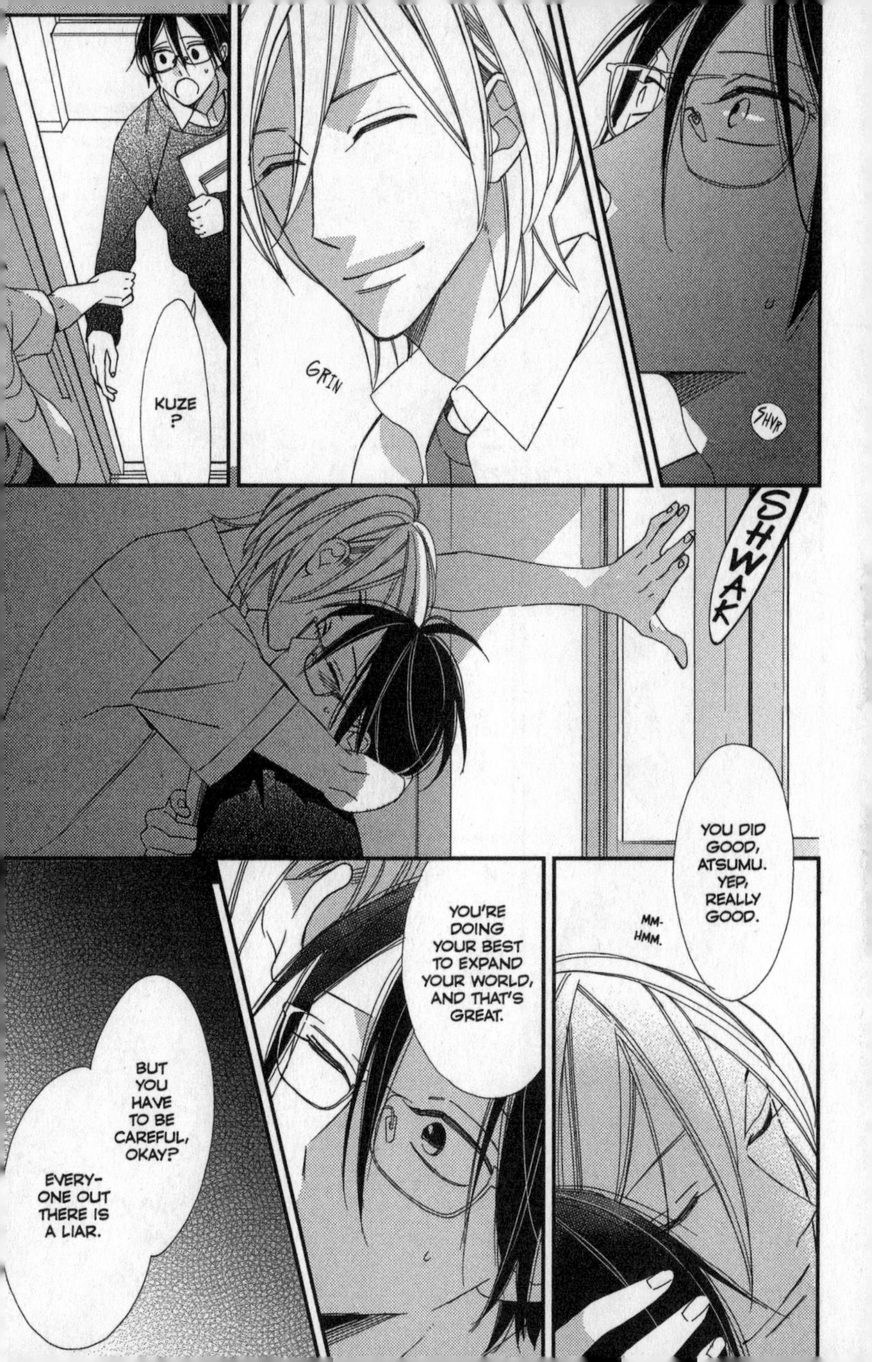
SHVR
GRIN
KUZE?
SHWAK
YOU DID GOOD, ATSUMU. YEP, REALLY GOOD.
MM-HMM.
YOU'RE DOING YOUR BEST TO EXPAND YOUR WORLD, AND THAT'S GREAT.
BUT YOU HAVE TO BE CAREFUL, OKAY?
EVERY-ONE OUT THERE IS A LIAR.

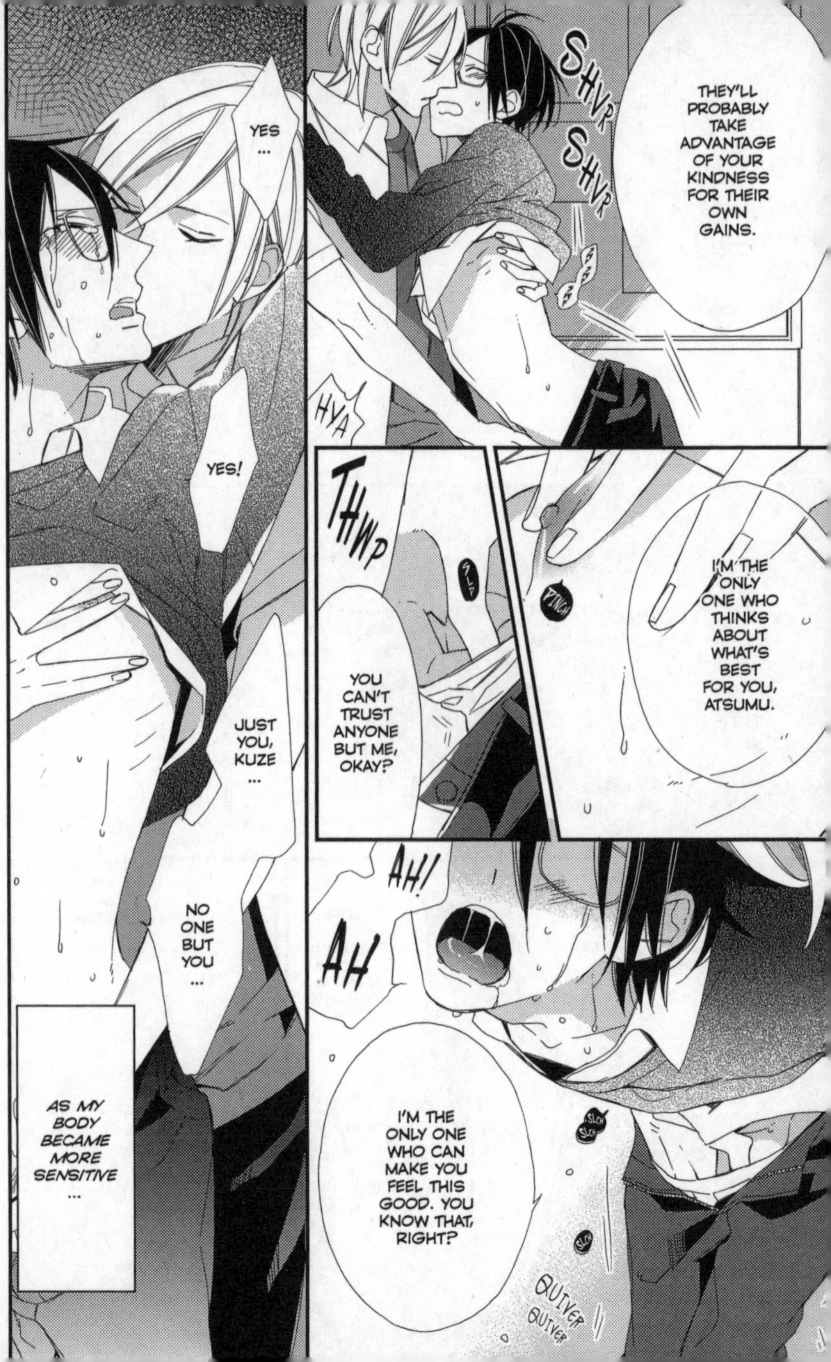
SHVR
SHVR
THEY'LL PROBABLY TAKE ADVANTAGE OF YOUR KINDNESS FOR THEIR OWN GAINS.
HYA
PINCH
I'M THE ONLY ONE WHO THINKS ABOUT WHAT'S BEST FOR YOU, ATSUMU.
THWP
SLP
YOU CAN'T TRUST ANYONE BUT ME, OKAY?
AH!
AH
I'M THE ONLY ONE WHO CAN MAKE YOU FEEL THIS GOOD. YOU KNOW THAT, RIGHT?
SLCH
SLCH
SLCH
QUIVER
QUIVER
YES ...
YES!
JUST YOU, KUZE ...
NO ONE BUT YOU ...
AS MY BODY BECAME MORE SENSITIVE ...

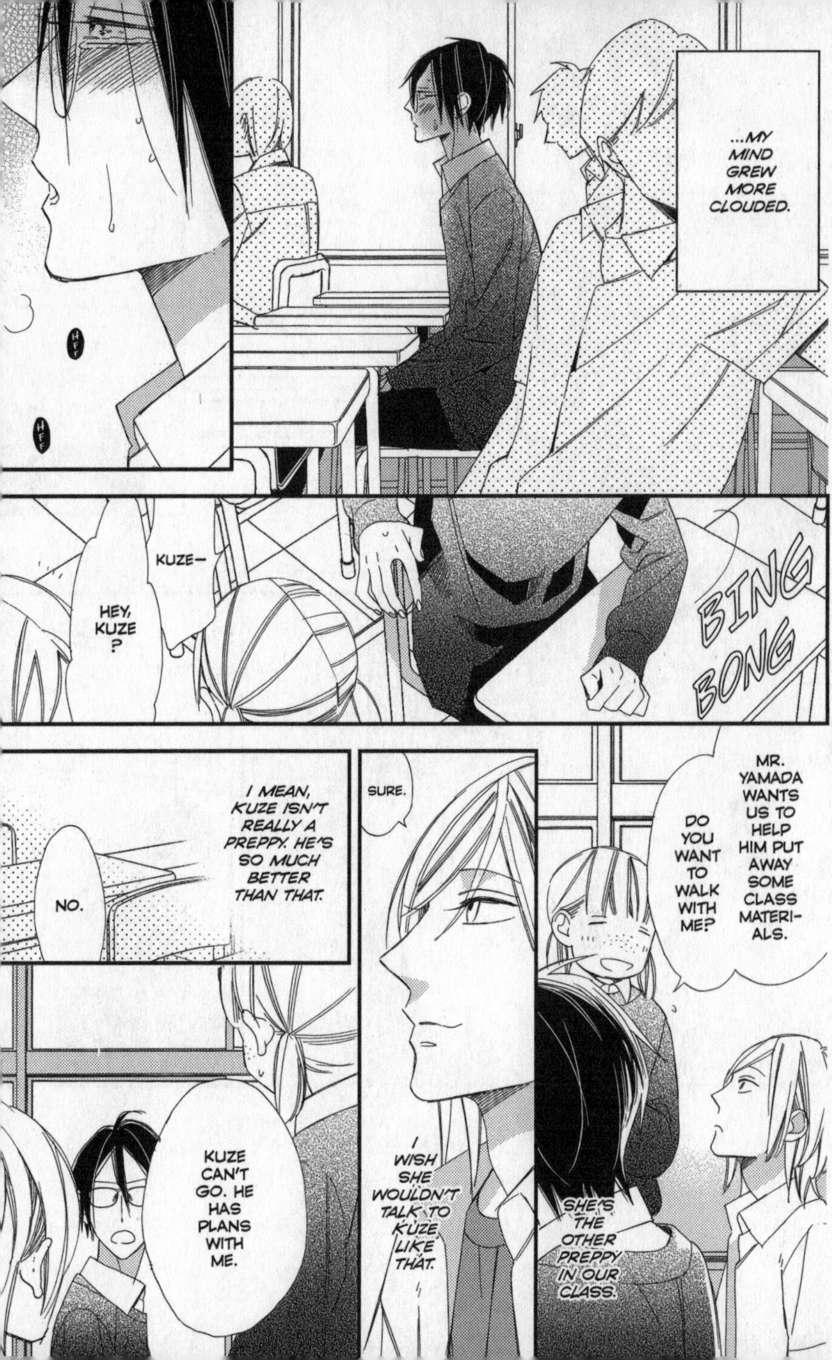

...MY MIND GREW MORE CLOUDED.
HFF
HFF
BING BONG
KUZE—
HEY, KUZE?
MR. YAMADA WANTS US TO HELP HIM PUT AWAY SOME CLASS MATERIALS.
DO YOU WANT TO WALK WITH ME?
SHE'S THE OTHER PREPPY IN OUR CLASS.
SURE.
I WISH SHE WOULDN'T TALK TO KUZE LIKE THAT.
I MEAN, KUZE ISN'T REALLY A PREPPY. HE'S SO MUCH BETTER THAN THAT.
NO.
KUZE CAN'T GO. HE HAS PLANS WITH ME.

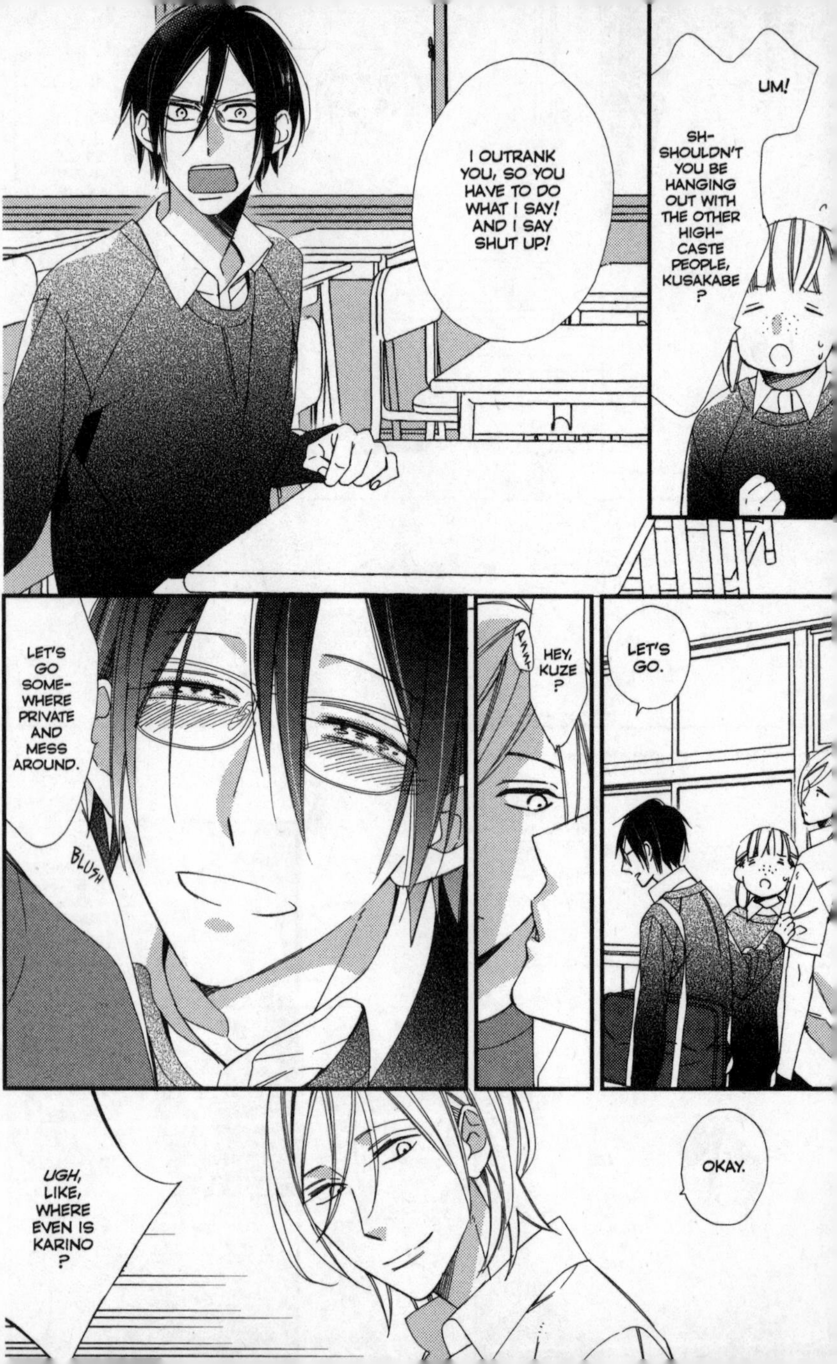
UM!
SH-SHOULDN'T YOU BE HANGING OUT WITH THE OTHER HIGH-CASTE PEOPLE, KUSAKABE?
I OUTRANK YOU, SO YOU HAVE TO DO WHAT I SAY! AND I SAY SHUT UP!
LET'S GO.
HEY, KUZE?
LET'S GO SOMEWHERE PRIVATE AND MESS AROUND.
BLUSH
OKAY.
UGH, LIKE, WHERE EVEN IS KARINO?

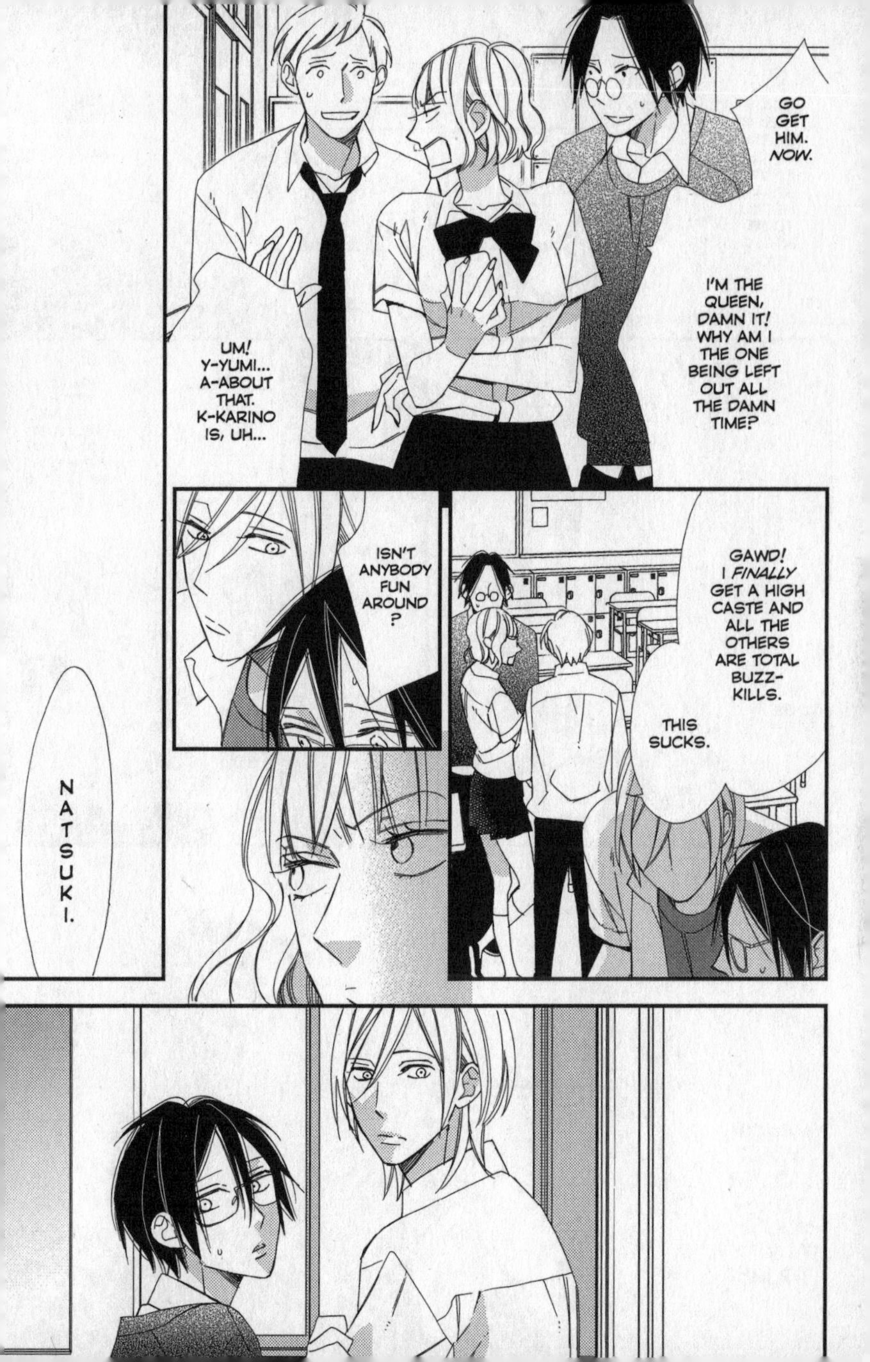
GO GET HIM. *NOW.*
I'M THE QUEEN, DAMN IT! WHY AM I THE ONE BEING LEFT OUT ALL THE DAMN TIME?
UM! Y-YUMI... A-ABOUT THAT. K-KARINO IS, UH...
GAWD! I *FINALLY* GET A HIGH CASTE AND ALL THE OTHERS ARE TOTAL BUZZ-KILLS.
THIS SUCKS.
ISN'T ANYBODY FUN AROUND?
NATSUKI.

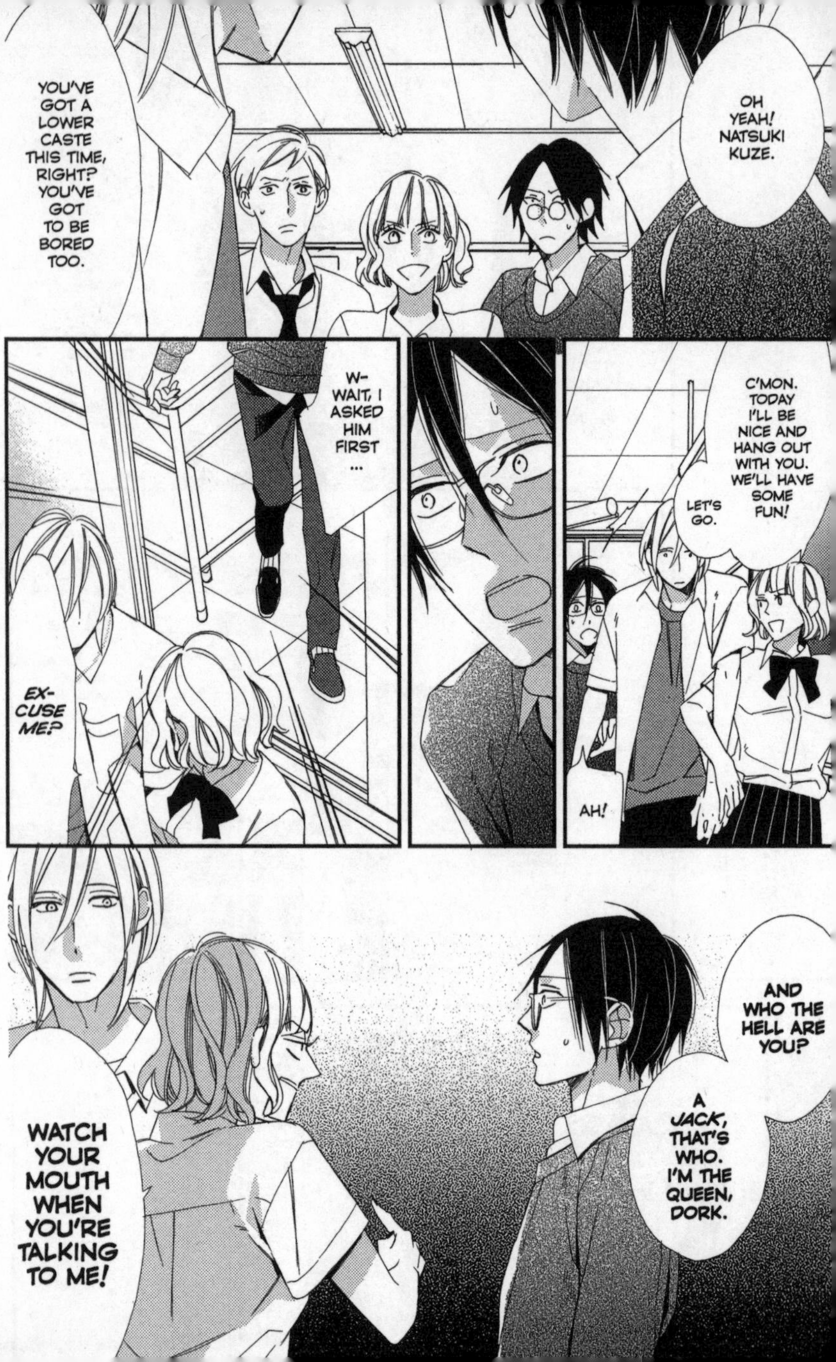
OH YEAH! NATSUKI KUZE.
YOU'VE GOT A LOWER CASTE THIS TIME, RIGHT? YOU'VE GOT TO BE BORED TOO.
C'MON. TODAY I'LL BE NICE AND HANG OUT WITH YOU. WE'LL HAVE SOME FUN!
LET'S GO.
AH!
W-WAIT, I ASKED HIM FIRST ...
EX-CUSE ME?
AND WHO THE HELL ARE YOU?
A *JACK*, THAT'S WHO. I'M THE QUEEN, DORK.
WATCH YOUR MOUTH WHEN YOU'RE TALKING TO ME!

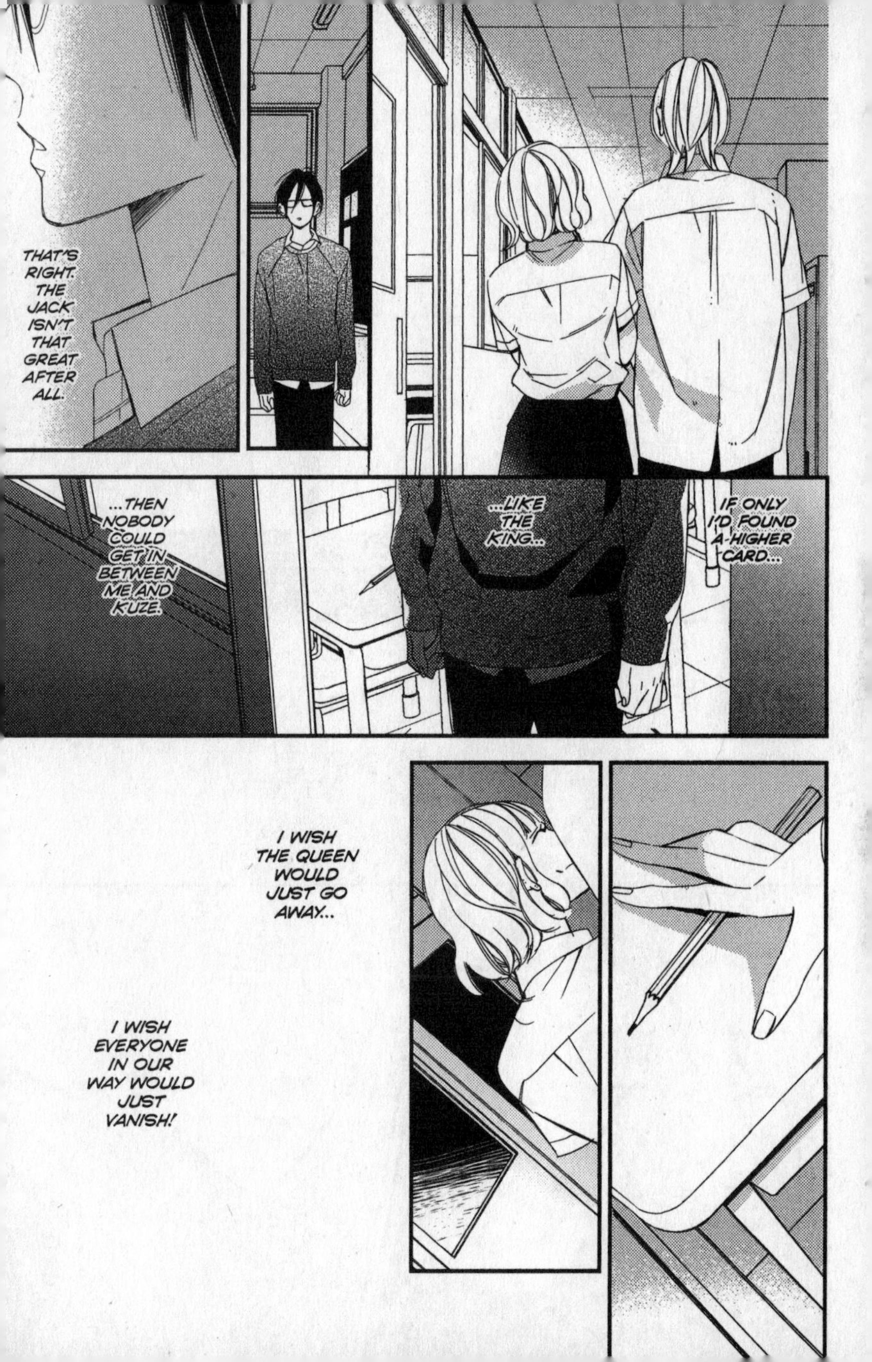
THAT'S RIGHT. THE JACK ISN'T THAT GREAT AFTER ALL.
IF ONLY I'D FOUND A HIGHER CARD...
...LIKE THE KING...
...THEN NOBODY COULD GET IN BETWEEN ME AND KUZE.
I WISH THE QUEEN WOULD JUST GO AWAY...
I WISH EVERYONE IN OUR WAY WOULD JUST VANISH!

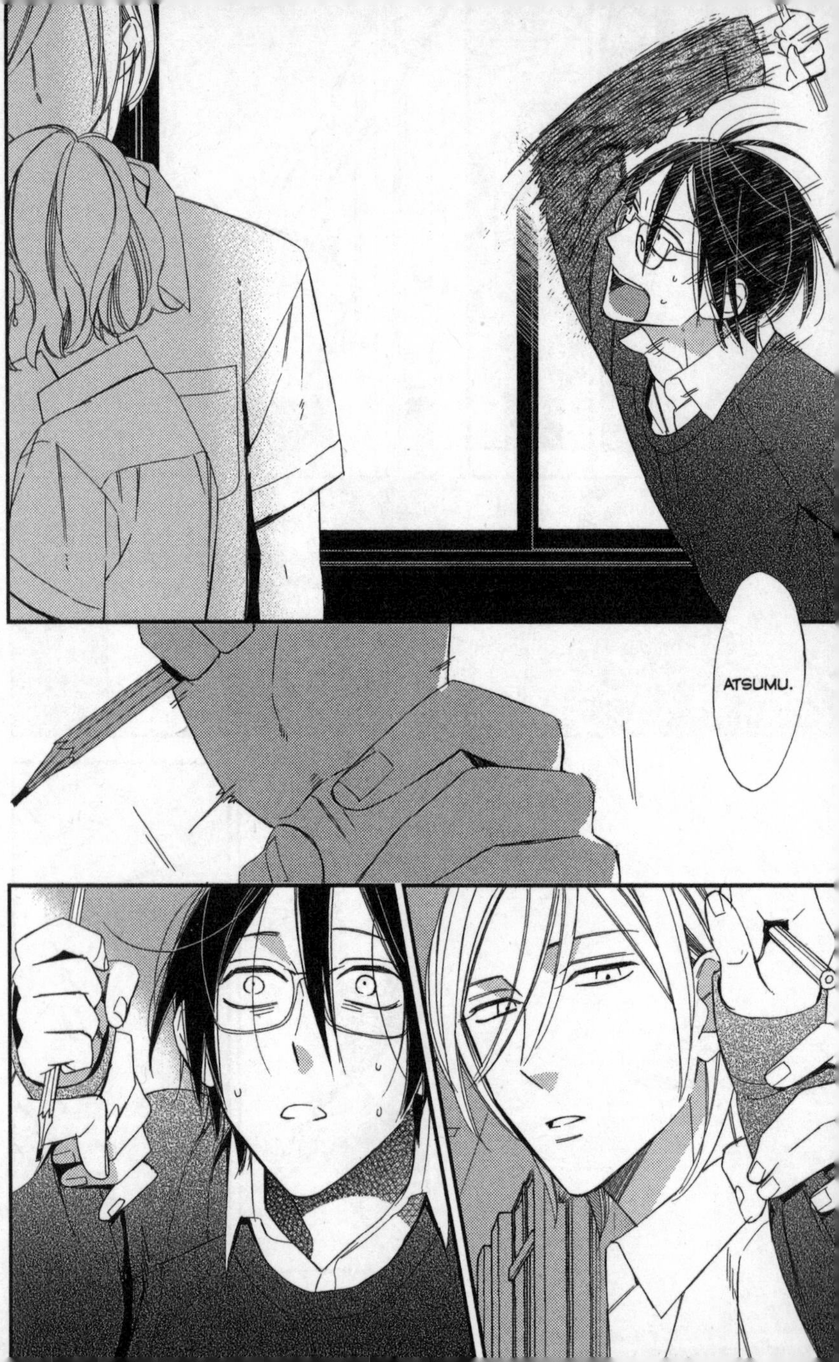
ATSUMU.

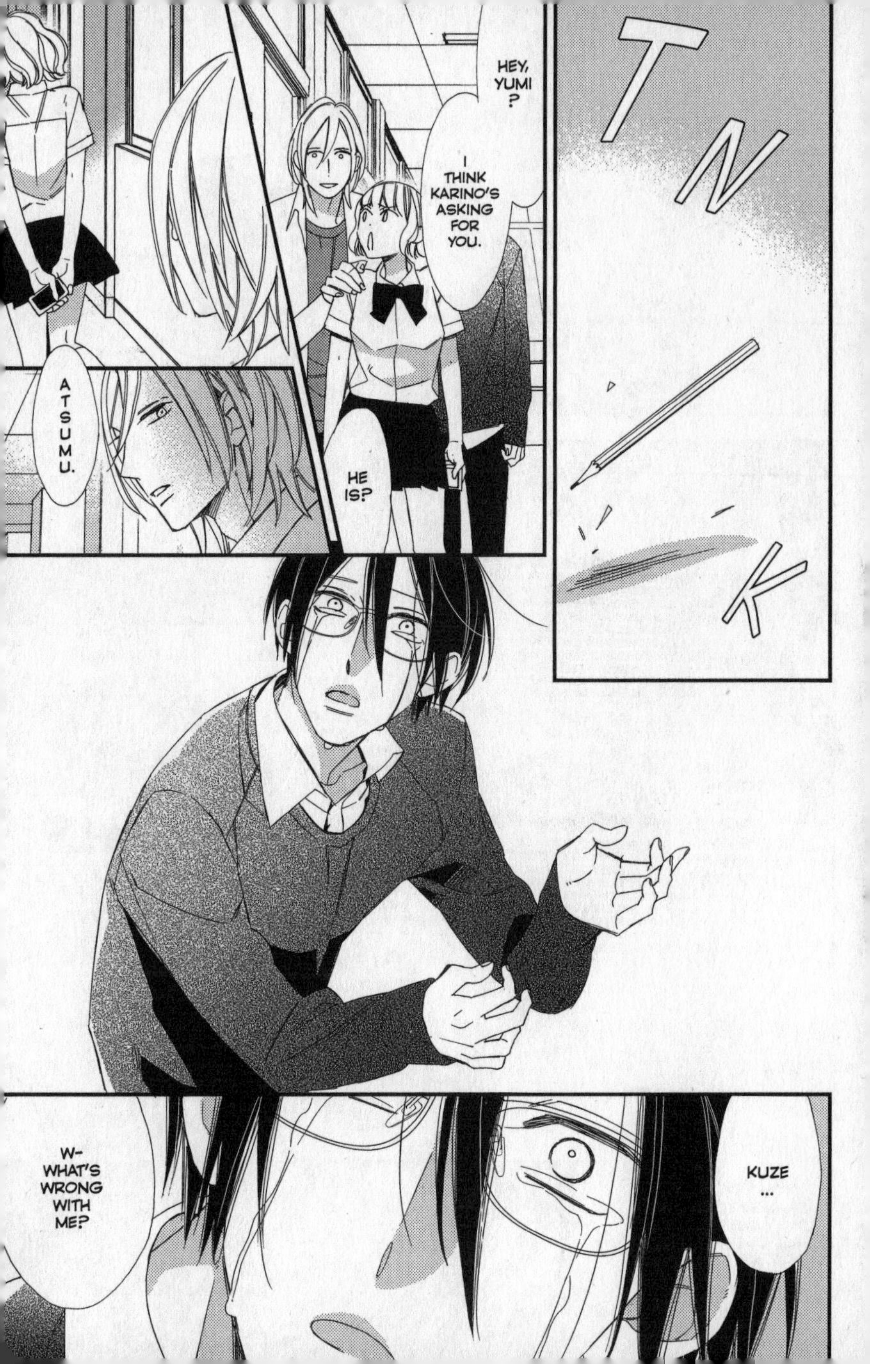
TNK
HEY, YUMI?
I THINK KARINO'S ASKING FOR YOU.
HE IS?
ATSUMU.
KUZE...
W-WHAT'S WRONG WITH ME?

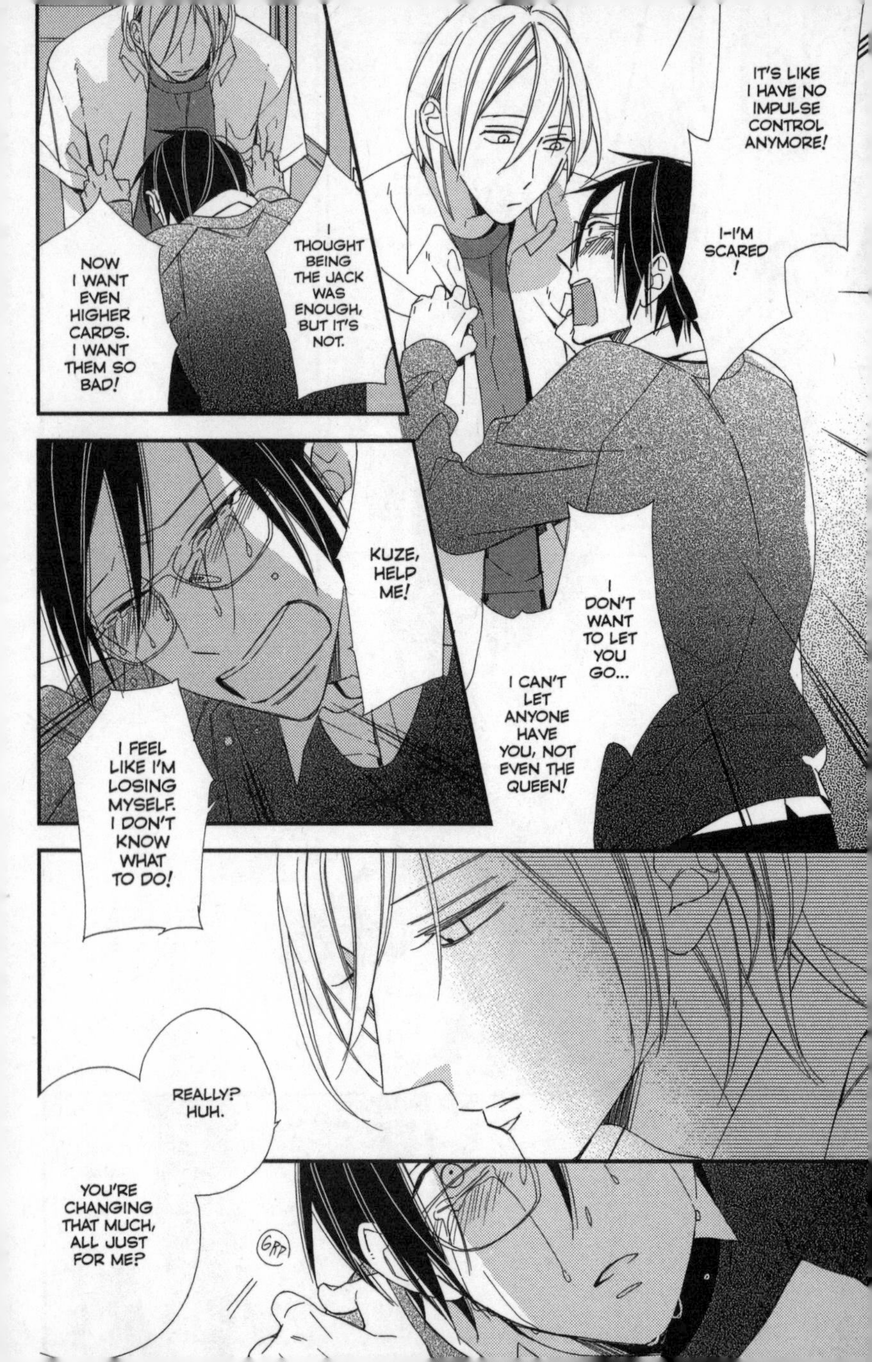
IT'S LIKE I HAVE NO IMPULSE CONTROL ANYMORE!
I-I'M SCARED!
I DON'T WANT TO LET YOU GO...
I CAN'T LET ANYONE HAVE YOU, NOT EVEN THE QUEEN!
I THOUGHT BEING THE JACK WAS ENOUGH, BUT IT'S NOT.
NOW I WANT EVEN HIGHER CARDS. I WANT THEM SO BAD!
KUZE, HELP ME!
I FEEL LIKE I'M LOSING MYSELF. I DON'T KNOW WHAT TO DO!
REALLY? HUH.
YOU'RE CHANGING THAT MUCH, ALL JUST FOR ME?
GRP

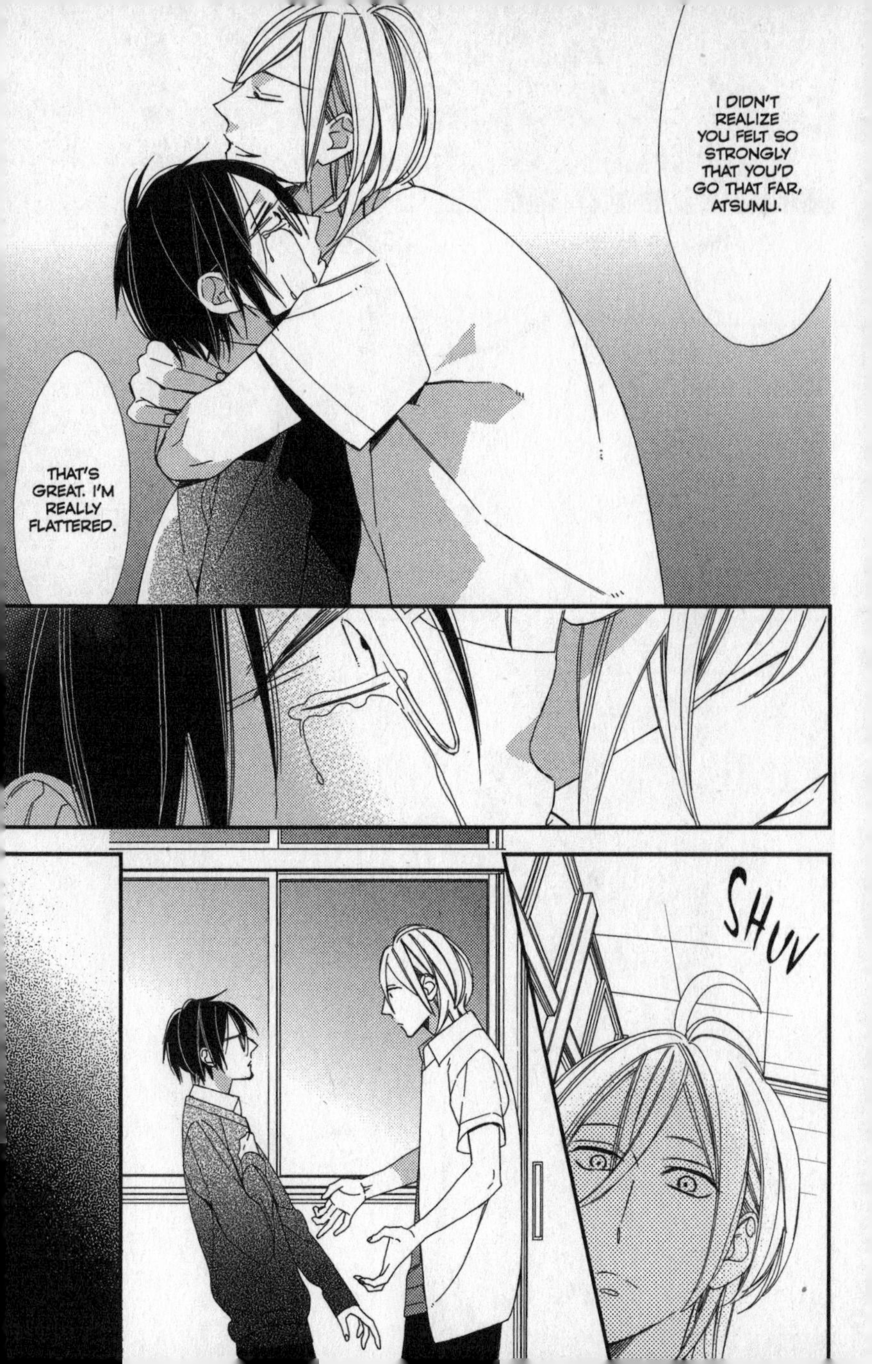
I DIDN'T REALIZE YOU FELT SO STRONGLY THAT YOU'D GO THAT FAR, ATSUMU.
THAT'S GREAT. I'M REALLY FLATTERED.
SHUV

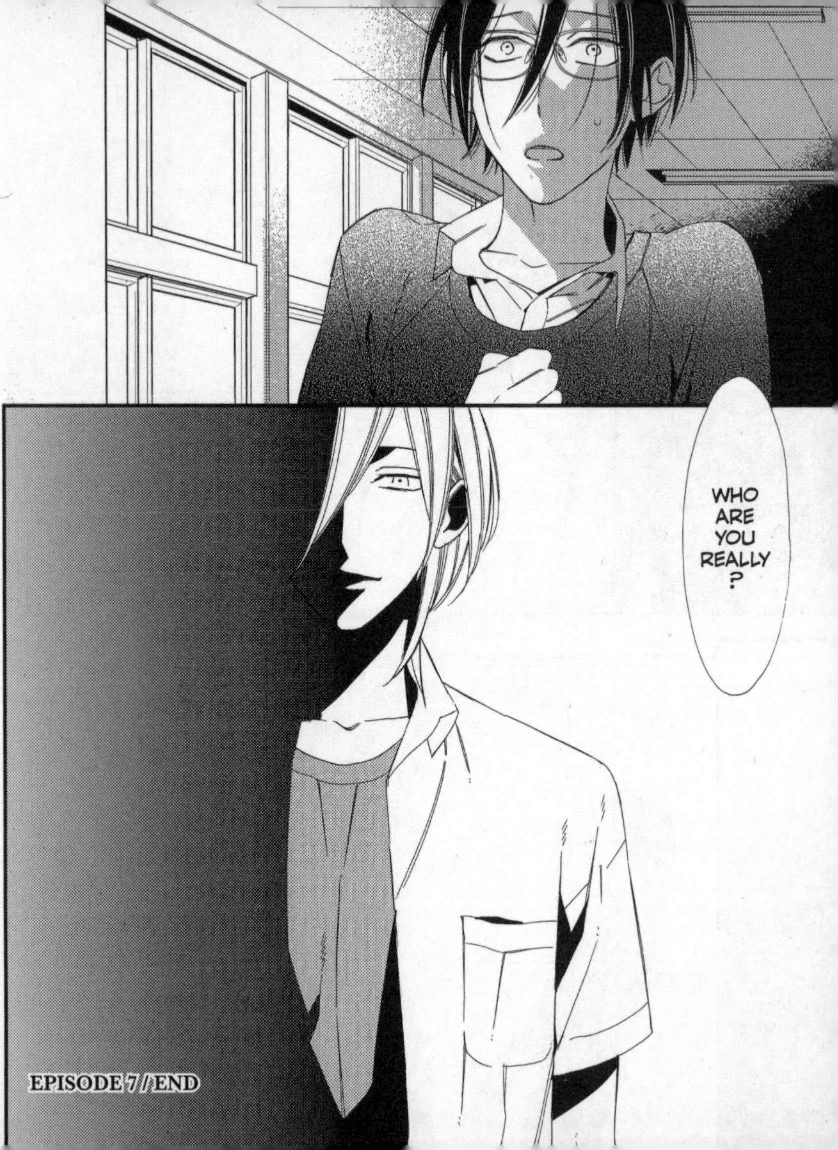
WHO ARE YOU REALLY ?
EPISODE 7 / END

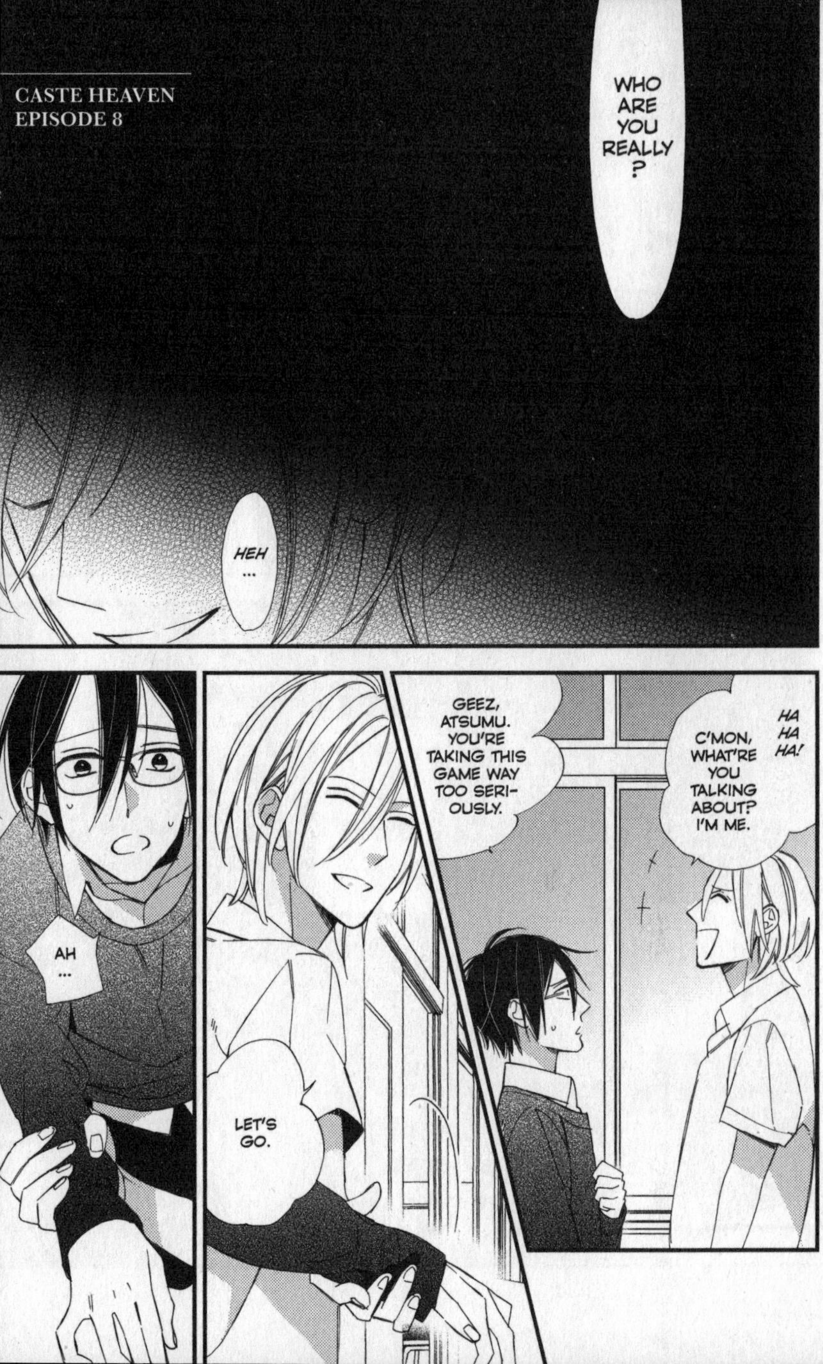
CASTE HEAVEN
EPISODE 8
WHO ARE YOU REALLY?
HEH...
HA HA HA!
C'MON, WHAT'RE YOU TALKING ABOUT? I'M ME.
GEEZ, ATSUMU. YOU'RE TAKING THIS GAME WAY TOO SERIOUSLY.
LET'S GO.
AH...

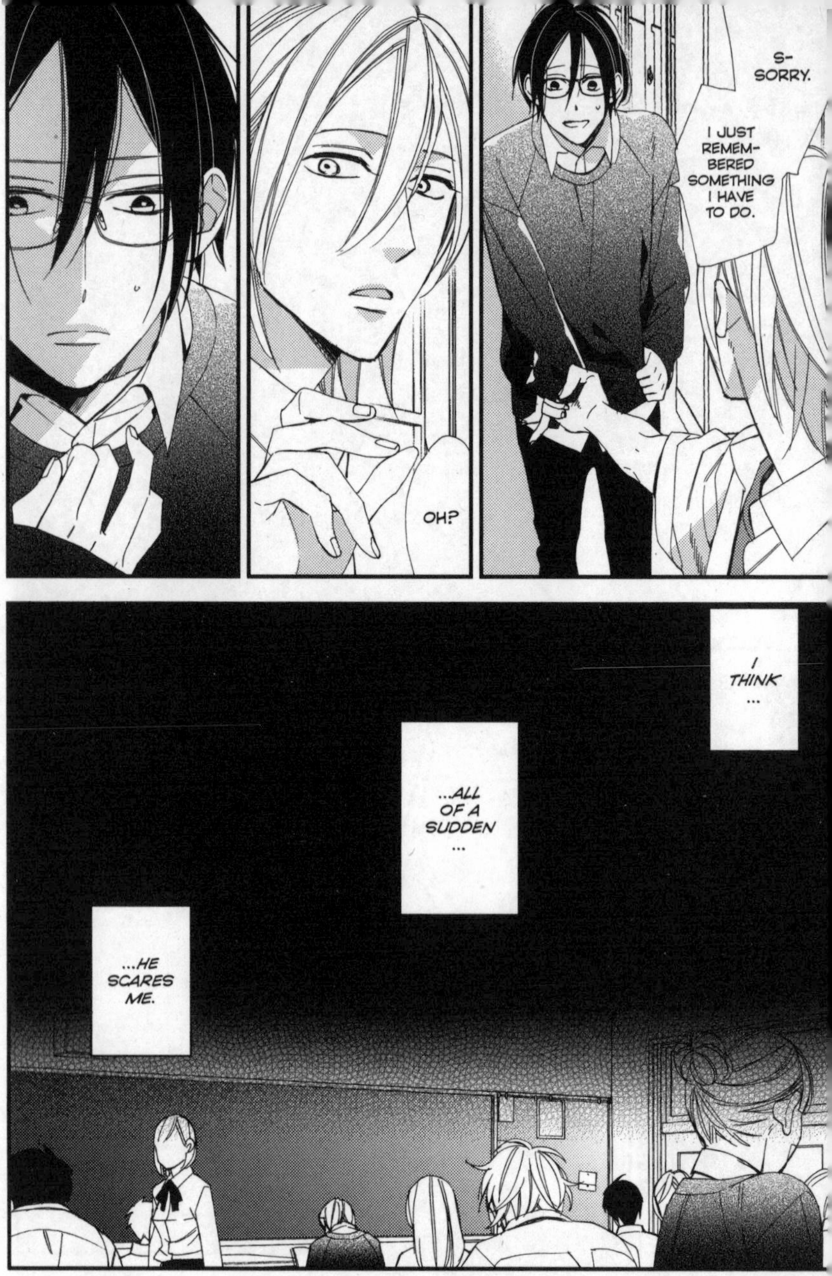
S-
SORRY.
I JUST REMEM-BERED SOMETHING I HAVE TO DO.
OH?
I THINK ...
...ALL OF A SUDDEN ...
...HE SCARES ME.

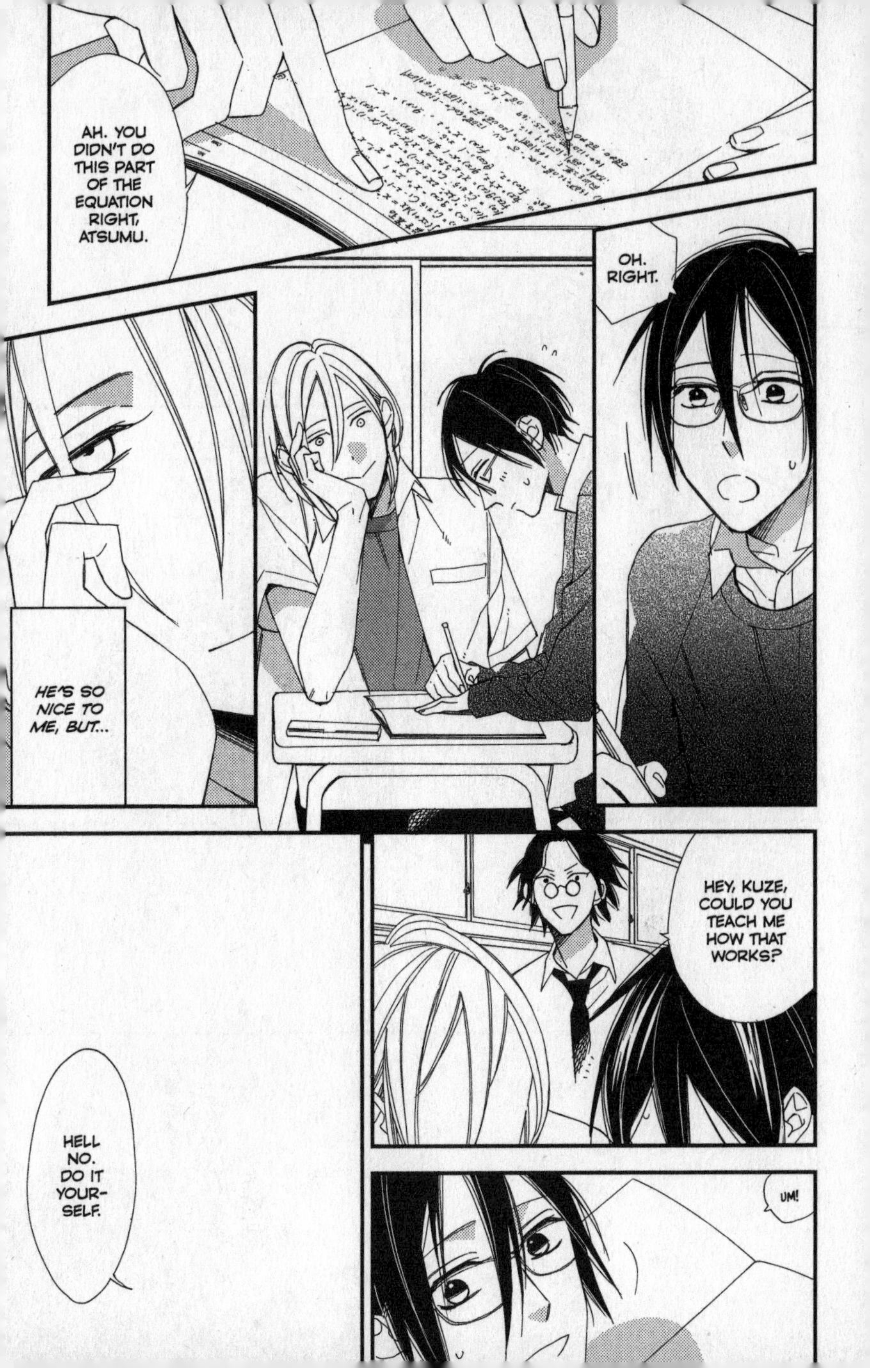
AH. YOU DIDN'T DO THIS PART OF THE EQUATION RIGHT, ATSUMU.
OH. RIGHT.
HE'S SO NICE TO ME, BUT...
HEY, KUZE, COULD YOU TEACH ME HOW THAT WORKS?
UM!
HELL NO. DO IT YOURSELF.

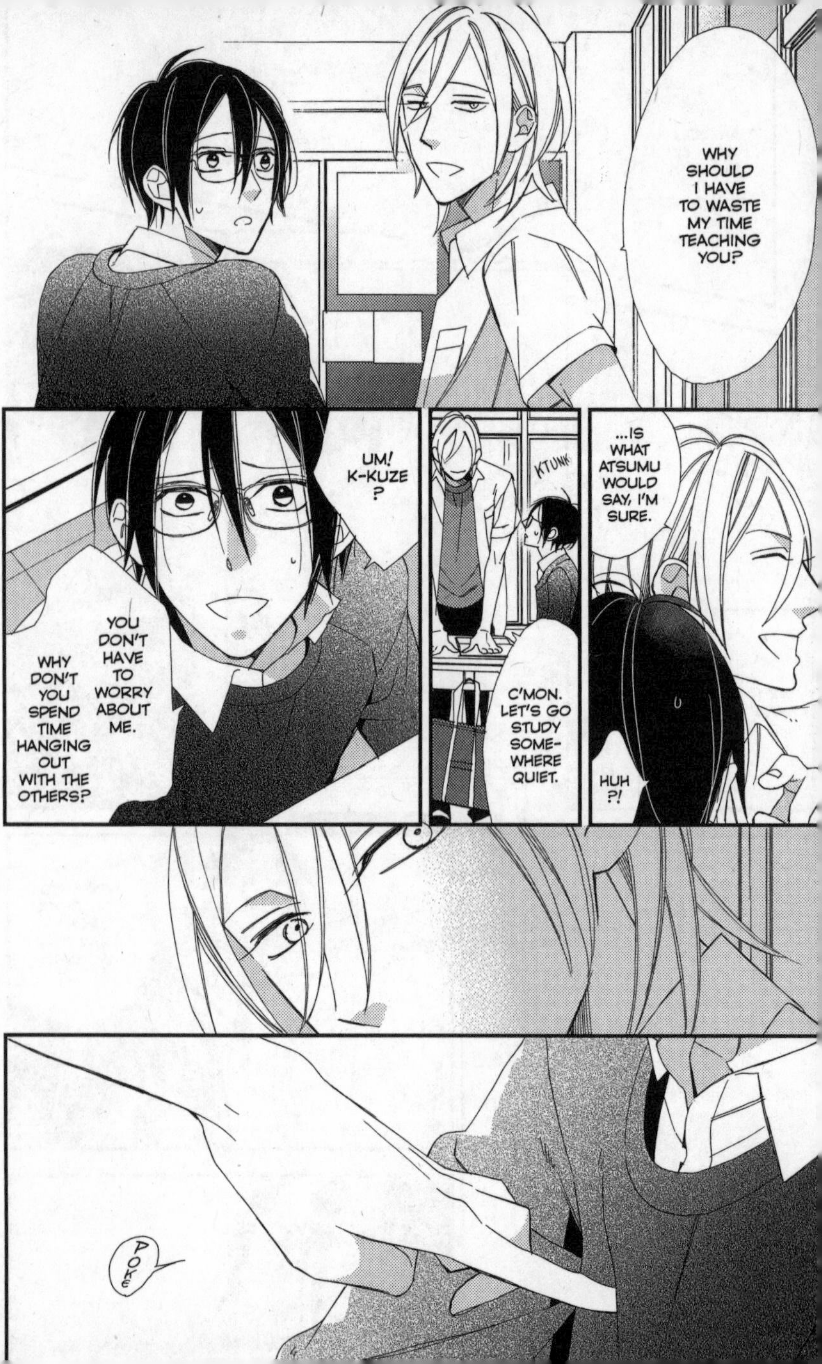
WHY SHOULD I HAVE TO WASTE MY TIME TEACHING YOU?
...IS WHAT ATSUMU WOULD SAY, I'M SURE.
HUH ?!
KTUNK
C'MON. LET'S GO STUDY SOME-WHERE QUIET.
UM! K-KUZE ?
YOU DON'T HAVE TO WORRY ABOUT ME.
WHY DON'T YOU SPEND TIME HANGING OUT WITH THE OTHERS?
POKE

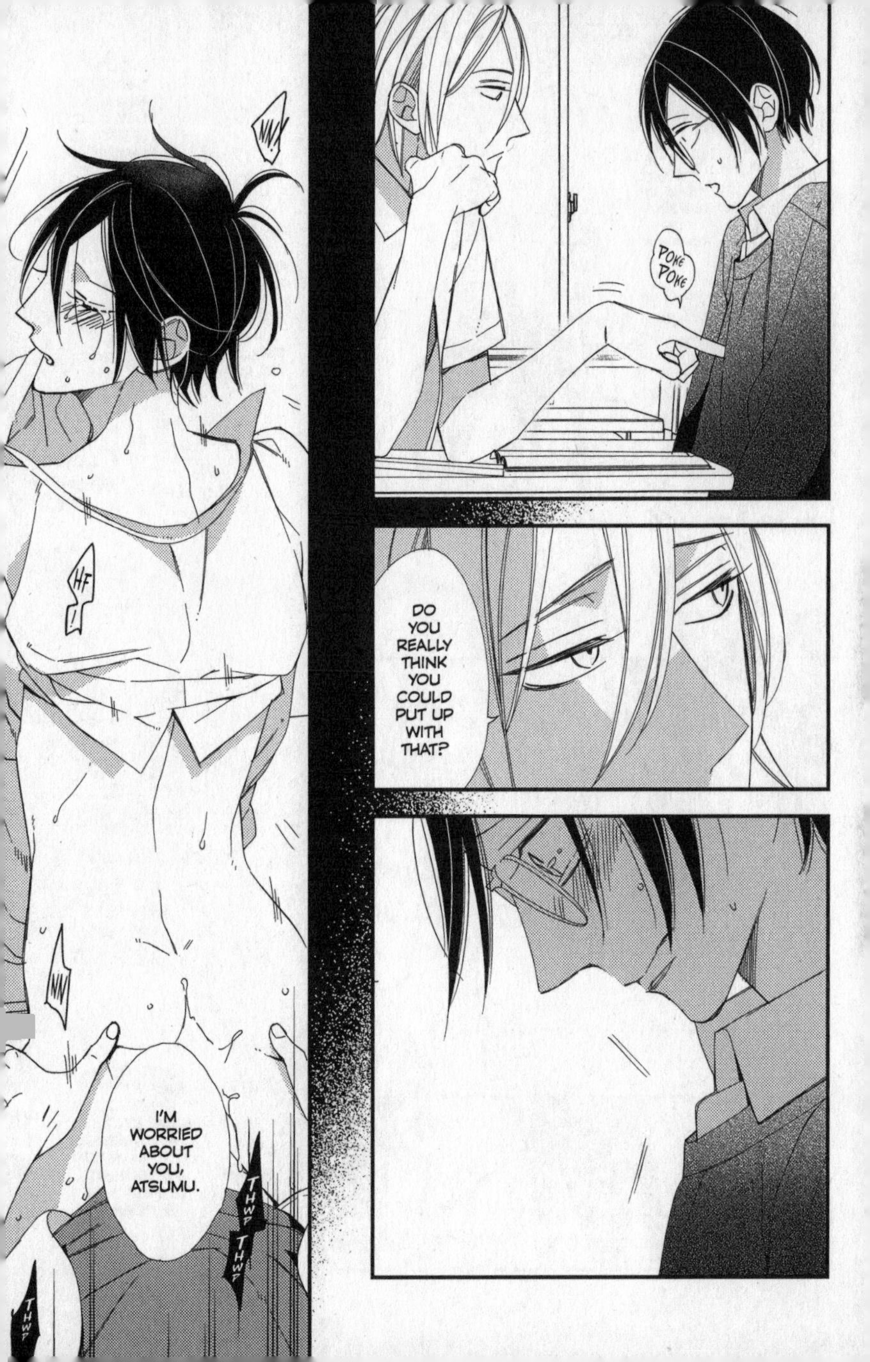
POKE POKE
DO YOU REALLY THINK YOU COULD PUT UP WITH THAT?
NN!
HF
NN
I'M WORRIED ABOUT YOU, ATSUMU.
THWP THWP
THWP

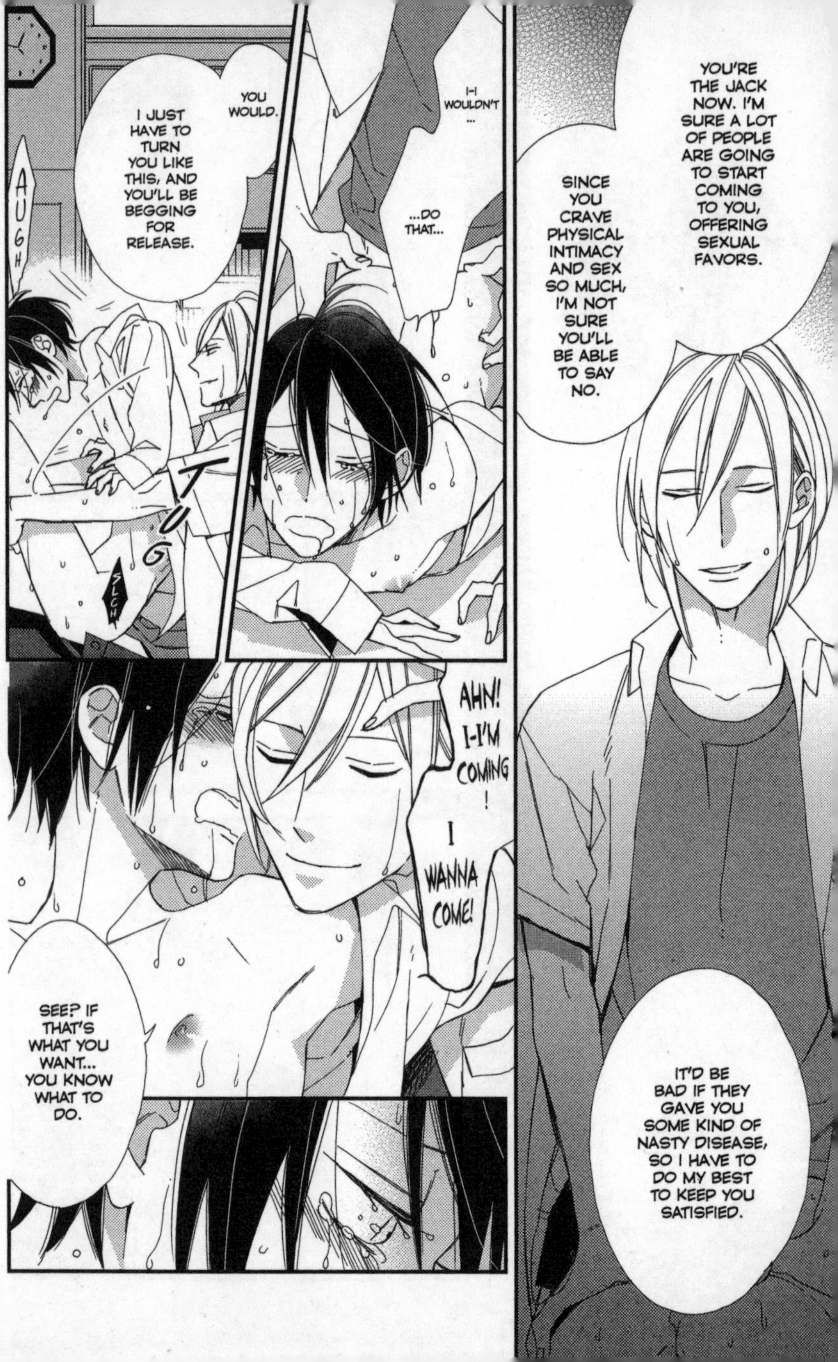
YOU'RE THE JACK NOW. I'M SURE A LOT OF PEOPLE ARE GOING TO START COMING TO YOU, OFFERING SEXUAL FAVORS.
SINCE YOU CRAVE PHYSICAL INTIMACY AND SEX SO MUCH, I'M NOT SURE YOU'LL BE ABLE TO SAY NO.
IT'D BE BAD IF THEY GAVE YOU SOME KIND OF NASTY DISEASE, SO I HAVE TO DO MY BEST TO KEEP YOU SATISFIED.
I-I WOULDN'T ...
...DO THAT...
YOU WOULD.
I JUST HAVE TO TURN YOU LIKE THIS, AND YOU'LL BE BEGGING FOR RELEASE.
AUGH
TUG
SLCH
AHN! I-I'M COMING!
I WANNA COME!
SEE? IF THAT'S WHAT YOU WANT... YOU KNOW WHAT TO DO.

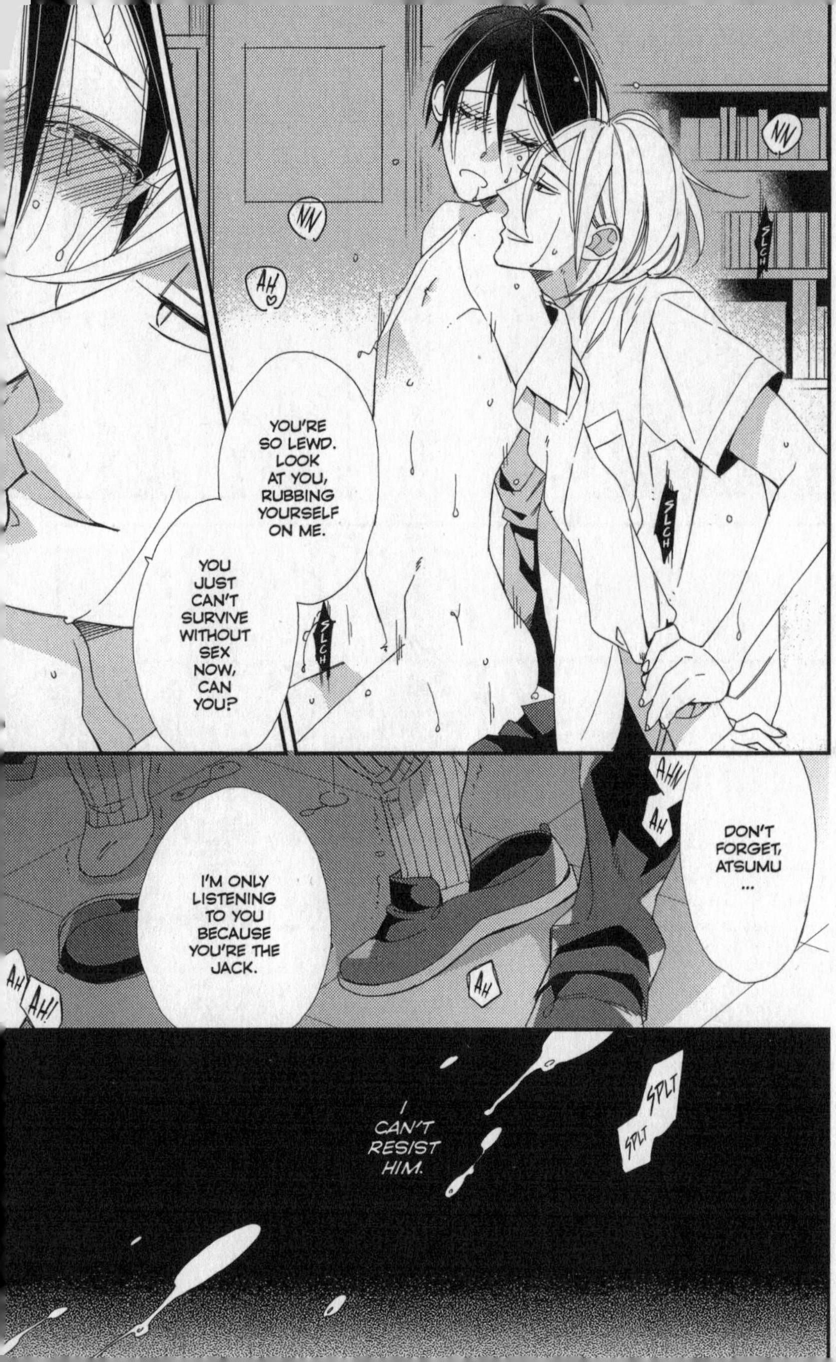
NN
SLCH
NN
AH ♡
YOU'RE SO LEWD. LOOK AT YOU, RUBBING YOURSELF ON ME.
SLCH
YOU JUST CAN'T SURVIVE WITHOUT SEX NOW, CAN YOU?
SLCH
DON'T FORGET, ATSUMU...
AHN
AH
I'M ONLY LISTENING TO YOU BECAUSE YOU'RE THE JACK.
AH
AH!
AH!
SPLT
SPLT
I CAN'T RESIST HIM.

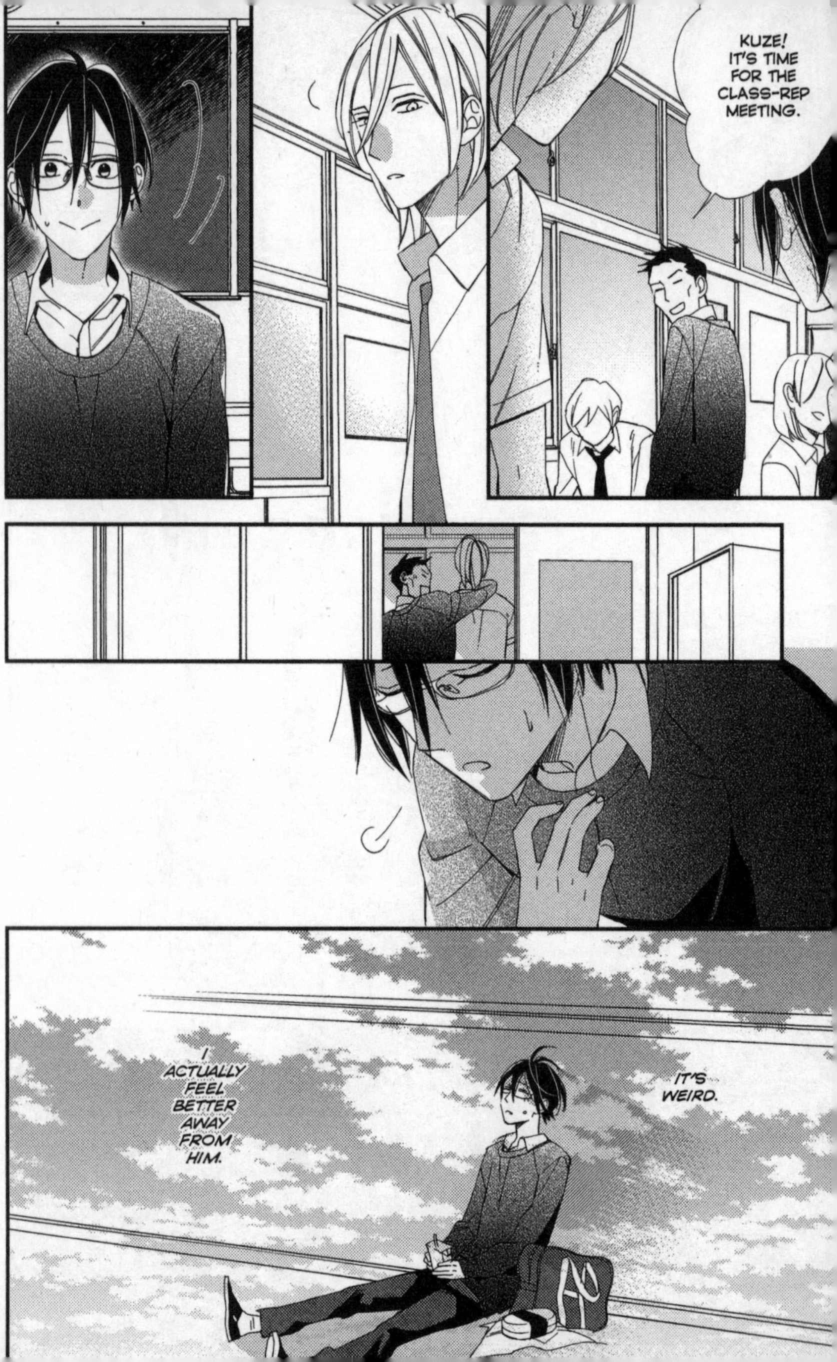
KUZE! IT'S TIME FOR THE CLASS-REP MEETING.
IT'S WEIRD.
I ACTUALLY FEEL BETTER AWAY FROM HIM.

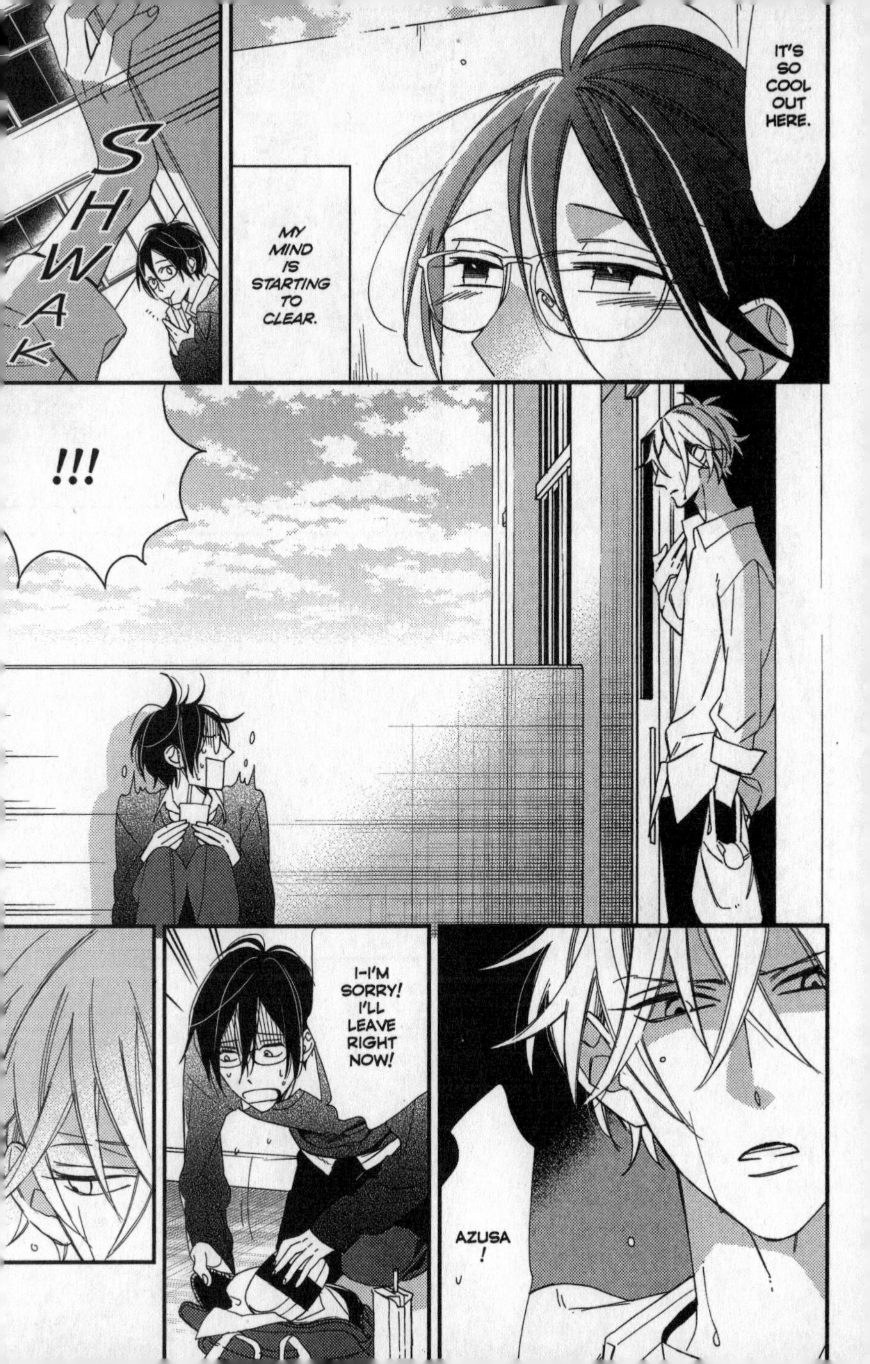
IT'S SO COOL OUT HERE.
MY MIND IS STARTING TO CLEAR.
SHWAK
!!!
AZUSA!
I-I'M SORRY! I'LL LEAVE RIGHT NOW!

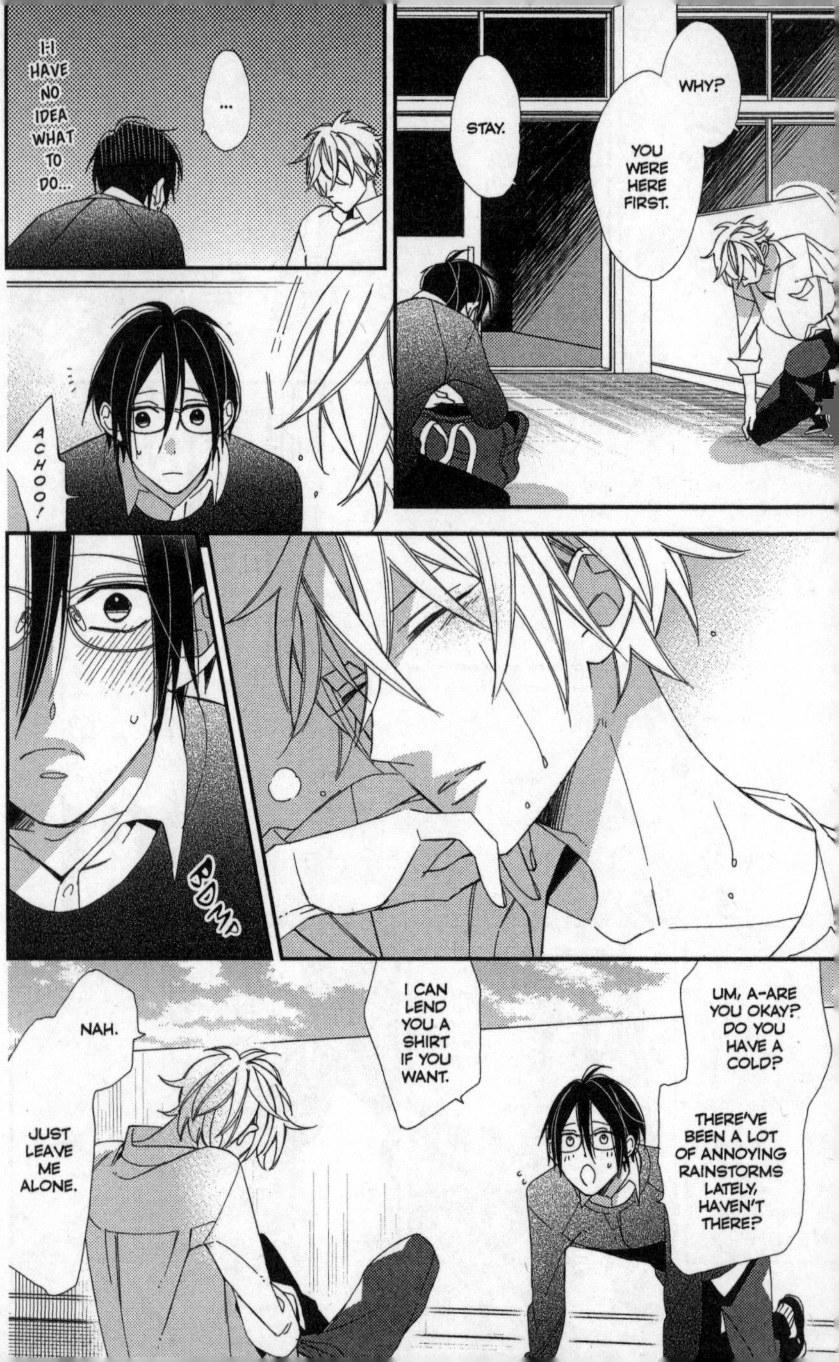
WHY? YOU WERE HERE FIRST.
STAY.
...
I-I HAVE NO IDEA WHAT TO DO...
ACHOO!
BDMP
UM, A-ARE YOU OKAY? DO YOU HAVE A COLD?
THERE'VE BEEN A LOT OF ANNOYING RAINSTORMS LATELY, HAVEN'T THERE?
I CAN LEND YOU A SHIRT IF YOU WANT.
NAH.
JUST LEAVE ME ALONE.

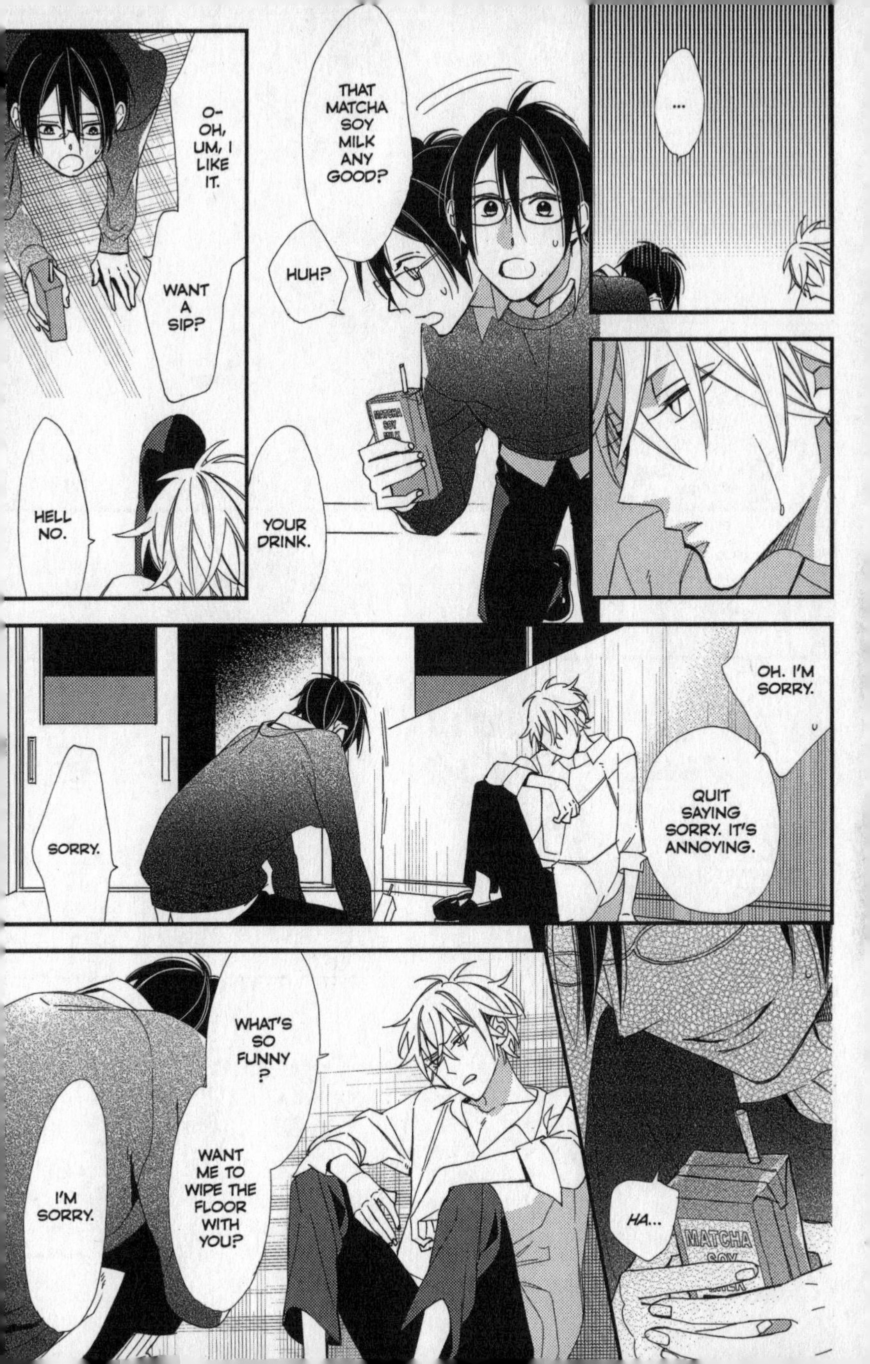
...
THAT MATCHA SOY MILK ANY GOOD?
HUH?
YOUR DRINK.
MATCHA SOY MILK
O-OH, UM, I LIKE IT.
WANT A SIP?
HELL NO.
OH. I'M SORRY.
QUIT SAYING SORRY. IT'S ANNOYING.
SORRY.
HA...
WHAT'S SO FUNNY?
WANT ME TO WIPE THE FLOOR WITH YOU?
I'M SORRY.

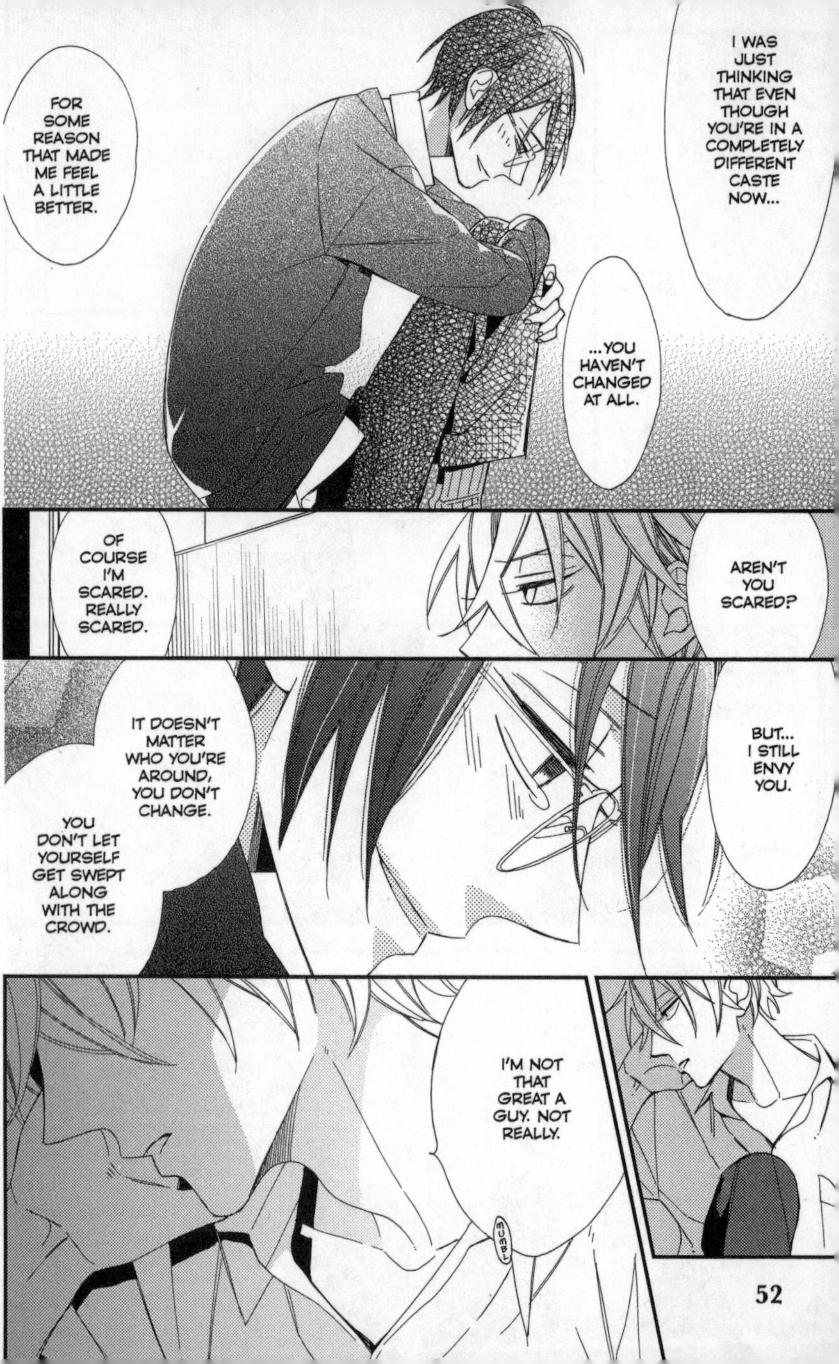
I WAS JUST THINKING THAT EVEN THOUGH YOU'RE IN A COMPLETELY DIFFERENT CASTE NOW...
...YOU HAVEN'T CHANGED AT ALL.
FOR SOME REASON THAT MADE ME FEEL A LITTLE BETTER.
AREN'T YOU SCARED?
OF COURSE I'M SCARED. REALLY SCARED.
BUT... I STILL ENVY YOU.
IT DOESN'T MATTER WHO YOU'RE AROUND, YOU DON'T CHANGE.
YOU DON'T LET YOURSELF GET SWEPT ALONG WITH THE CROWD.
I'M NOT THAT GREAT A GUY. NOT REALLY.

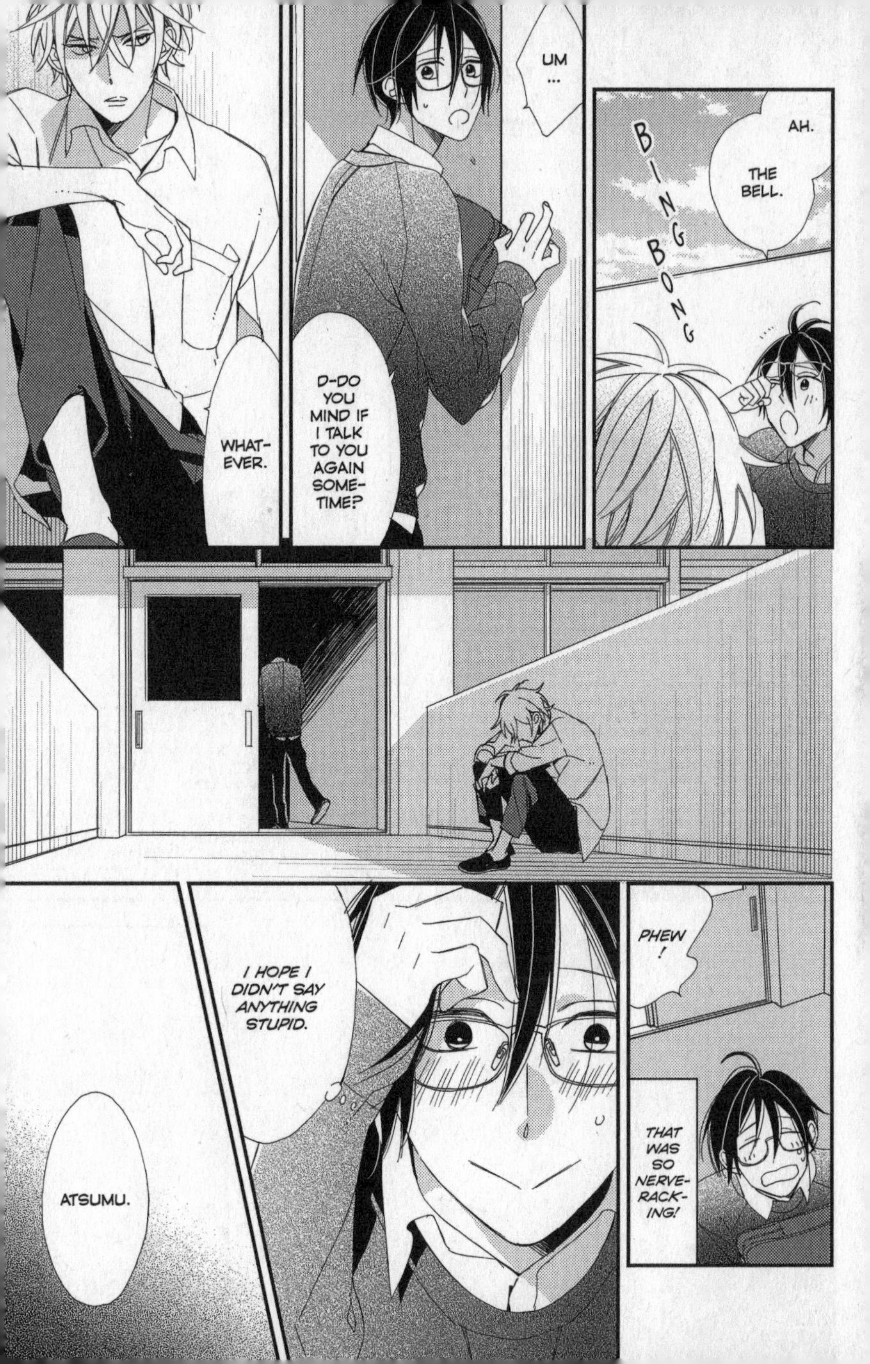
AH.
THE BELL.
BING BONG
UM ...
D-DO YOU MIND IF I TALK TO YOU AGAIN SOME-TIME?
WHAT-EVER.
PHEW!
THAT WAS SO NERVE-RACK-ING!
I HOPE I DIDN'T SAY ANYTHING STUPID.
ATSUMU.

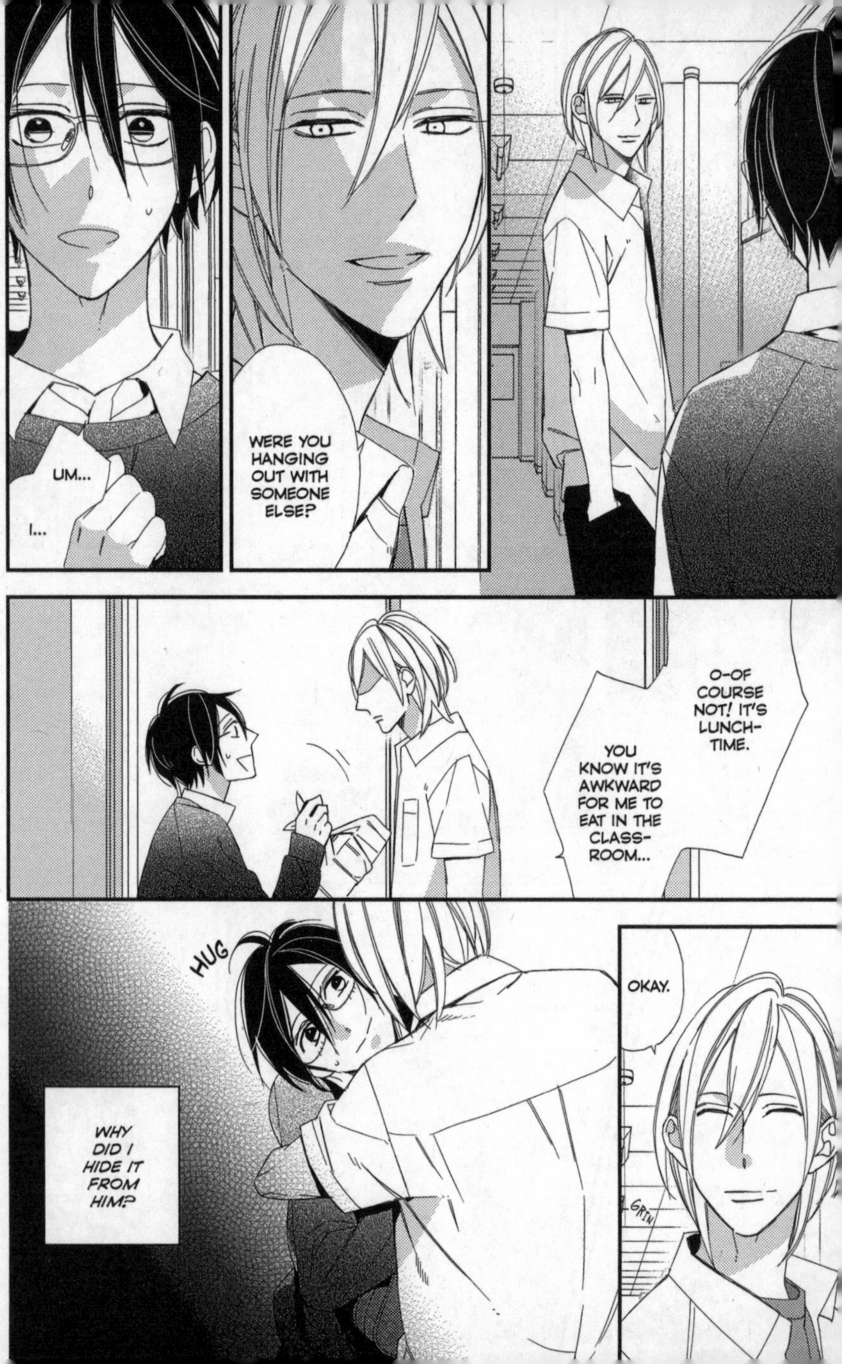
WERE YOU HANGING OUT WITH SOMEONE ELSE?
UM...
I...
O-OF COURSE NOT! IT'S LUNCH-TIME.
YOU KNOW IT'S AWKWARD FOR ME TO EAT IN THE CLASS-ROOM...
OKAY.
GRIN
HUG
WHY DID I HIDE IT FROM HIM?

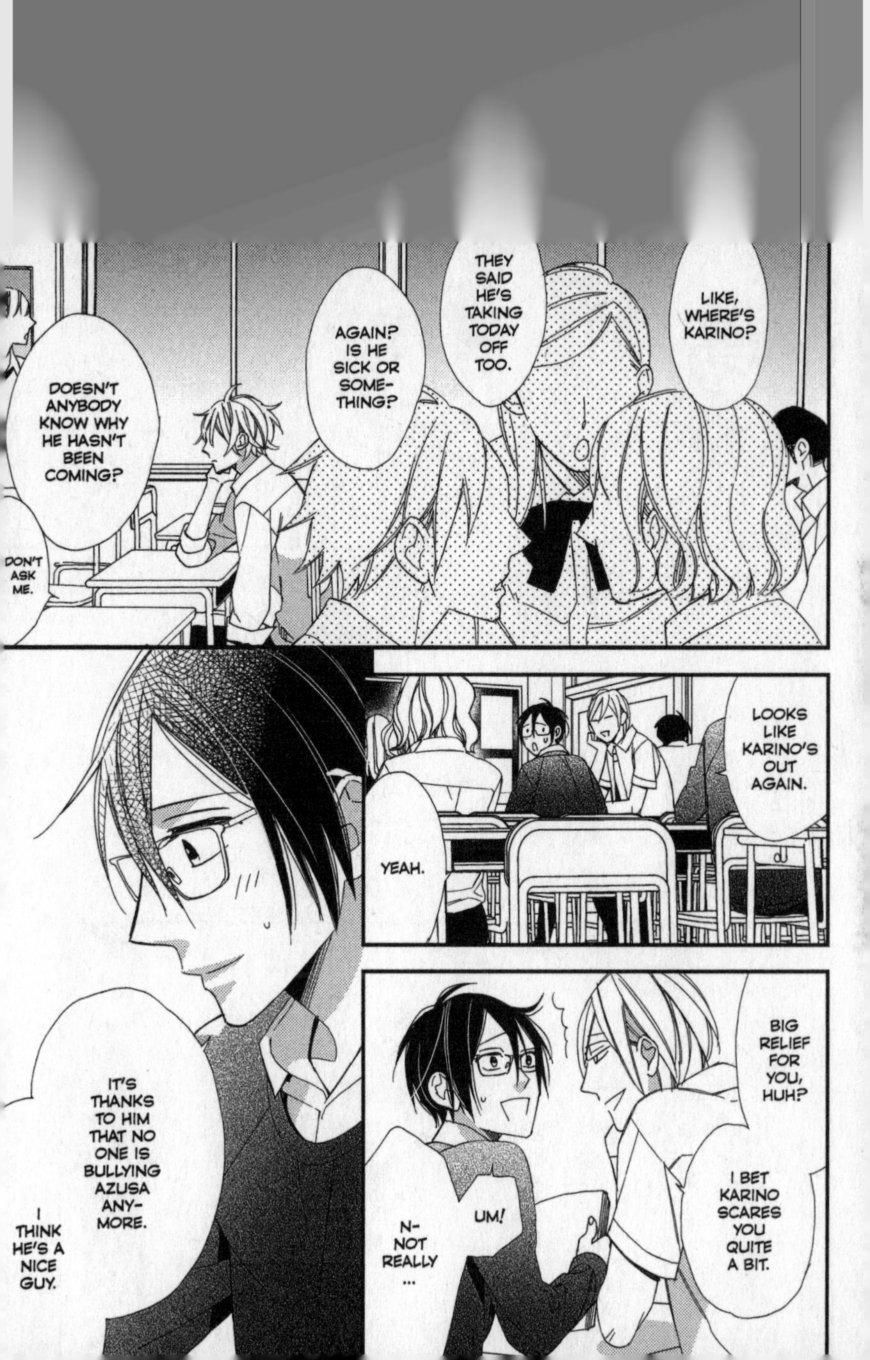
LIKE, WHERE'S KARINO?
THEY SAID HE'S TAKING TODAY OFF TOO.
AGAIN? IS HE SICK OR SOME-THING?
DOESN'T ANYBODY KNOW WHY HE HASN'T BEEN COMING?
DON'T ASK ME.
LOOKS LIKE KARINO'S OUT AGAIN.
YEAH.
BIG RELIEF FOR YOU, HUH?
I BET KARINO SCARES YOU QUITE A BIT.
UM!
N-NOT REALLY...
IT'S THANKS TO HIM THAT NO ONE IS BULLYING AZUSA ANY-MORE.
I THINK HE'S A NICE GUY.

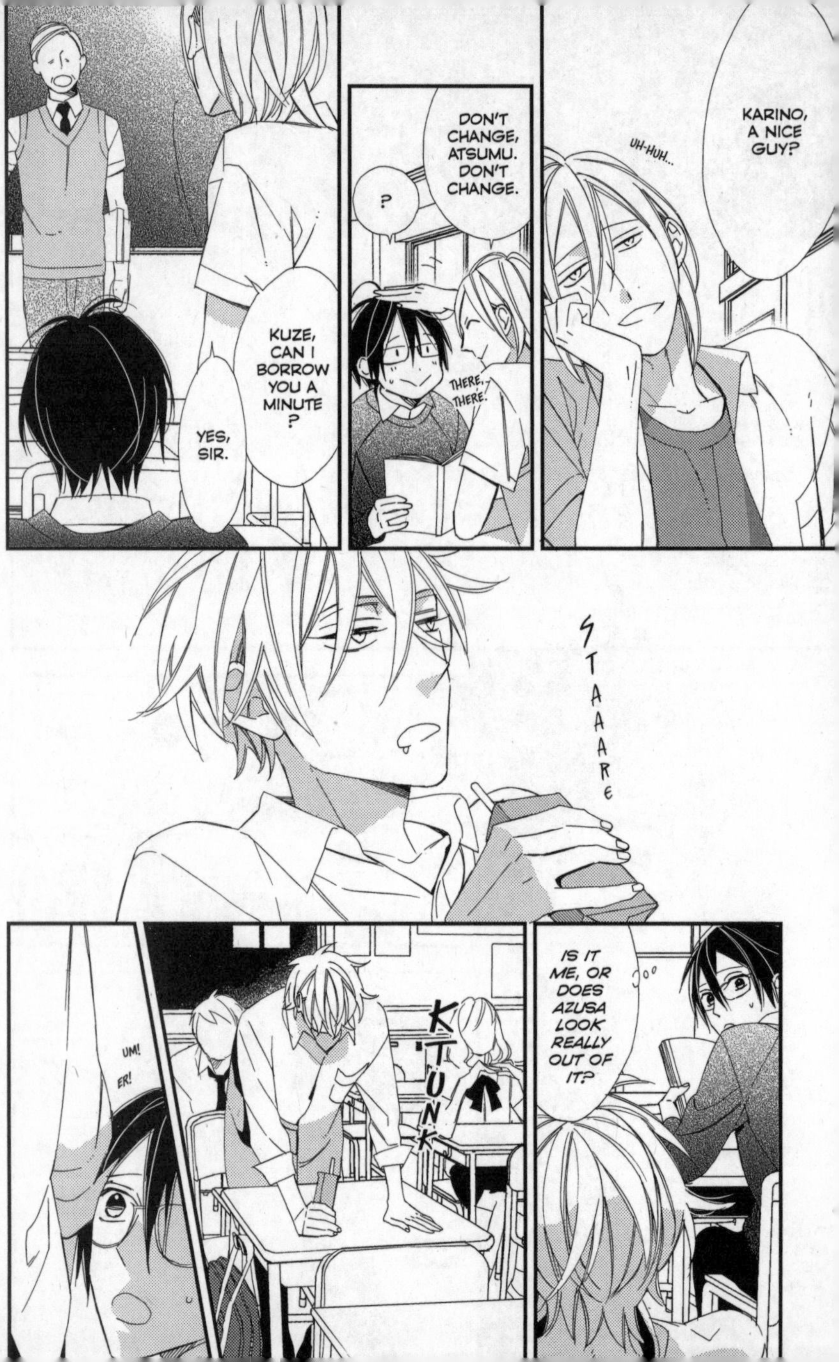
KARINO, A NICE GUY?
UH-HUH...
DON'T CHANGE, ATSUMU. DON'T CHANGE.
?
THERE, THERE.
KUZE, CAN I BORROW YOU A MINUTE?
YES, SIR.
STAAARE
IS IT ME, OR DOES AZUSA LOOK REALLY OUT OF IT?
KTUNK
UM! ER!

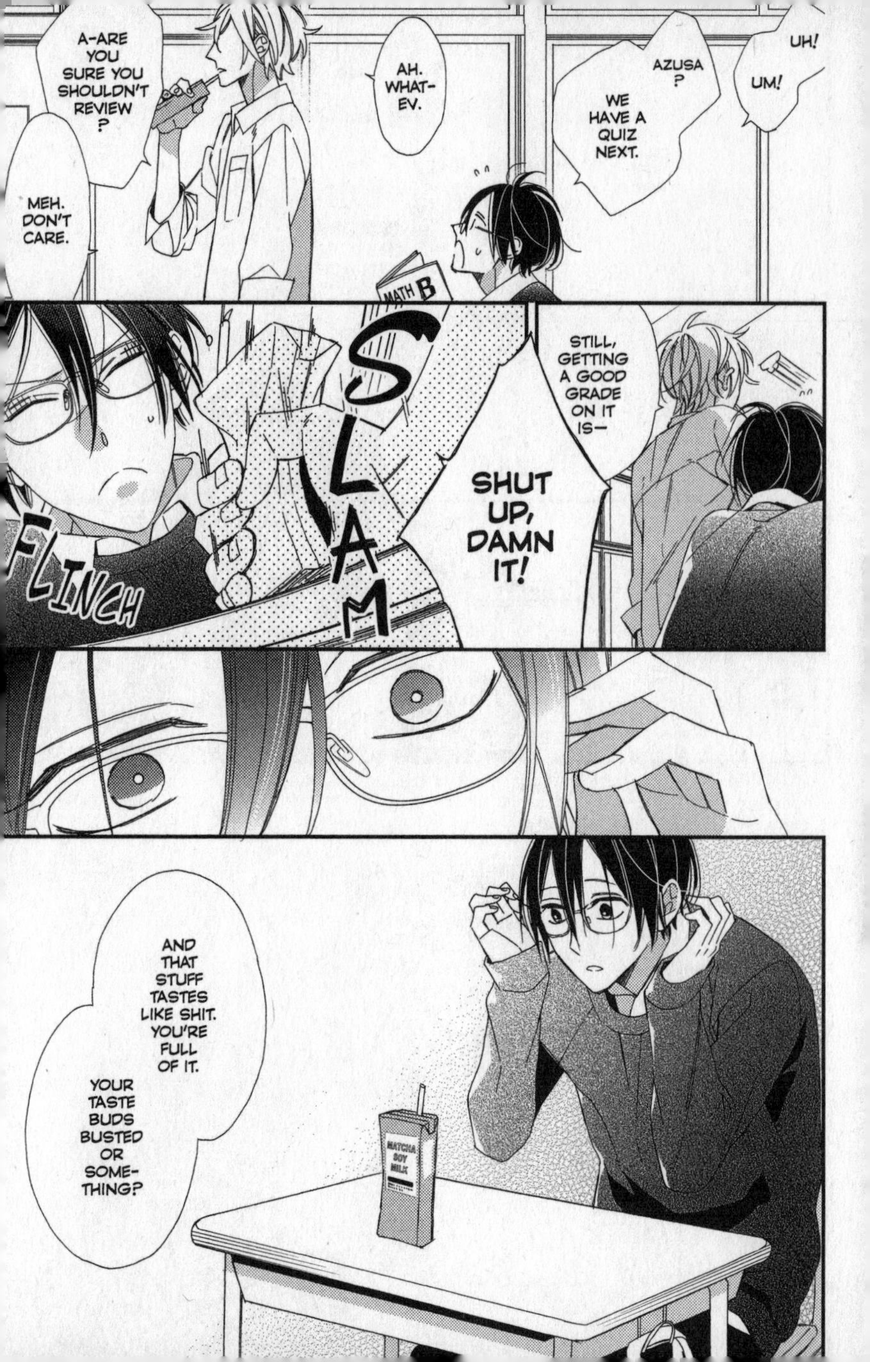
UH!
UM!
AZUSA?
WE HAVE A QUIZ NEXT.
AH. WHAT-EV.
A-ARE YOU SURE YOU SHOULDN'T REVIEW?
MEH. DON'T CARE.
MATH B
STILL, GETTING A GOOD GRADE ON IT IS—
SHUT UP, DAMN IT!
SLAM
FLINCH
AND THAT STUFF TASTES LIKE SHIT. YOU'RE FULL OF IT.
YOUR TASTE BUDS BUSTED OR SOME-THING?
MATCHA SOY MILK

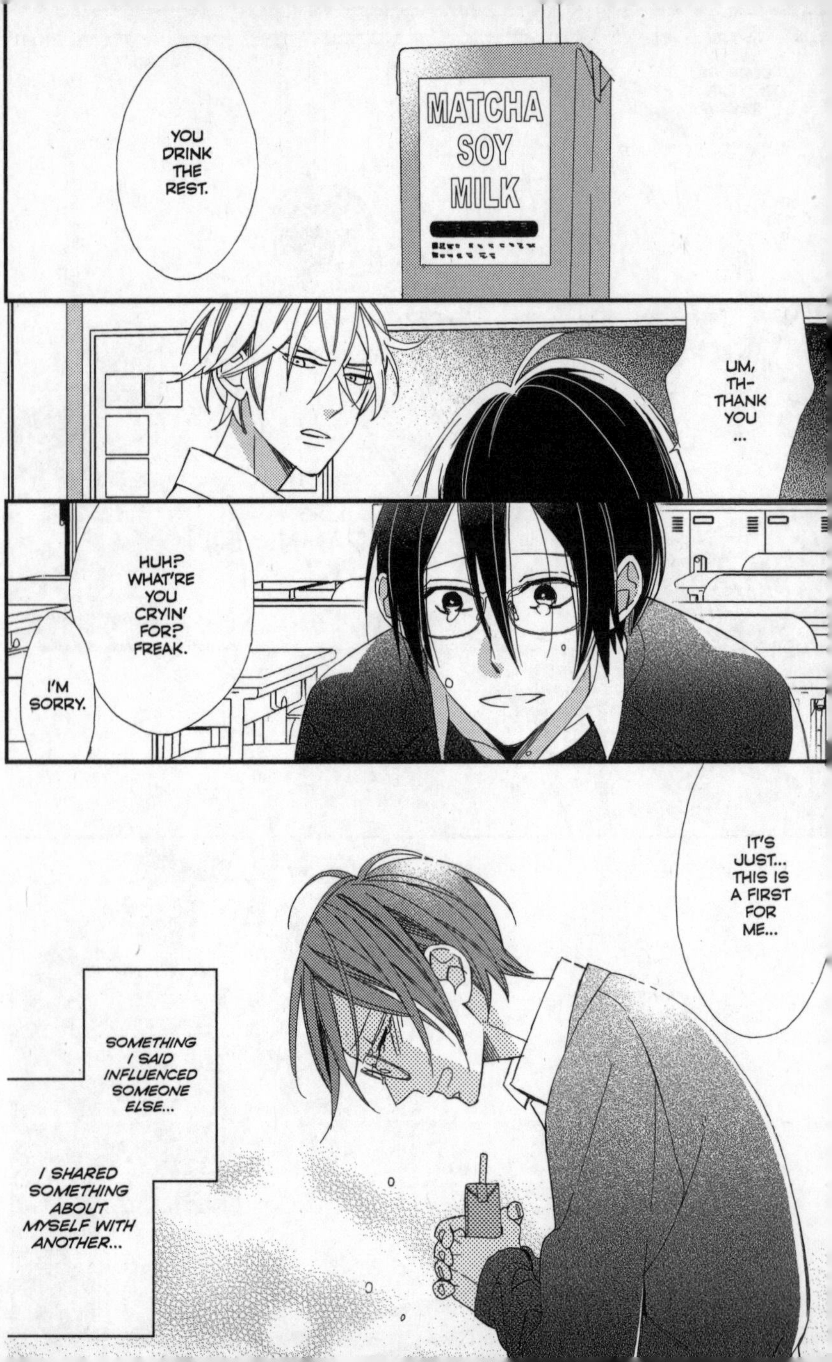
MATCHA SOY MILK
YOU DRINK THE REST.
UM, TH-THANK YOU...
HUH? WHAT'RE YOU CRYIN' FOR? FREAK.
I'M SORRY.
IT'S JUST... THIS IS A FIRST FOR ME...
SOMETHING I SAID INFLUENCED SOMEONE ELSE...
I SHARED SOMETHING ABOUT MYSELF WITH ANOTHER...

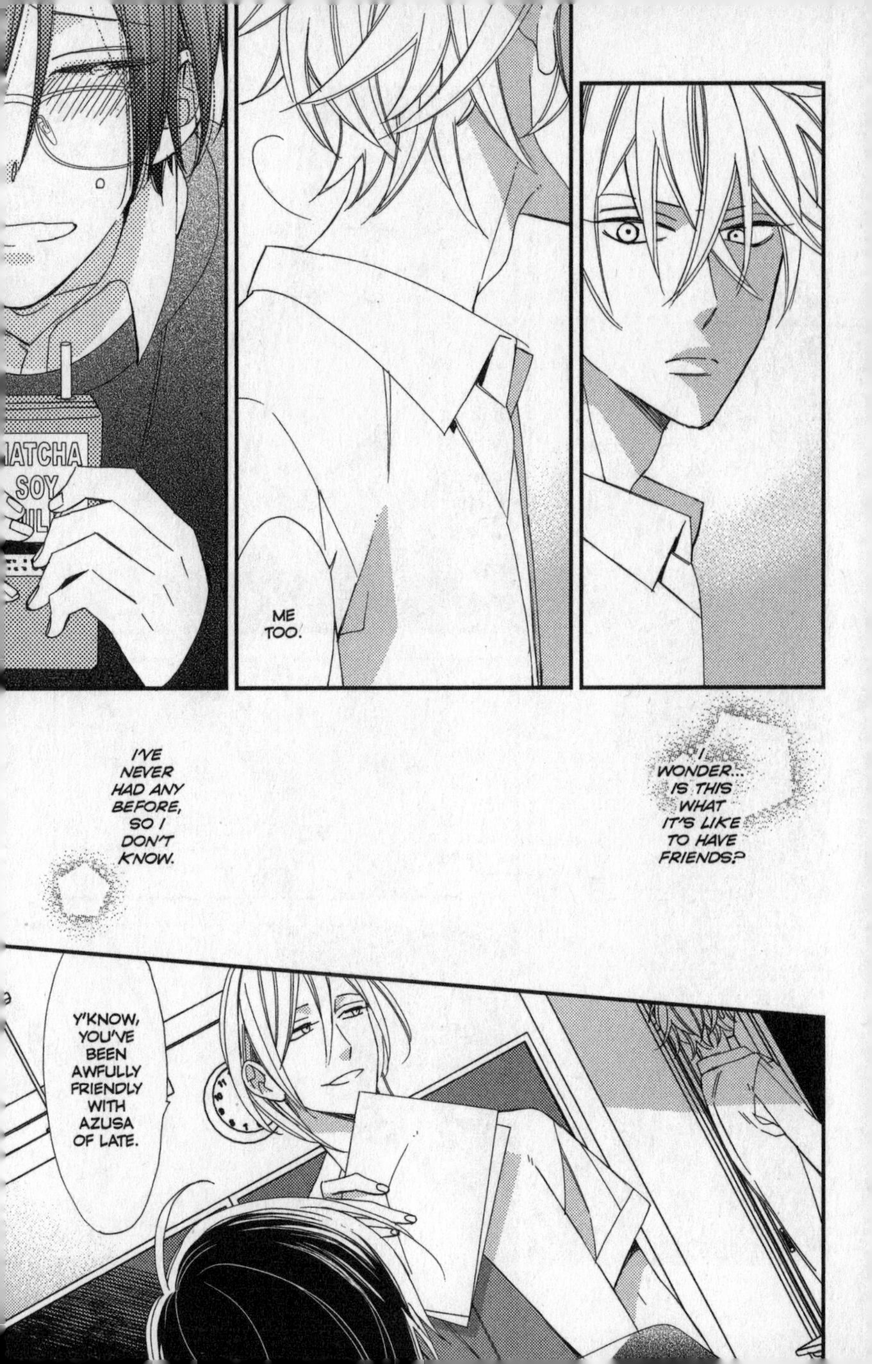
ME TOO.
ATCHA
SOY
I WONDER... IS THIS WHAT IT'S LIKE TO HAVE FRIENDS?
I'VE NEVER HAD ANY BEFORE, SO I DON'T KNOW.
Y'KNOW, YOU'VE BEEN AWFULLY FRIENDLY WITH AZUSA OF LATE.

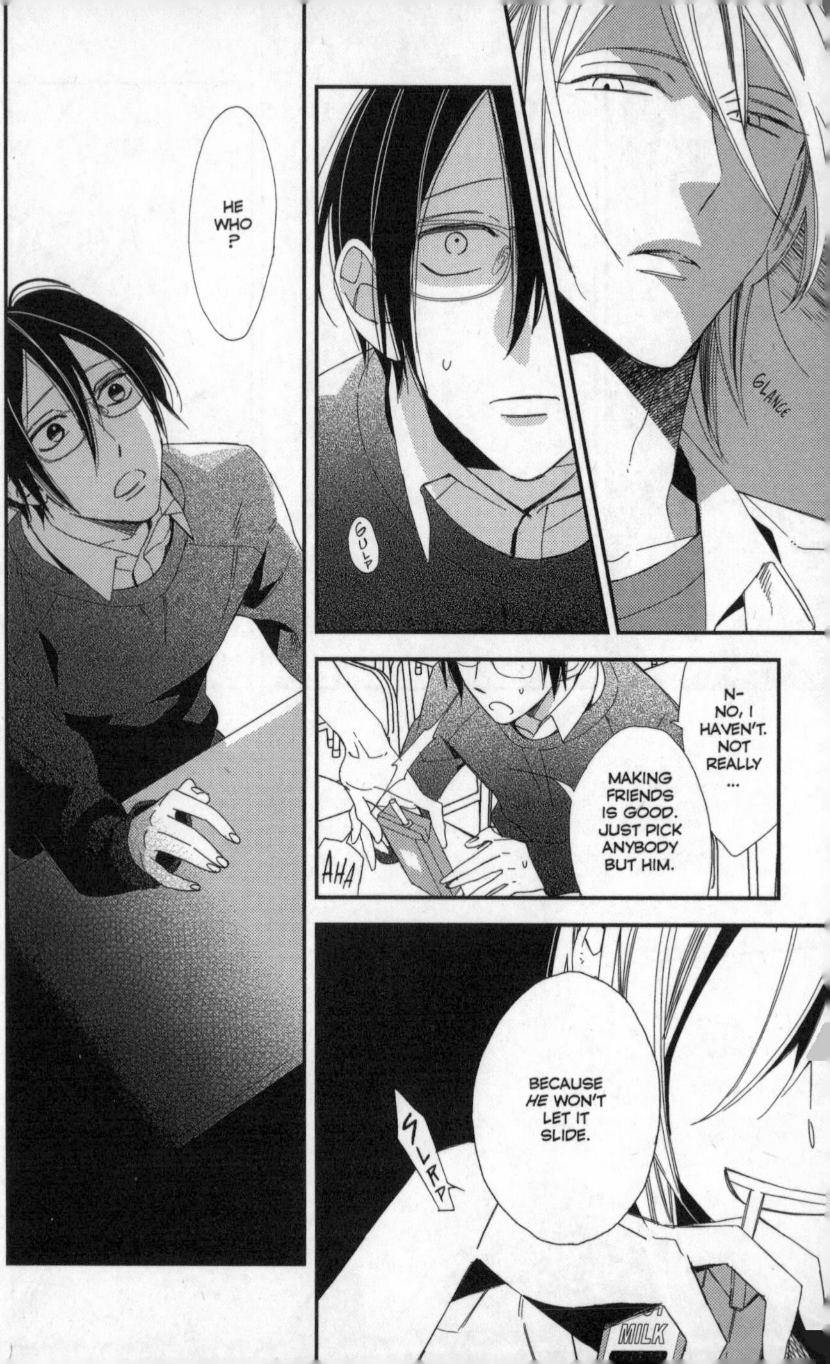
GLANCE
GULP
N-NO, I HAVEN'T. NOT REALLY ...
MAKING FRIENDS IS GOOD. JUST PICK ANYBODY BUT HIM.
AHA
BECAUSE *HE* WON'T LET IT SLIDE.
SLRP
MILK
HE WHO?

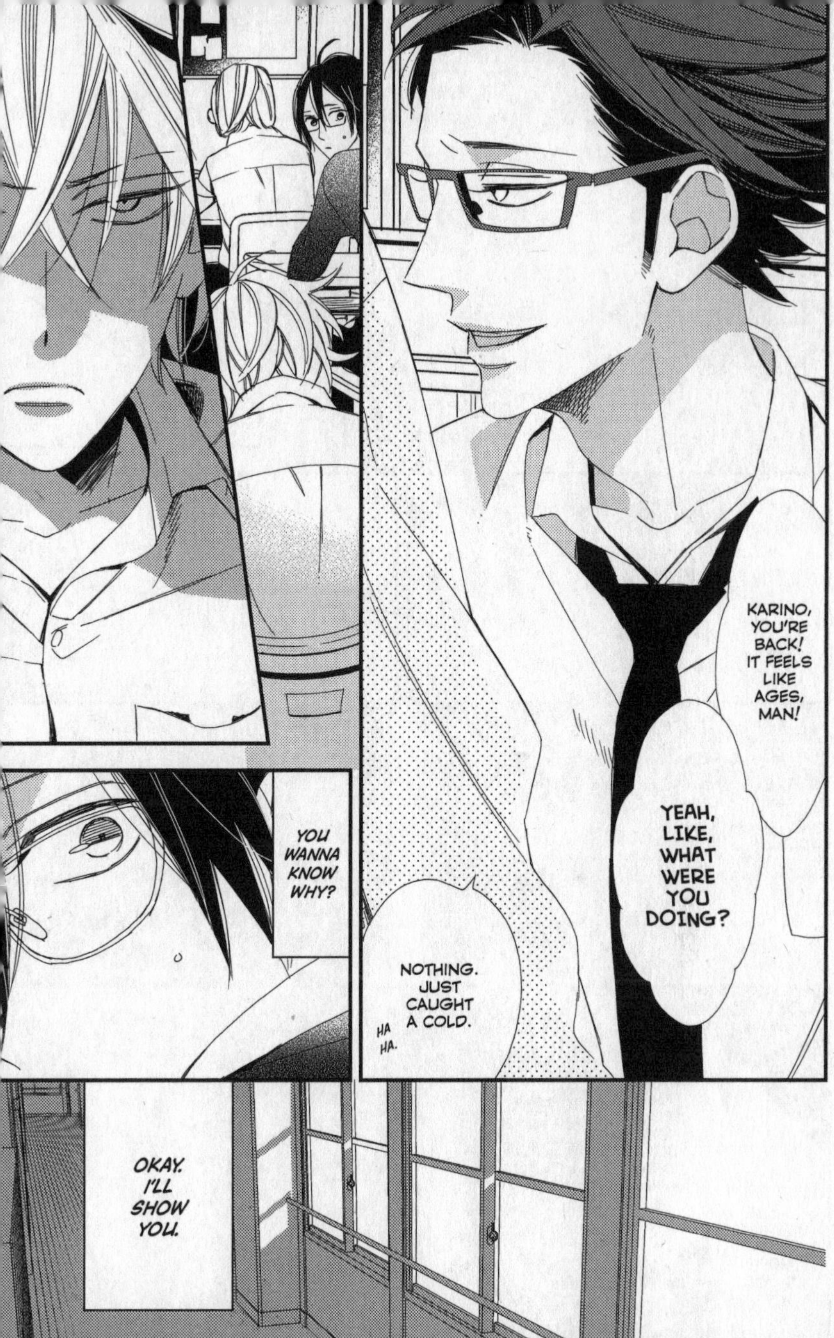
KARINO, YOU'RE BACK! IT FEELS LIKE AGES, MAN!
YEAH, LIKE, WHAT WERE YOU DOING?
NOTHING. JUST CAUGHT A COLD.
HA HA.
YOU WANNA KNOW WHY?
OKAY. I'LL SHOW YOU.

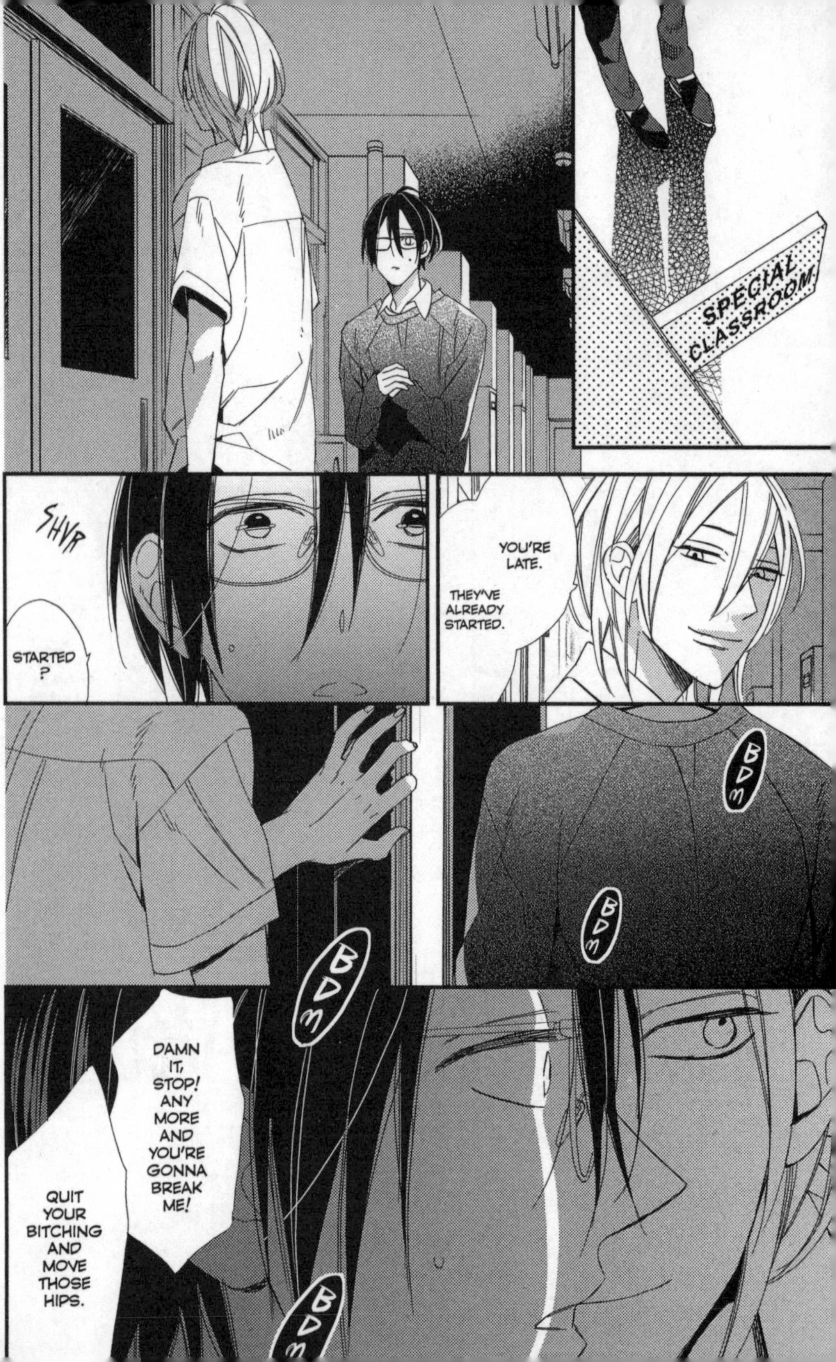
SPECIAL CLASSROOM
YOU'RE LATE.
THEY'VE ALREADY STARTED.
SHVR
STARTED?
BDM
BDM
BDM
DAMN IT, STOP! ANY MORE AND YOU'RE GONNA BREAK ME!
QUIT YOUR BITCHING AND MOVE THOSE HIPS.
BDM

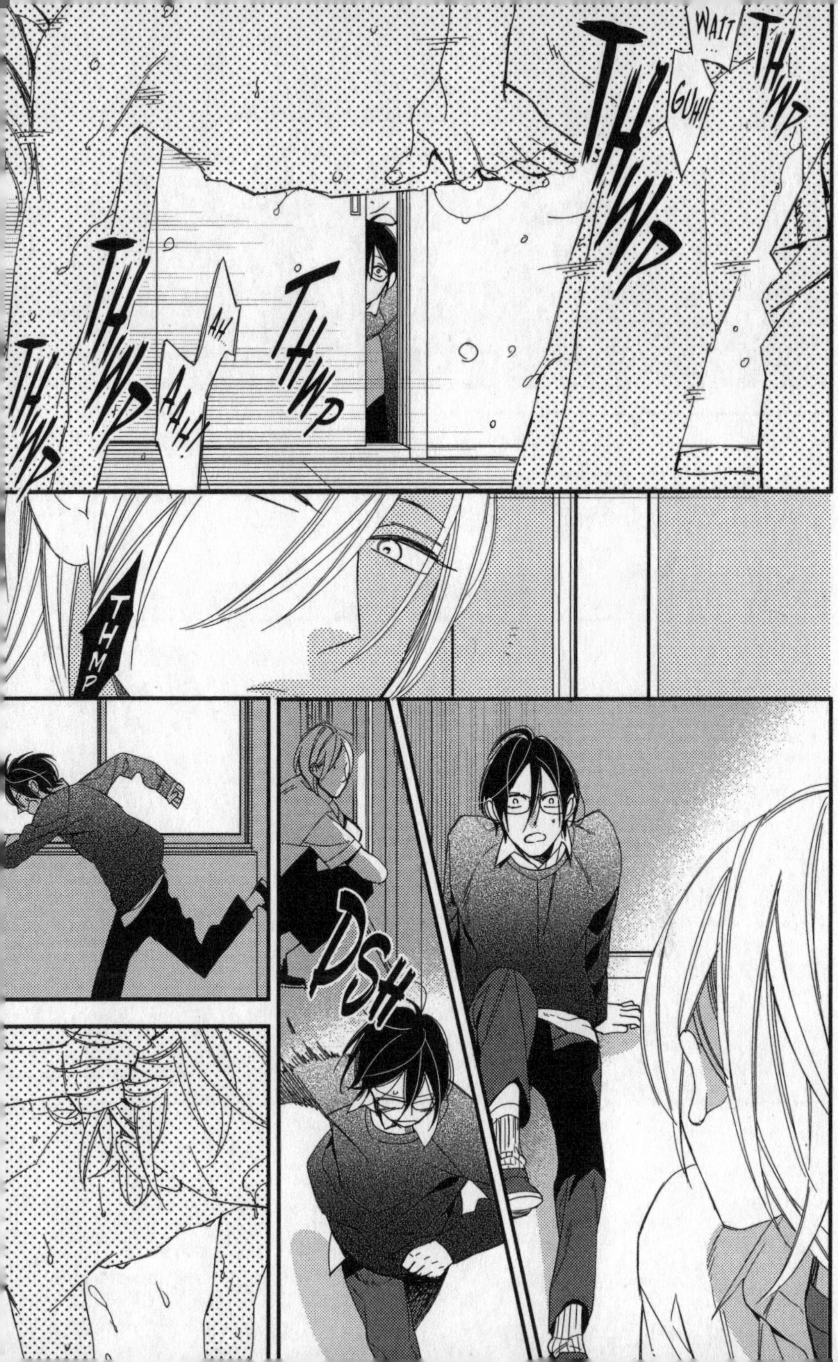
THWP
WAIT...
GUH!
THWP
THWP
AH AAH!
THWP
THWP
THMP
DSH

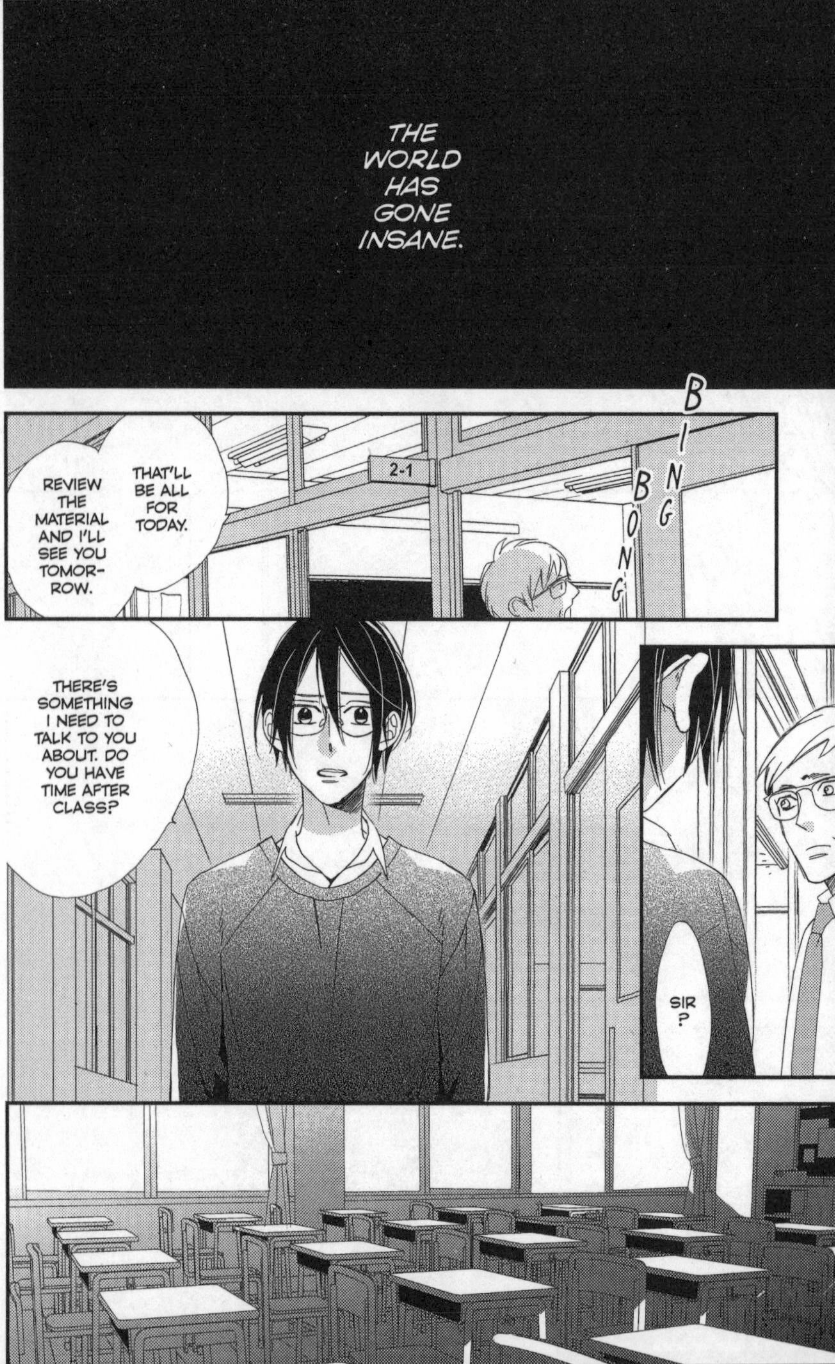
THE WORLD HAS GONE INSANE.
BING BONG
THAT'LL BE ALL FOR TODAY.
REVIEW THE MATERIAL AND I'LL SEE YOU TOMOR-ROW.
2-1
SIR?
THERE'S SOMETHING I NEED TO TALK TO YOU ABOUT. DO YOU HAVE TIME AFTER CLASS?

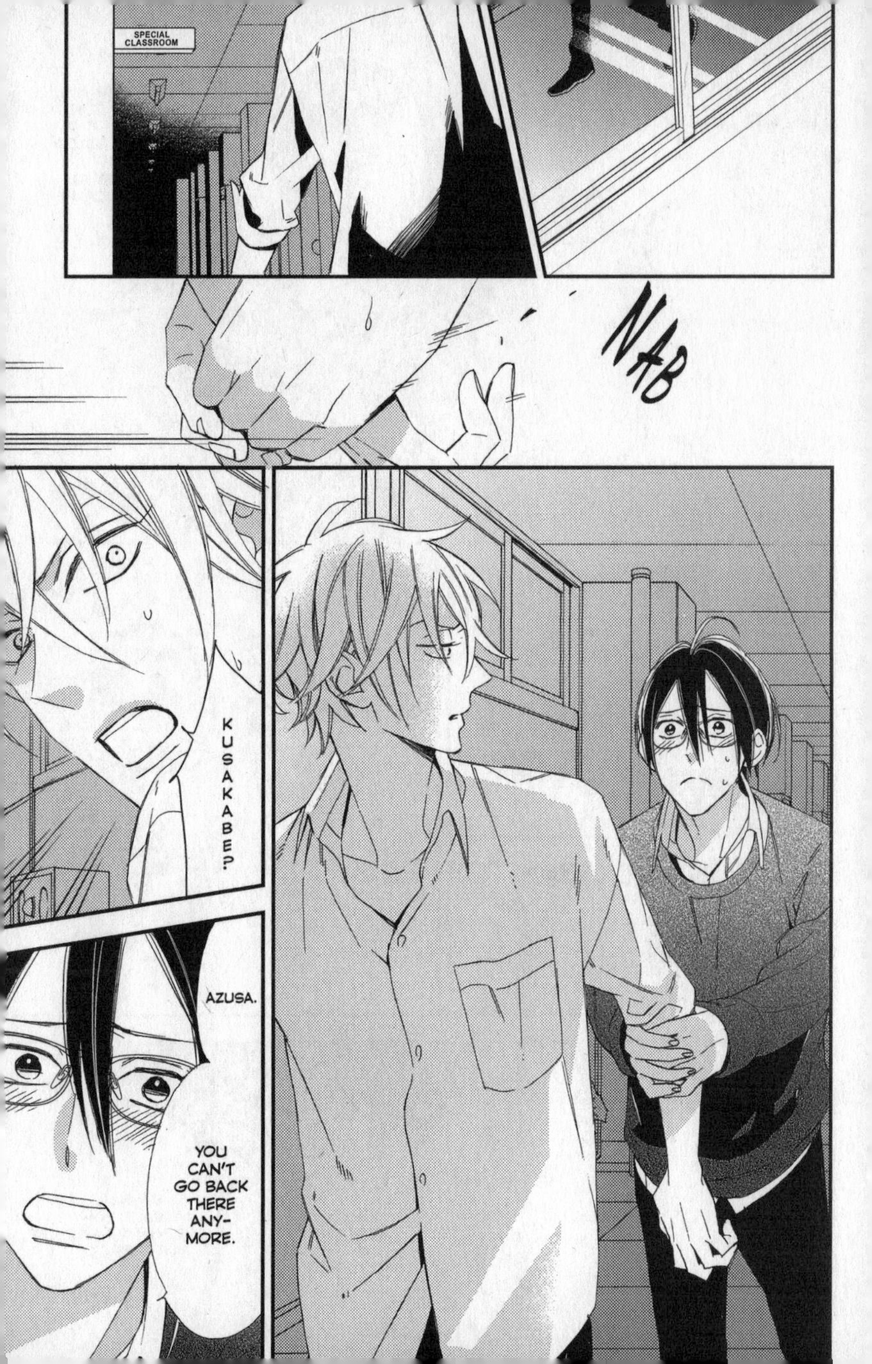
SPECIAL CLASSROOM
NAB
KUSAKABE?
AZUSA.
YOU CAN'T GO BACK THERE ANY-MORE.

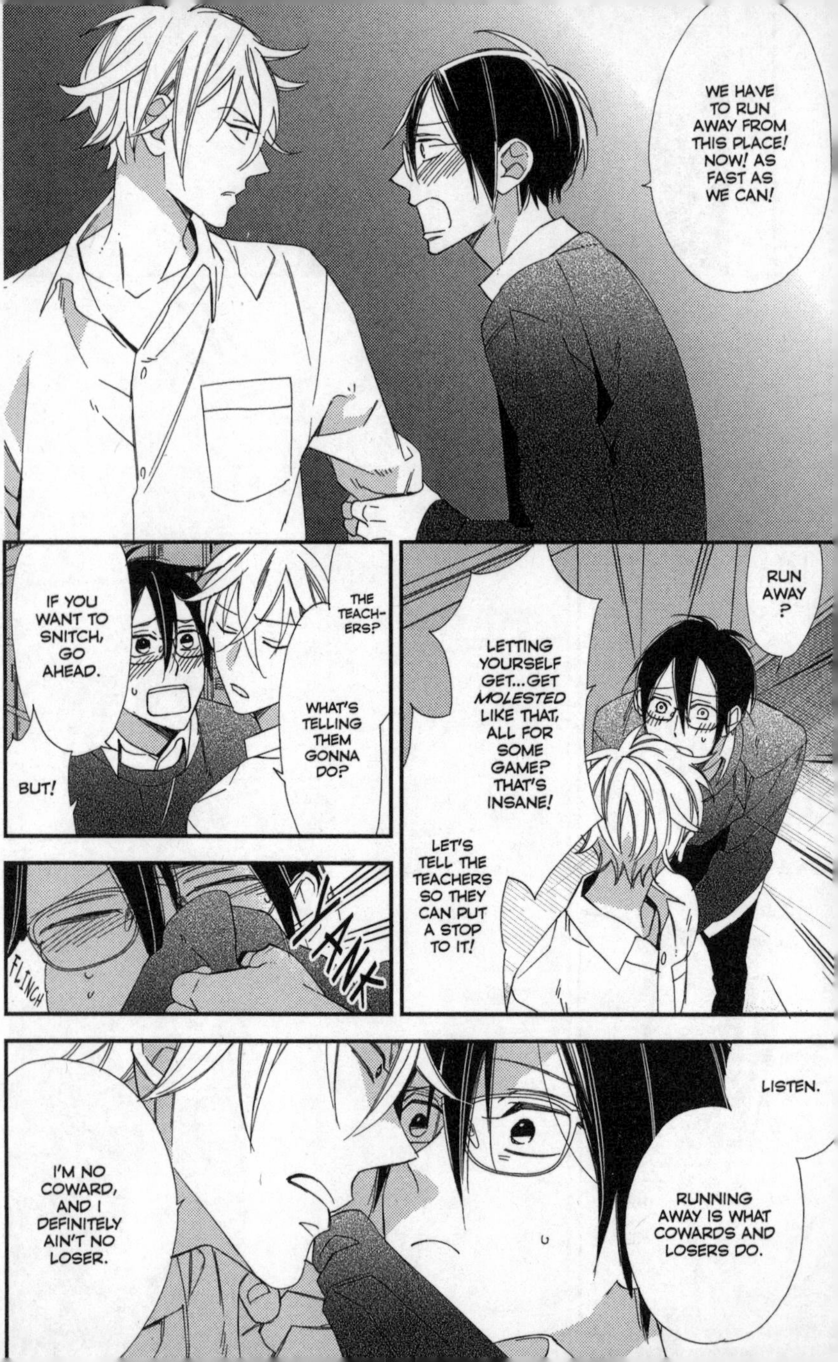
WE HAVE TO RUN AWAY FROM THIS PLACE! NOW! AS FAST AS WE CAN!
RUN AWAY?
LETTING YOURSELF GET...GET MOLESTED LIKE THAT, ALL FOR SOME GAME? THAT'S INSANE!
LET'S TELL THE TEACHERS SO THEY CAN PUT A STOP TO IT!
THE TEACHERS?
WHAT'S TELLING THEM GONNA DO?
IF YOU WANT TO SNITCH, GO AHEAD.
BUT!
YANK
FLINCH
LISTEN.
RUNNING AWAY IS WHAT COWARDS AND LOSERS DO.
I'M NO COWARD, AND I DEFINITELY AIN'T NO LOSER.

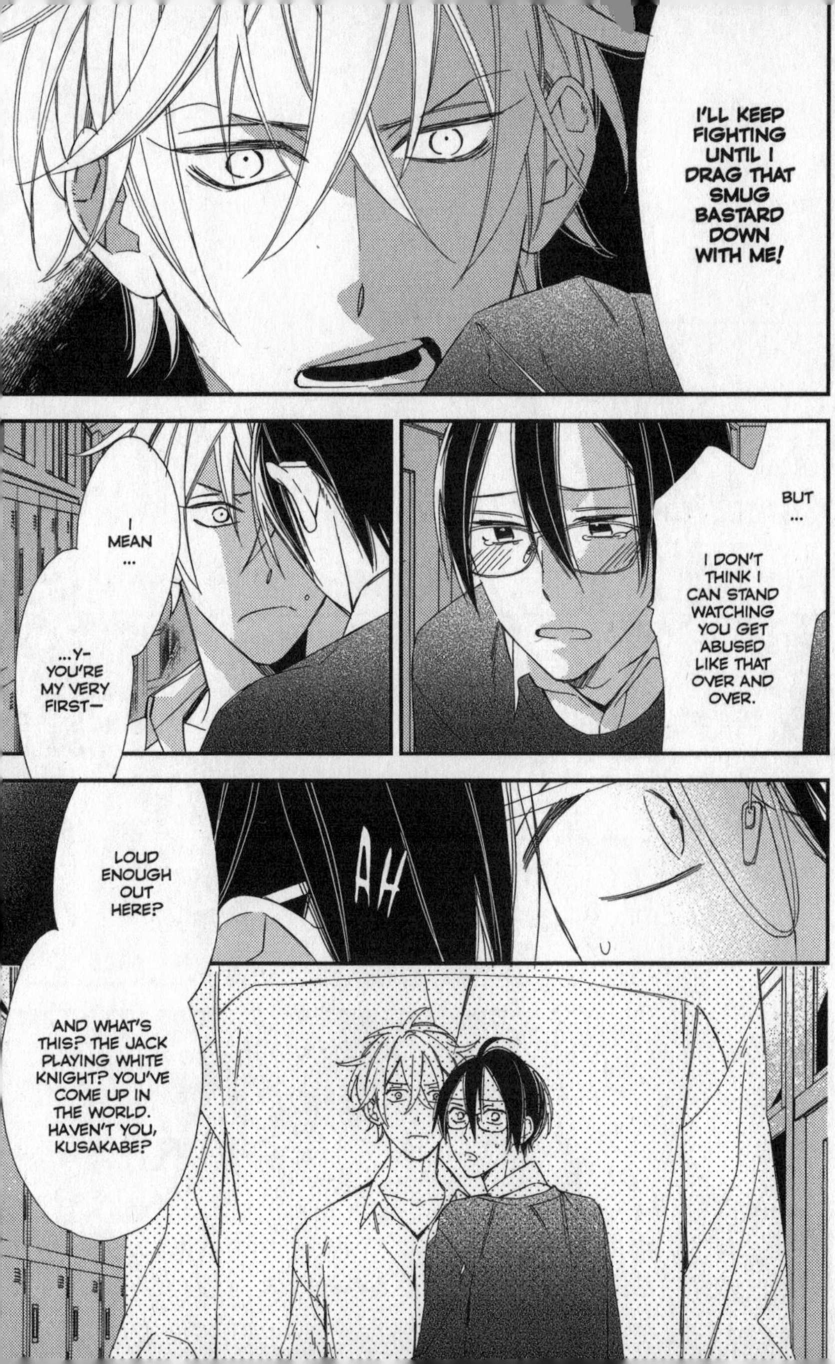
I'LL KEEP FIGHTING UNTIL I DRAG THAT SMUG BASTARD DOWN WITH ME!
BUT ...
I DON'T THINK I CAN STAND WATCHING YOU GET ABUSED LIKE THAT OVER AND OVER.
I MEAN ...
...Y-YOU'RE MY VERY FIRST—
AH
LOUD ENOUGH OUT HERE?
AND WHAT'S THIS? THE JACK PLAYING WHITE KNIGHT? YOU'VE COME UP IN THE WORLD. HAVEN'T YOU, KUSAKABE?

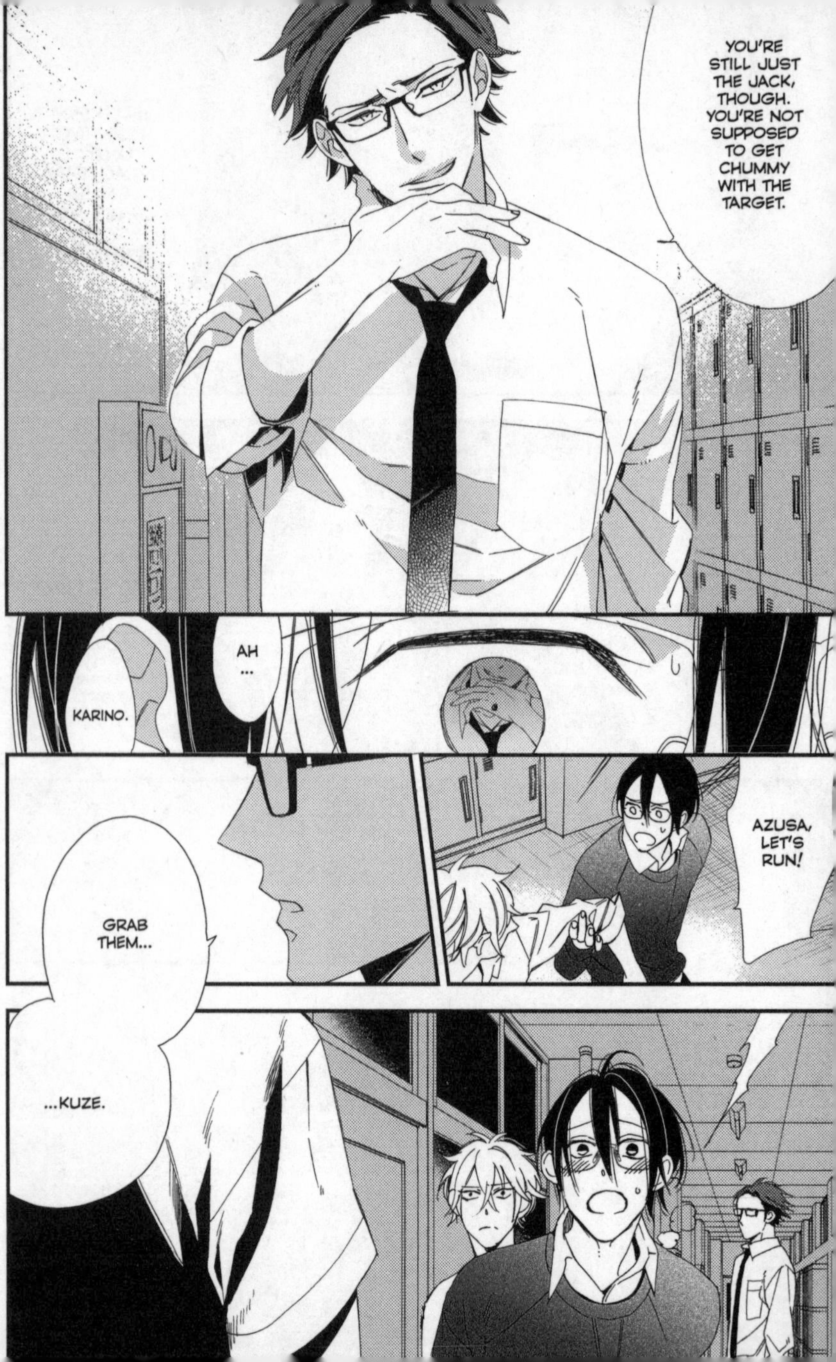
YOU'RE STILL JUST THE JACK, THOUGH. YOU'RE NOT SUPPOSED TO GET CHUMMY WITH THE TARGET.
AH ...
KARINO.
AZUSA, LET'S RUN!
GRAB THEM...
...KUZE.

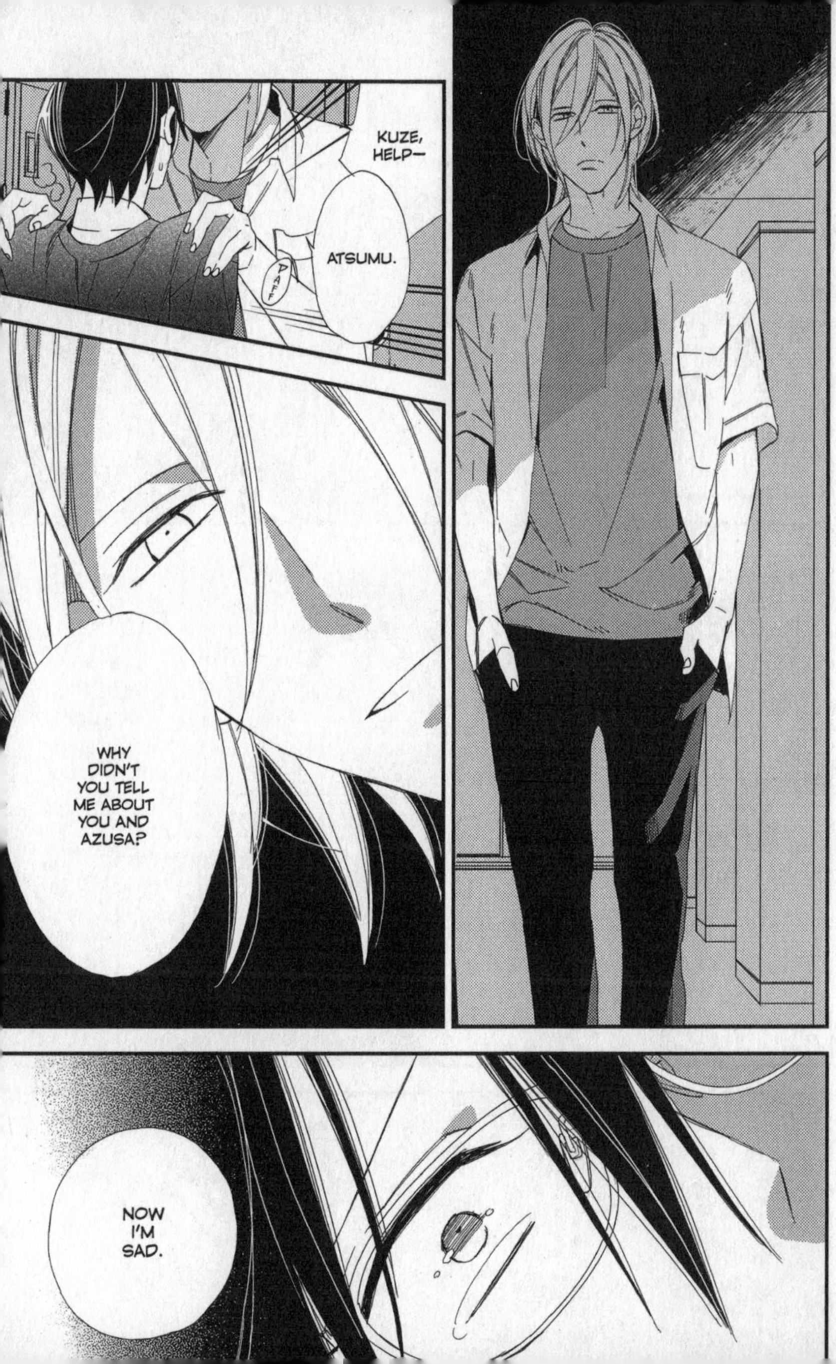
KUZE, HELP—
ATSUMU.
PAFF
WHY DIDN'T YOU TELL ME ABOUT YOU AND AZUSA?
NOW I'M SAD.

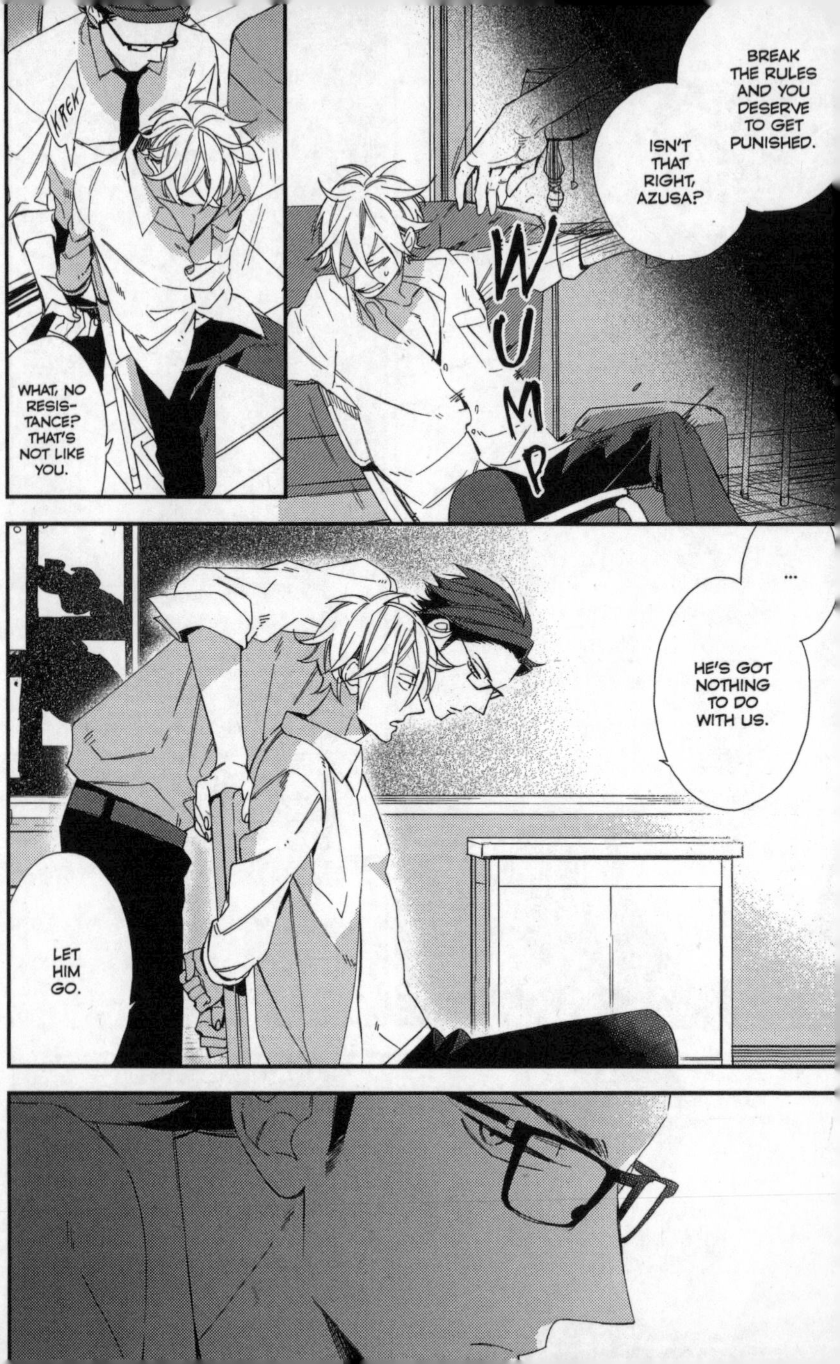
BREAK THE RULES AND YOU DESERVE TO GET PUNISHED.
ISN'T THAT RIGHT, AZUSA?
WUMP
KREK
WHAT, NO RESIS-TANCE? THAT'S NOT LIKE YOU.
...
HE'S GOT NOTHING TO DO WITH US.
LET HIM GO.

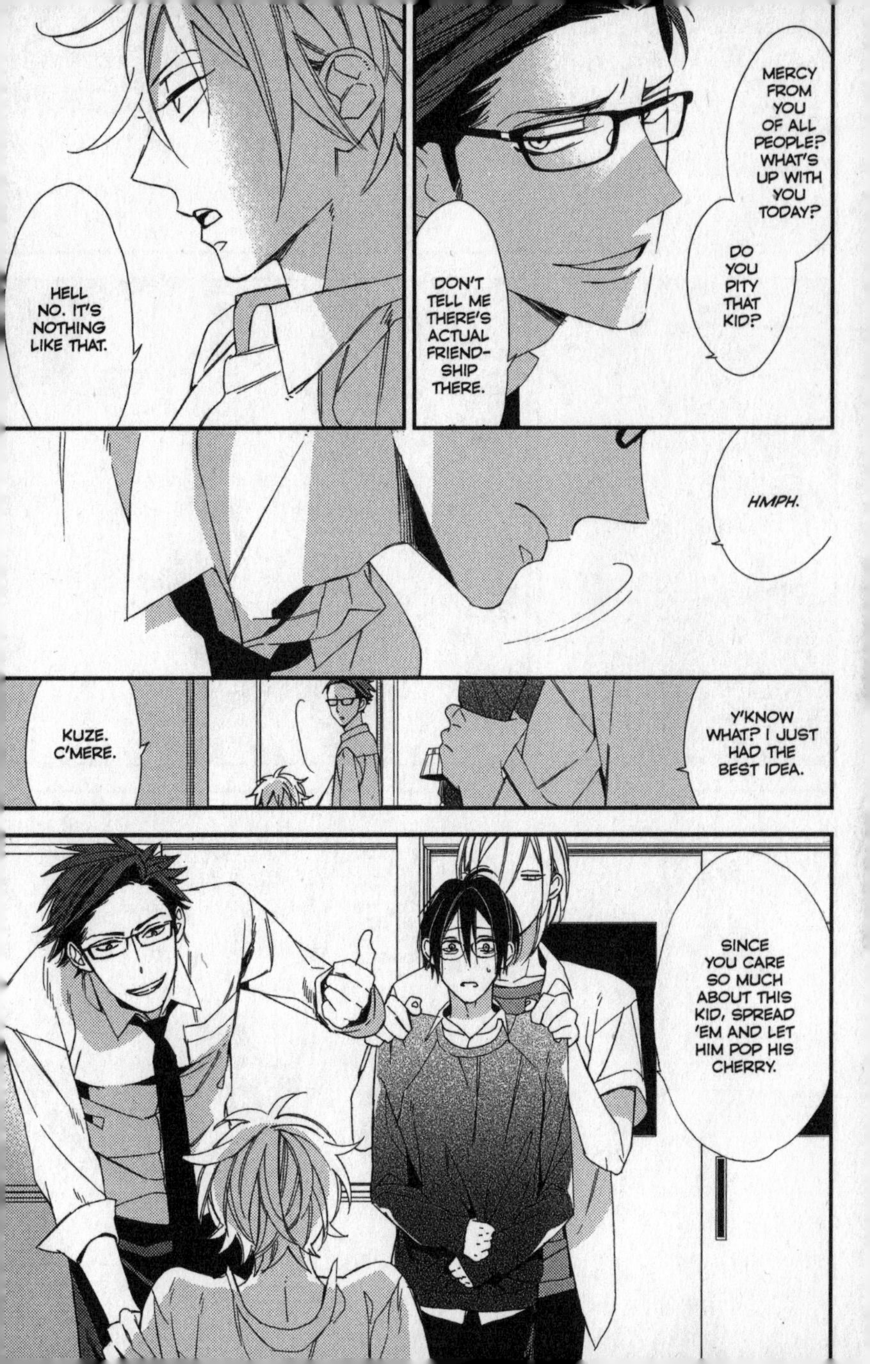
MERCY FROM YOU OF ALL PEOPLE? WHAT'S UP WITH YOU TODAY?
DO YOU PITY THAT KID?
DON'T TELL ME THERE'S ACTUAL FRIEND-SHIP THERE.
HELL NO. IT'S NOTHING LIKE THAT.
HMPH.
Y'KNOW WHAT? I JUST HAD THE BEST IDEA.
KUZE. C'MERE.
SINCE YOU CARE SO MUCH ABOUT THIS KID, SPREAD 'EM AND LET HIM POP HIS CHERRY.

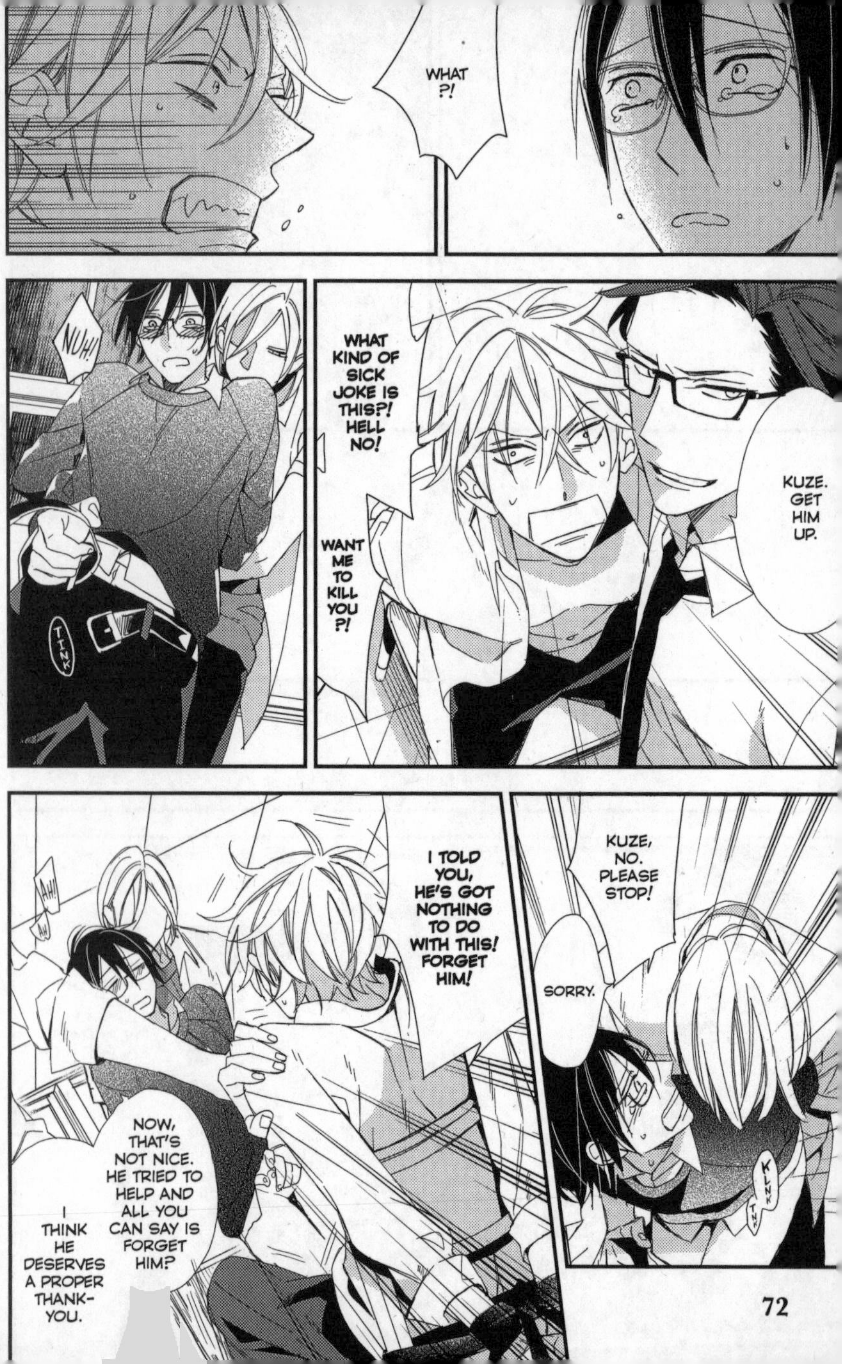
WHAT ?!
KUZE. GET HIM UP.
WHAT KIND OF SICK JOKE IS THIS?! HELL NO!
WANT ME TO KILL YOU ?!
NUH!
TINK
KUZE, NO. PLEASE STOP!
SORRY.
KLNK
TNK
I TOLD YOU, HE'S GOT NOTHING TO DO WITH THIS! FORGET HIM!
AH!
AH
NOW, THAT'S NOT NICE. HE TRIED TO HELP AND ALL YOU CAN SAY IS FORGET HIM?
I THINK HE DESERVES A PROPER THANK-YOU.

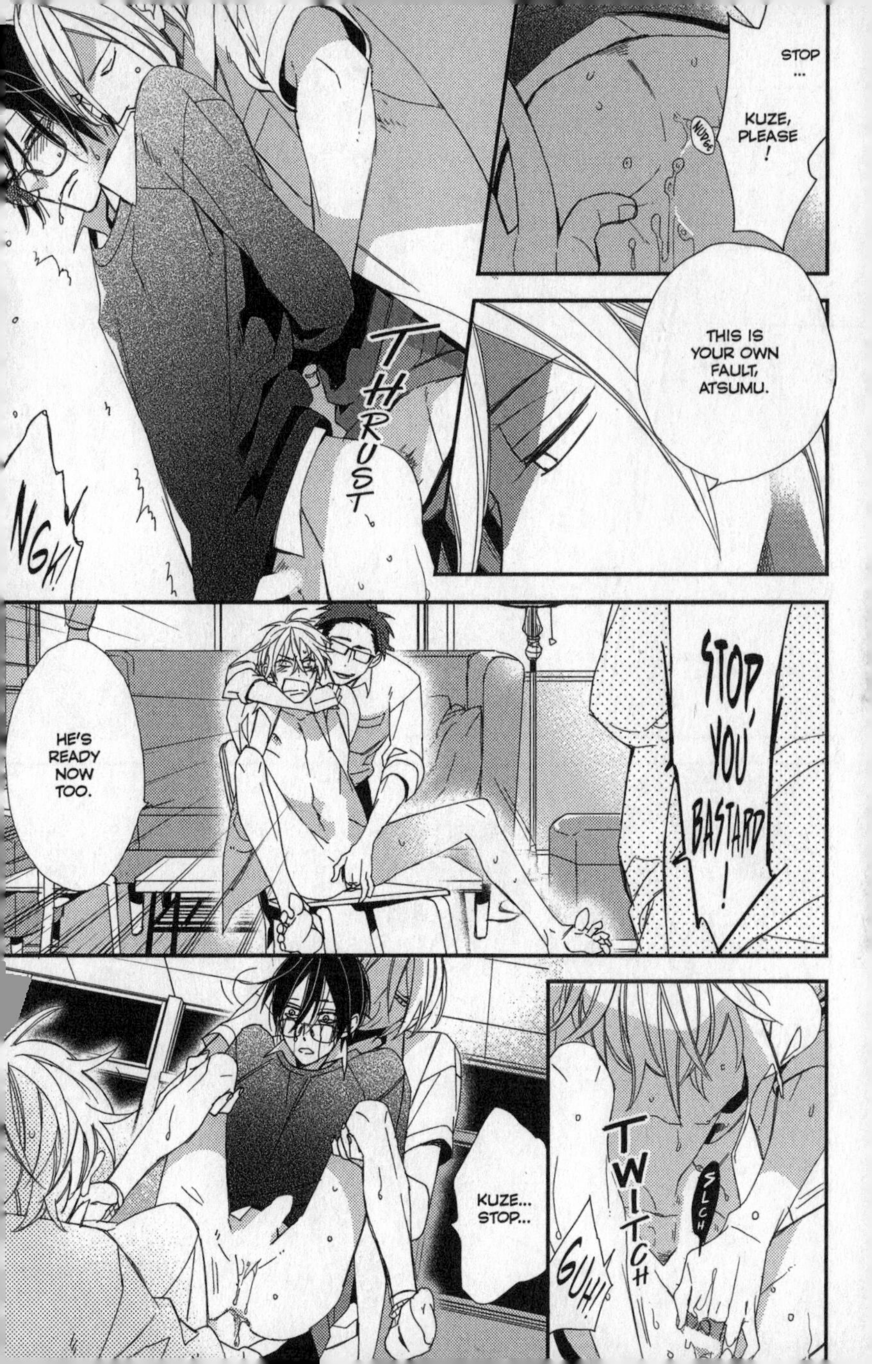
STOP ...
KUZE, PLEASE!
NUDGE
THIS IS YOUR OWN FAULT, ATSUMU.
THRUST
NGK!
STOP, YOU BASTARD!
HE'S READY NOW TOO.
TWITCH
SLCH
GUH!
KUZE... STOP...

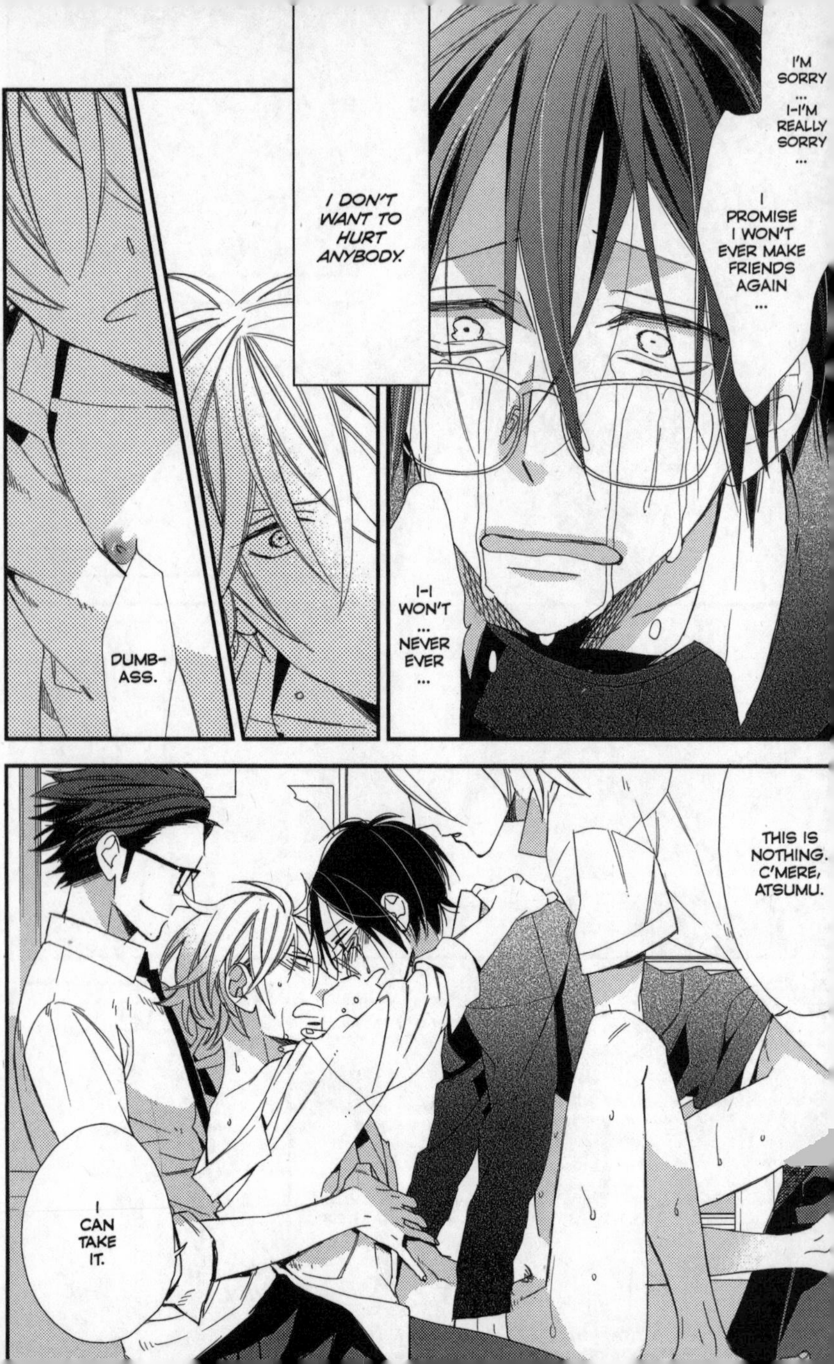
I'M SORRY ... I-I'M REALLY SORRY ...
I PROMISE I WON'T EVER MAKE FRIENDS AGAIN ...
I-I WON'T ... NEVER EVER ...
I DON'T WANT TO HURT ANYBODY.
DUMB-ASS.
THIS IS NOTHING. C'MERE, ATSUMU.
I CAN TAKE IT.

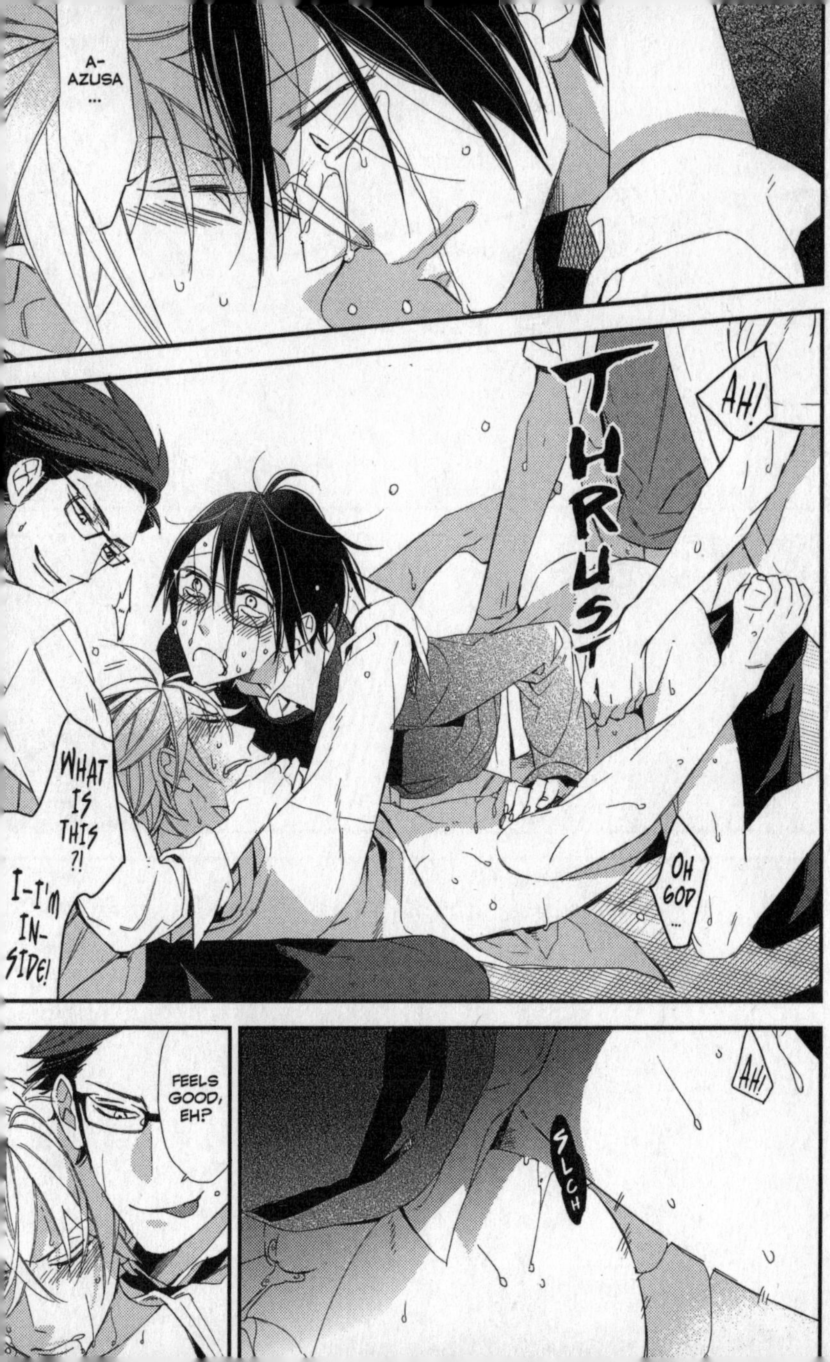
A-AZUSA ...
AH!
THRUST
OH GOD ...
WHAT IS THIS ?!
I-I'M IN-SIDE!
AH!
SLCH
FEELS GOOD, EH?

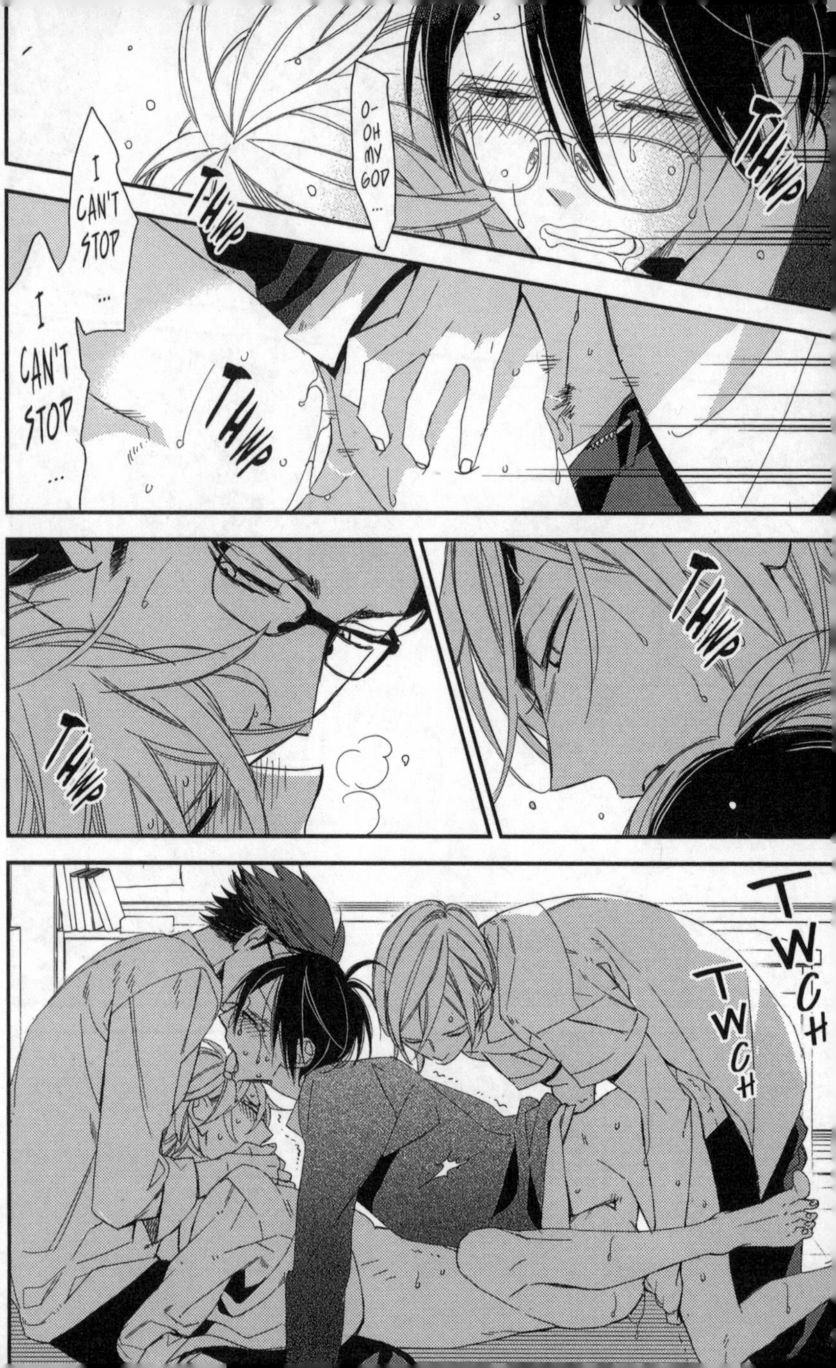
THWP
O-OH MY GOD ...
THWP
I CAN'T STOP ...
I CAN'T STOP ...
THWP
THWP
THWP
TWCH
TWCH

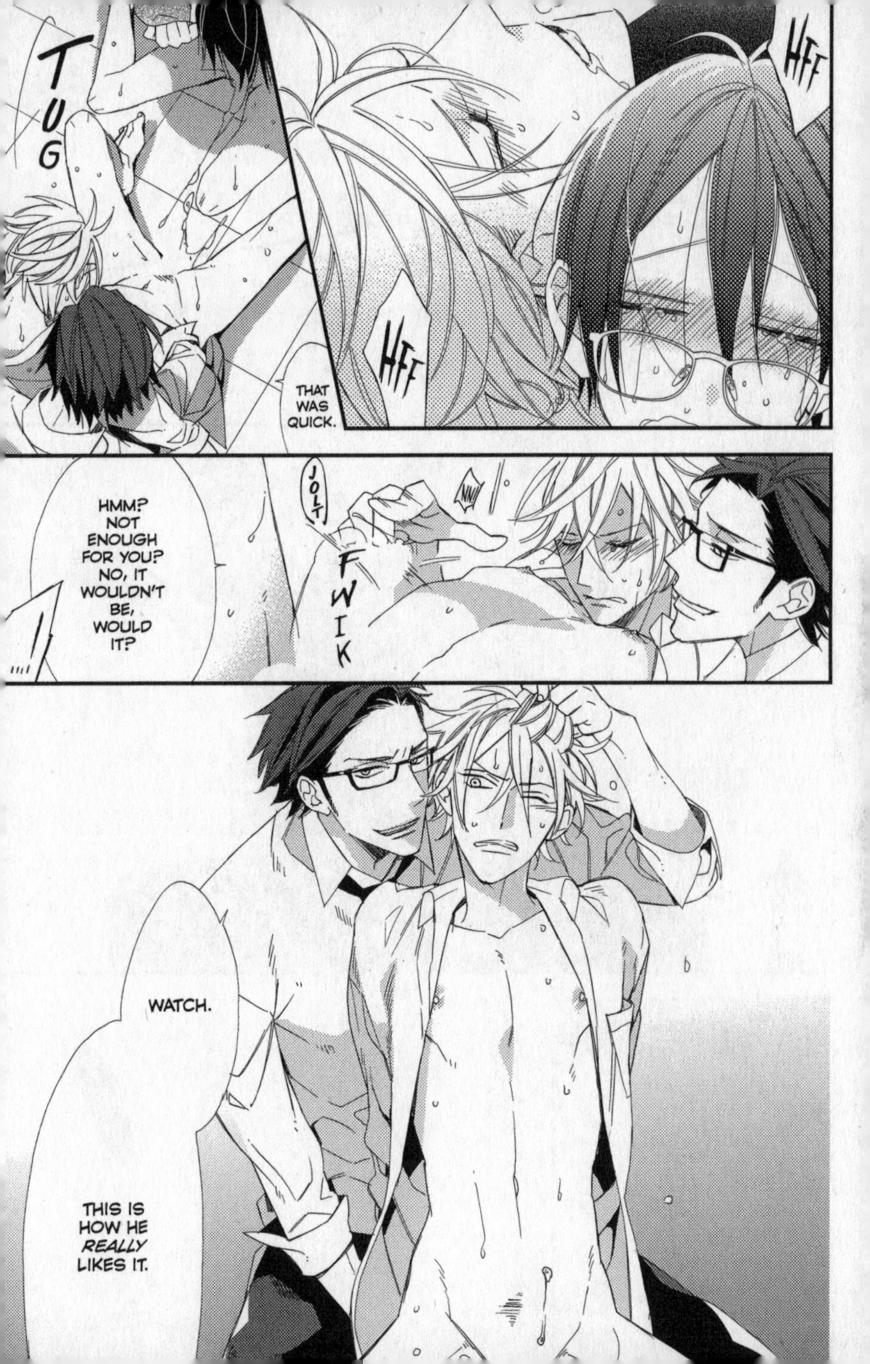
HFF
HFF
THAT WAS QUICK.
TUG
NN!
JOLT
FWIK
HMM? NOT ENOUGH FOR YOU? NO, IT WOULDN'T BE, WOULD IT?
...!
WATCH.
THIS IS HOW HE *REALLY* LIKES IT.

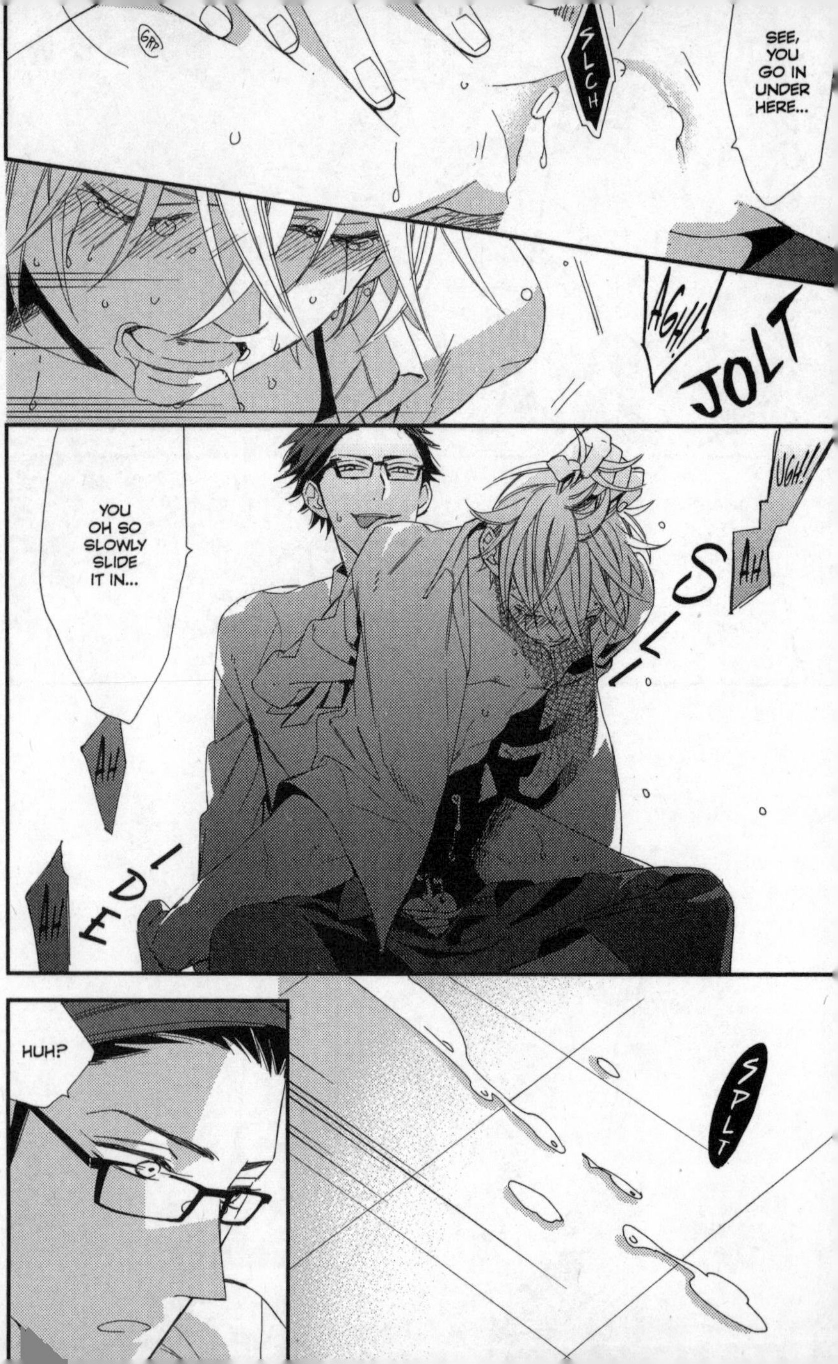
SEE, YOU GO IN UNDER HERE...
SLCH
GRP
JOLT
AGH!!
UGH!!
AH
SLIIDE
YOU OH SO SLOWLY SLIDE IT IN...
AH
AH
SPLT
HUH?

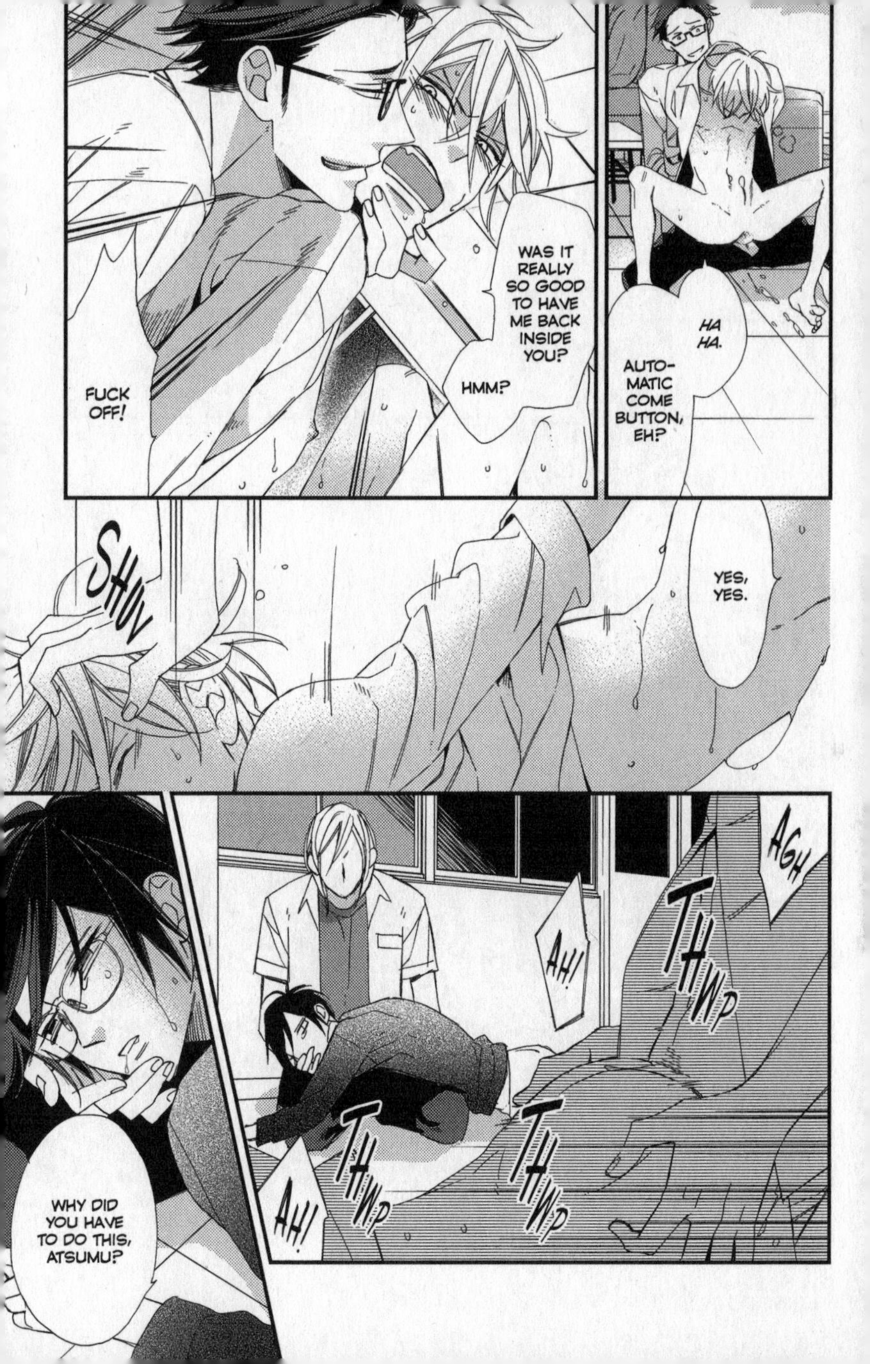
HA HA.
AUTOMATIC COME BUTTON, EH?
WAS IT REALLY SO GOOD TO HAVE ME BACK INSIDE YOU?
HMM?
FUCK OFF!
YES, YES.
SHUV
AGH
THWP
AH!
THWP
THWP
AH!
WHY DID YOU HAVE TO DO THIS, ATSUMU?

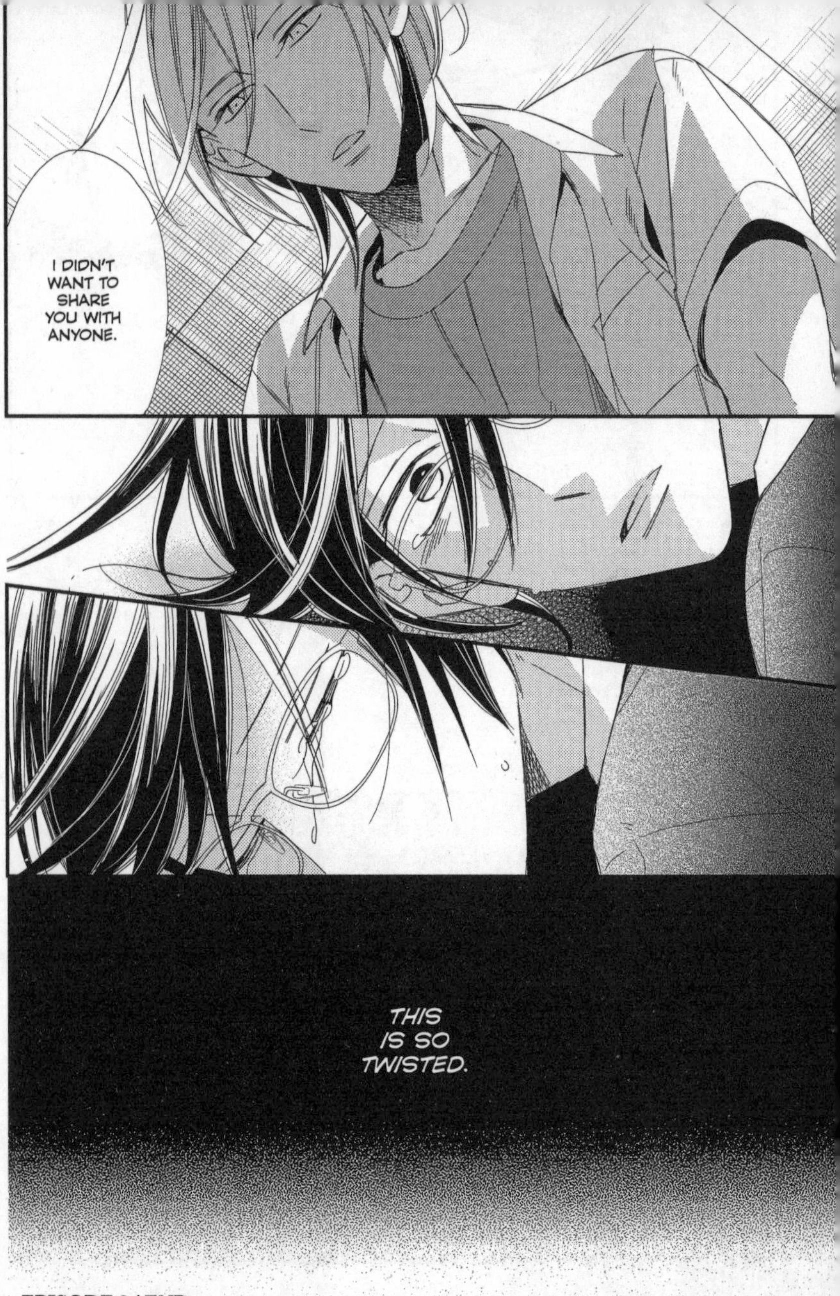
I DIDN'T WANT TO SHARE YOU WITH ANYONE.
THIS IS SO TWISTED.

EPISODE 8 / END

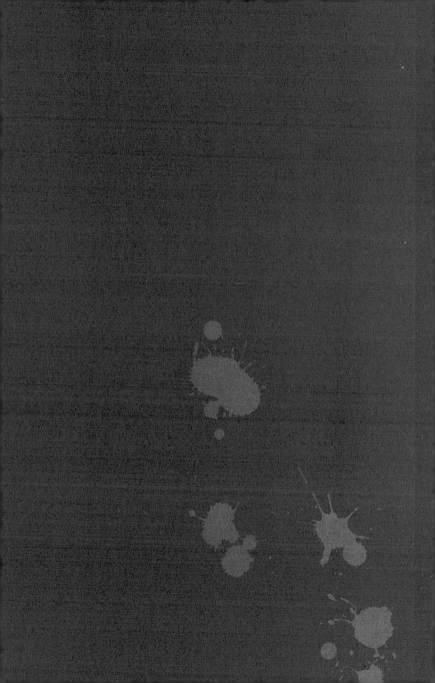

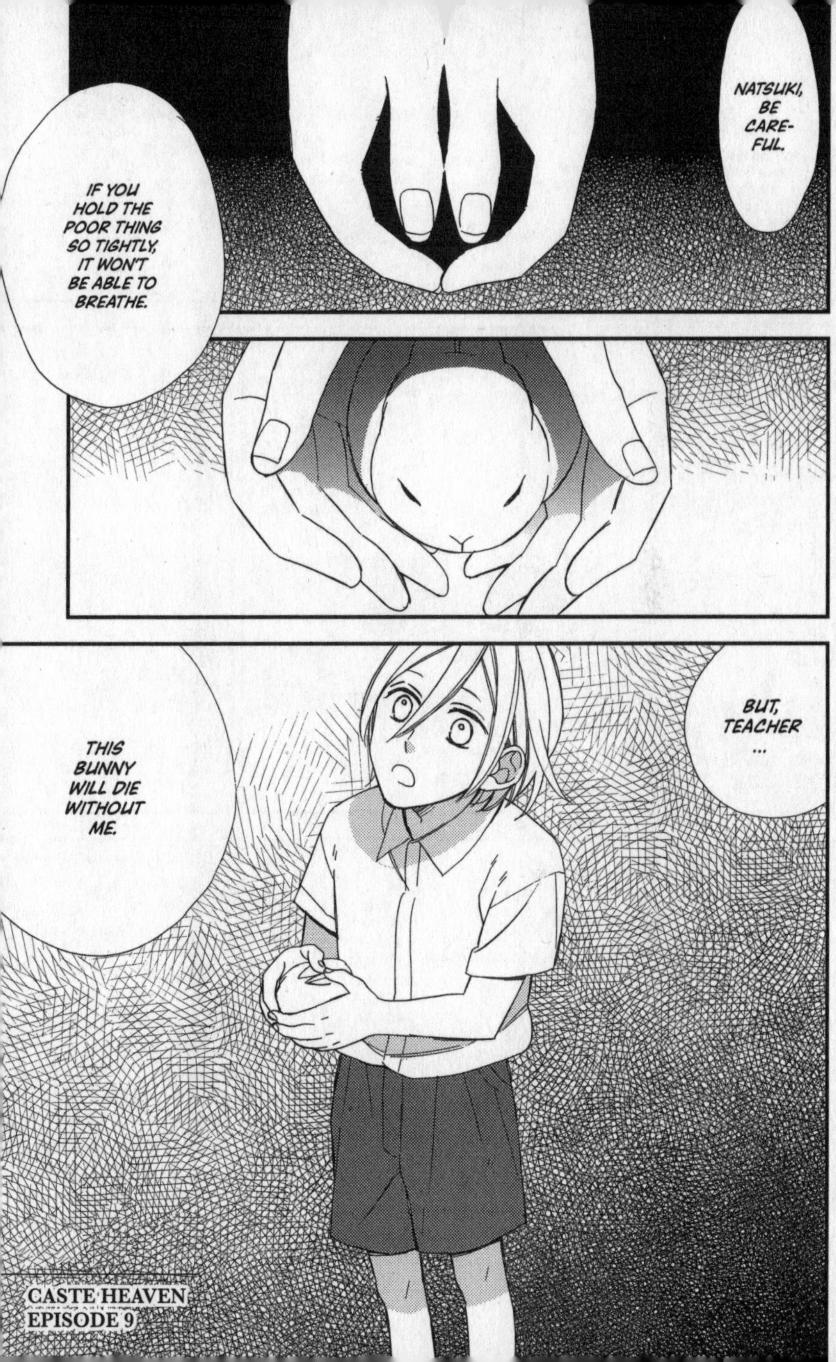
NATSUKI, BE CARE-FUL.
IF YOU HOLD THE POOR THING SO TIGHTLY, IT WON'T BE ABLE TO BREATHE.
BUT, TEACHER ...
THIS BUNNY WILL DIE WITHOUT ME.
CASTE HEAVEN
EPISODE 9

AFTER I WAS BORN, MY MOTHER WAS AFFLICTED WITH A BAD CASE OF POSTPARTUM ANXIETY. SHE COULDN'T STAND THE THOUGHT OF ANYONE—EVEN MY FATHER—COMING ANYWHERE NEAR ME.

SHE REMAINED THAT WAY UNTIL I STARTED PRESCHOOL AT THREE YEARS OLD.

AFTER ENTERING ELEMENTARY SCHOOL, ONE OF MY FAVORITE THINGS TO DO WAS CHORES IN THE SCHOOL'S RABBIT HUTCH.

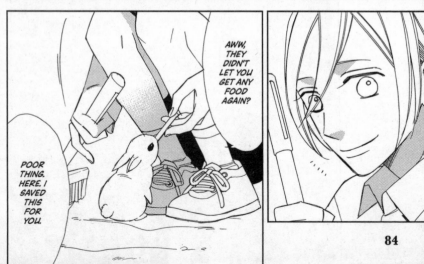

AWW, THEY DIDN'T LET YOU GET ANY FOOD AGAIN?

POOR THING. HERE. I SAVED THIS FOR YOU.

84

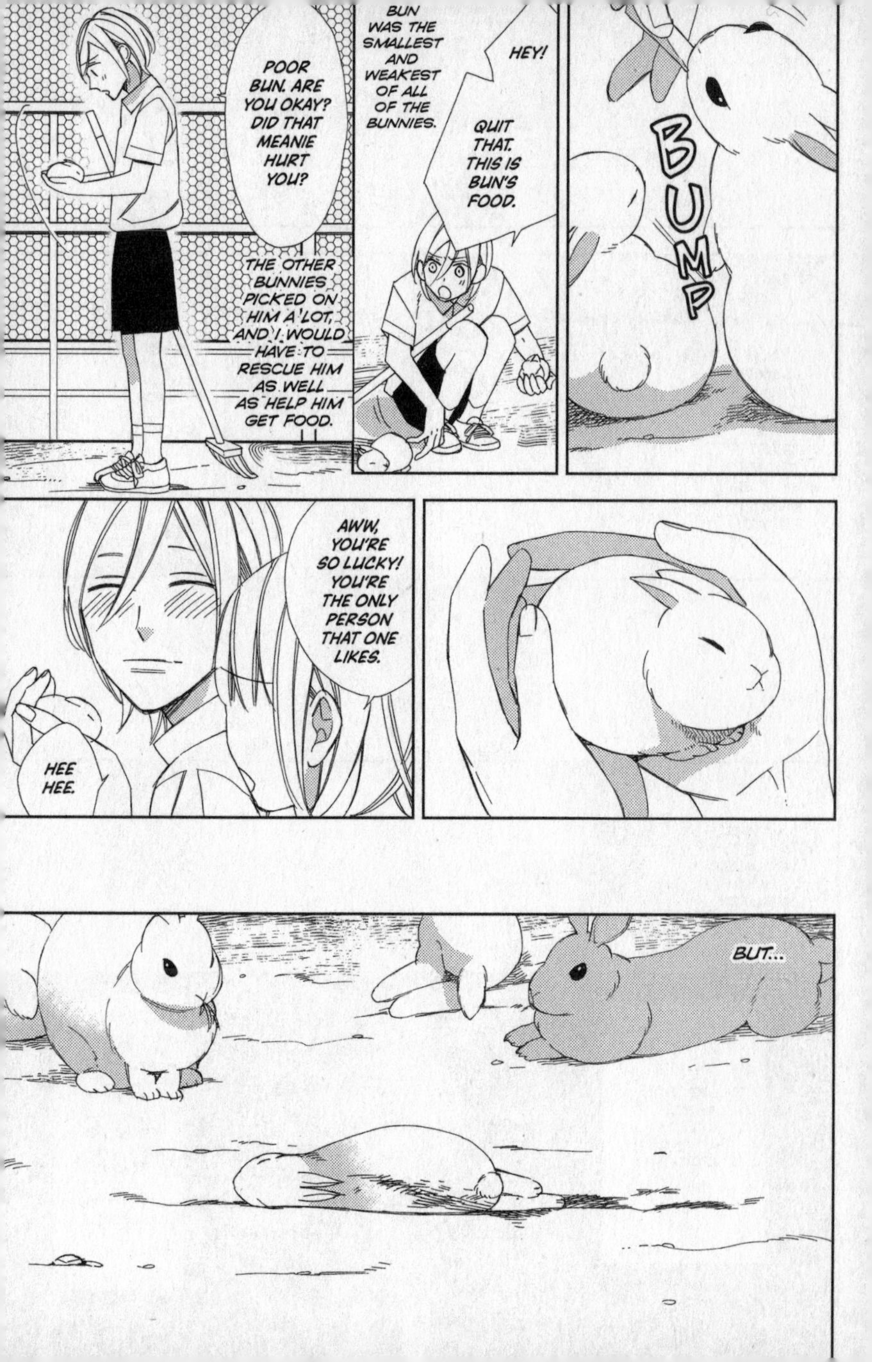
BUMP
HEY!
QUIT THAT. THIS IS BUN'S FOOD.
BUN WAS THE SMALLEST AND WEAKEST OF ALL OF THE BUNNIES.
POOR BUN. ARE YOU OKAY? DID THAT MEANIE HURT YOU?
THE OTHER BUNNIES PICKED ON HIM A LOT, AND I WOULD HAVE TO RESCUE HIM AS WELL AS HELP HIM GET FOOD.
AWW, YOU'RE SO LUCKY! YOU'RE THE ONLY PERSON THAT ONE LIKES.
HEE HEE.
BUT...

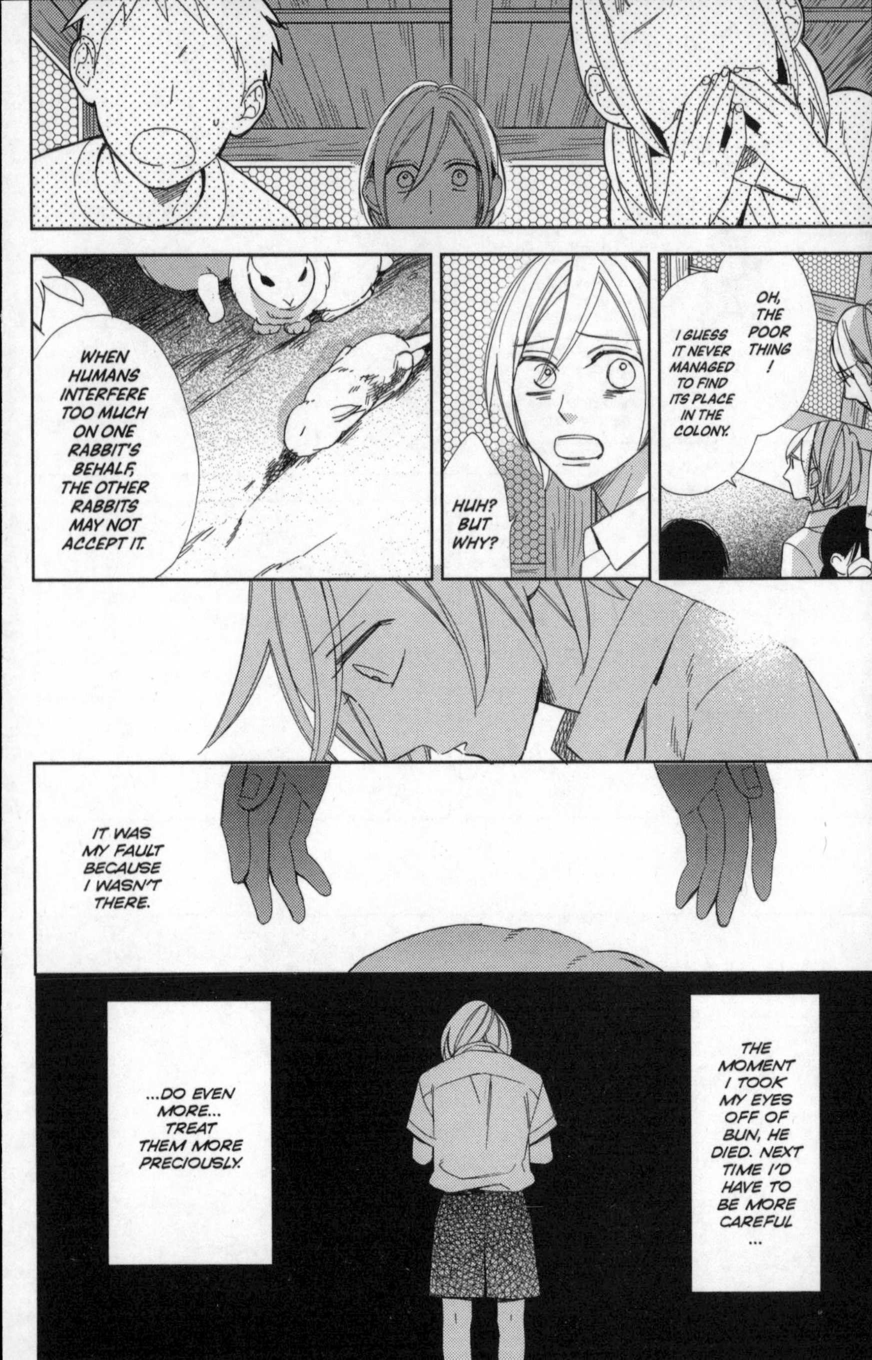
OH, THE POOR THING!
I GUESS IT NEVER MANAGED TO FIND ITS PLACE IN THE COLONY.
HUH? BUT WHY?
WHEN HUMANS INTERFERE TOO MUCH ON ONE RABBIT'S BEHALF, THE OTHER RABBITS MAY NOT ACCEPT IT.
IT WAS MY FAULT BECAUSE I WASN'T THERE.
THE MOMENT I TOOK MY EYES OFF OF BUN, HE DIED. NEXT TIME I'D HAVE TO BE MORE CAREFUL...
...DO EVEN MORE... TREAT THEM MORE PRECIOUSLY.

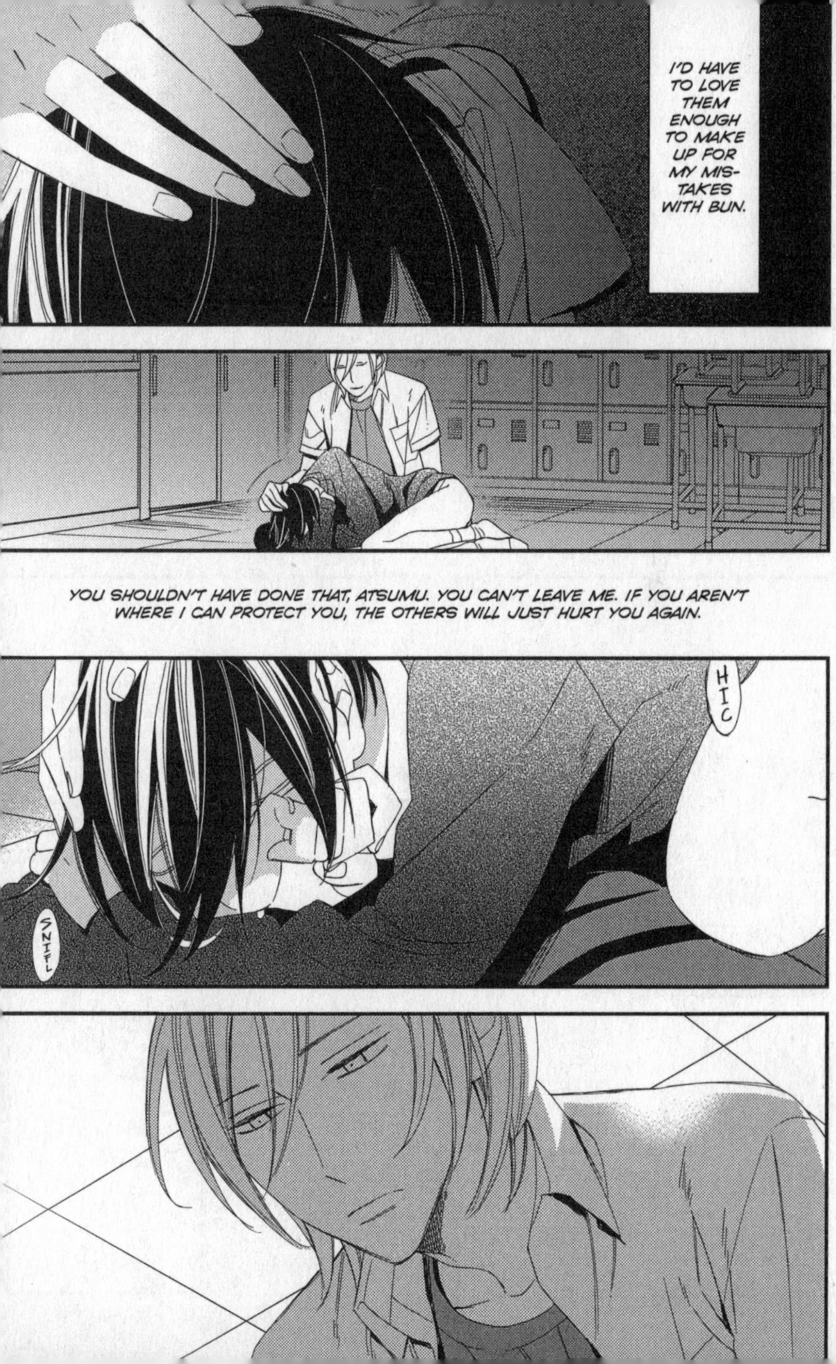
I'D HAVE TO LOVE THEM ENOUGH TO MAKE UP FOR MY MIS-TAKES WITH BUN.
YOU SHOULDN'T HAVE DONE THAT, ATSUMU. YOU CAN'T LEAVE ME. IF YOU AREN'T WHERE I CAN PROTECT YOU, THE OTHERS WILL JUST HURT YOU AGAIN.
HIC
SNIFL

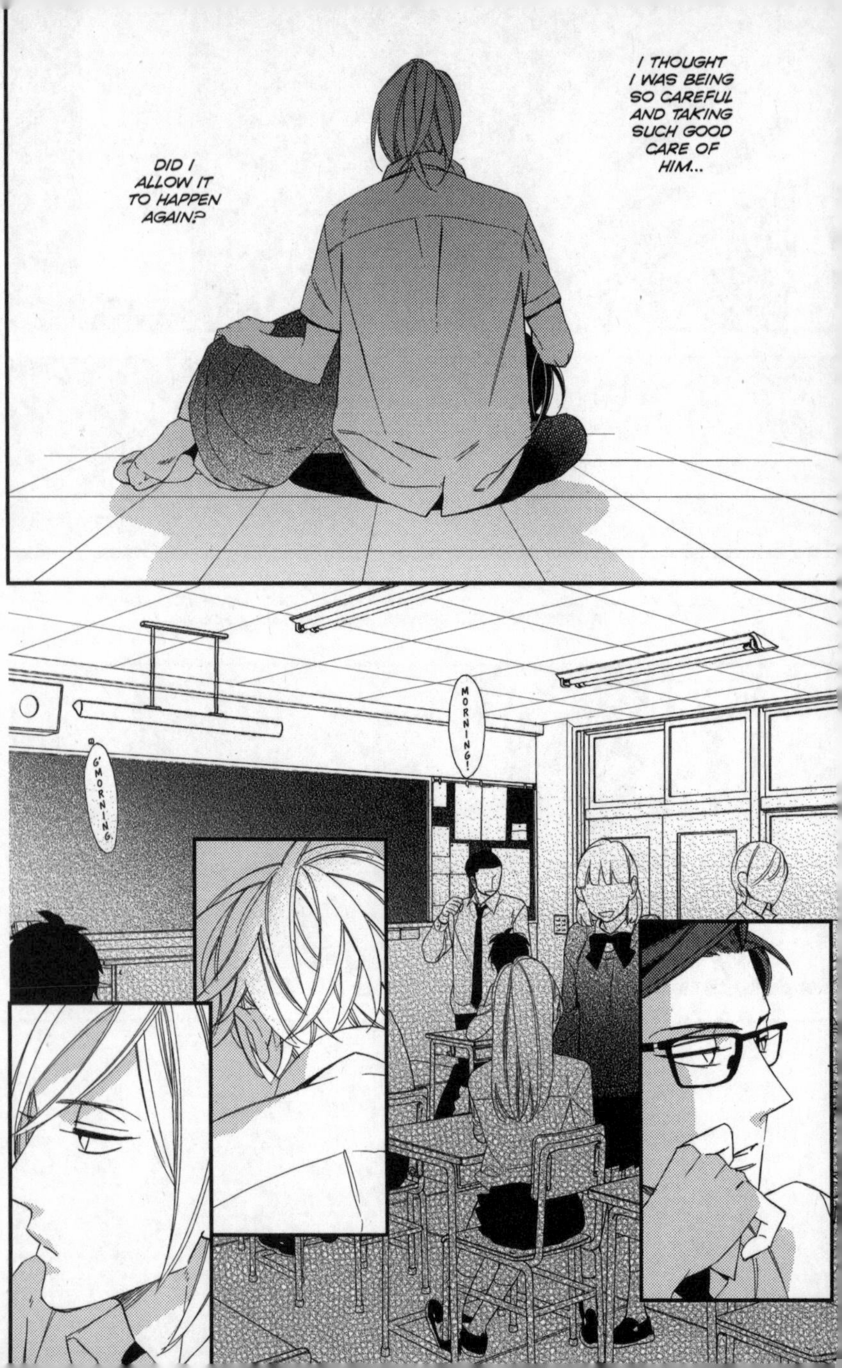
I THOUGHT I WAS BEING SO CAREFUL AND TAKING SUCH GOOD CARE OF HIM...
DID I ALLOW IT TO HAPPEN AGAIN?
MORNING!
G'MORNING.

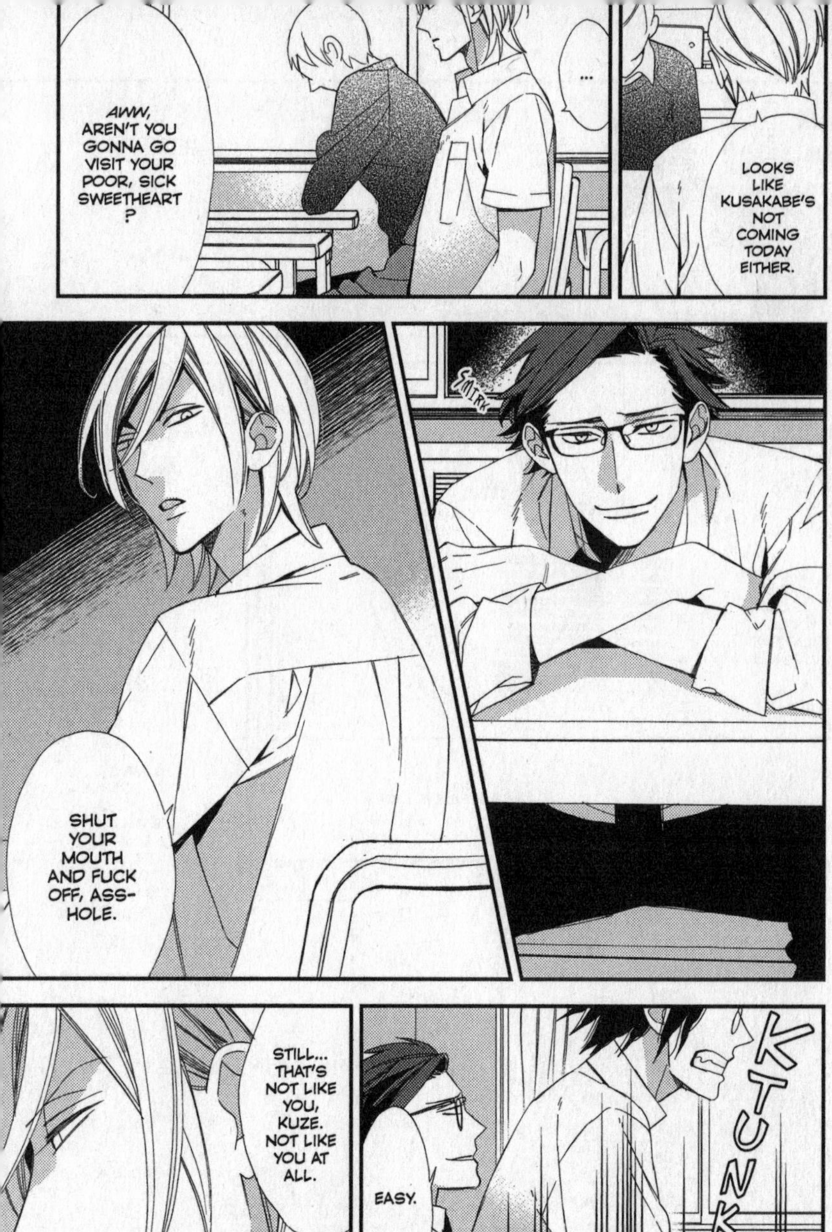
LOOKS LIKE KUSAKABE'S NOT COMING TODAY EITHER.
...
AWW, AREN'T YOU GONNA GO VISIT YOUR POOR, SICK SWEETHEART?
SMIRK
SHUT YOUR MOUTH AND FUCK OFF, ASS-HOLE.
KTUNK
EASY.
STILL... THAT'S NOT LIKE YOU, KUZE. NOT LIKE YOU AT ALL.

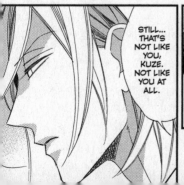

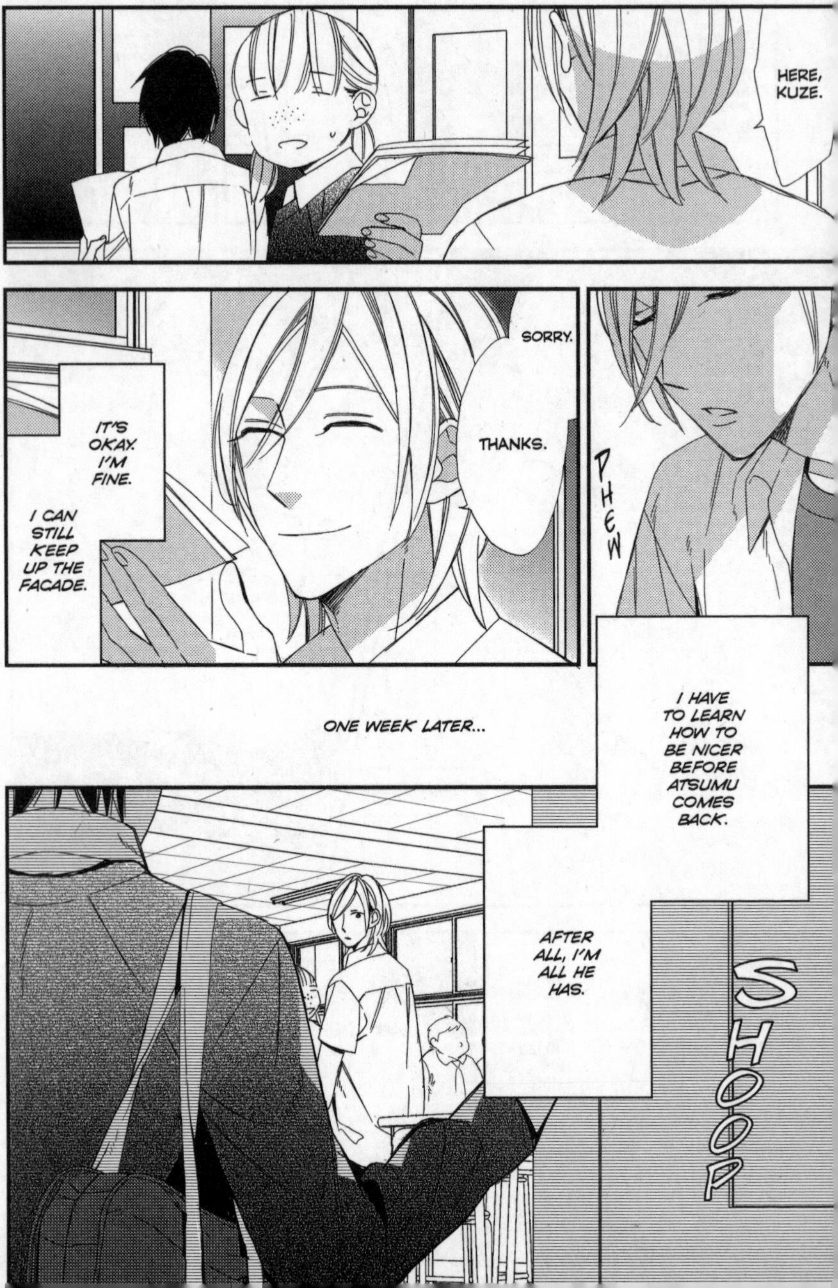
HERE, KUZE.
PHEW
SORRY.
THANKS.
IT'S OKAY. I'M FINE.
I CAN STILL KEEP UP THE FACADE.
I HAVE TO LEARN HOW TO BE NICER BEFORE ATSUMU COMES BACK.
ONE WEEK LATER...
AFTER ALL, I'M ALL HE HAS.
SHOOP

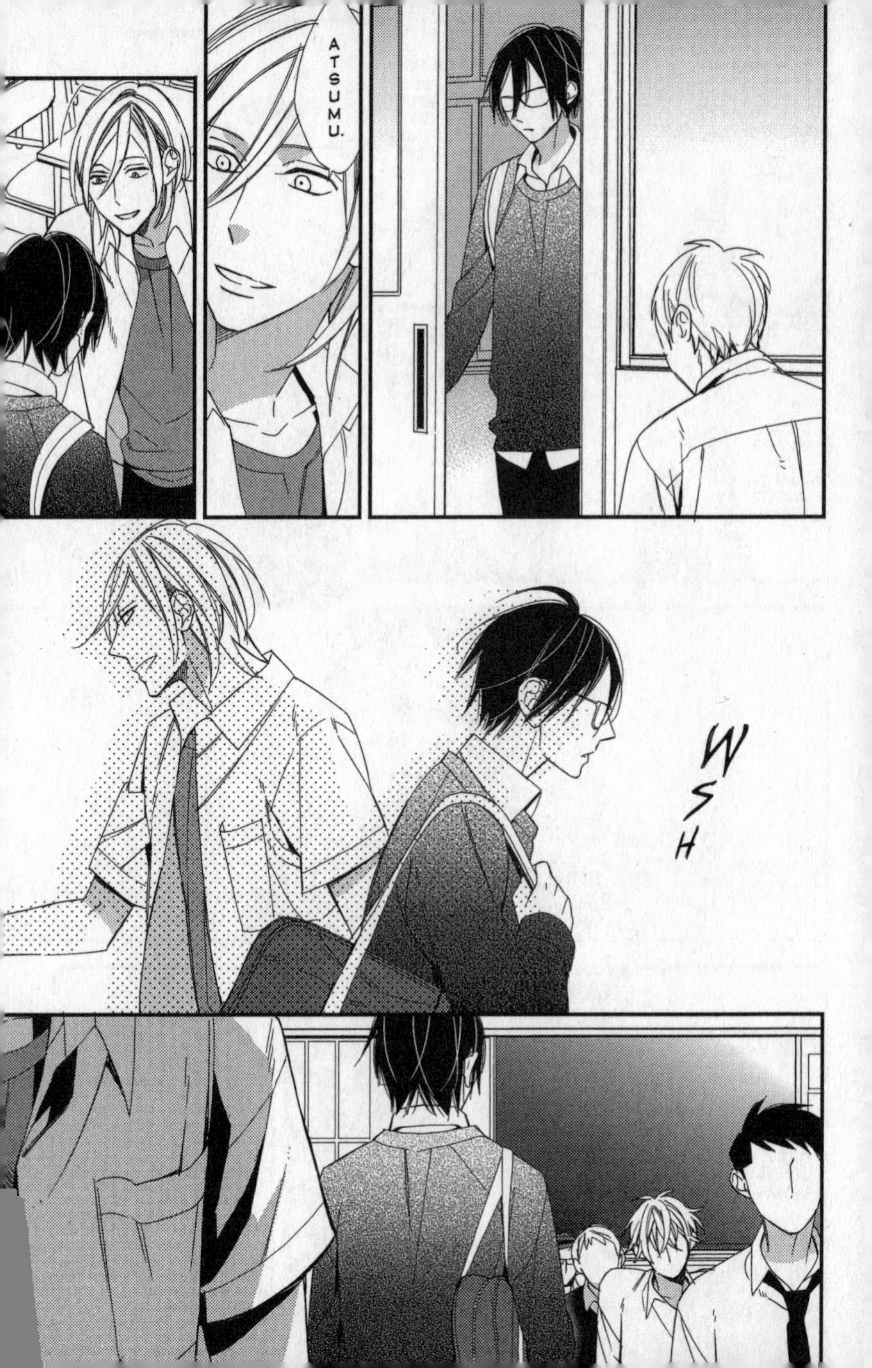
ATSUMU.
WSH

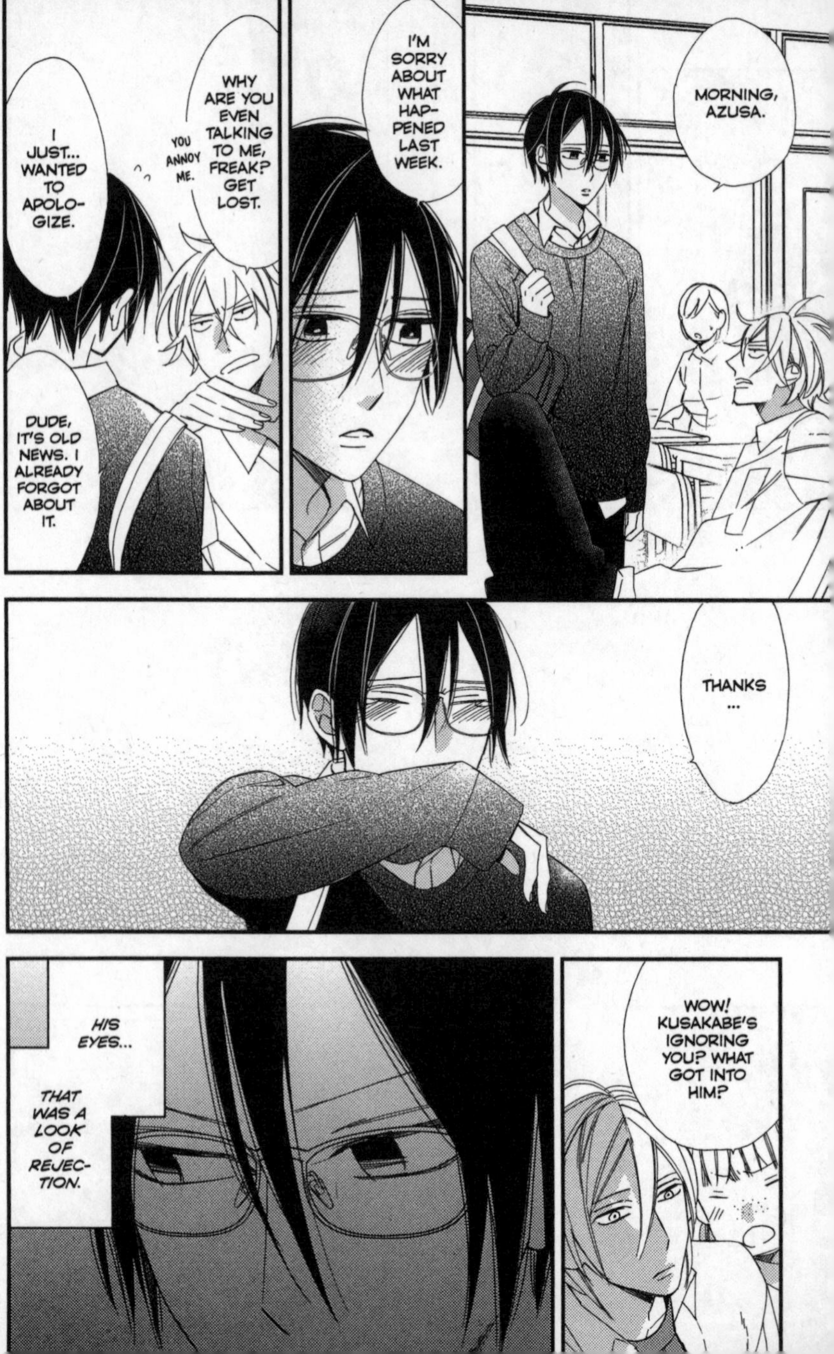
MORNING, AZUSA.
I'M SORRY ABOUT WHAT HAP-PENED LAST WEEK.
WHY ARE YOU EVEN TALKING TO ME, FREAK? GET LOST.
YOU ANNOY ME.
I JUST... WANTED TO APOLO-GIZE.
DUDE, IT'S OLD NEWS. I ALREADY FORGOT ABOUT IT.
THANKS ...
WOW! KUSAKABE'S IGNORING YOU? WHAT GOT INTO HIM?
HIS EYES...
THAT WAS A LOOK OF REJEC-TION.

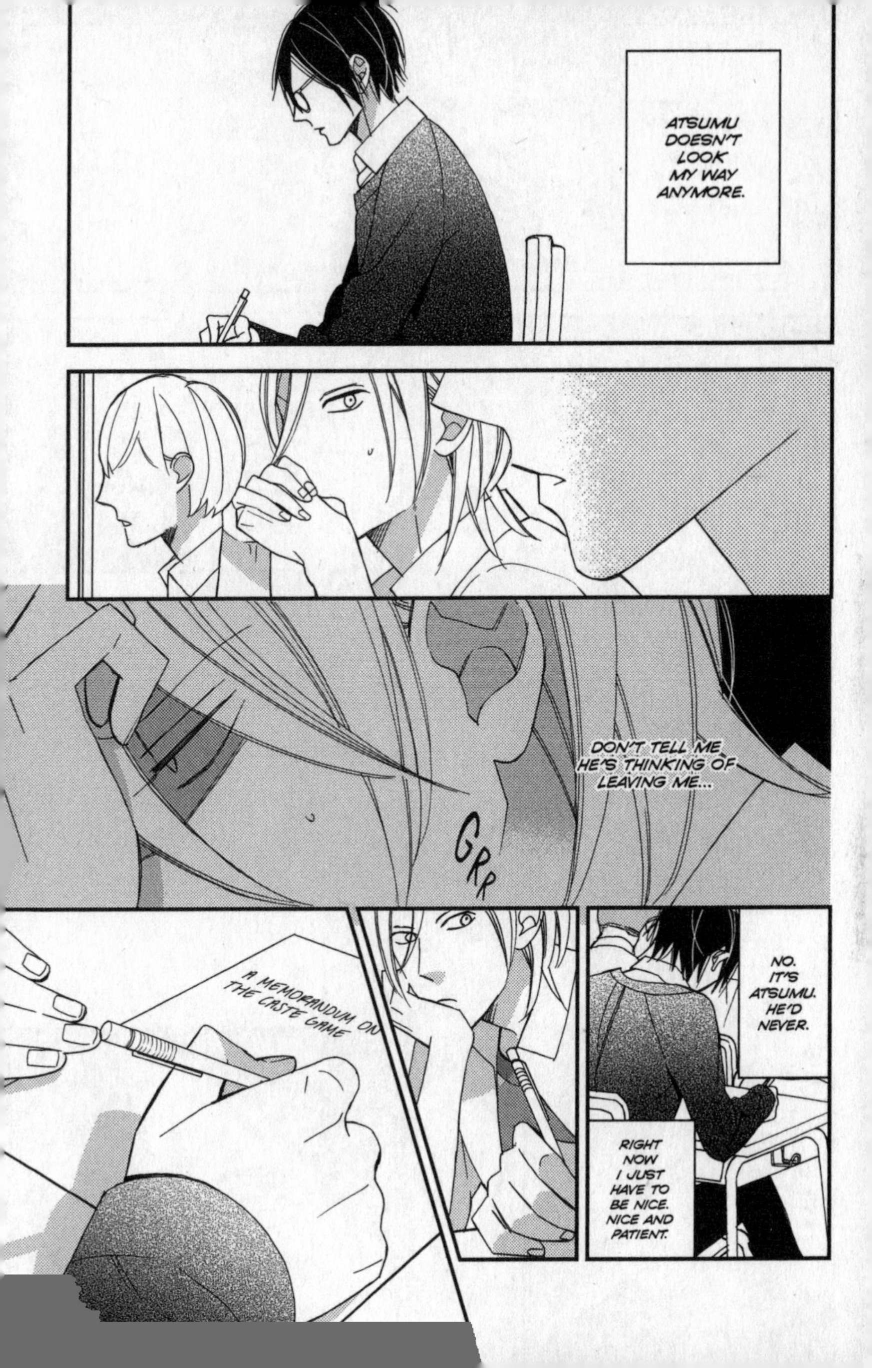
ATSUMU DOESN'T LOOK MY WAY ANYMORE.
DON'T TELL ME HE'S THINKING OF LEAVING ME...
GRR
NO. IT'S ATSUMU. HE'D NEVER.
RIGHT NOW I JUST HAVE TO BE NICE. NICE AND PATIENT.
A MEMORANDUM ON THE CASTE GAME

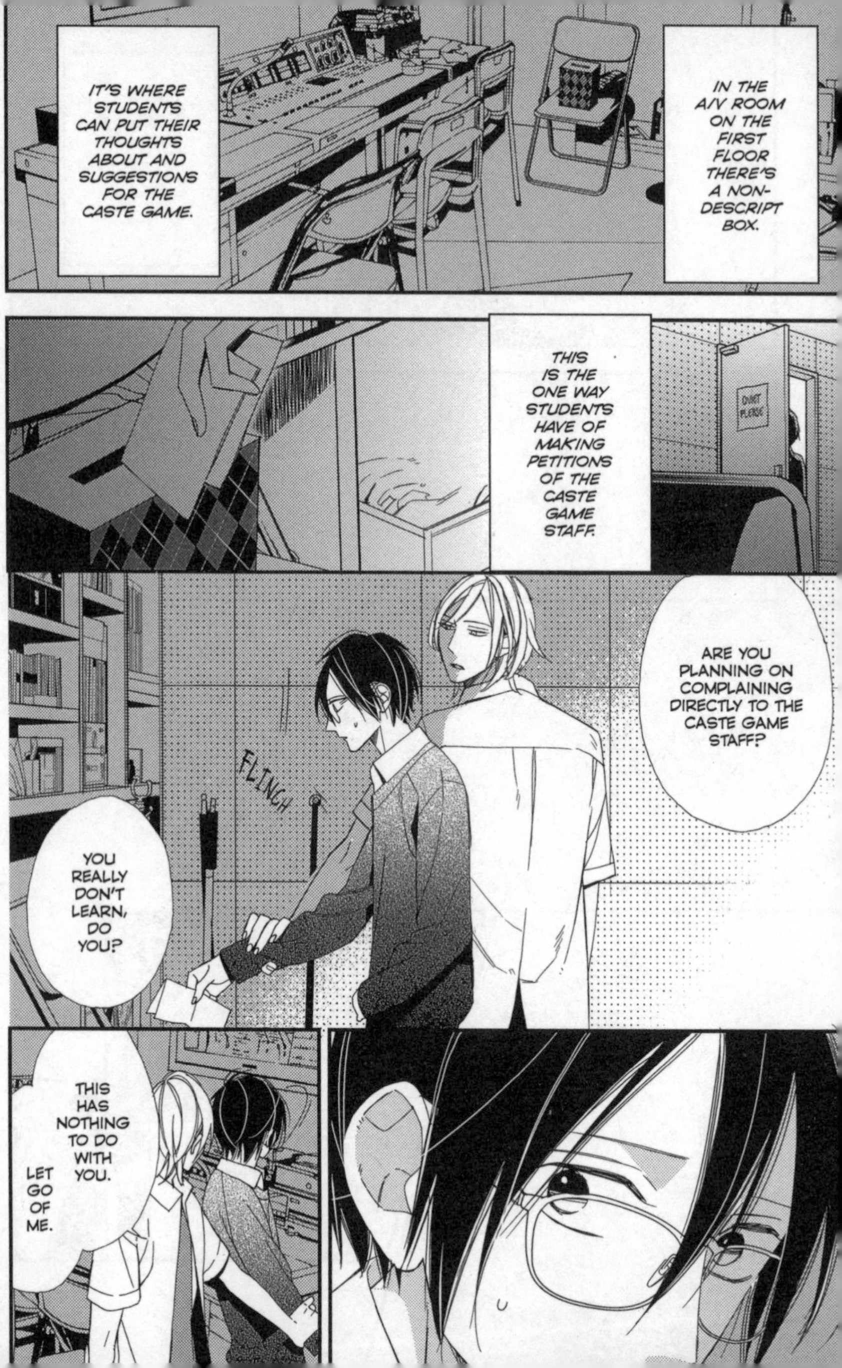
IN THE A/V ROOM ON THE FIRST FLOOR THERE'S A NON-DESCRIPT BOX.
IT'S WHERE STUDENTS CAN PUT THEIR THOUGHTS ABOUT AND SUGGESTIONS FOR THE CASTE GAME.
QUIET PLEASE
THIS IS THE ONE WAY STUDENTS HAVE OF MAKING PETITIONS OF THE CASTE GAME STAFF.
ARE YOU PLANNING ON COMPLAINING DIRECTLY TO THE CASTE GAME STAFF?
FLINCH
YOU REALLY DON'T LEARN, DO YOU?
THIS HAS NOTHING TO DO WITH YOU.
LET GO OF ME.

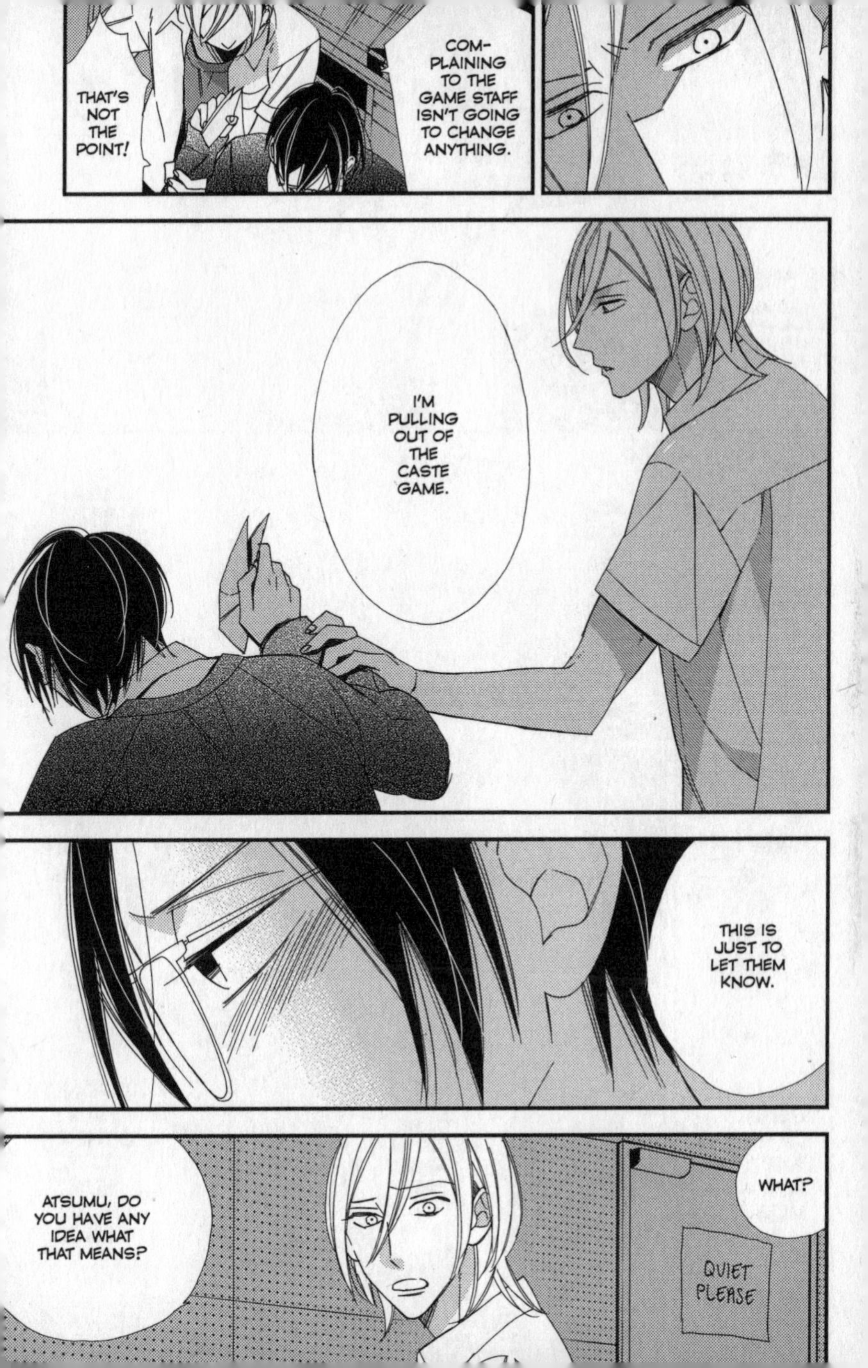
COM-PLAINING TO THE GAME STAFF ISN'T GOING TO CHANGE ANYTHING.
THAT'S NOT THE POINT!
I'M PULLING OUT OF THE CASTE GAME.
THIS IS JUST TO LET THEM KNOW.
WHAT?
ATSUMU, DO YOU HAVE ANY IDEA WHAT THAT MEANS?
QUIET PLEASE

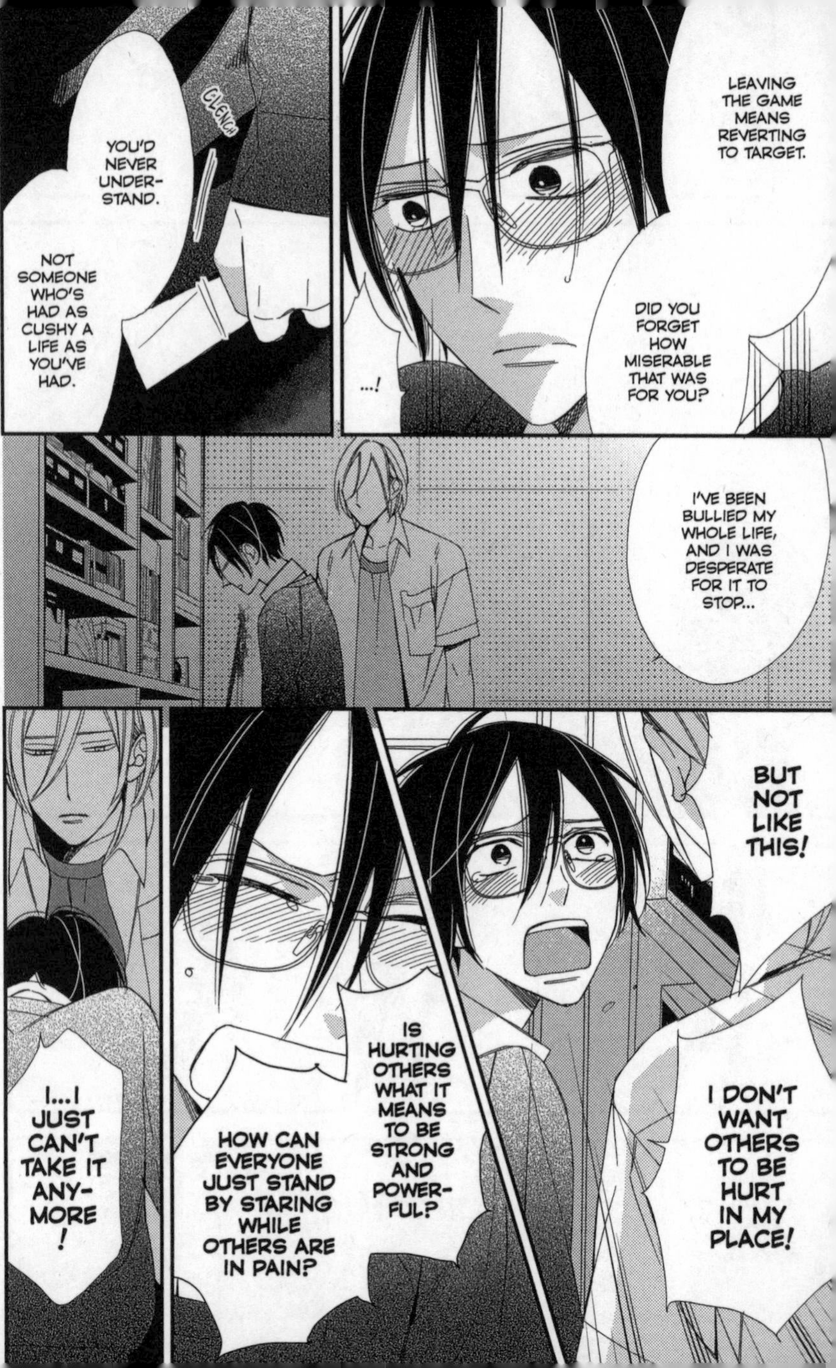
LEAVING THE GAME MEANS REVERTING TO TARGET.
DID YOU FORGET HOW MISERABLE THAT WAS FOR YOU?
...!
YOU'D NEVER UNDER-STAND.
CLENCH
NOT SOMEONE WHO'S HAD AS CUSHY A LIFE AS YOU'VE HAD.
I'VE BEEN BULLIED MY WHOLE LIFE, AND I WAS DESPERATE FOR IT TO STOP...
BUT NOT LIKE THIS!
I DON'T WANT OTHERS TO BE HURT IN MY PLACE!
IS HURTING OTHERS WHAT IT MEANS TO BE STRONG AND POWER-FUL?
HOW CAN EVERYONE JUST STAND BY STARING WHILE OTHERS ARE IN PAIN?
I...I JUST CAN'T TAKE IT ANY-MORE!

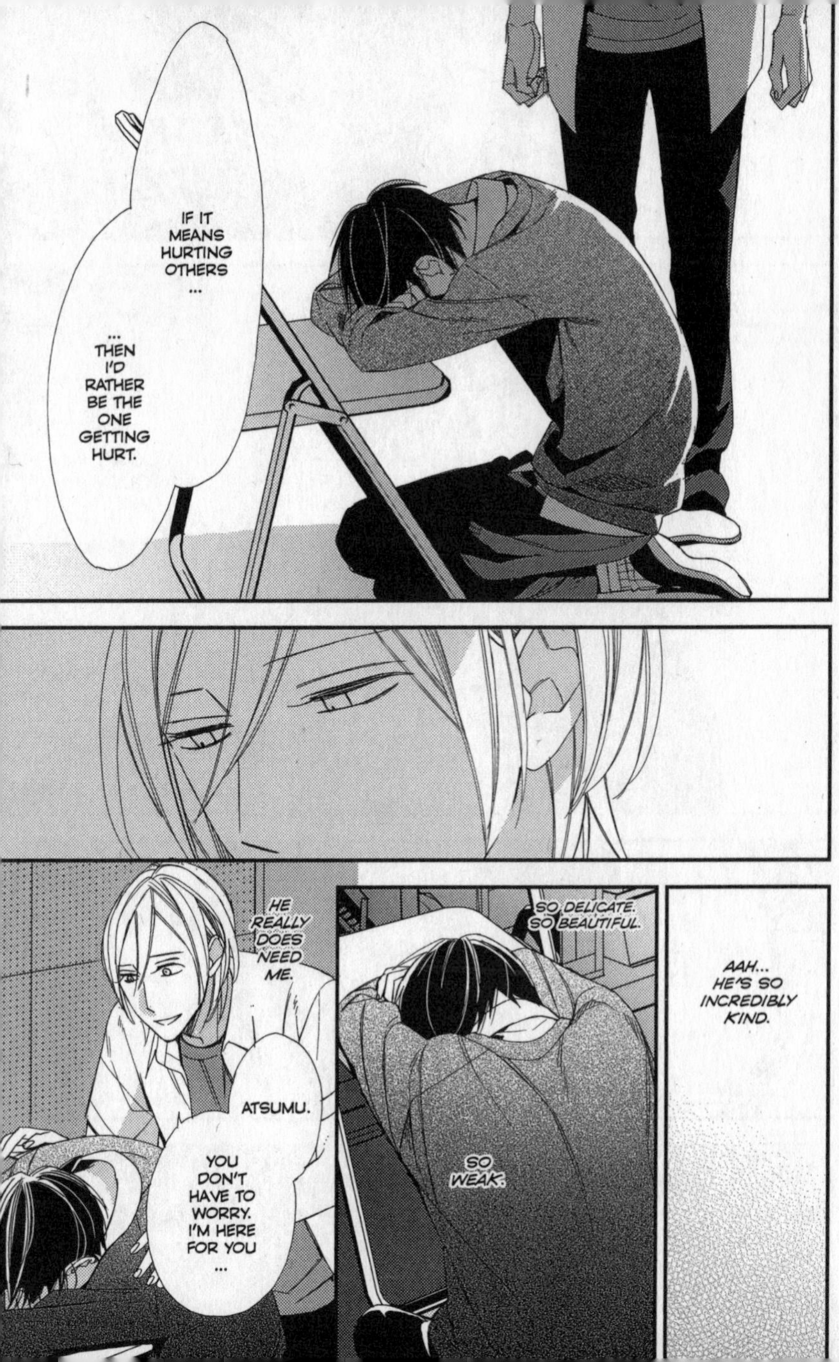
IF IT MEANS HURTING OTHERS ...
... THEN I'D RATHER BE THE ONE GETTING HURT.
AAH... HE'S SO INCREDIBLY KIND.
SO DELICATE. SO BEAUTIFUL.
SO WEAK.
HE REALLY DOES NEED ME.
ATSUMU.
YOU DON'T HAVE TO WORRY. I'M HERE FOR YOU ...

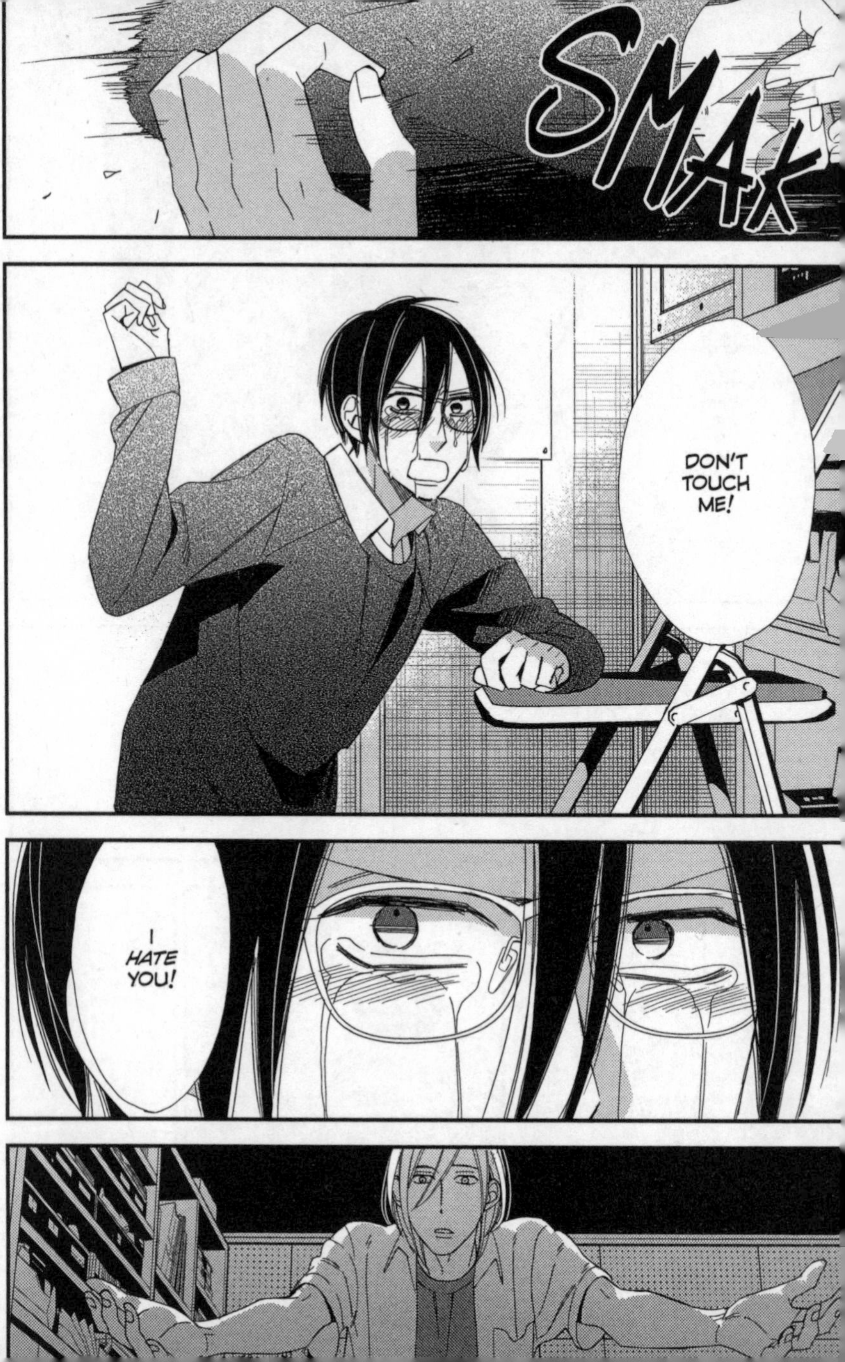
SMAK
DON'T TOUCH ME!
I HATE YOU!

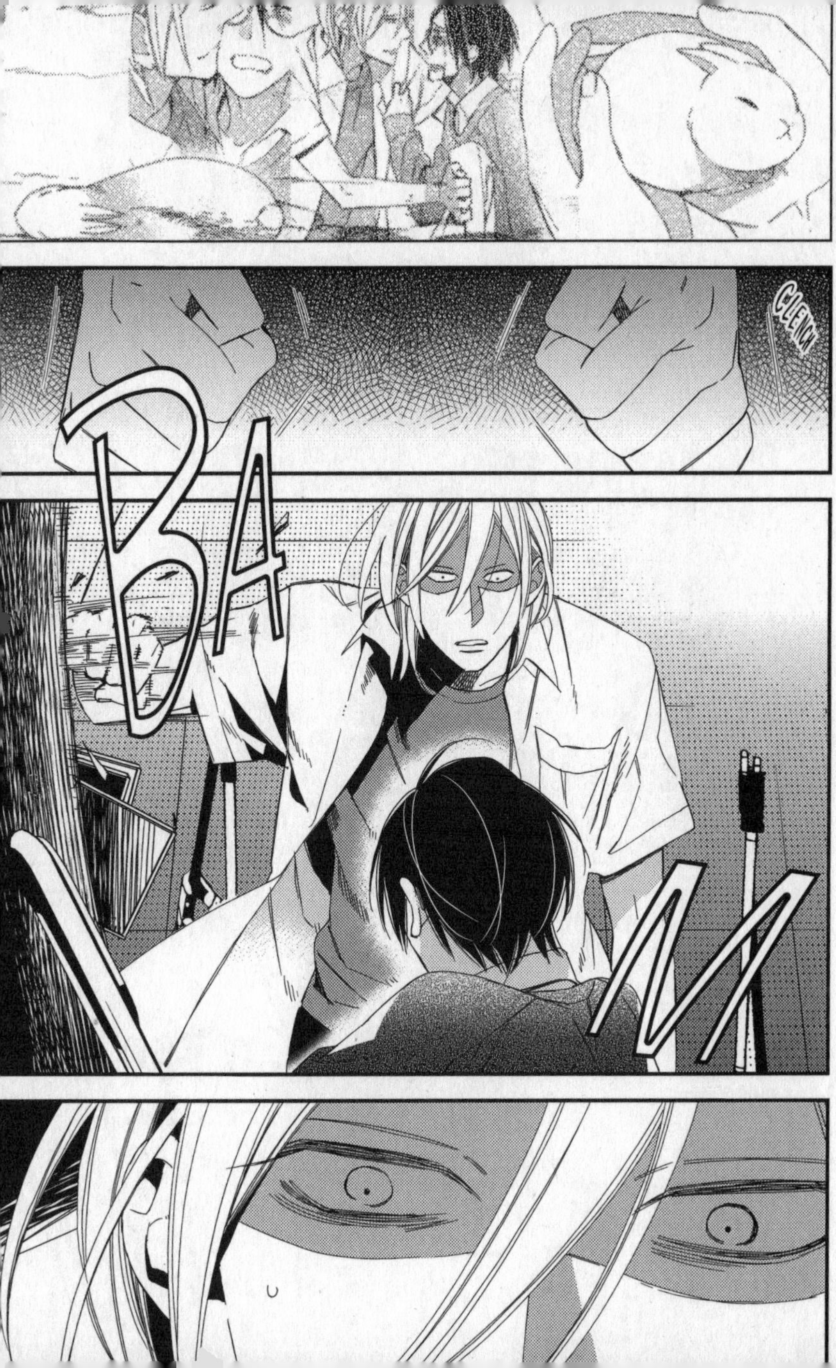
CLENCH
BAM

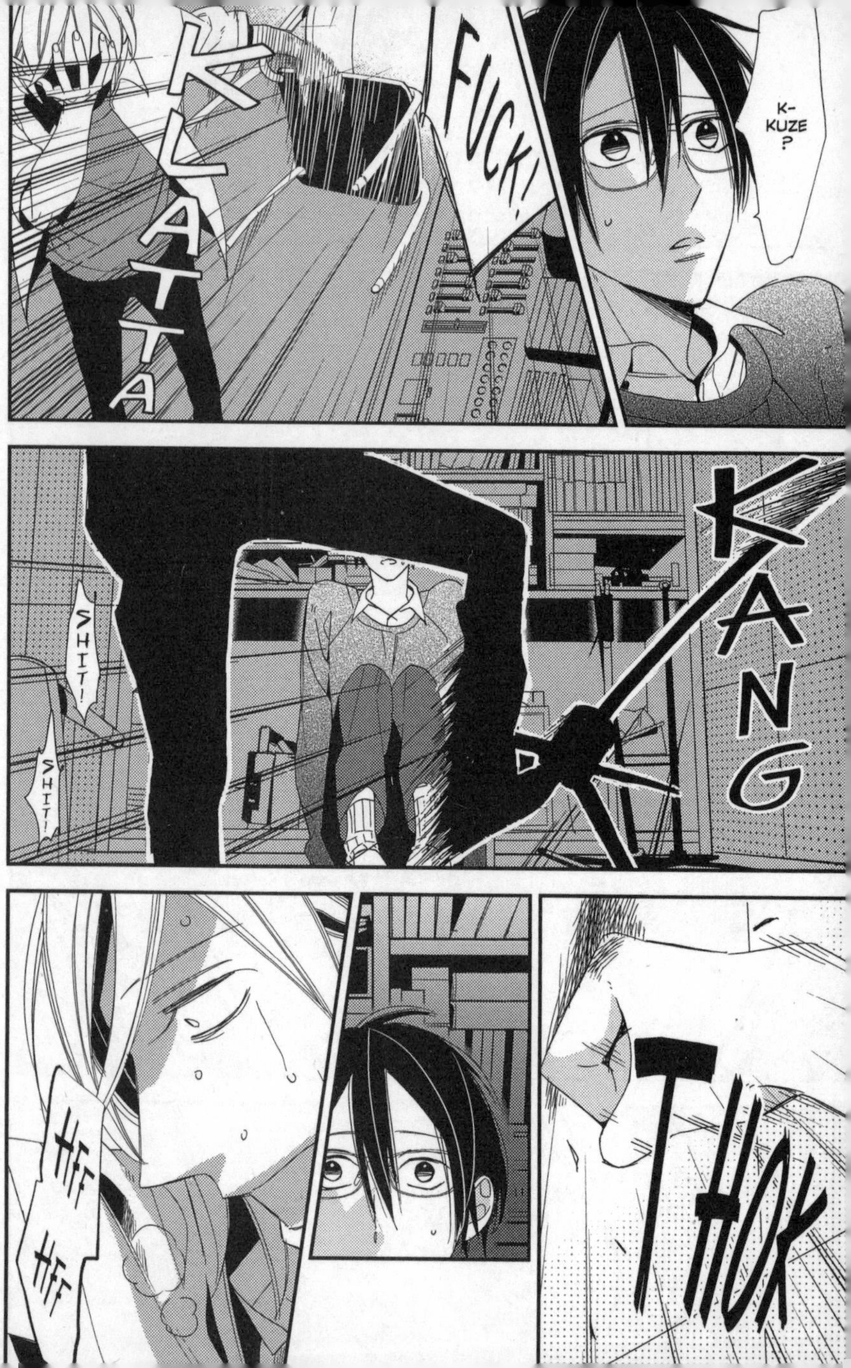
K-KUZE?
FUCK!
KLATTA
KANG
SHIT!
SHIT!
THOK
HFF
HFF

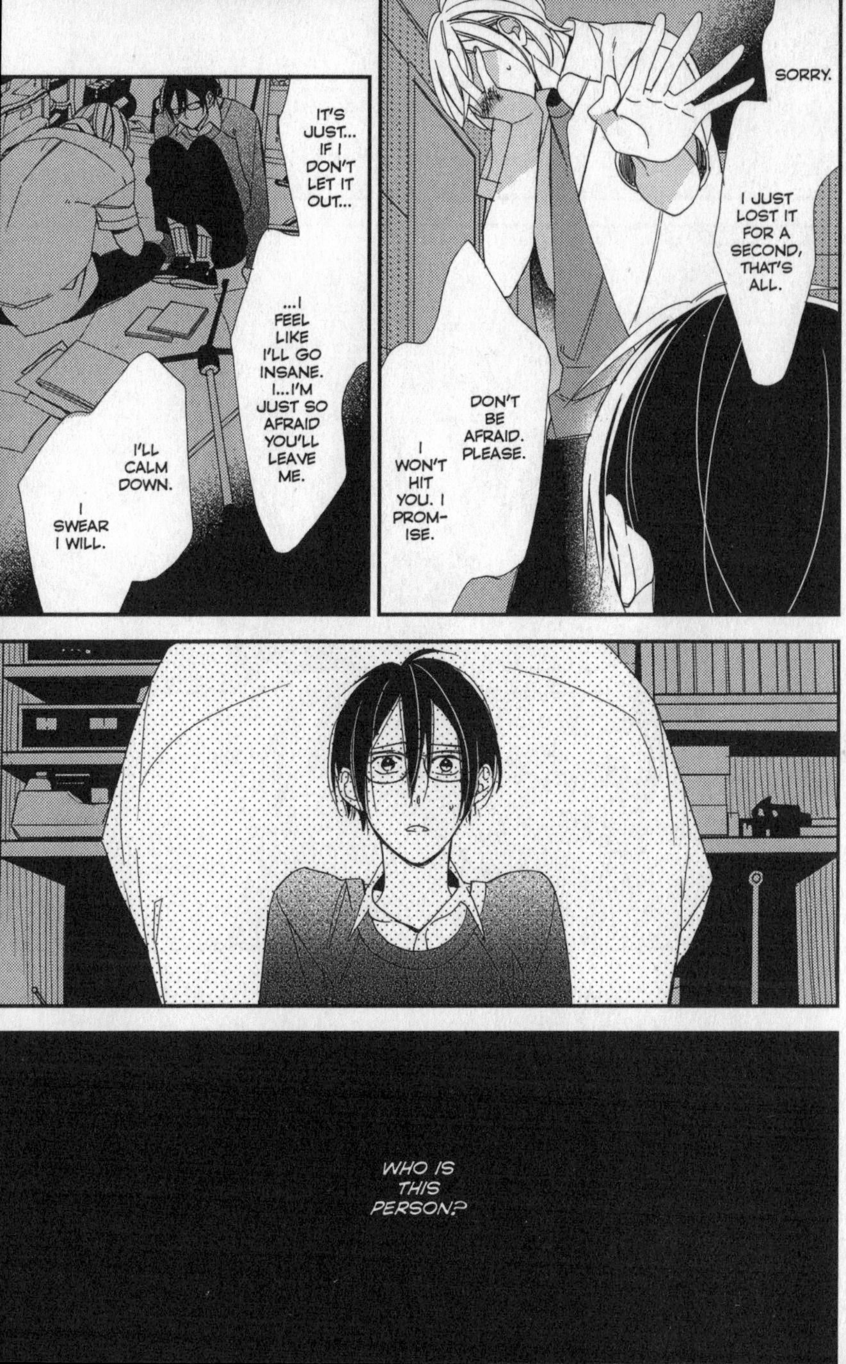
SORRY.
I JUST LOST IT FOR A SECOND, THAT'S ALL.
DON'T BE AFRAID. PLEASE.
I WON'T HIT YOU. I PROMISE.
IT'S JUST... IF I DON'T LET IT OUT...
...I FEEL LIKE I'LL GO INSANE. I...I'M JUST SO AFRAID YOU'LL LEAVE ME.
I'LL CALM DOWN.
I SWEAR I WILL.
WHO IS THIS PERSON?

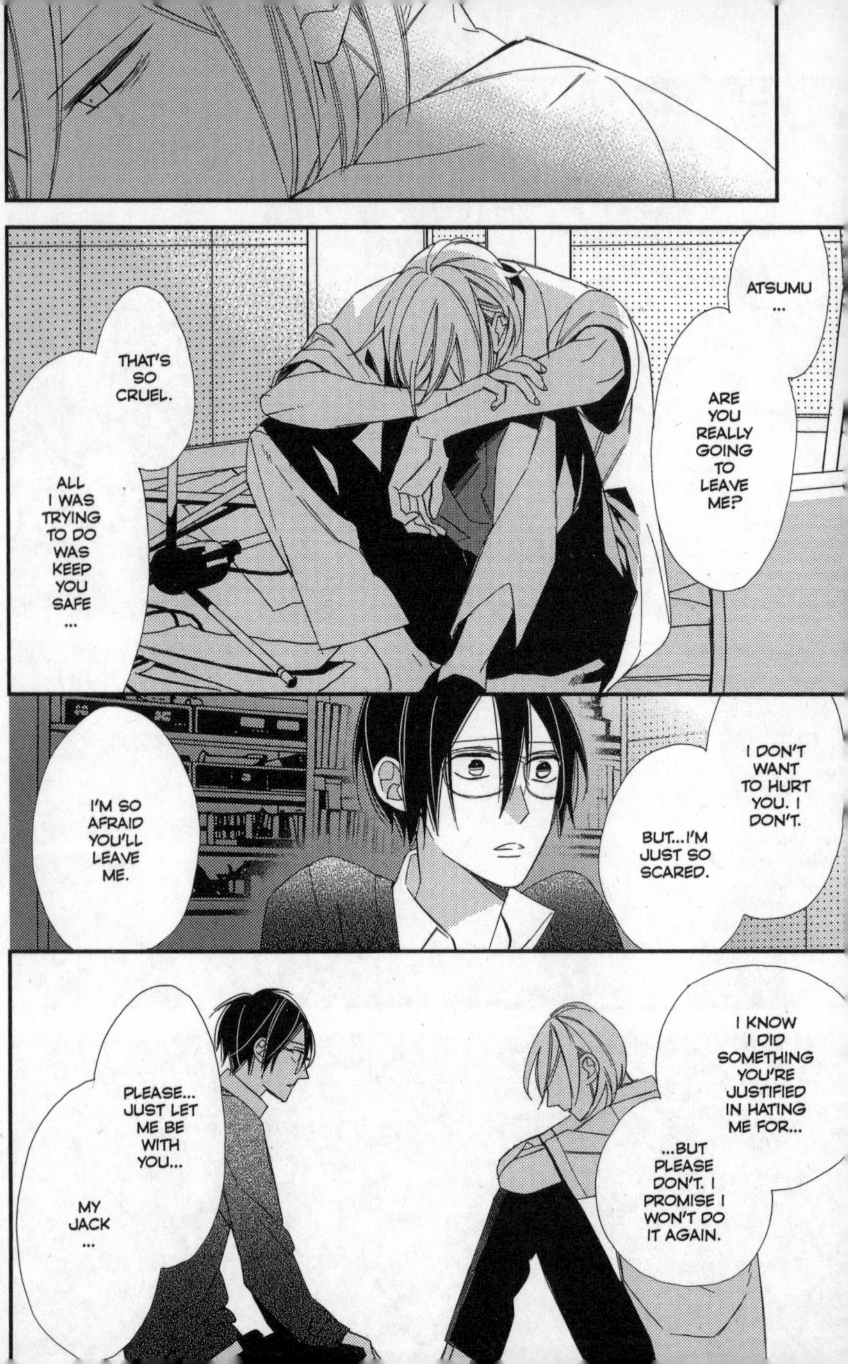
ATSUMU ...
ARE YOU REALLY GOING TO LEAVE ME?
THAT'S SO CRUEL.
ALL I WAS TRYING TO DO WAS KEEP YOU SAFE ...
I DON'T WANT TO HURT YOU. I DON'T.
BUT...I'M JUST SO SCARED.
I'M SO AFRAID YOU'LL LEAVE ME.
I KNOW I DID SOMETHING YOU'RE JUSTIFIED IN HATING ME FOR...
...BUT PLEASE DON'T. I PROMISE I WON'T DO IT AGAIN.
PLEASE... JUST LET ME BE WITH YOU...
MY JACK ...

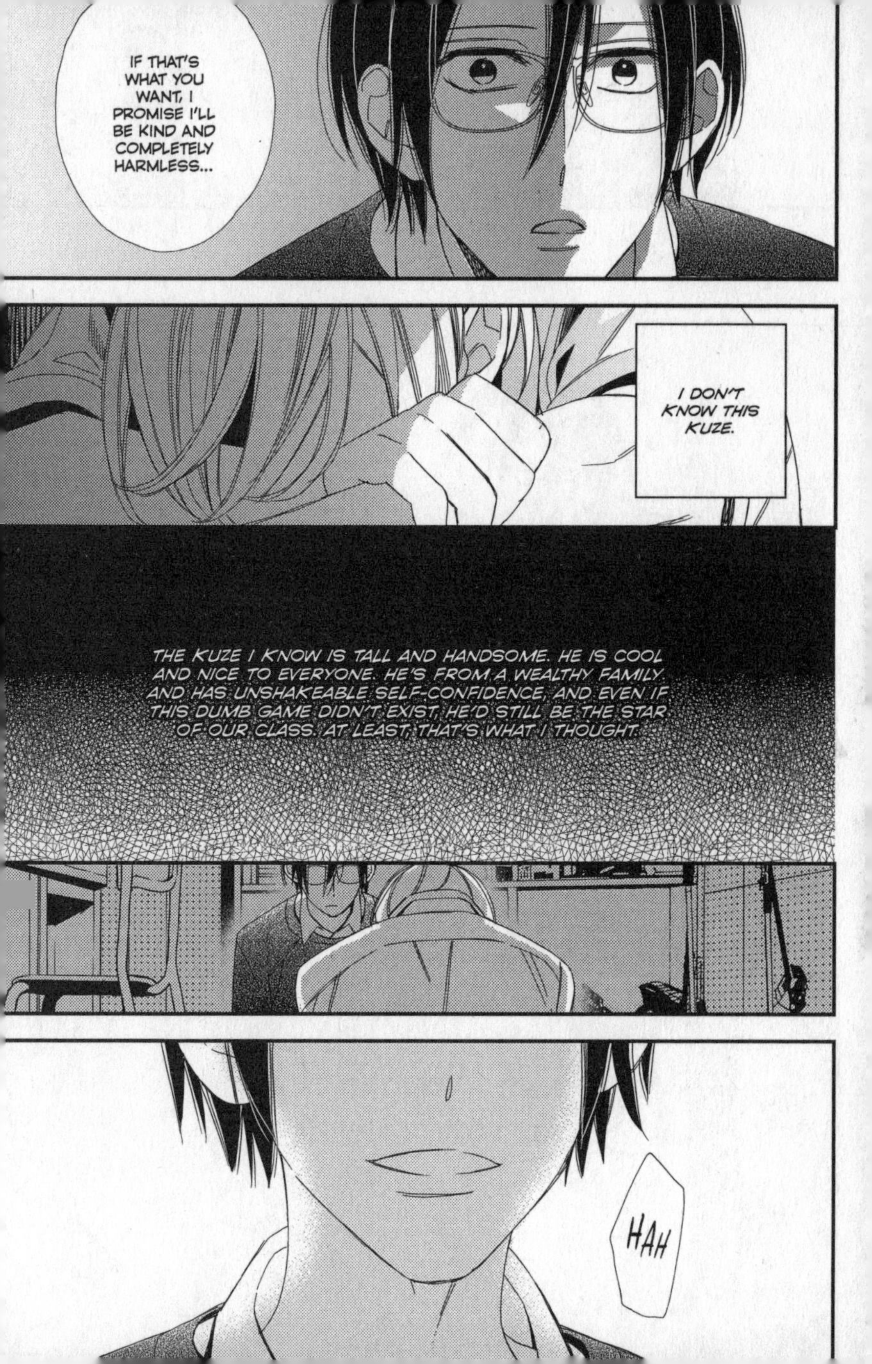
IF THAT'S WHAT YOU WANT, I PROMISE I'LL BE KIND AND COMPLETELY HARMLESS...
I DON'T KNOW THIS KUZE.
THE KUZE I KNOW IS TALL AND HANDSOME. HE IS COOL AND NICE TO EVERYONE. HE'S FROM A WEALTHY FAMILY AND HAS UNSHAKEABLE SELF-CONFIDENCE, AND EVEN IF THIS DUMB GAME DIDN'T EXIST, HE'D STILL BE THE STAR OF OUR CLASS. AT LEAST, THAT'S WHAT I THOUGHT.
HAH

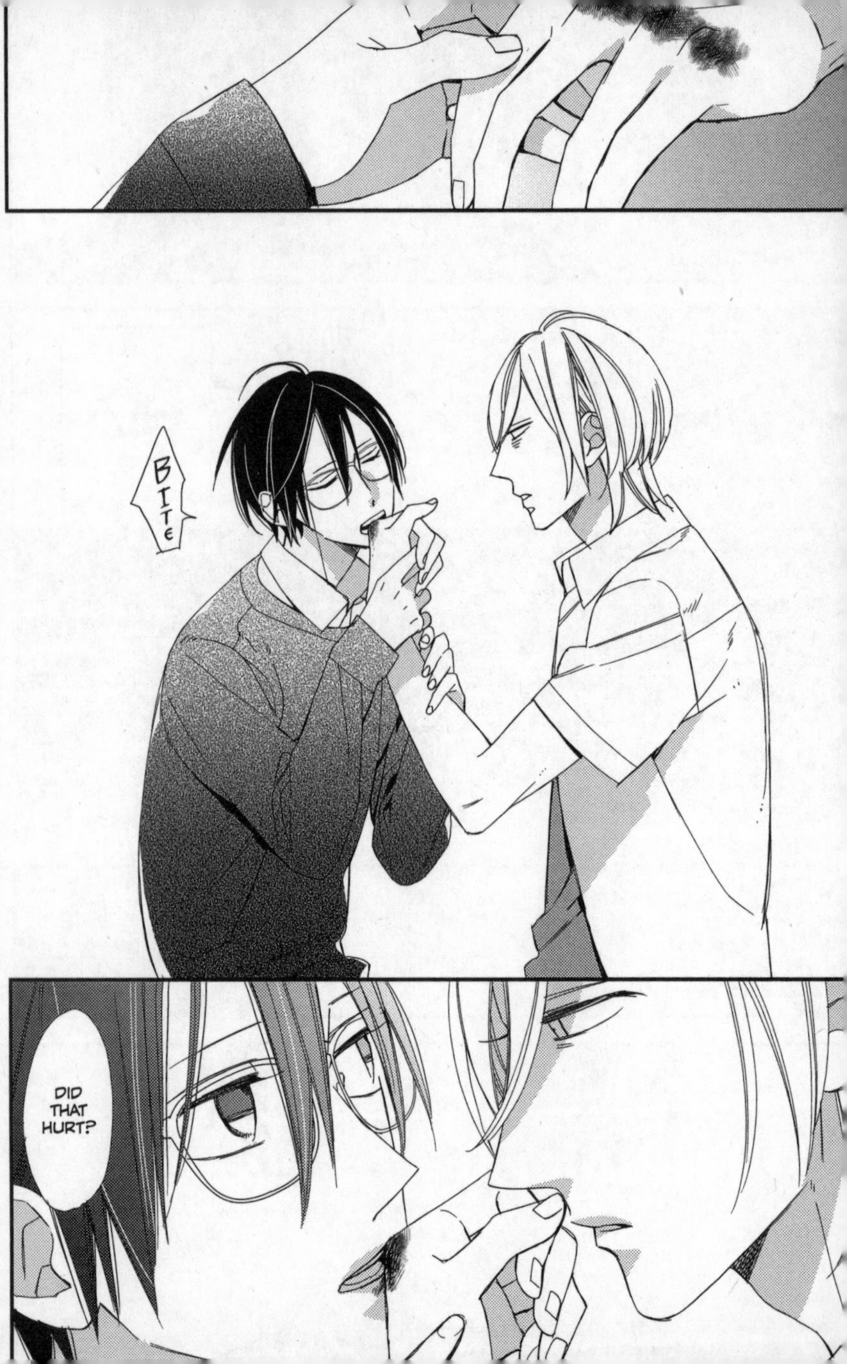
BITE
DID THAT HURT?

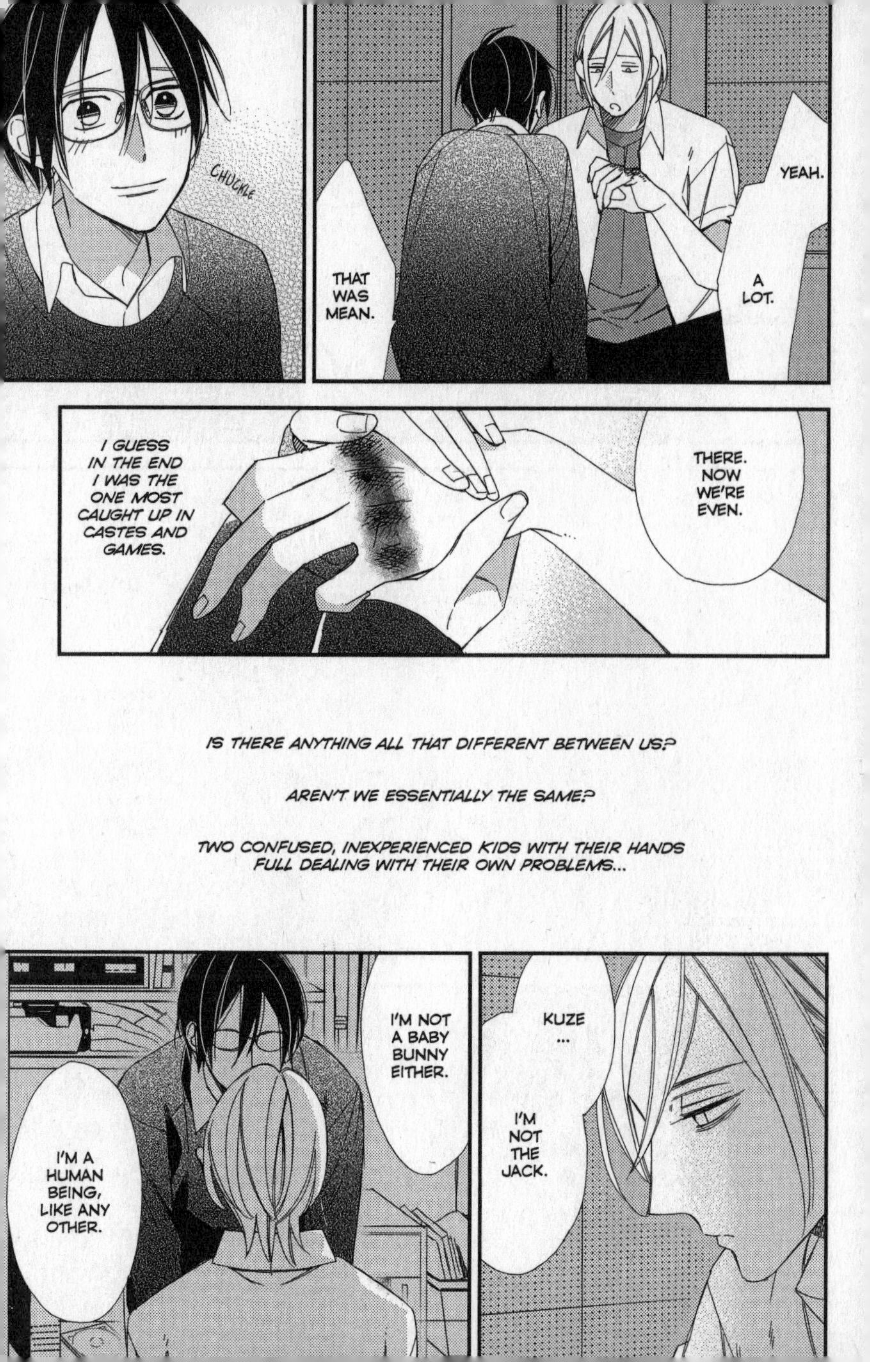
YEAH.
A LOT.
THAT WAS MEAN.
CHUCKLE
THERE. NOW WE'RE EVEN.
I GUESS IN THE END I WAS THE ONE MOST CAUGHT UP IN CASTES AND GAMES.
IS THERE ANYTHING ALL THAT DIFFERENT BETWEEN US?
AREN'T WE ESSENTIALLY THE SAME?
TWO CONFUSED, INEXPERIENCED KIDS WITH THEIR HANDS FULL DEALING WITH THEIR OWN PROBLEMS...
KUZE...
I'M NOT THE JACK.
I'M NOT A BABY BUNNY EITHER.
I'M A HUMAN BEING, LIKE ANY OTHER.

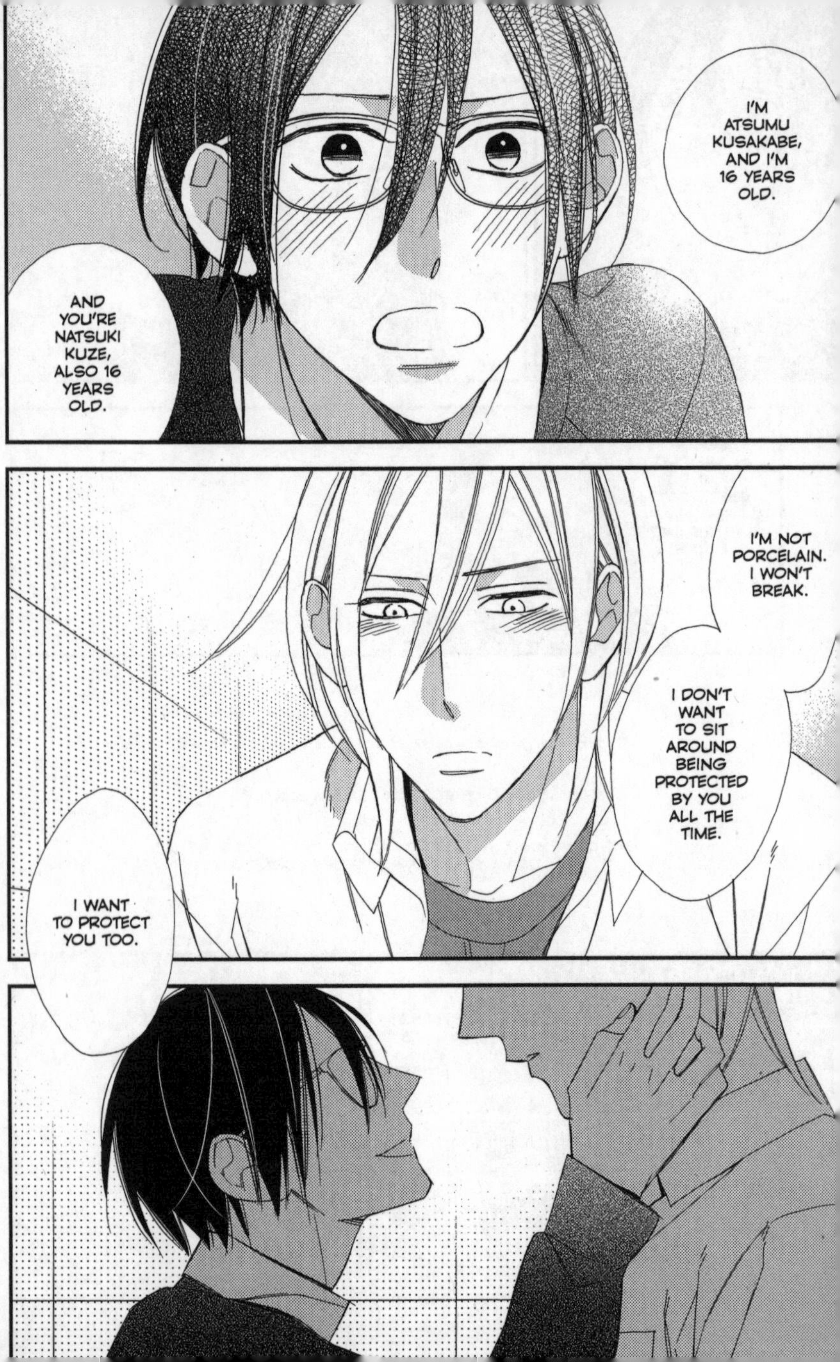
I'M ATSUMU KUSAKABE, AND I'M 16 YEARS OLD.
AND YOU'RE NATSUKI KUZE, ALSO 16 YEARS OLD.
I'M NOT PORCELAIN. I WON'T BREAK.
I DON'T WANT TO SIT AROUND BEING PROTECTED BY YOU ALL THE TIME.
I WANT TO PROTECT YOU TOO.

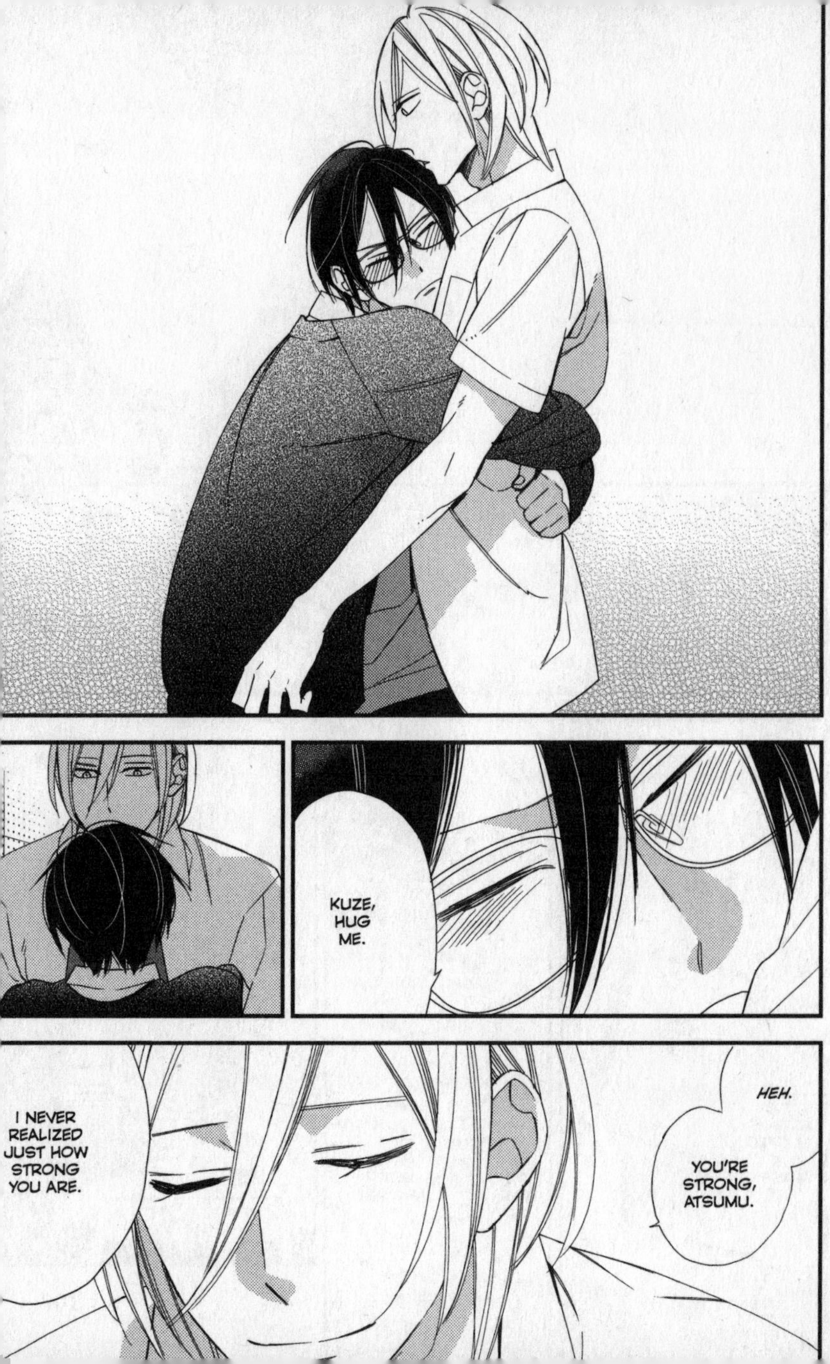
KUZE, HUG ME.
HEH.
YOU'RE STRONG, ATSUMU.
I NEVER REALIZED JUST HOW STRONG YOU ARE.

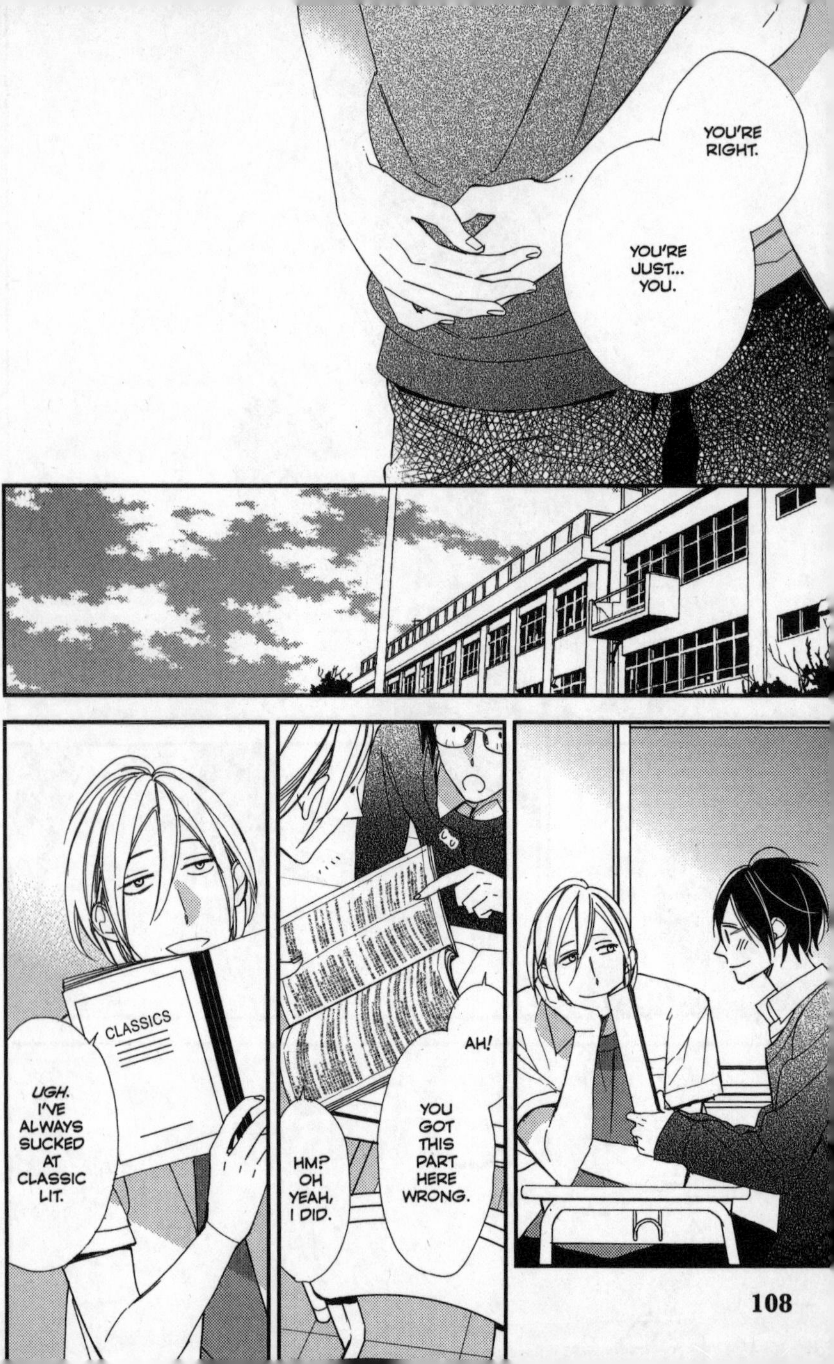
YOU'RE RIGHT.
YOU'RE JUST... YOU.
AH!
YOU GOT THIS PART HERE WRONG.
HM? OH YEAH, I DID.
CLASSICS
UGH. I'VE ALWAYS SUCKED AT CLASSIC LIT.

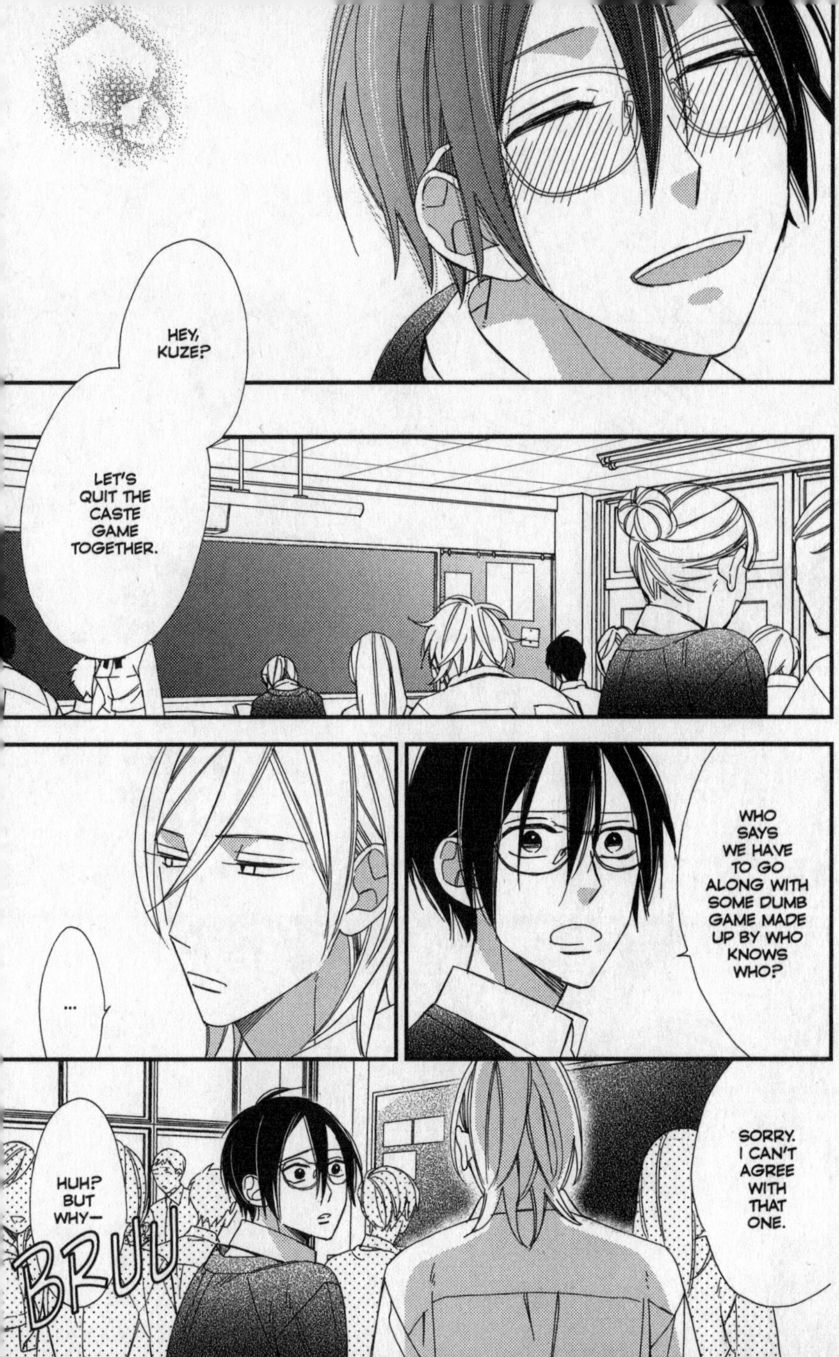
HEY, KUZE?
LET'S QUIT THE CASTE GAME TOGETHER.
WHO SAYS WE HAVE TO GO ALONG WITH SOME DUMB GAME MADE UP BY WHO KNOWS WHO?
...
SORRY. I CAN'T AGREE WITH THAT ONE.
HUH? BUT WHY—
BRUU

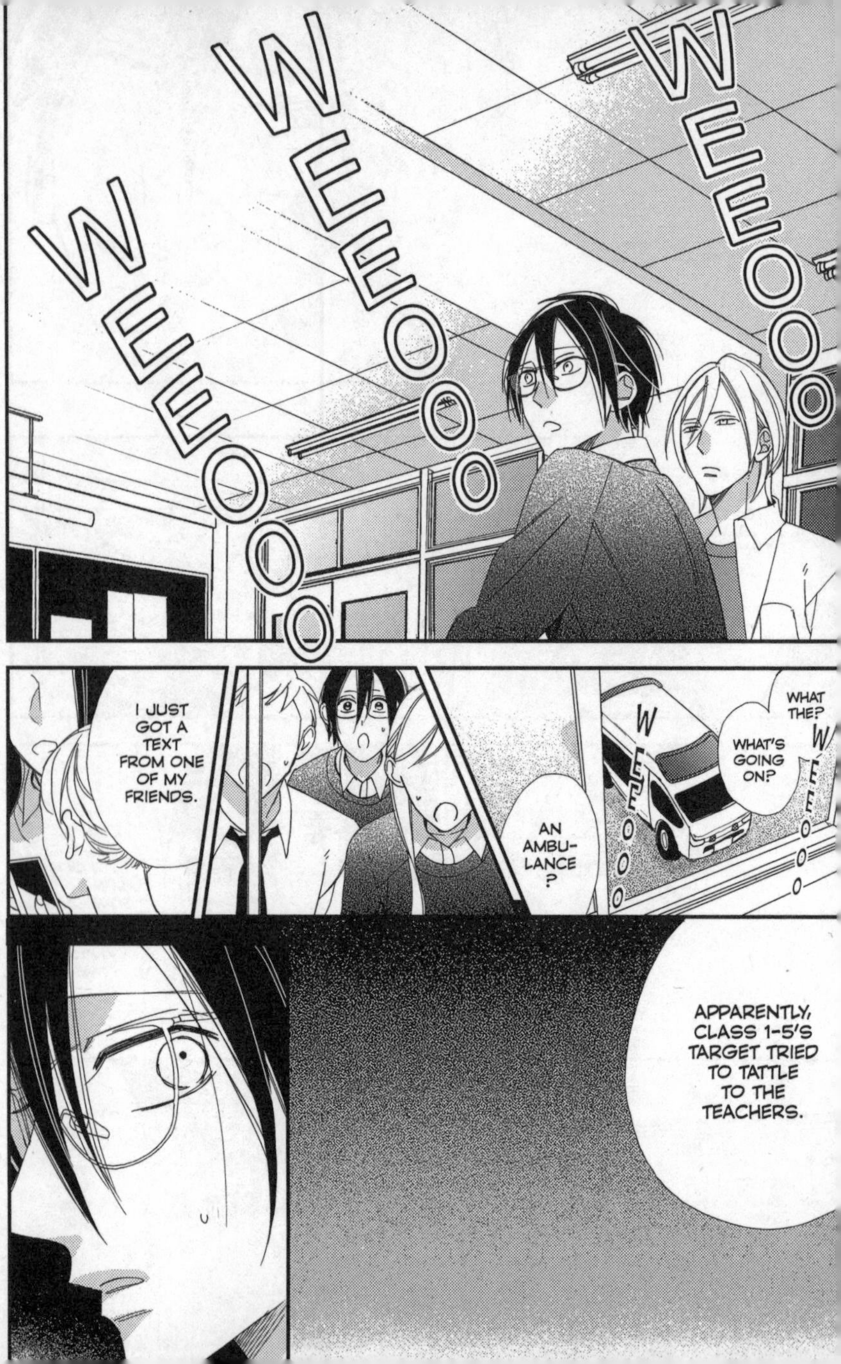

WEEOOOO
WEEOOOOO
WEEOOOO
WEEOOO
WHAT THE?
WHAT'S GOING ON?
WEEOOOO
AN AMBU-LANCE?
I JUST GOT A TEXT FROM ONE OF MY FRIENDS.
APPARENTLY, CLASS 1-5'S TARGET TRIED TO TATTLE TO THE TEACHERS.

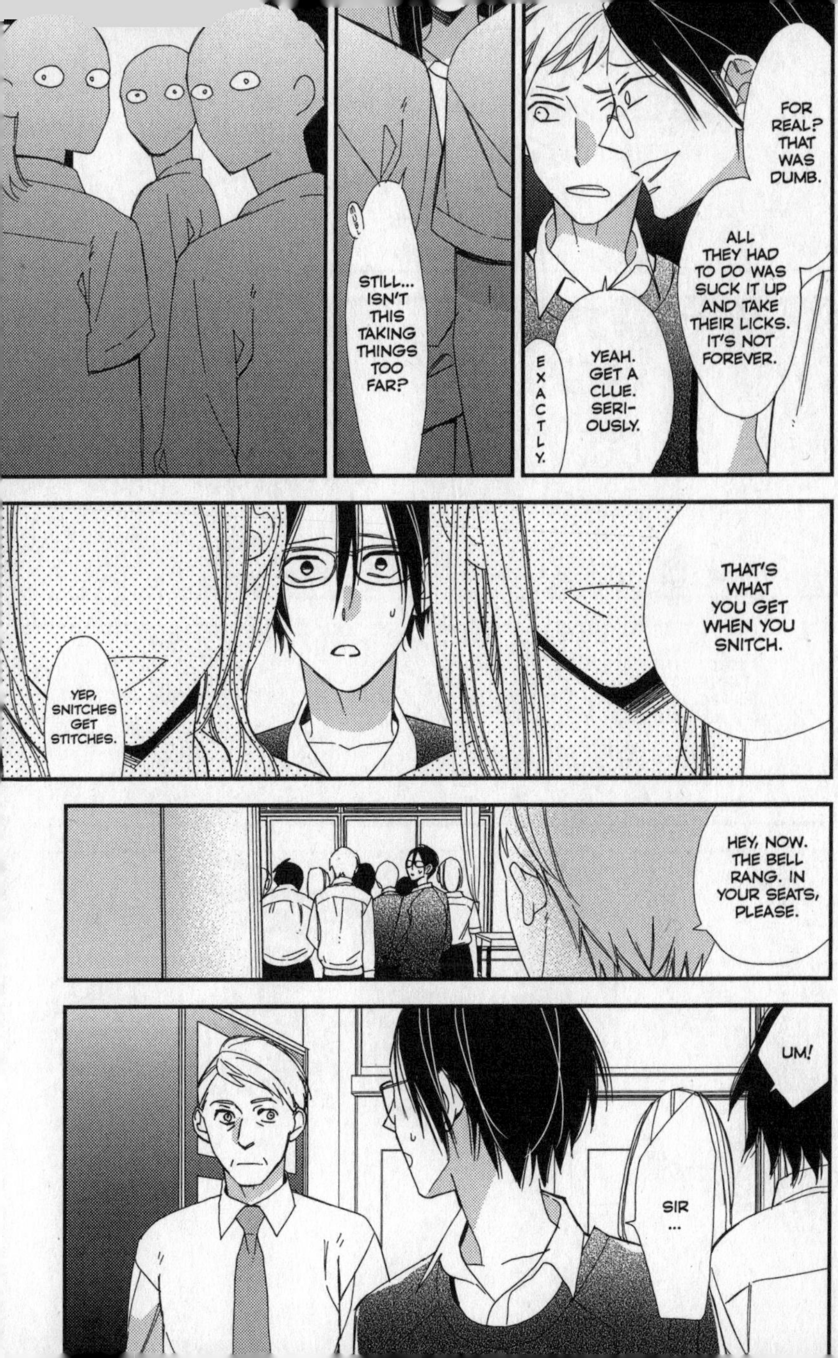
FOR REAL? THAT WAS DUMB.
ALL THEY HAD TO DO WAS SUCK IT UP AND TAKE THEIR LICKS. IT'S NOT FOREVER.
YEAH. GET A CLUE. SERIOUSLY.
EXACTLY.
STILL... ISN'T THIS TAKING THINGS TOO FAR?
THAT'S WHAT YOU GET WHEN YOU SNITCH.
YEP, SNITCHES GET STITCHES.
HEY, NOW. THE BELL RANG. IN YOUR SEATS, PLEASE.
UM!
SIR...

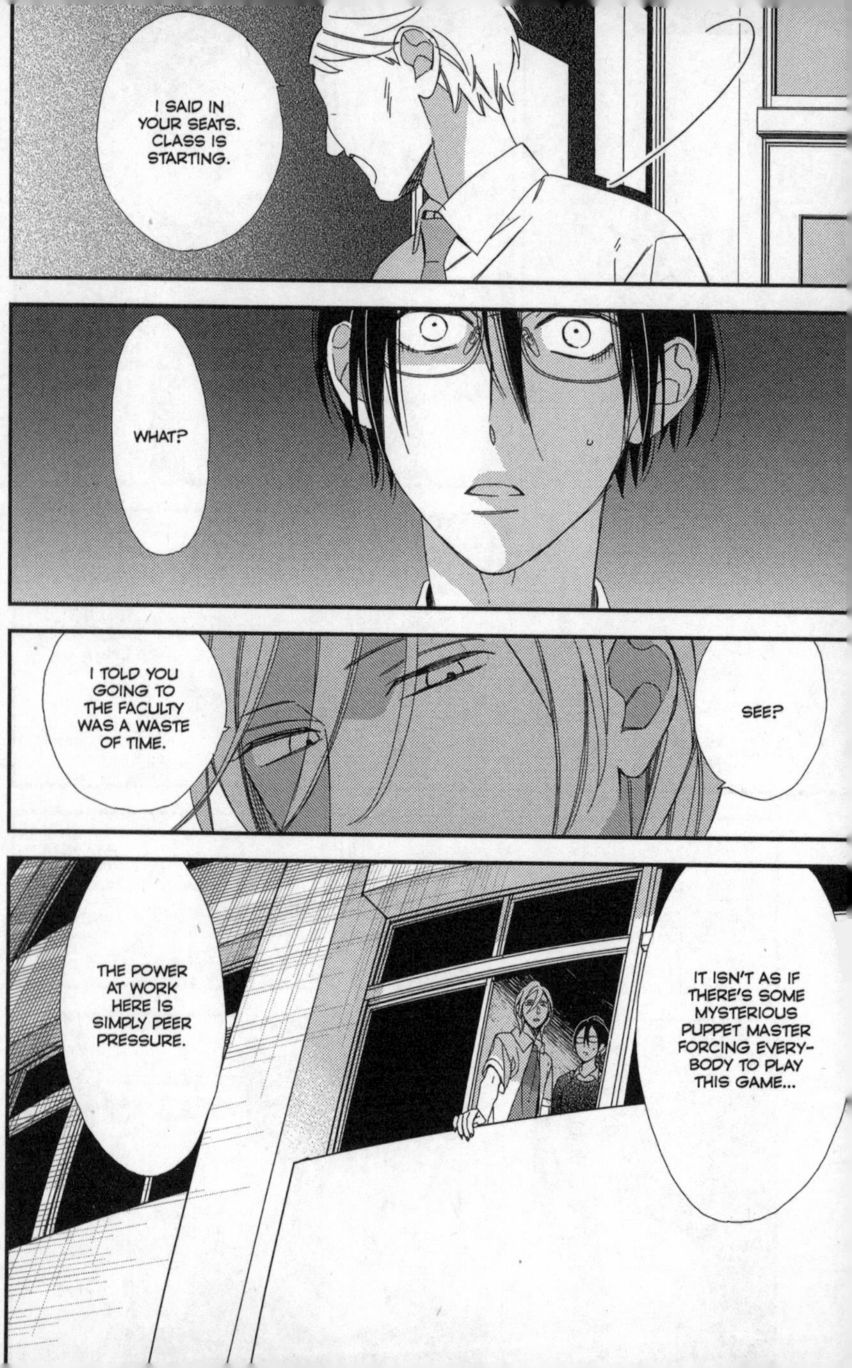
I SAID IN YOUR SEATS. CLASS IS STARTING.
WHAT?
SEE?
I TOLD YOU GOING TO THE FACULTY WAS A WASTE OF TIME.
IT ISN'T AS IF THERE'S SOME MYSTERIOUS PUPPET MASTER FORCING EVERY-BODY TO PLAY THIS GAME...
THE POWER AT WORK HERE IS SIMPLY PEER PRESSURE.

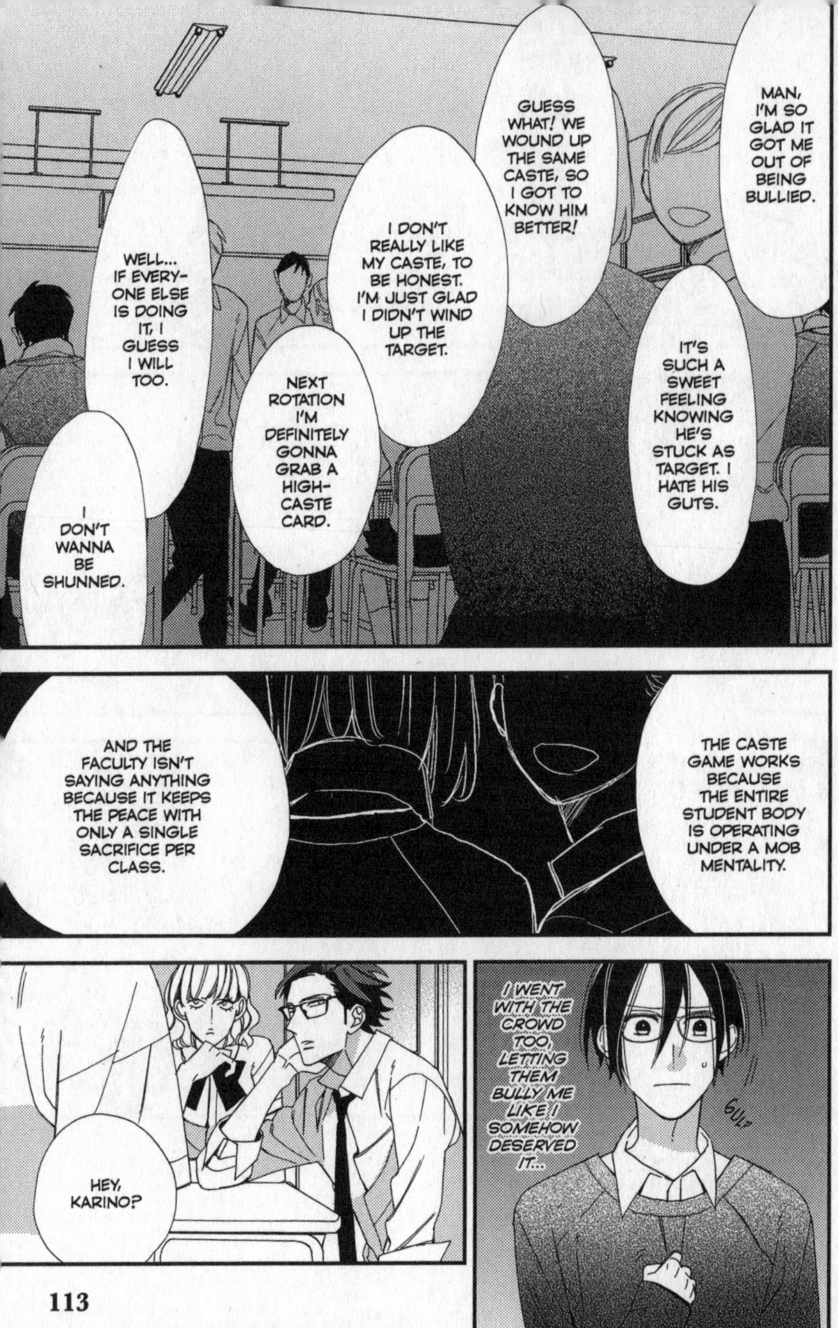
MAN, I'M SO GLAD IT GOT ME OUT OF BEING BULLIED.
GUESS WHAT! WE WOUND UP THE SAME CASTE, SO I GOT TO KNOW HIM BETTER!
IT'S SUCH A SWEET FEELING KNOWING HE'S STUCK AS TARGET. I HATE HIS GUTS.
I DON'T REALLY LIKE MY CASTE, TO BE HONEST. I'M JUST GLAD I DIDN'T WIND UP THE TARGET.
WELL... IF EVERYONE ELSE IS DOING IT, I GUESS I WILL TOO.
NEXT ROTATION I'M DEFINITELY GONNA GRAB A HIGH-CASTE CARD.
I DON'T WANNA BE SHUNNED.
THE CASTE GAME WORKS BECAUSE THE ENTIRE STUDENT BODY IS OPERATING UNDER A MOB MENTALITY.
AND THE FACULTY ISN'T SAYING ANYTHING BECAUSE IT KEEPS THE PEACE WITH ONLY A SINGLE SACRIFICE PER CLASS.
I WENT WITH THE CROWD TOO, LETTING THEM BULLY ME LIKE I SOMEHOW DESERVED IT...
GULP
HEY, KARINO?

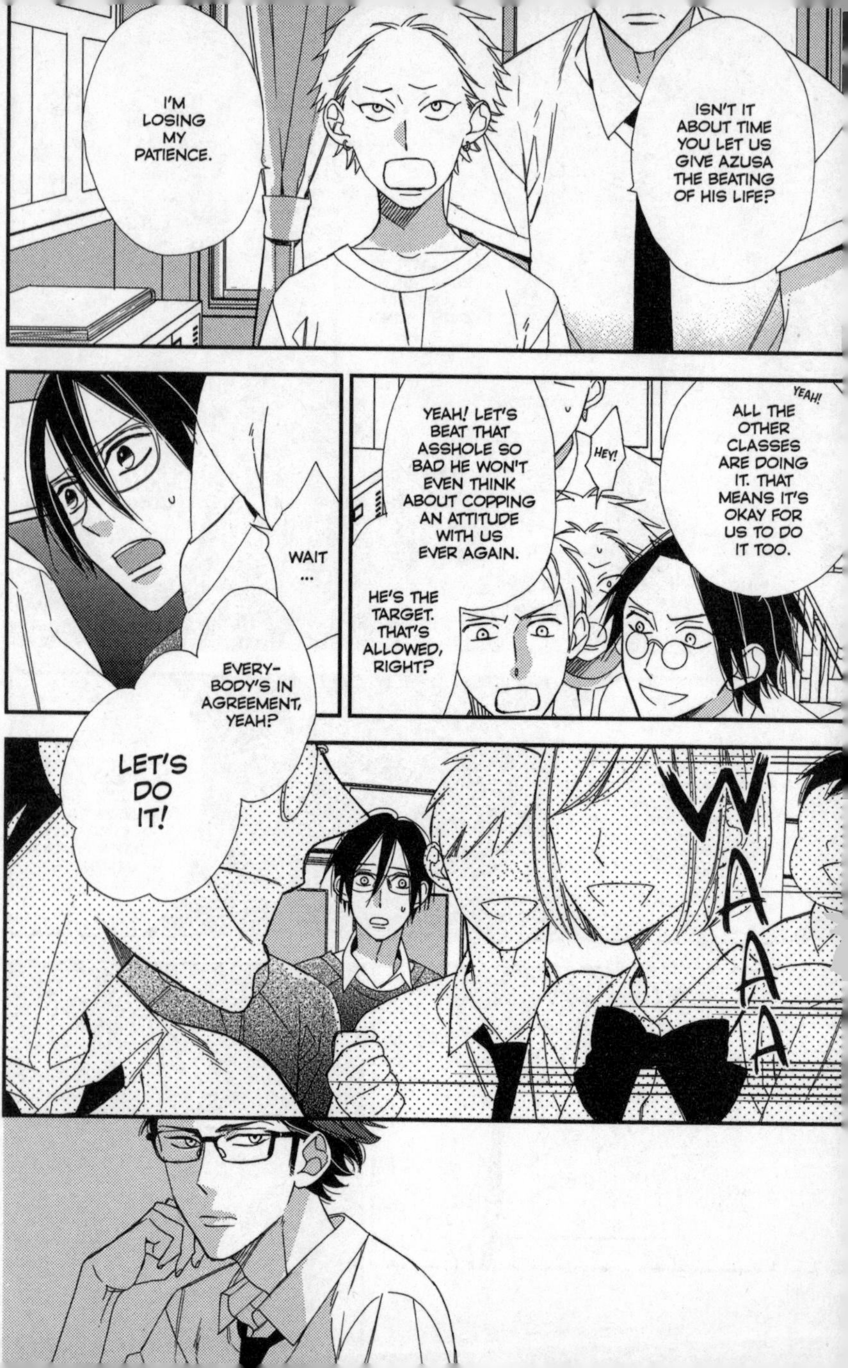
ISN'T IT ABOUT TIME YOU LET US GIVE AZUSA THE BEATING OF HIS LIFE?
I'M LOSING MY PATIENCE.
YEAH!
ALL THE OTHER CLASSES ARE DOING IT. THAT MEANS IT'S OKAY FOR US TO DO IT TOO.
HEY!
YEAH! LET'S BEAT THAT ASSHOLE SO BAD HE WON'T EVEN THINK ABOUT COPPING AN ATTITUDE WITH US EVER AGAIN.
HE'S THE TARGET. THAT'S ALLOWED, RIGHT?
WAIT ...
EVERY-BODY'S IN AGREEMENT, YEAH?
WAAA
LET'S DO IT!

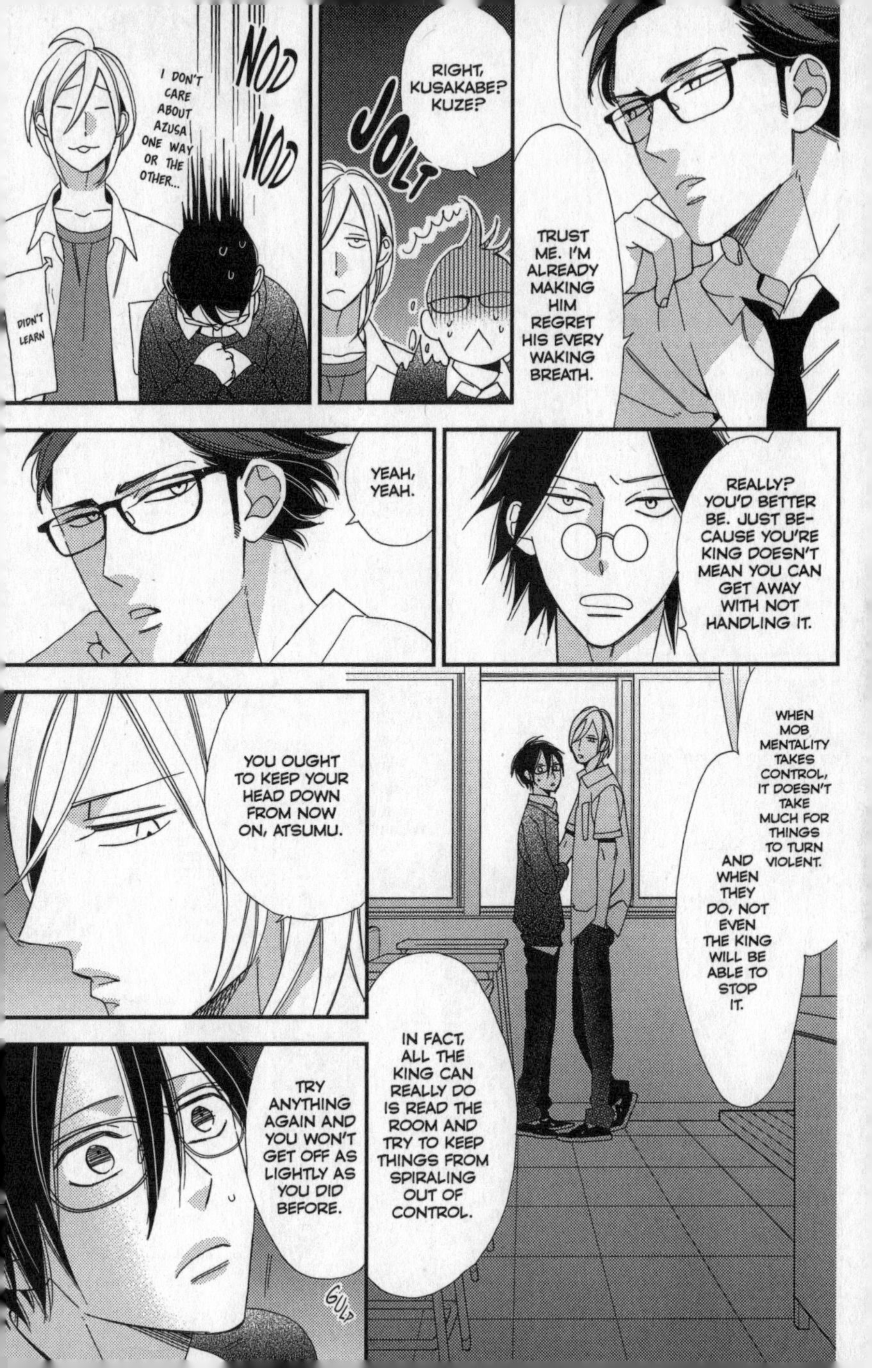
TRUST ME. I'M ALREADY MAKING HIM REGRET HIS EVERY WAKING BREATH.
RIGHT, KUSAKABE? KUZE?
JOLT
NOD NOD
I DON'T CARE ABOUT AZUSA ONE WAY OR THE OTHER...
DIDN'T LEARN
REALLY? YOU'D BETTER BE. JUST BE-CAUSE YOU'RE KING DOESN'T MEAN YOU CAN GET AWAY WITH NOT HANDLING IT.
YEAH, YEAH.
WHEN MOB MENTALITY TAKES CONTROL, IT DOESN'T TAKE MUCH FOR THINGS TO TURN VIOLENT.
AND WHEN THEY DO, NOT EVEN THE KING WILL BE ABLE TO STOP IT.
IN FACT, ALL THE KING CAN REALLY DO IS READ THE ROOM AND TRY TO KEEP THINGS FROM SPIRALING OUT OF CONTROL.
YOU OUGHT TO KEEP YOUR HEAD DOWN FROM NOW ON, ATSUMU.
TRY ANYTHING AGAIN AND YOU WON'T GET OFF AS LIGHTLY AS YOU DID BEFORE.
GULP

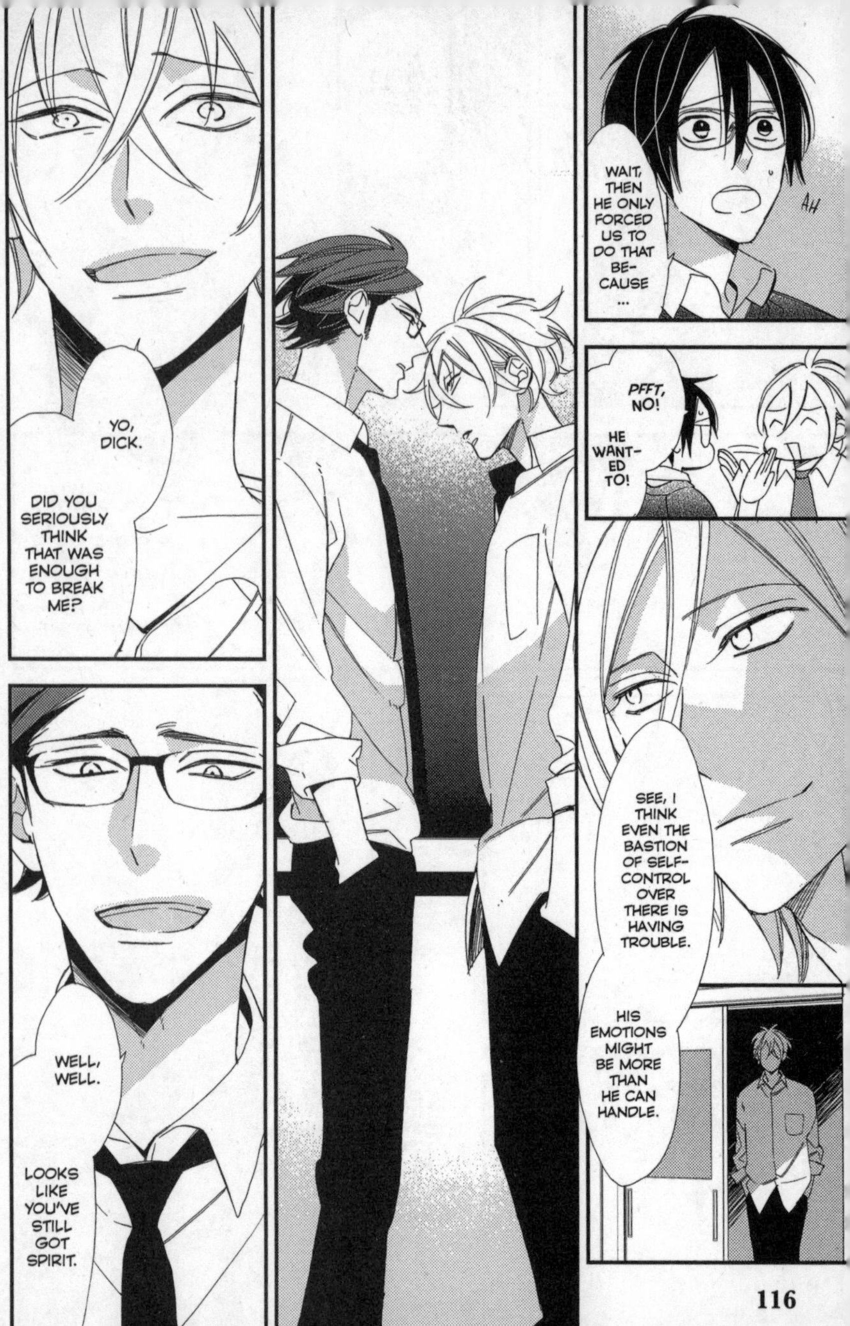
WAIT, THEN HE ONLY FORCED US TO DO THAT BE- CAUSE ...
AH
PFFT, NO!
HE WANT- ED TO!
SEE, I THINK EVEN THE BASTION OF SELF- CONTROL OVER THERE IS HAVING TROUBLE.
HIS EMOTIONS MIGHT BE MORE THAN HE CAN HANDLE.
YO, DICK.
DID YOU SERIOUSLY THINK THAT WAS ENOUGH TO BREAK ME?
WELL, WELL.
LOOKS LIKE YOU'VE STILL GOT SPIRIT.

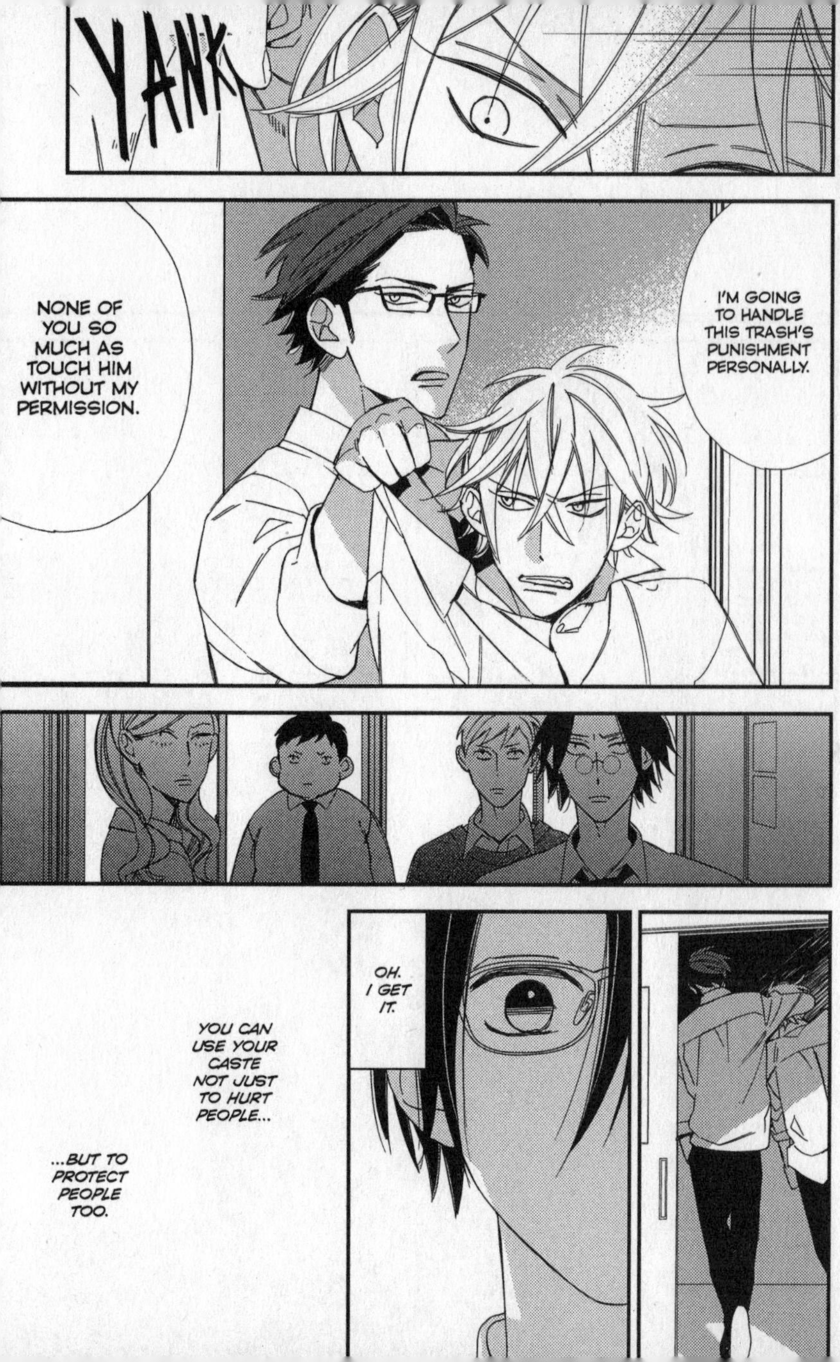
YANK
I'M GOING TO HANDLE THIS TRASH'S PUNISHMENT PERSONALLY.
NONE OF YOU SO MUCH AS TOUCH HIM WITHOUT MY PERMISSION.
OH. I GET IT.
YOU CAN USE YOUR CASTE NOT JUST TO HURT PEOPLE...
...BUT TO PROTECT PEOPLE TOO.

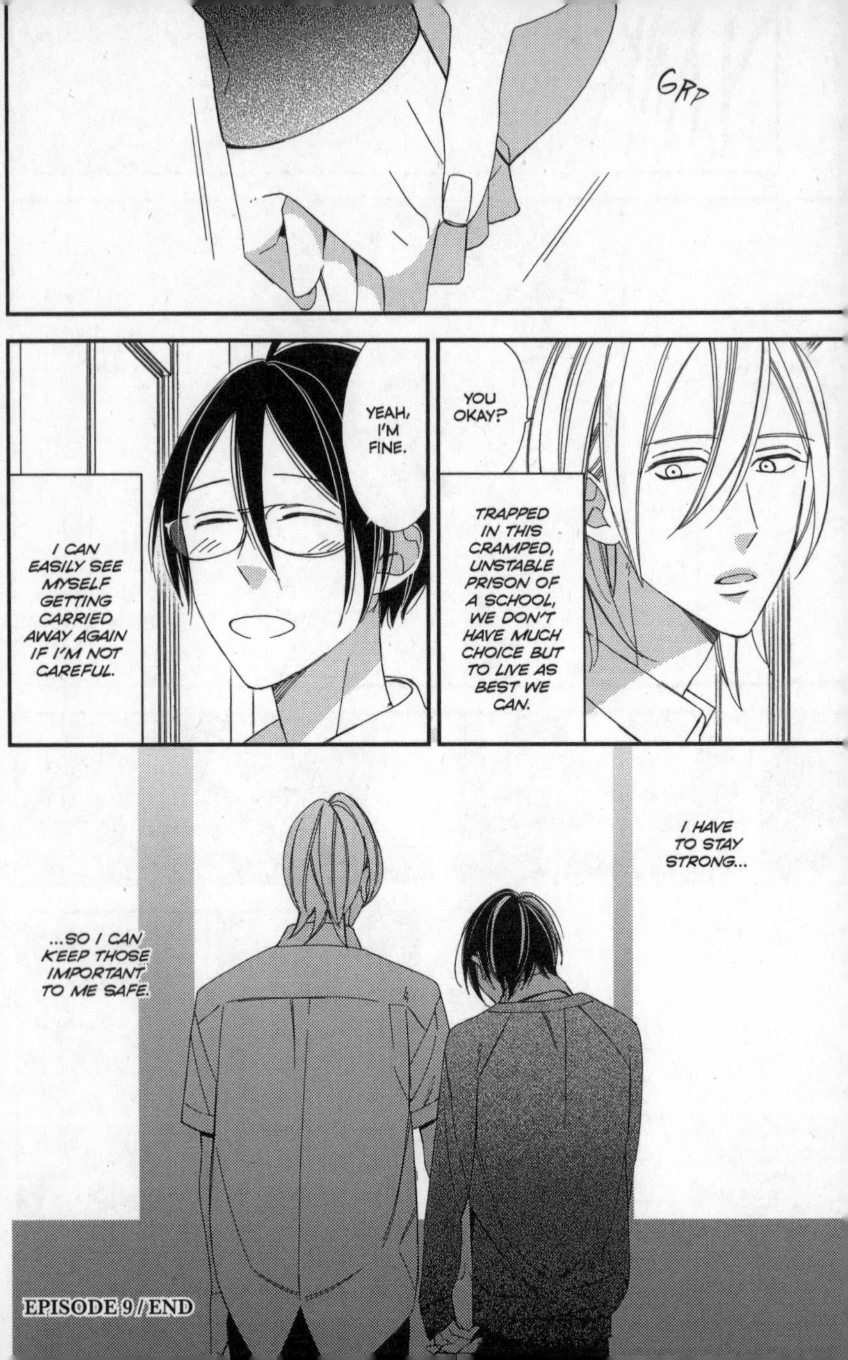
GRP
YOU OKAY?
TRAPPED IN THIS CRAMPED, UNSTABLE PRISON OF A SCHOOL, WE DON'T HAVE MUCH CHOICE BUT TO LIVE AS BEST WE CAN.
YEAH, I'M FINE.
I CAN EASILY SEE MYSELF GETTING CARRIED AWAY AGAIN IF I'M NOT CAREFUL.
I HAVE TO STAY STRONG...
...SO I CAN KEEP THOSE IMPORTANT TO ME SAFE.
EPISODE 9 / END

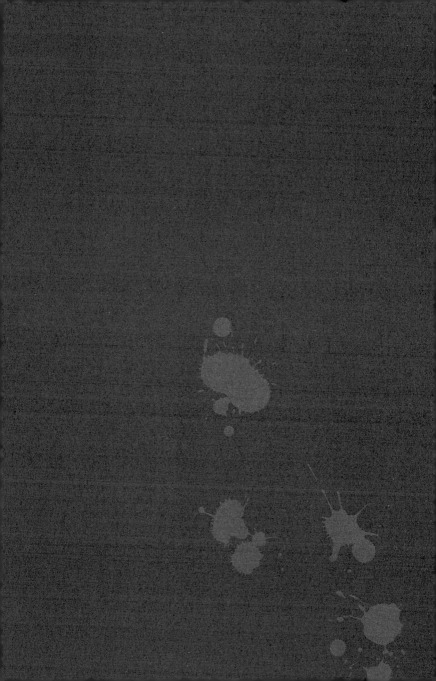

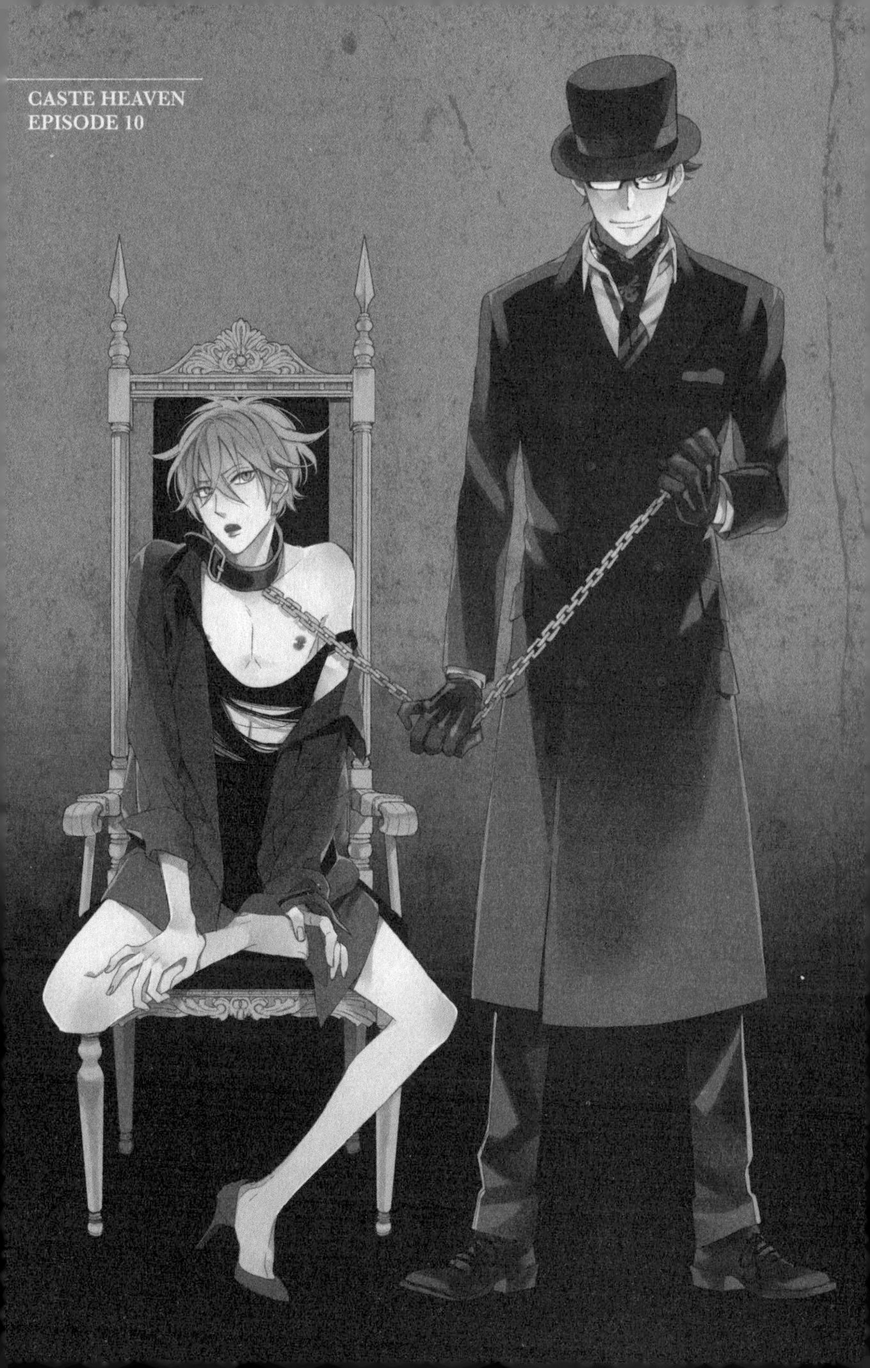
CASTE HEAVEN
EPISODE 10

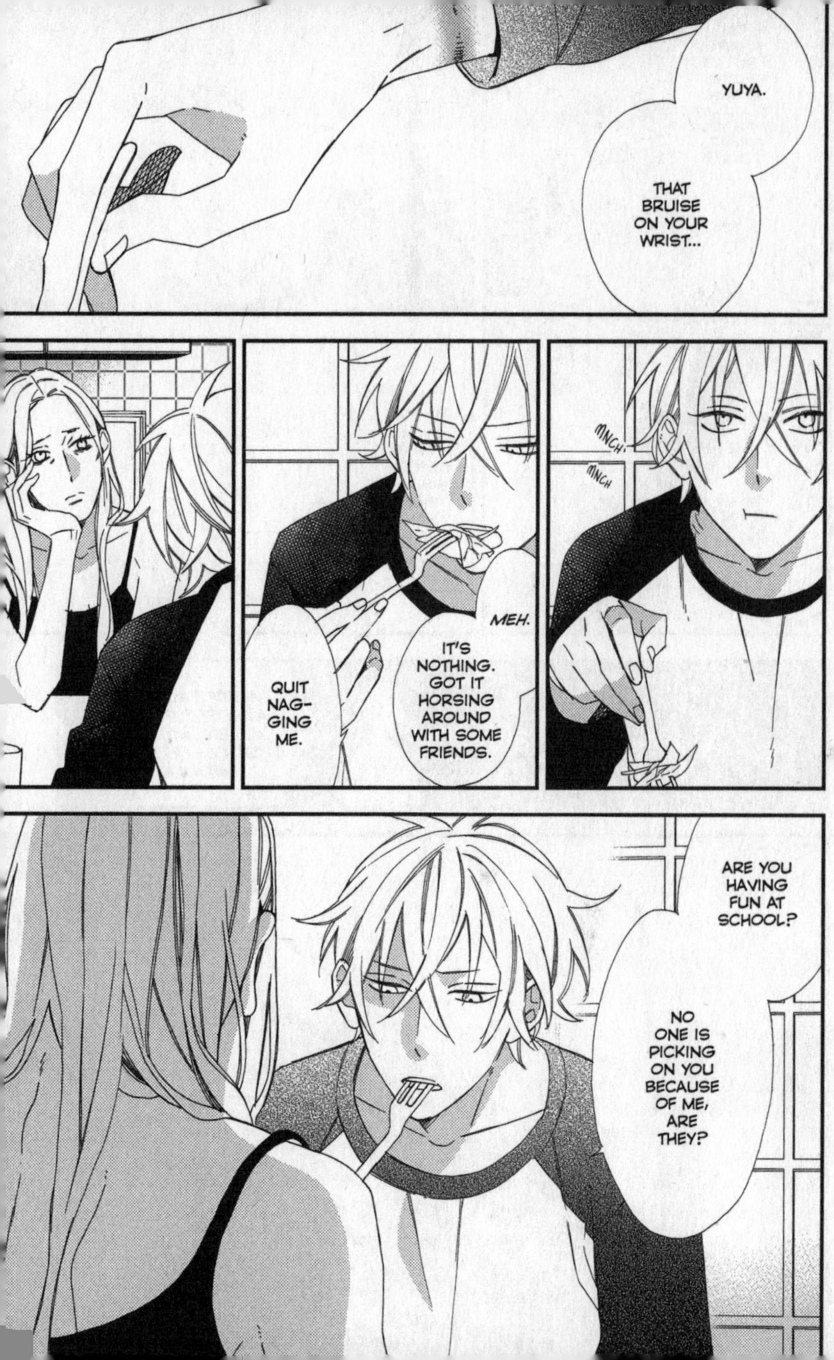
YUYA.
THAT BRUISE ON YOUR WRIST...
MNCH
MNCH
MEH.
IT'S NOTHING. GOT IT HORSING AROUND WITH SOME FRIENDS.
QUIT NAG-GING ME.
ARE YOU HAVING FUN AT SCHOOL?
NO ONE IS PICKING ON YOU BECAUSE OF ME, ARE THEY?

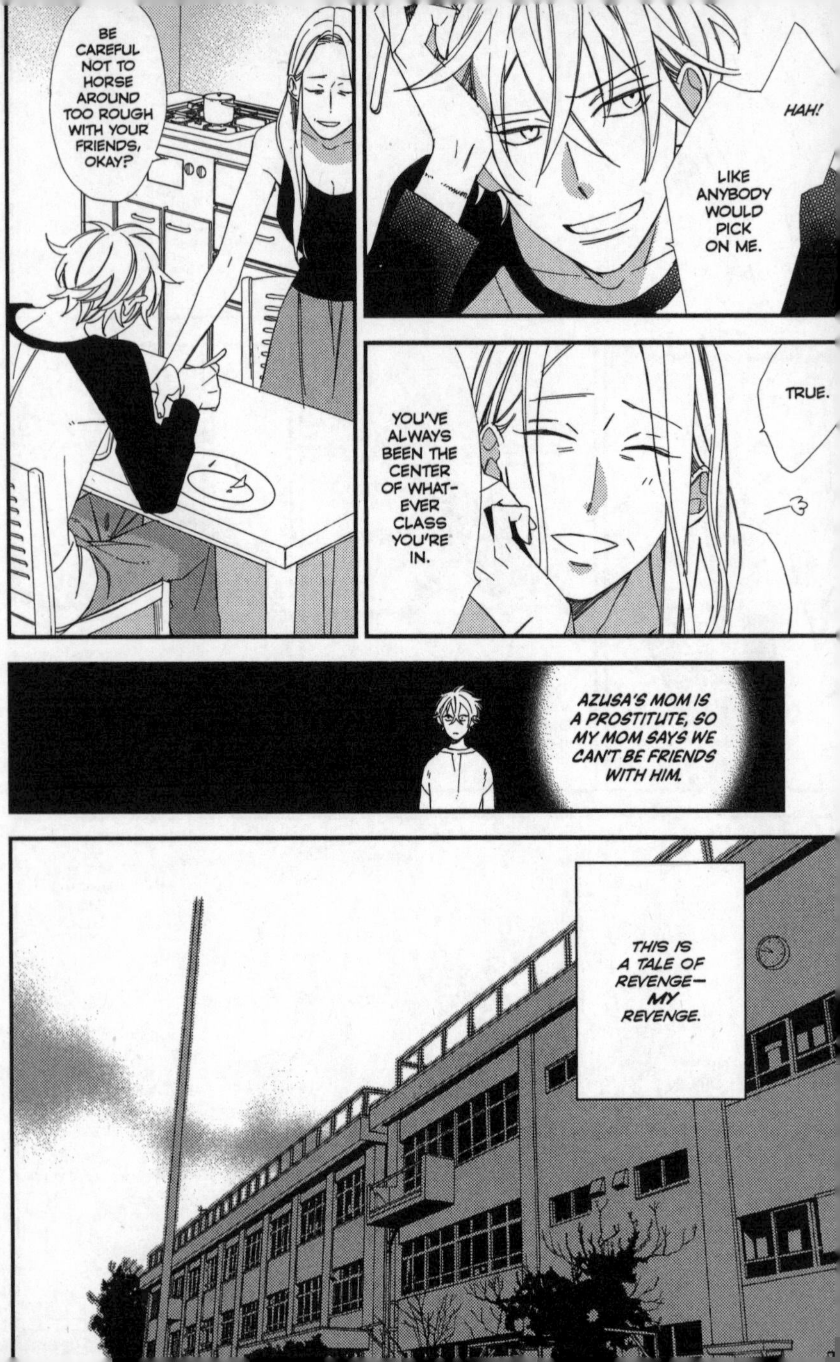
HAH!
LIKE ANYBODY WOULD PICK ON ME.
TRUE.
YOU'VE ALWAYS BEEN THE CENTER OF WHAT-EVER CLASS YOU'RE IN.
BE CAREFUL NOT TO HORSE AROUND TOO ROUGH WITH YOUR FRIENDS, OKAY?
AZUSA'S MOM IS A PROSTITUTE, SO MY MOM SAYS WE CAN'T BE FRIENDS WITH HIM.
THIS IS A TALE OF REVENGE—MY REVENGE.

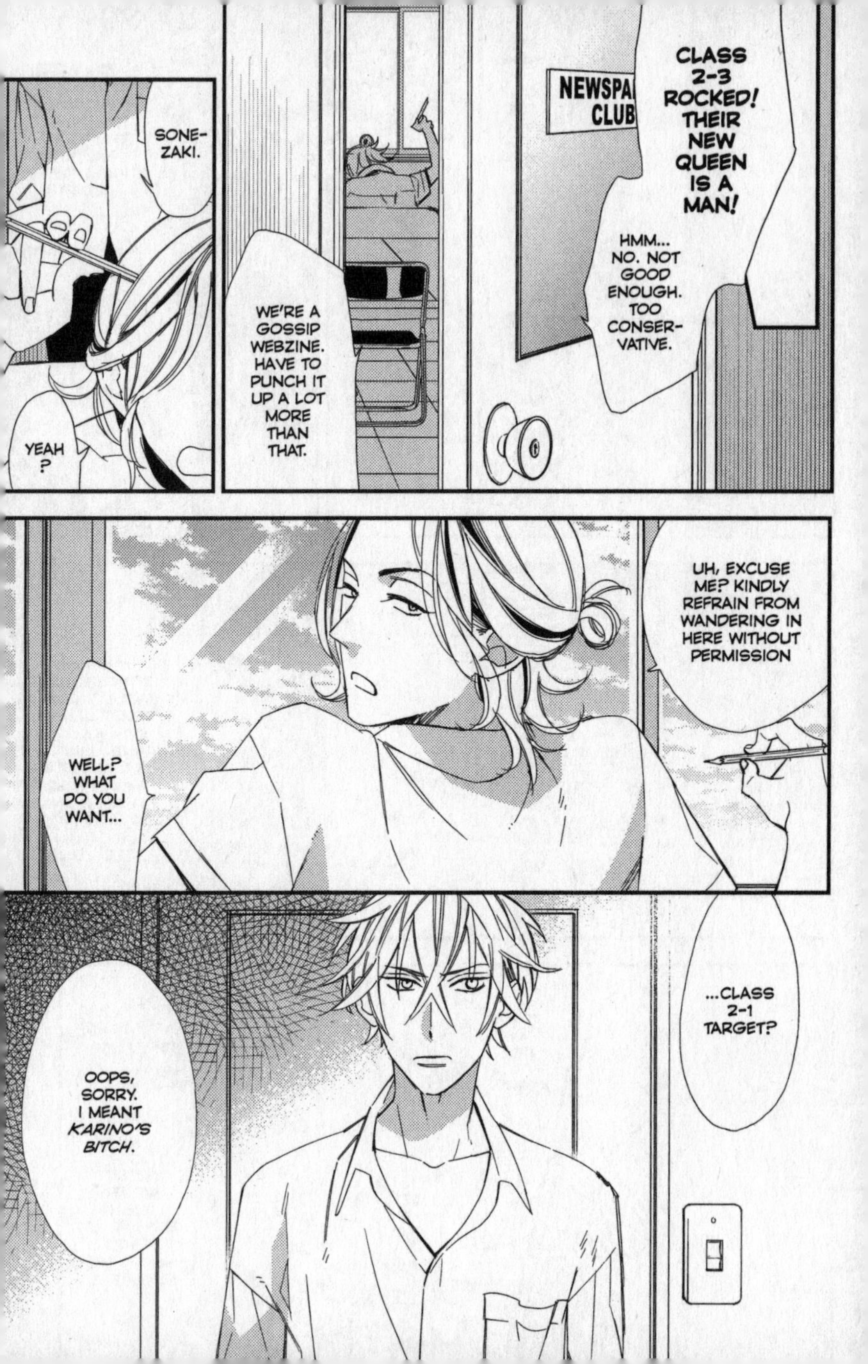
CLASS 2-3 ROCKED! THEIR NEW QUEEN IS A MAN!
NEWSPA CLUB
HMM... NO. NOT GOOD ENOUGH. TOO CONSER-VATIVE.
WE'RE A GOSSIP WEBZINE. HAVE TO PUNCH IT UP A LOT MORE THAN THAT.
SONE-ZAKI.
YEAH?
UH, EXCUSE ME? KINDLY REFRAIN FROM WANDERING IN HERE WITHOUT PERMISSION
WELL? WHAT DO YOU WANT...
...CLASS 2-1 TARGET?
OOPS, SORRY. I MEANT *KARINO'S BITCH*.

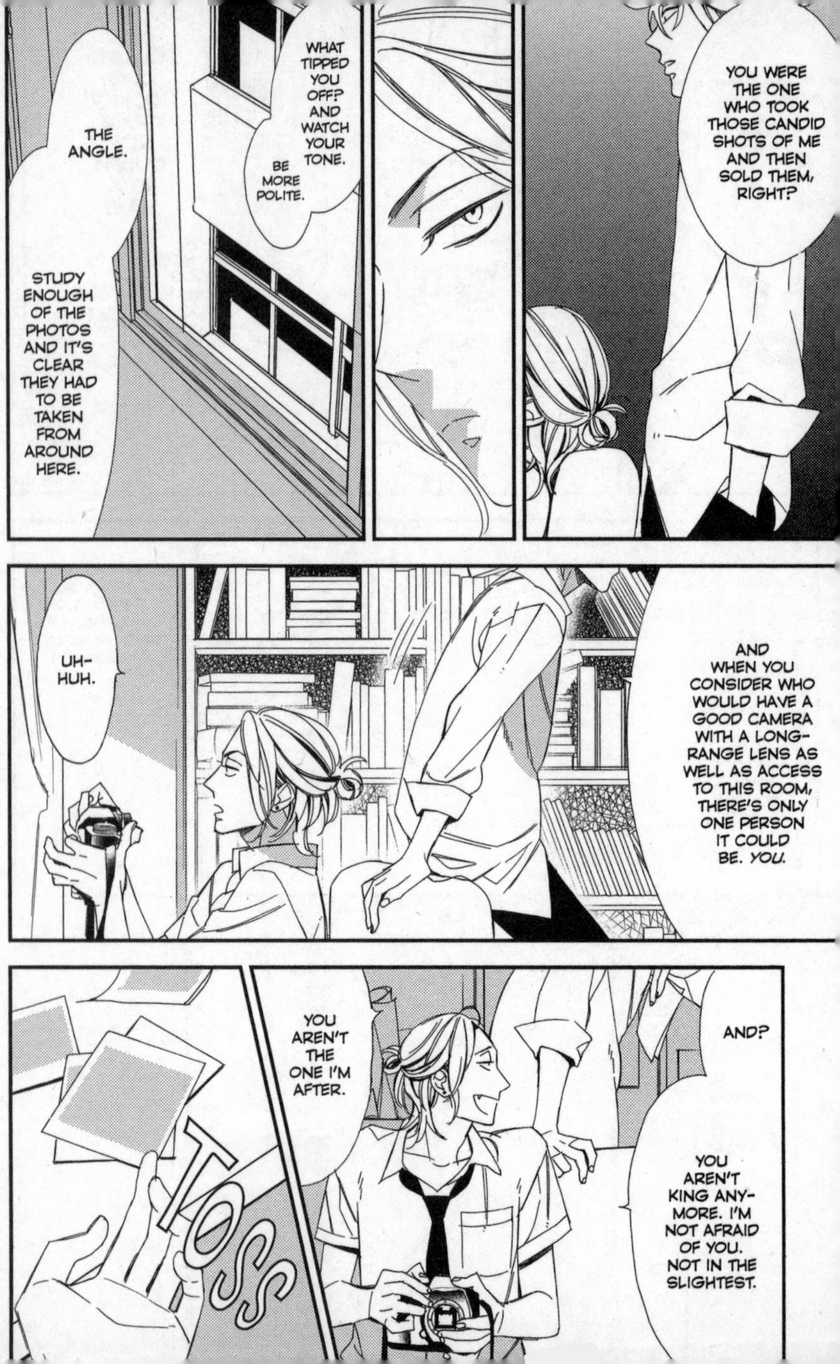
YOU WERE THE ONE WHO TOOK THOSE CANDID SHOTS OF ME AND THEN SOLD THEM, RIGHT?
WHAT TIPPED YOU OFF? AND WATCH YOUR TONE.
BE MORE POLITE.
THE ANGLE.
STUDY ENOUGH OF THE PHOTOS AND IT'S CLEAR THEY HAD TO BE TAKEN FROM AROUND HERE.
AND WHEN YOU CONSIDER WHO WOULD HAVE A GOOD CAMERA WITH A LONG-RANGE LENS AS WELL AS ACCESS TO THIS ROOM, THERE'S ONLY ONE PERSON IT COULD BE. *YOU.*
UH-HUH.
AND?
YOU AREN'T KING ANYMORE. I'M NOT AFRAID OF YOU. NOT IN THE SLIGHTEST.
YOU AREN'T THE ONE I'M AFTER.
TOSS

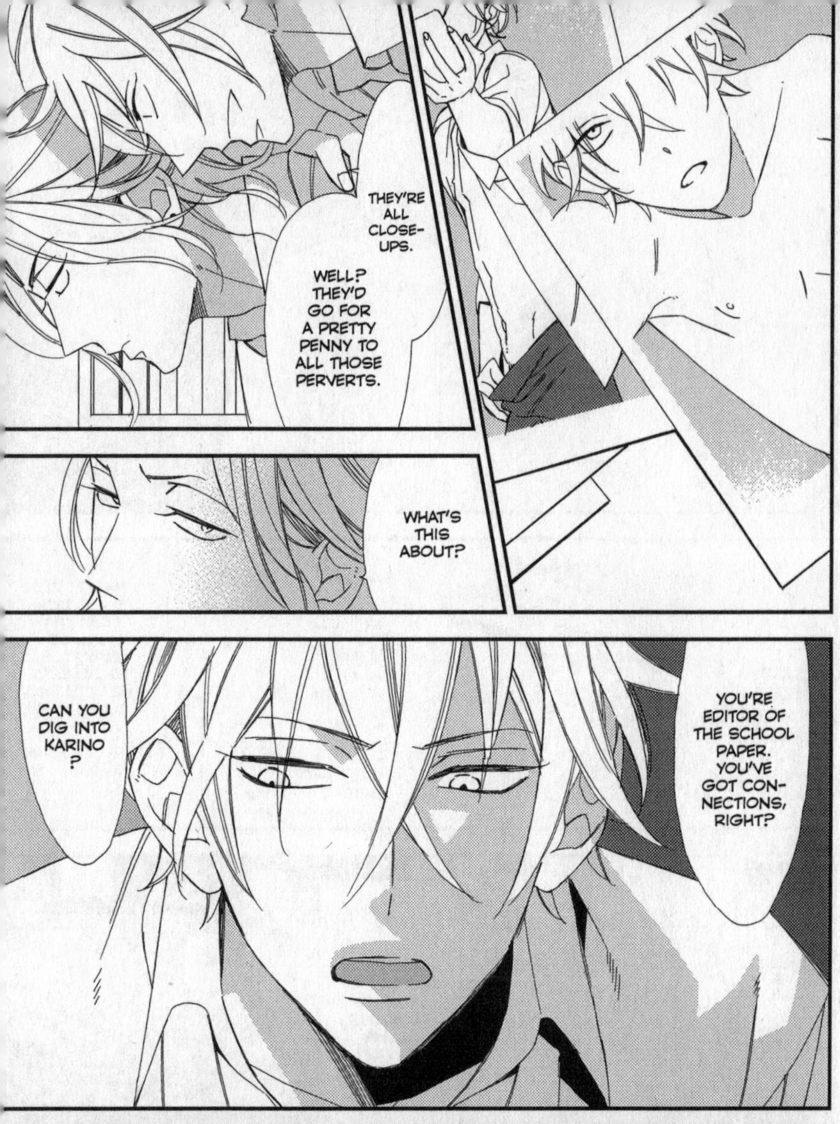
THEY'RE ALL CLOSE-UPS.
WELL? THEY'D GO FOR A PRETTY PENNY TO ALL THOSE PERVERTS.
WHAT'S THIS ABOUT?
YOU'RE EDITOR OF THE SCHOOL PAPER. YOU'VE GOT CONNECTIONS, RIGHT?
CAN YOU DIG INTO KARINO?

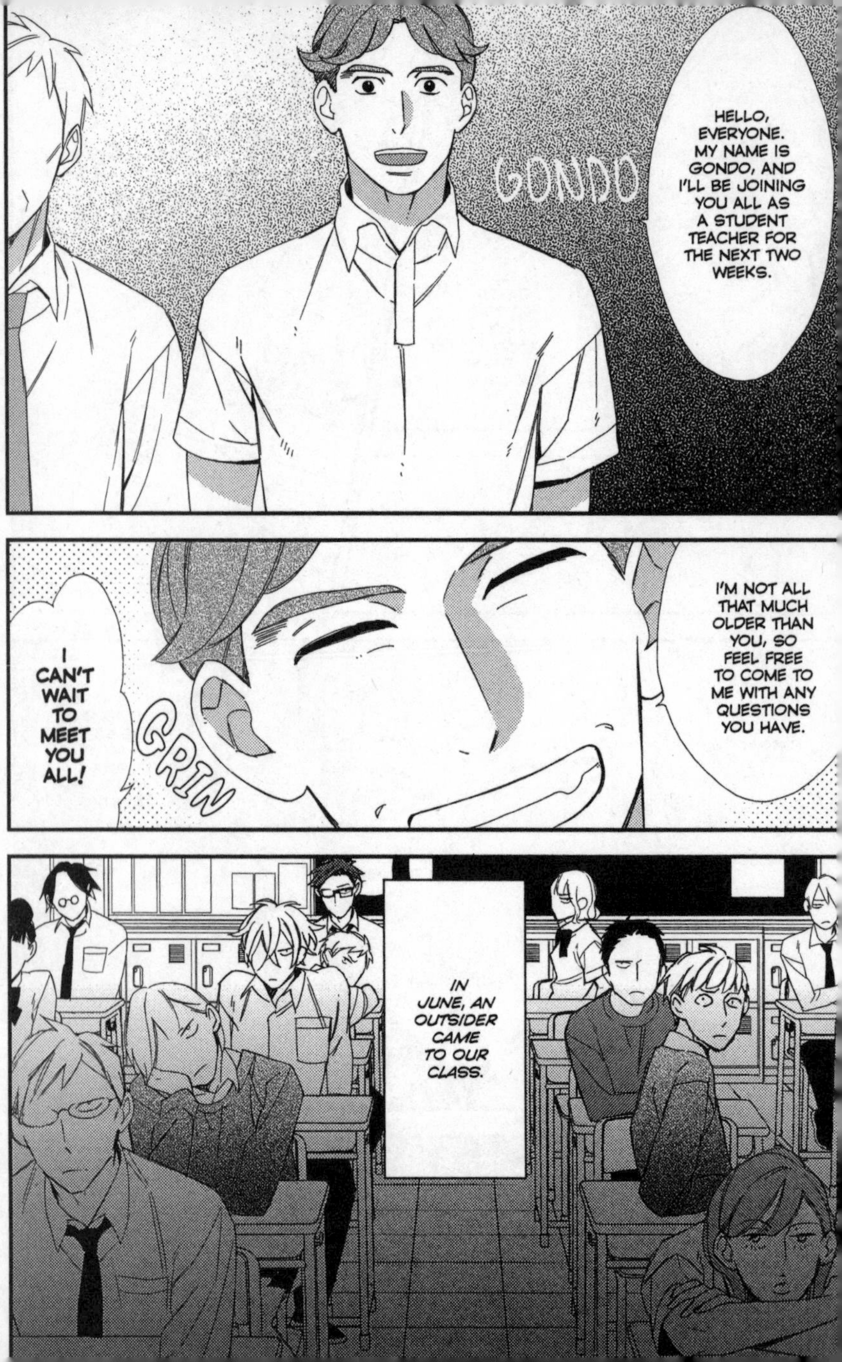
HELLO, EVERYONE. MY NAME IS GONDO, AND I'LL BE JOINING YOU ALL AS A STUDENT TEACHER FOR THE NEXT TWO WEEKS.
GONDO
I'M NOT ALL THAT MUCH OLDER THAN YOU, SO FEEL FREE TO COME TO ME WITH ANY QUESTIONS YOU HAVE.
GRIN
I CAN'T WAIT TO MEET YOU ALL!
IN JUNE, AN OUTSIDER CAME TO OUR CLASS.

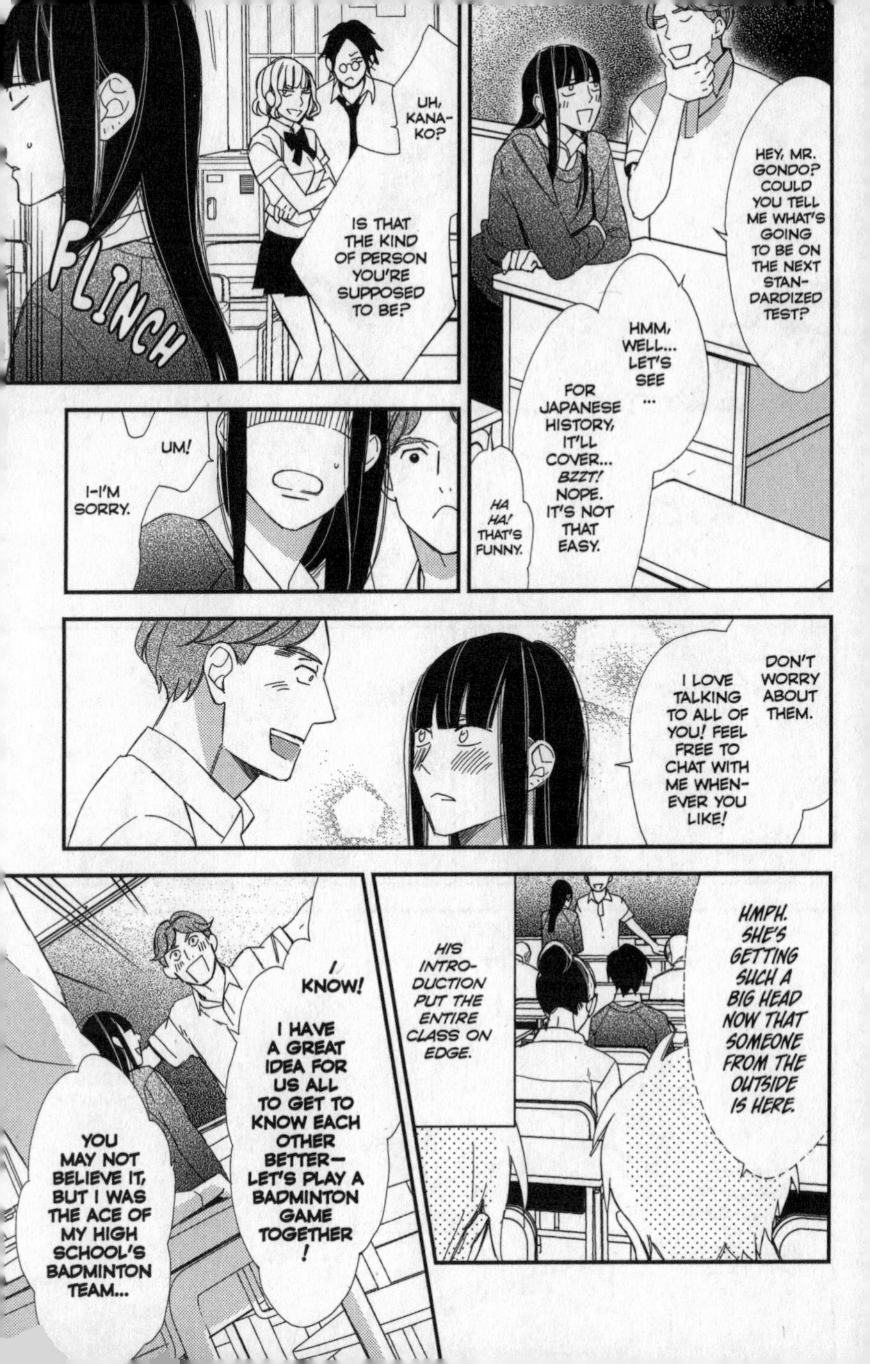
HEY, MR. GONDO? COULD YOU TELL ME WHAT'S GOING TO BE ON THE NEXT STANDARDIZED TEST?
HMM, WELL... LET'S SEE ...
FOR JAPANESE HISTORY, IT'LL COVER... BZZT! NOPE. IT'S NOT THAT EASY.
HA HA! THAT'S FUNNY.
UH, KANAKO?
IS THAT THE KIND OF PERSON YOU'RE SUPPOSED TO BE?
FLINCH
UM!
I-I'M SORRY.
DON'T WORRY ABOUT THEM.
I LOVE TALKING TO ALL OF YOU! FEEL FREE TO CHAT WITH ME WHENEVER YOU LIKE!
HMPH. SHE'S GETTING SUCH A BIG HEAD NOW THAT SOMEONE FROM THE OUTSIDE IS HERE.
HIS INTRODUCTION PUT THE ENTIRE CLASS ON EDGE.
I KNOW!
I HAVE A GREAT IDEA FOR US ALL TO GET TO KNOW EACH OTHER BETTER—LET'S PLAY A BADMINTON GAME TOGETHER!
YOU MAY NOT BELIEVE IT, BUT I WAS THE ACE OF MY HIGH SCHOOL'S BADMINTON TEAM...

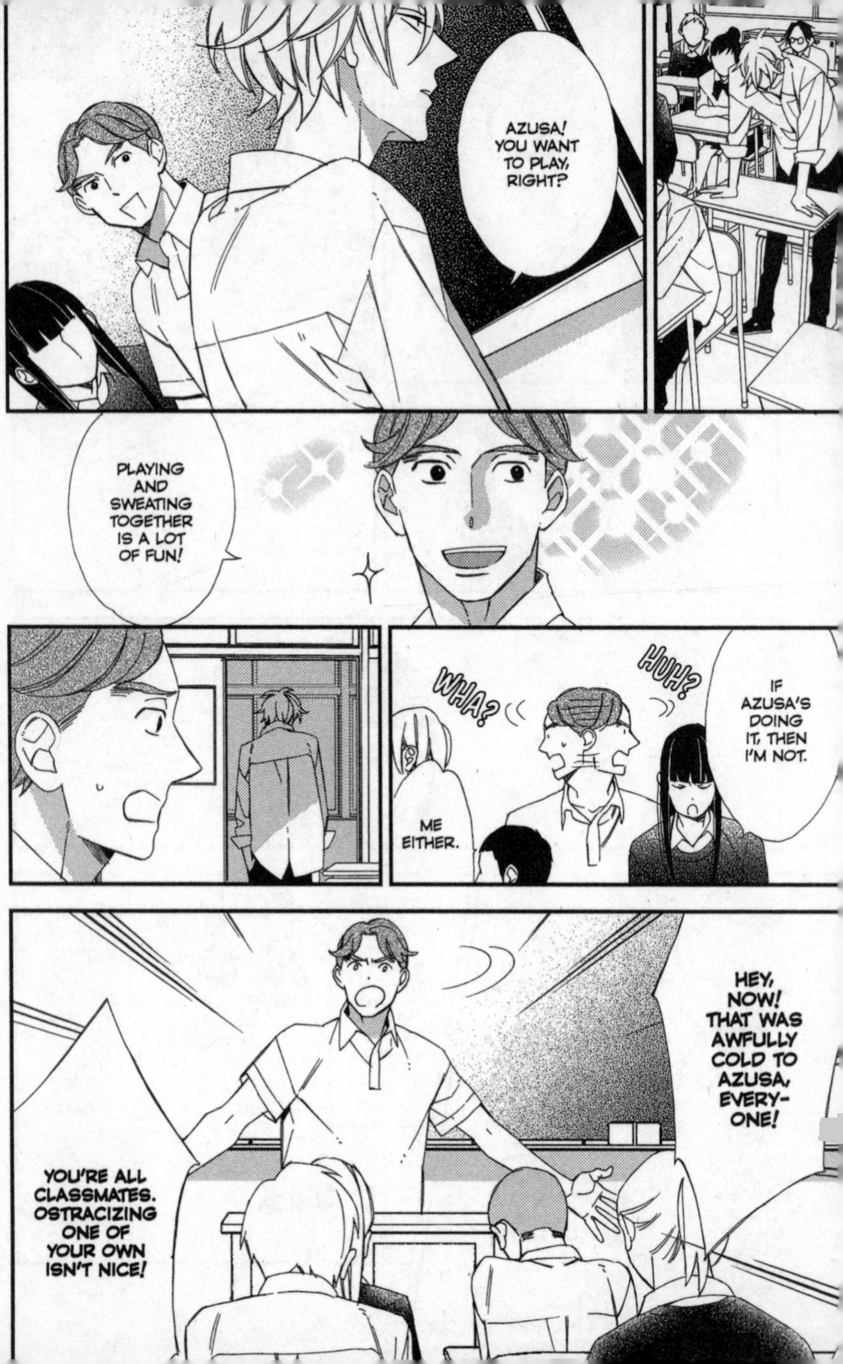
AZUSA! YOU WANT TO PLAY, RIGHT?
PLAYING AND SWEATING TOGETHER IS A LOT OF FUN!
IF AZUSA'S DOING IT, THEN I'M NOT.
HUH?
WHA?
ME EITHER.
HEY, NOW! THAT WAS AWFULLY COLD TO AZUSA, EVERYONE!
YOU'RE ALL CLASSMATES. OSTRACIZING ONE OF YOUR OWN ISN'T NICE!

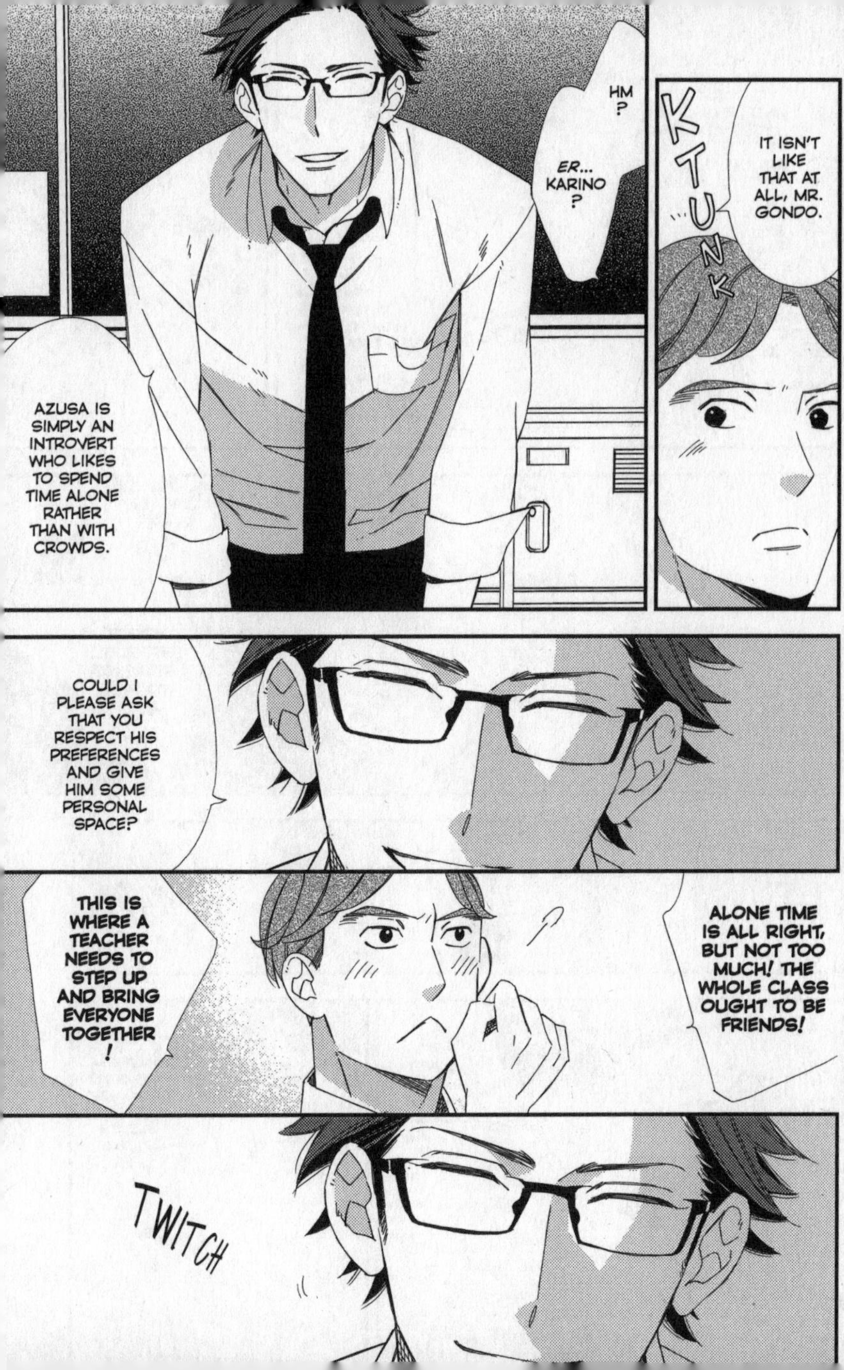
KTUNK
...
IT ISN'T LIKE THAT AT ALL, MR. GONDO.
HM?
ER... KARINO?
AZUSA IS SIMPLY AN INTROVERT WHO LIKES TO SPEND TIME ALONE RATHER THAN WITH CROWDS.
COULD I PLEASE ASK THAT YOU RESPECT HIS PREFERENCES AND GIVE HIM SOME PERSONAL SPACE?
ALONE TIME IS ALL RIGHT, BUT NOT TOO MUCH! THE WHOLE CLASS OUGHT TO BE FRIENDS!
THIS IS WHERE A TEACHER NEEDS TO STEP UP AND BRING EVERYONE TOGETHER!
TWITCH

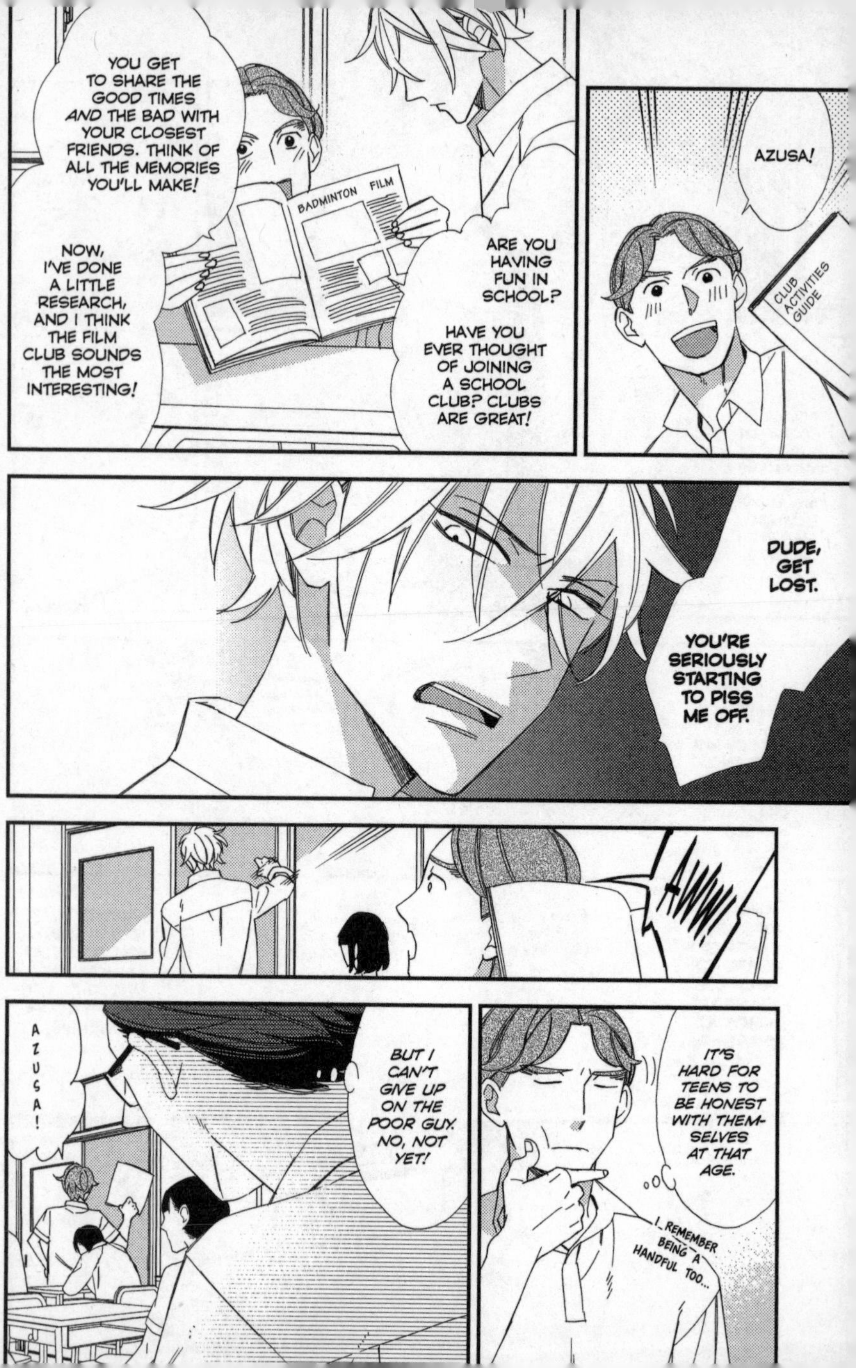
AZUSA!
CLUB ACTIVITIES GUIDE
ARE YOU HAVING FUN IN SCHOOL?
HAVE YOU EVER THOUGHT OF JOINING A SCHOOL CLUB? CLUBS ARE GREAT!
YOU GET TO SHARE THE GOOD TIMES *AND* THE BAD WITH YOUR CLOSEST FRIENDS. THINK OF ALL THE MEMORIES YOU'LL MAKE!
BADMINTON FILM
NOW, I'VE DONE A LITTLE RESEARCH, AND I THINK THE FILM CLUB SOUNDS THE MOST INTERESTING!
DUDE, GET LOST.
YOU'RE SERIOUSLY STARTING TO PISS ME OFF.
AWW!
IT'S HARD FOR TEENS TO BE HONEST WITH THEMSELVES AT THAT AGE.
I REMEMBER BEING A HANDFUL TOO...
BUT I CAN'T GIVE UP ON THE POOR GUY. NO, NOT YET!
AZUSA!

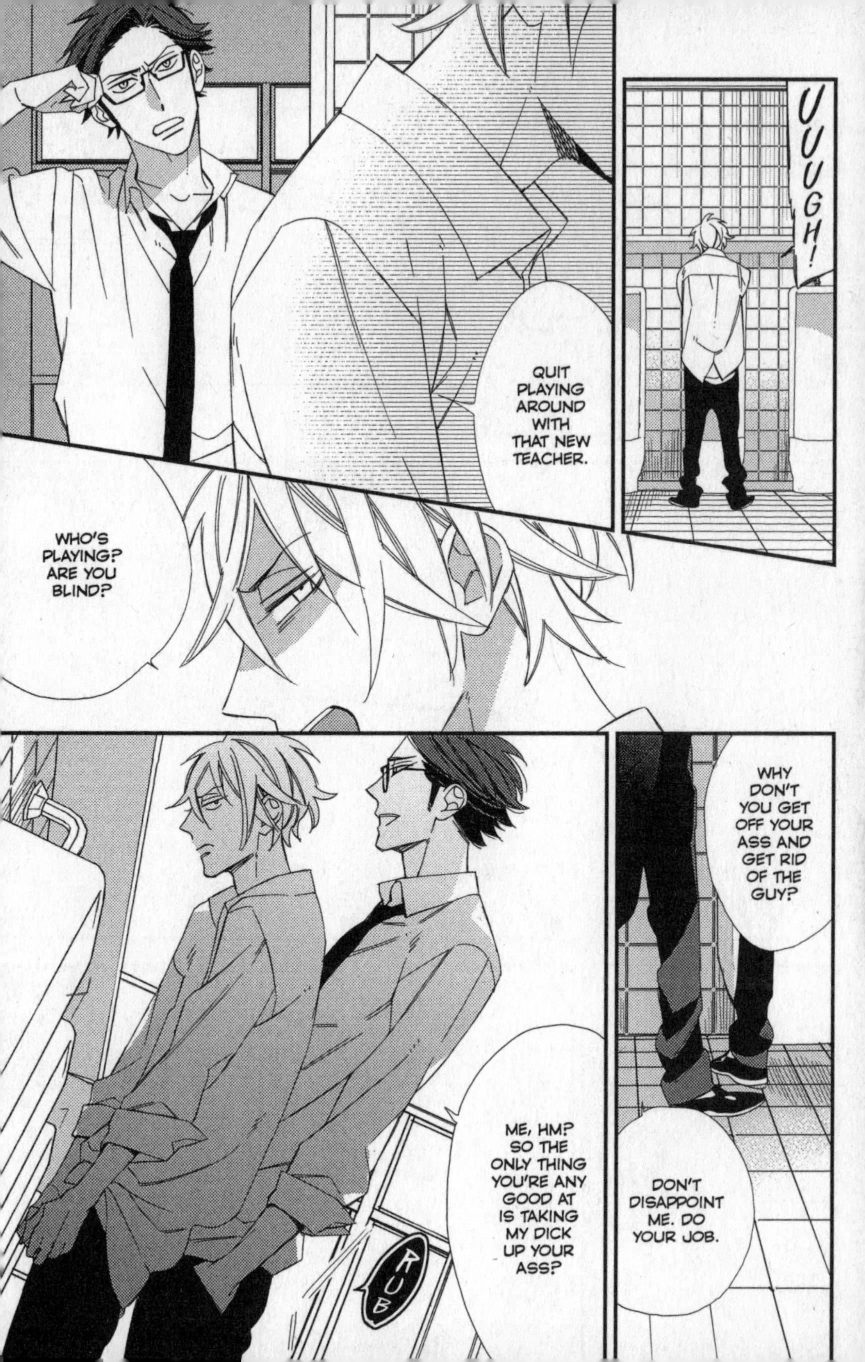
UUUUGH!
QUIT PLAYING AROUND WITH THAT NEW TEACHER.
WHO'S PLAYING? ARE YOU BLIND?
WHY DON'T YOU GET OFF YOUR ASS AND GET RID OF THE GUY?
DON'T DISAPPOINT ME. DO YOUR JOB.
ME, HM? SO THE ONLY THING YOU'RE ANY GOOD AT IS TAKING MY DICK UP YOUR ASS?
RUB

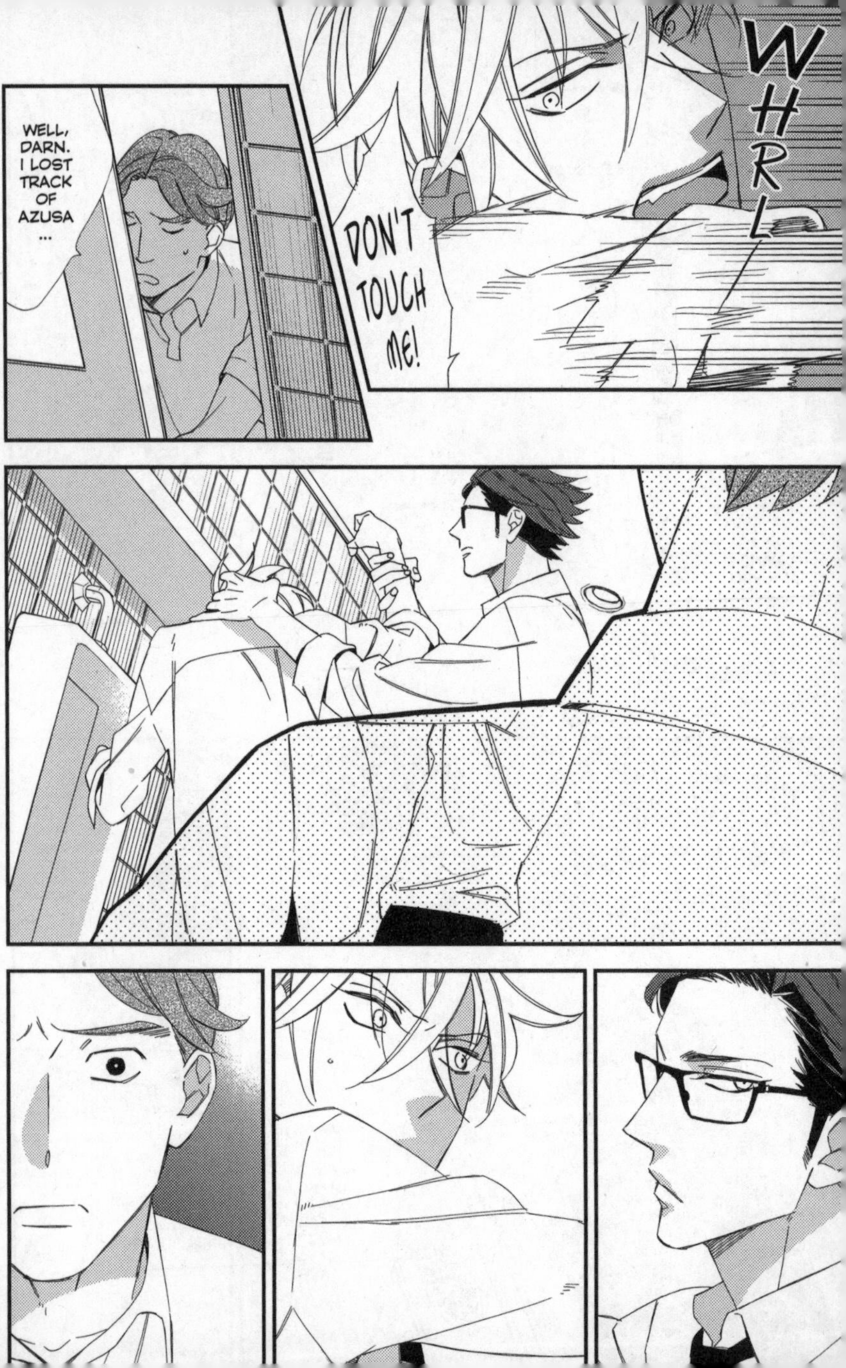
WHRL
DON'T TOUCH ME!
WELL, DARN. I LOST TRACK OF AZUSA ...

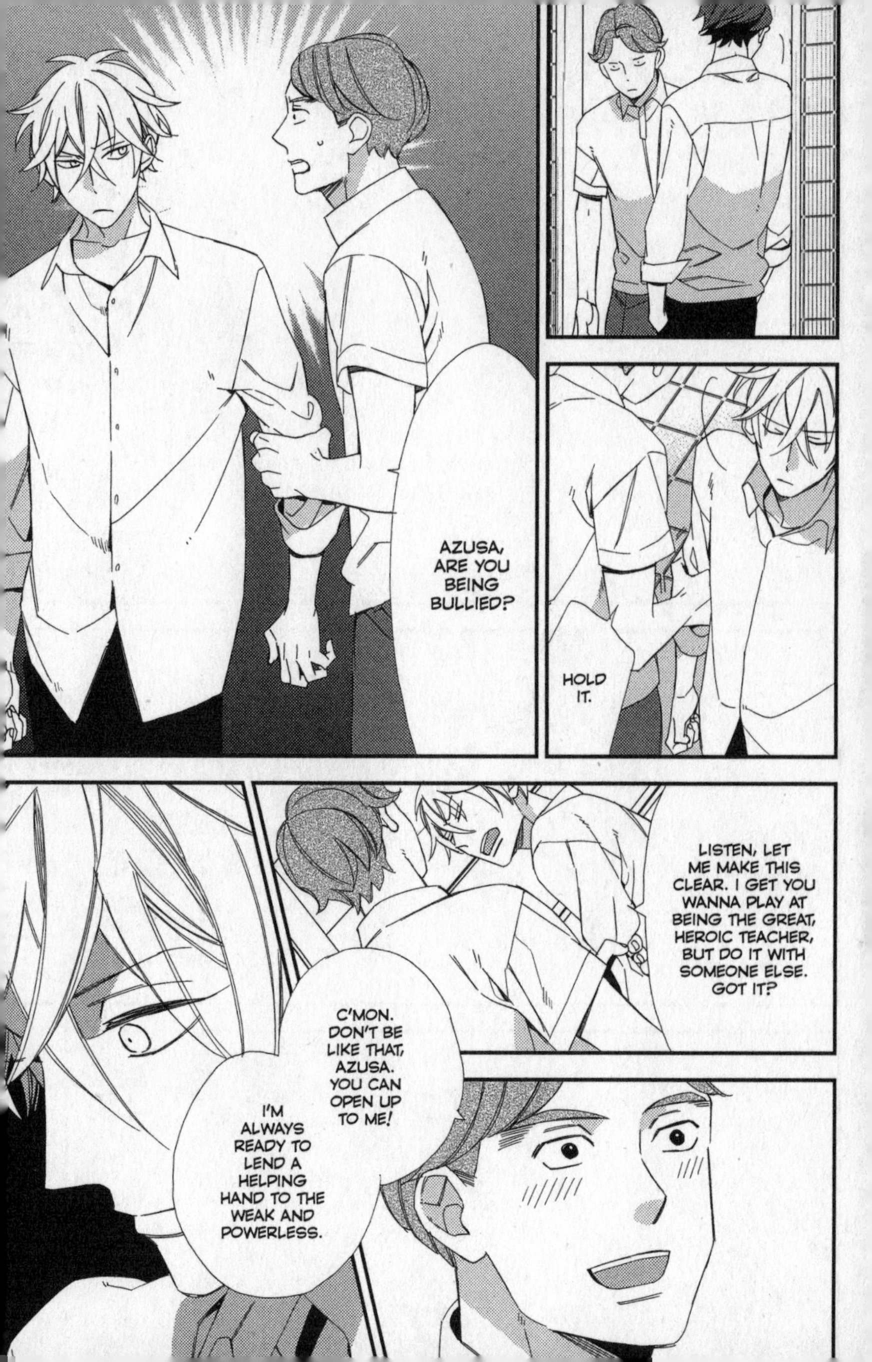
HOLD IT.
AZUSA, ARE YOU BEING BULLIED?
LISTEN, LET ME MAKE THIS CLEAR. I GET YOU WANNA PLAY AT BEING THE GREAT, HEROIC TEACHER, BUT DO IT WITH SOMEONE ELSE. GOT IT?
C'MON. DON'T BE LIKE THAT, AZUSA. YOU CAN OPEN UP TO ME!
I'M ALWAYS READY TO LEND A HELPING HAND TO THE WEAK AND POWERLESS.

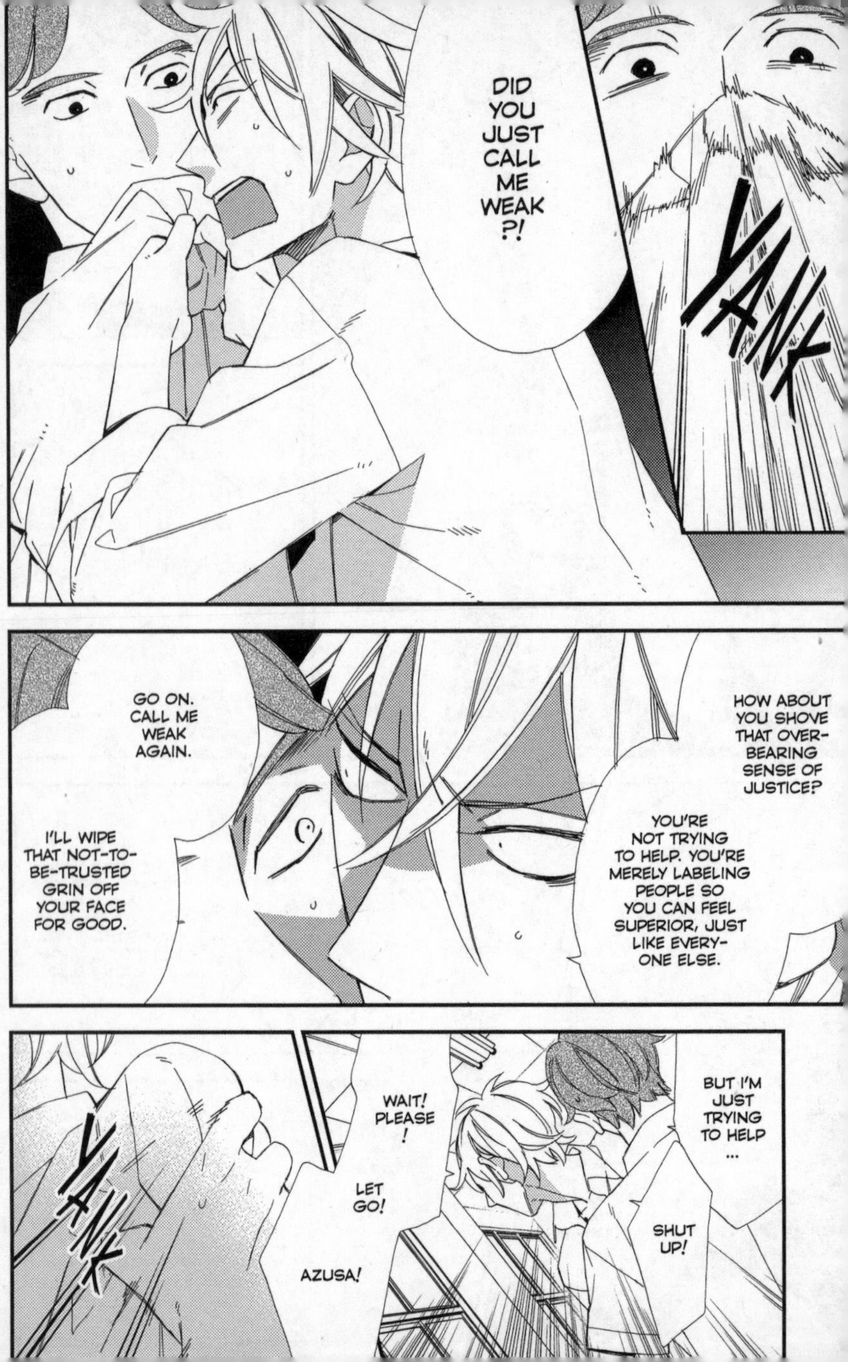
YANK
DID YOU JUST CALL ME WEAK?!
HOW ABOUT YOU SHOVE THAT OVER-BEARING SENSE OF JUSTICE?
YOU'RE NOT TRYING TO HELP. YOU'RE MERELY LABELING PEOPLE SO YOU CAN FEEL SUPERIOR, JUST LIKE EVERY-ONE ELSE.
GO ON. CALL ME WEAK AGAIN.
I'LL WIPE THAT NOT-TO-BE-TRUSTED GRIN OFF YOUR FACE FOR GOOD.
BUT I'M JUST TRYING TO HELP ...
SHUT UP!
WAIT! PLEASE!
LET GO!
AZUSA!
YANK

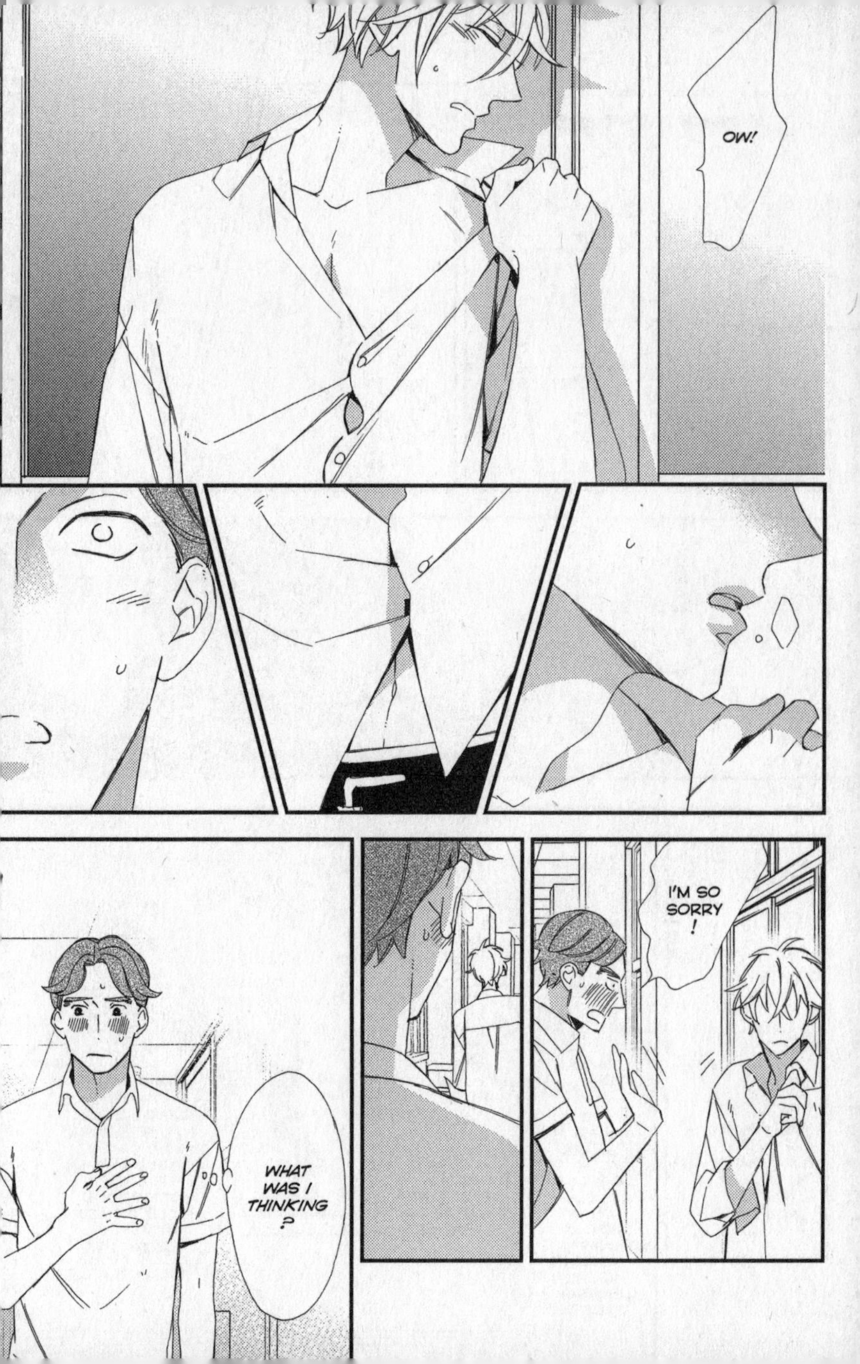
OW!
I'M SO SORRY!
WHAT WAS I THINKING?

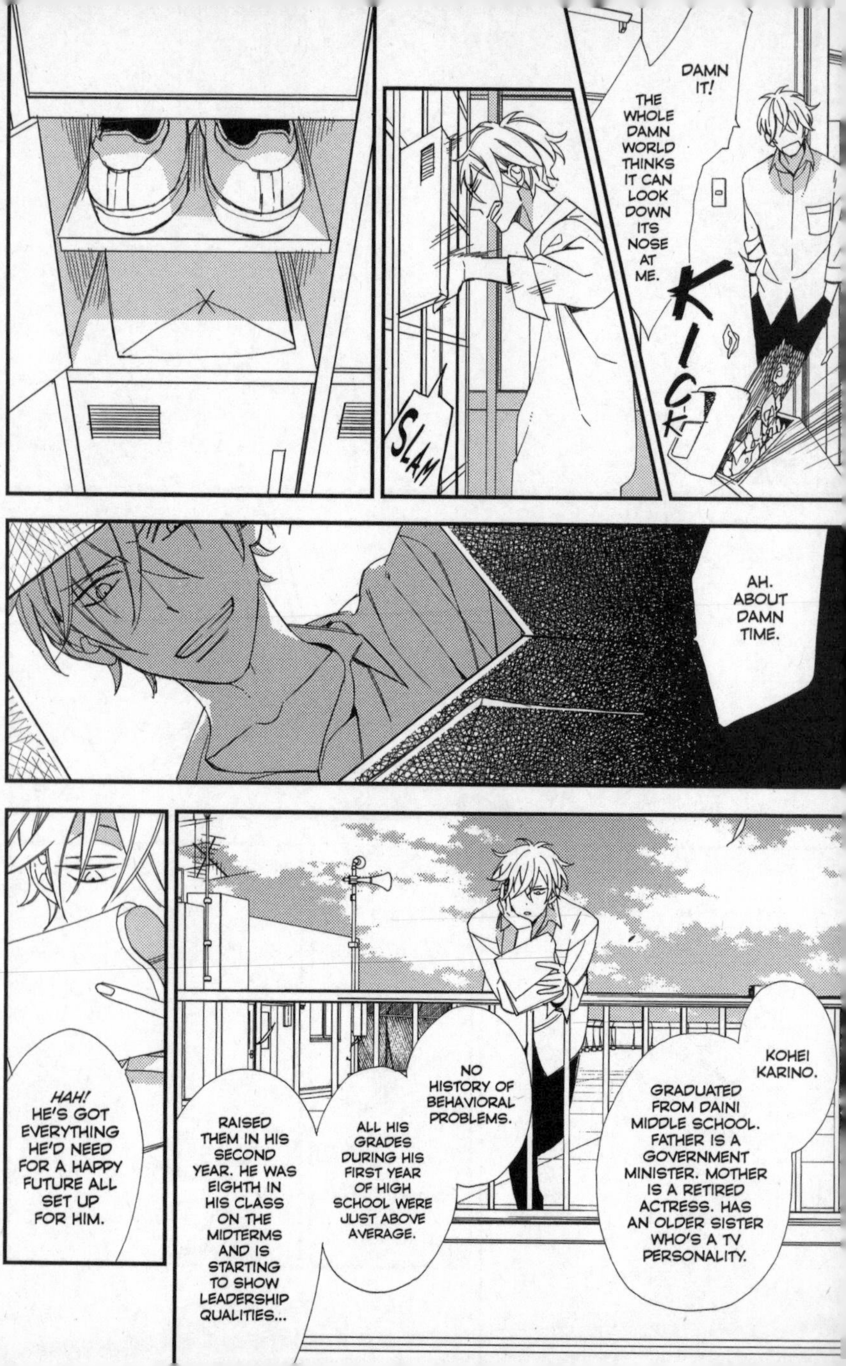
DAMN IT!
THE WHOLE DAMN WORLD THINKS IT CAN LOOK DOWN ITS NOSE AT ME.
KICK
SLAM
AH. ABOUT DAMN TIME.
KOHEI KARINO.
GRADUATED FROM DAINI MIDDLE SCHOOL. FATHER IS A GOVERNMENT MINISTER. MOTHER IS A RETIRED ACTRESS. HAS AN OLDER SISTER WHO'S A TV PERSONALITY.
NO HISTORY OF BEHAVIORAL PROBLEMS.
ALL HIS GRADES DURING HIS FIRST YEAR OF HIGH SCHOOL WERE JUST ABOVE AVERAGE.
RAISED THEM IN HIS SECOND YEAR. HE WAS EIGHTH IN HIS CLASS ON THE MIDTERMS AND IS STARTING TO SHOW LEADERSHIP QUALITIES...
HAH! HE'S GOT EVERYTHING HE'D NEED FOR A HAPPY FUTURE ALL SET UP FOR HIM.

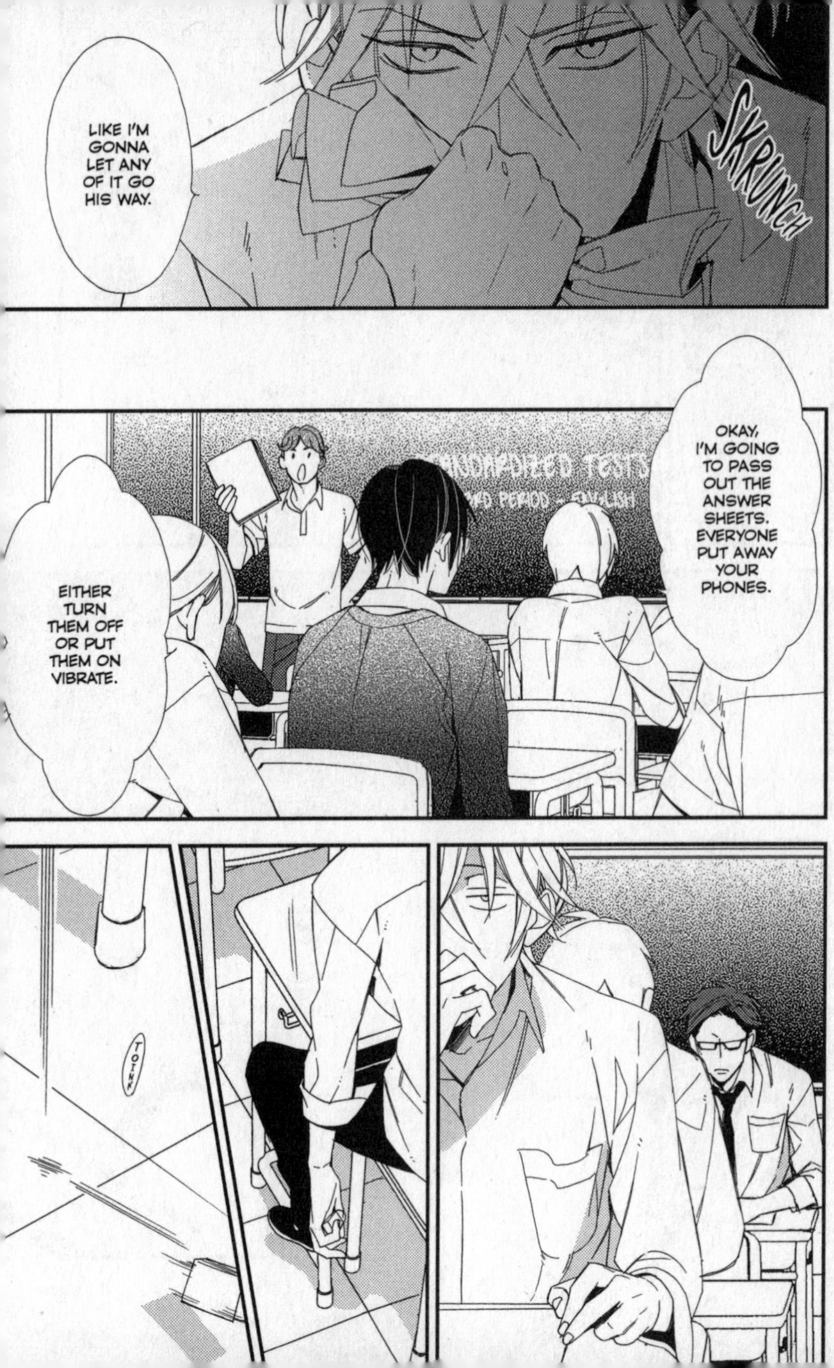
SKRUNCH
LIKE I'M GONNA LET ANY OF IT GO HIS WAY.
OKAY, I'M GOING TO PASS OUT THE ANSWER SHEETS. EVERYONE PUT AWAY YOUR PHONES.
EITHER TURN THEM OFF OR PUT THEM ON VIBRATE.
TOINK

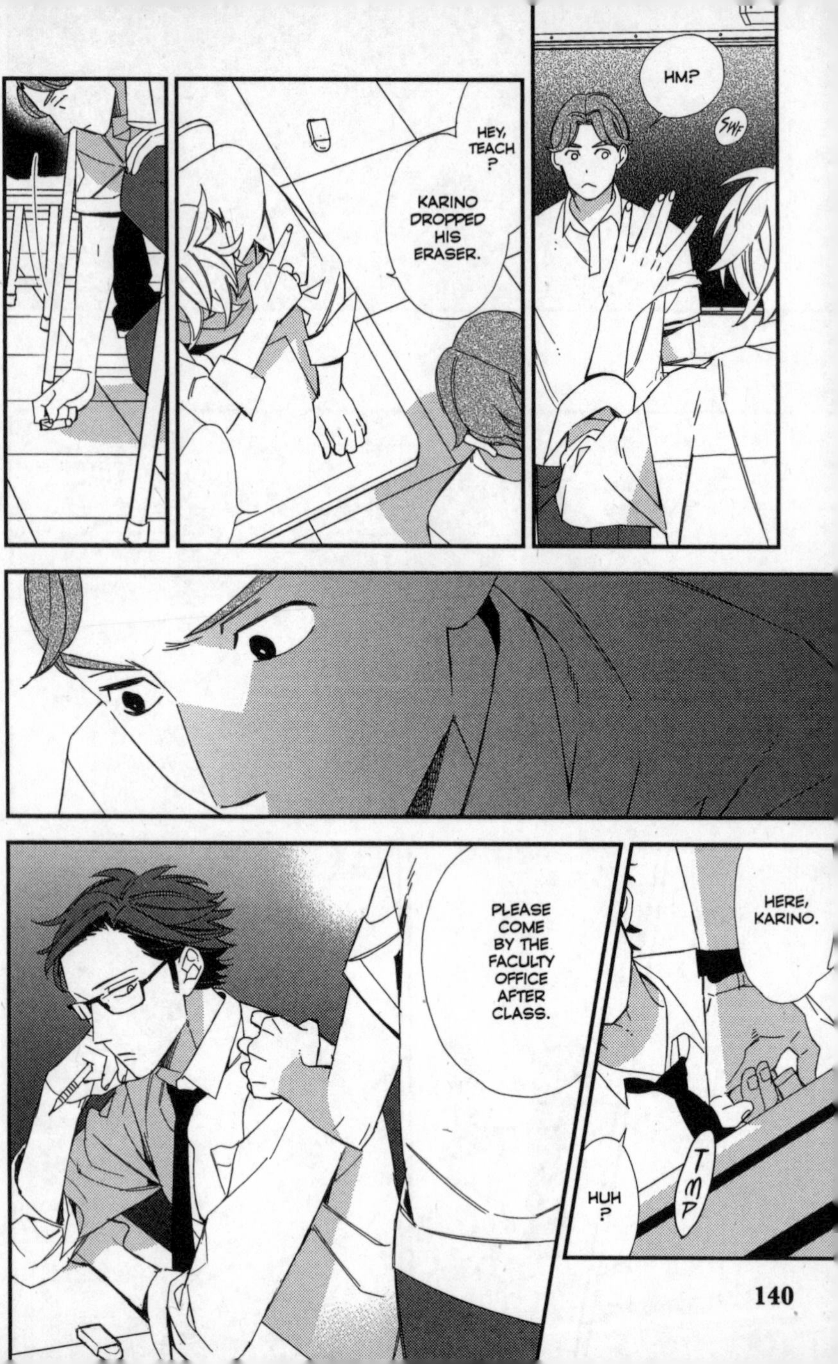
HM?
SWF
HEY, TEACH?
KARINO DROPPED HIS ERASER.
HERE, KARINO.
TMP
HUH?
PLEASE COME BY THE FACULTY OFFICE AFTER CLASS.

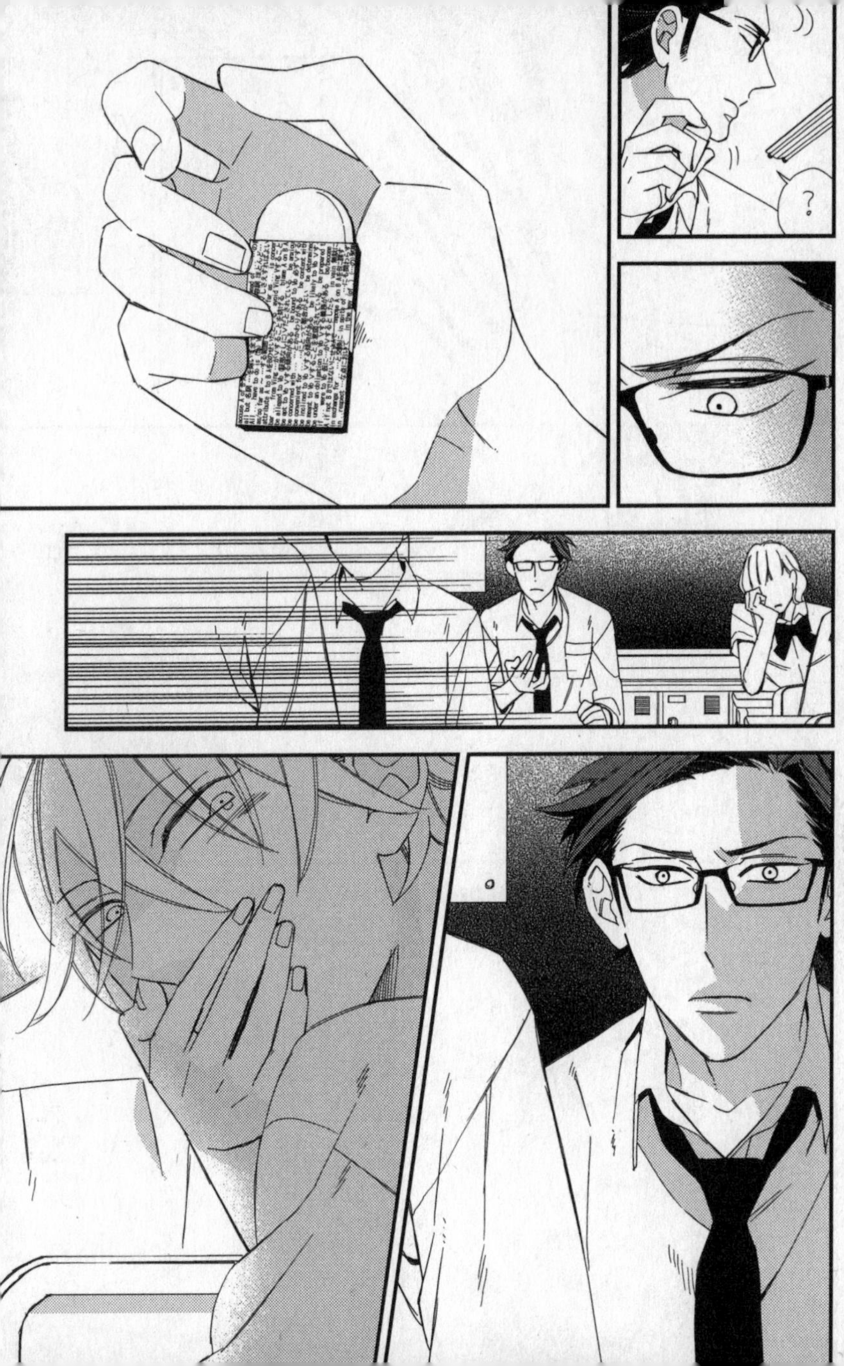
?

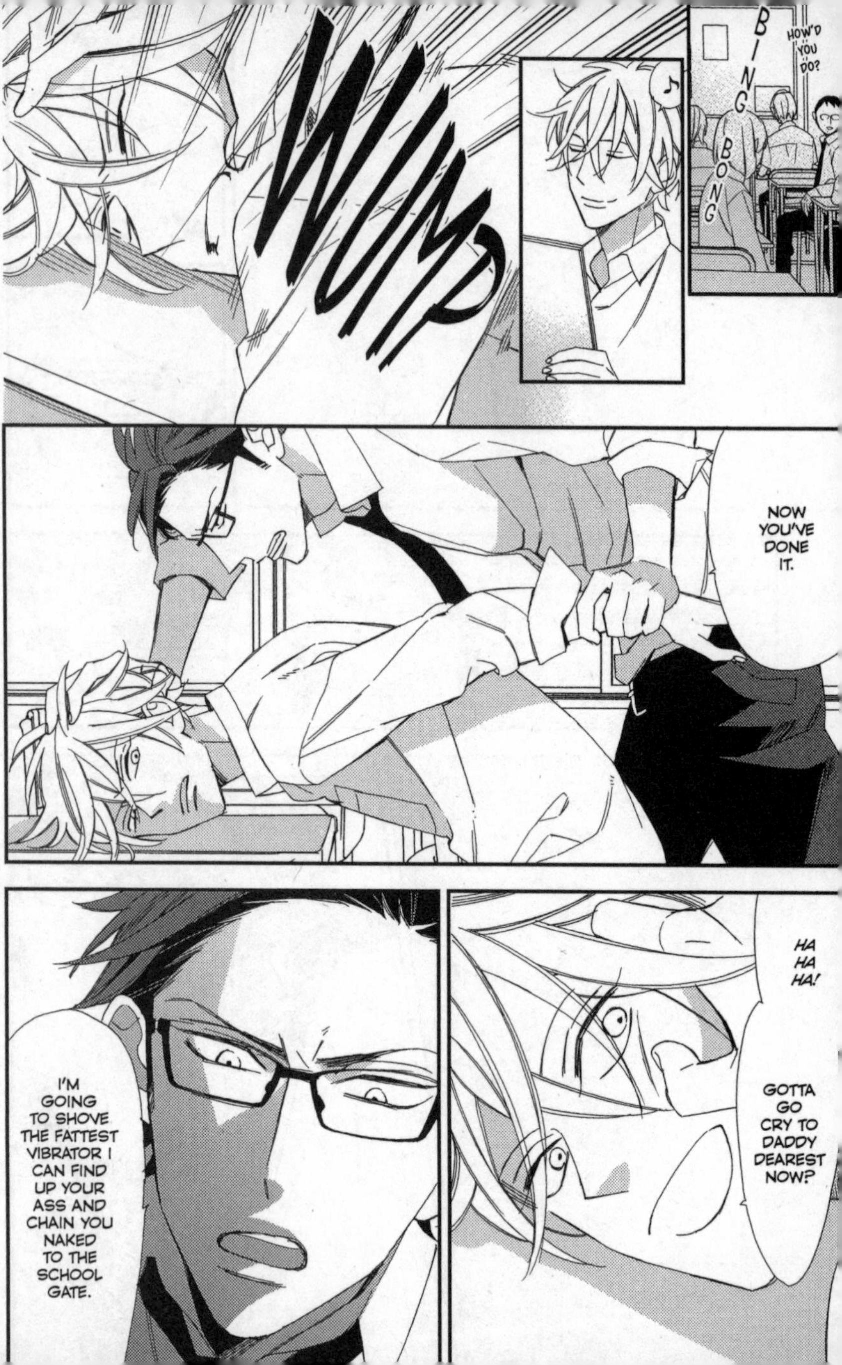
HOW'D YOU DO?
BING
BONG
WUMP
NOW YOU'VE DONE IT.
HA HA HA!
GOTTA GO CRY TO DADDY DEAREST NOW?
I'M GOING TO SHOVE THE FATTEST VIBRATOR I CAN FIND UP YOUR ASS AND CHAIN YOU NAKED TO THE SCHOOL GATE.

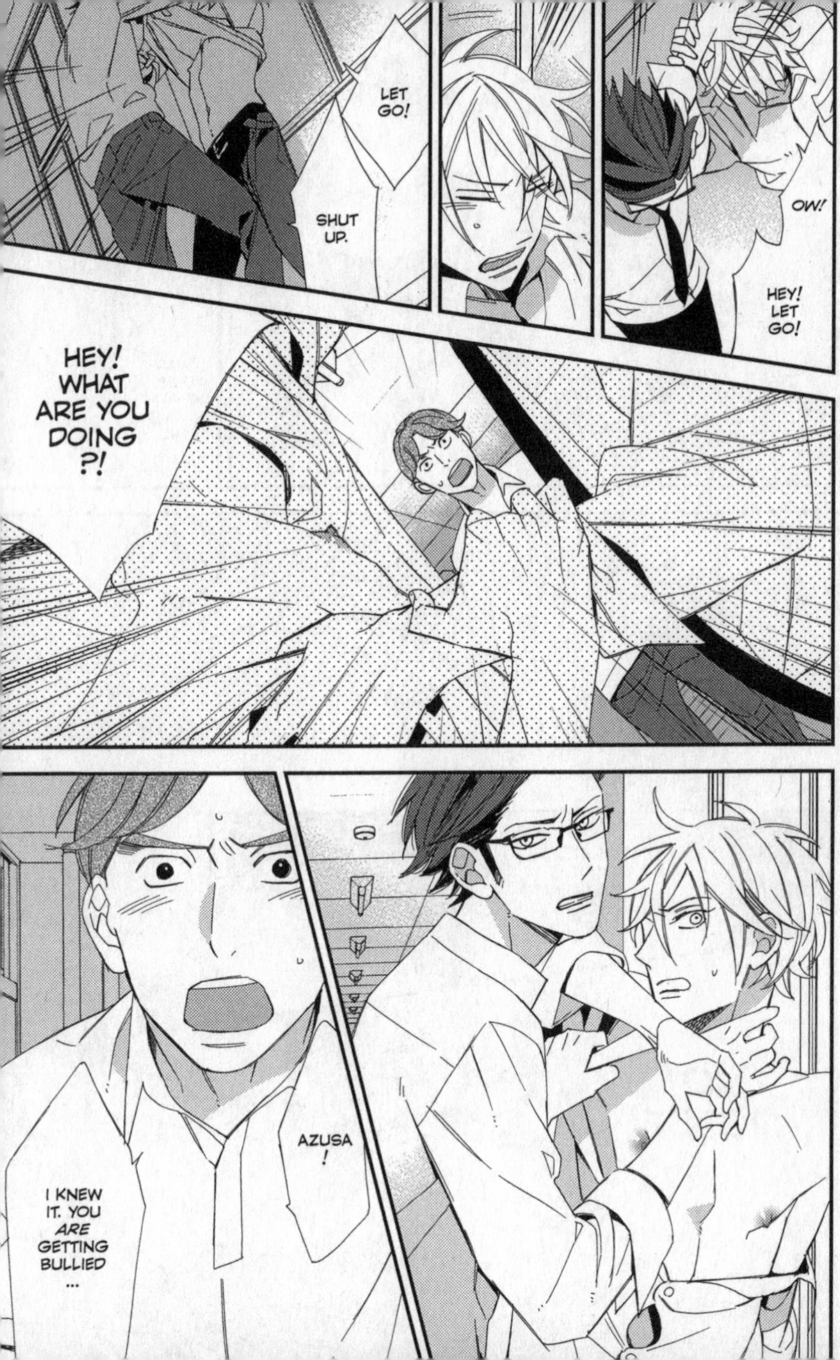
OW!
HEY! LET GO!
LET GO!
SHUT UP.
HEY! WHAT ARE YOU DOING?!
AZUSA!
I KNEW IT. YOU *ARE* GETTING BULLIED...

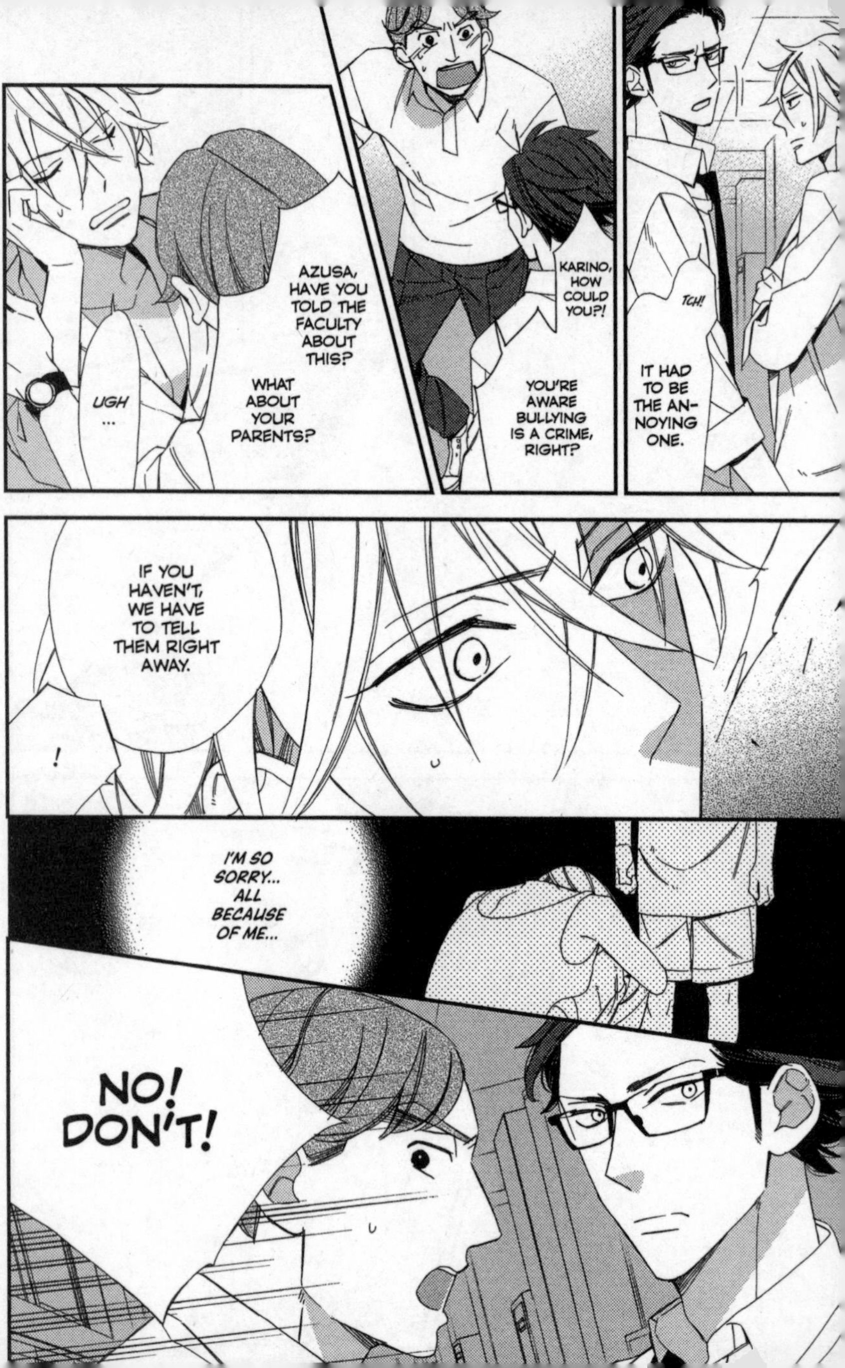
TCH!
IT HAD TO BE THE AN-NOYING ONE.
KARINO, HOW COULD YOU?!
YOU'RE AWARE BULLYING IS A CRIME, RIGHT?
AZUSA, HAVE YOU TOLD THE FACULTY ABOUT THIS?
WHAT ABOUT YOUR PARENTS?
UGH ...
IF YOU HAVEN'T, WE HAVE TO TELL THEM RIGHT AWAY.
!
I'M SO SORRY... ALL BECAUSE OF ME...
NO! DON'T!

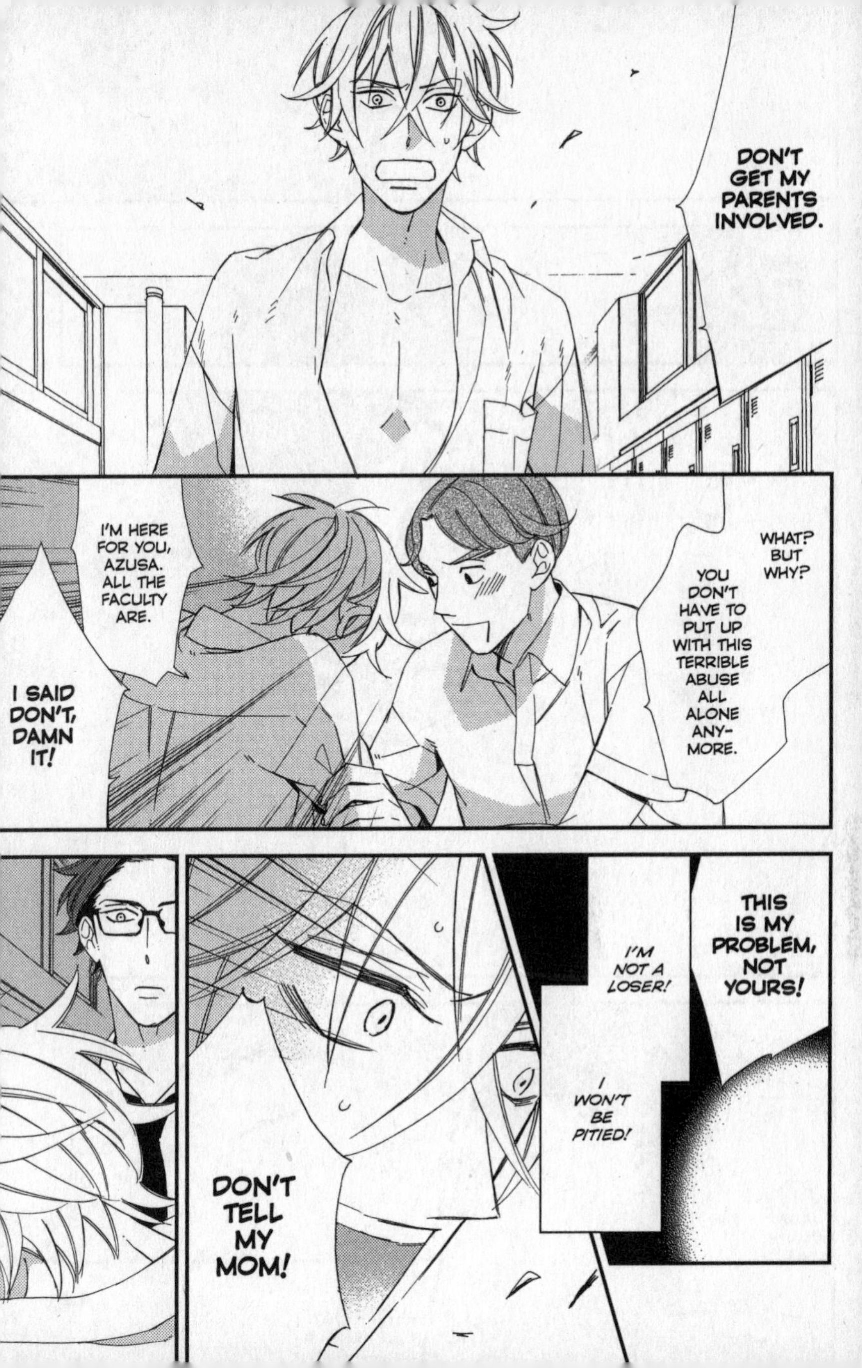
DON'T GET MY PARENTS INVOLVED.
WHAT? BUT WHY?
YOU DON'T HAVE TO PUT UP WITH THIS TERRIBLE ABUSE ALL ALONE ANY-MORE.
I'M HERE FOR YOU, AZUSA. ALL THE FACULTY ARE.
I SAID DON'T, DAMN IT!
THIS IS MY PROBLEM, NOT YOURS!
I'M NOT A LOSER!
I WON'T BE PITIED!
DON'T TELL MY MOM!

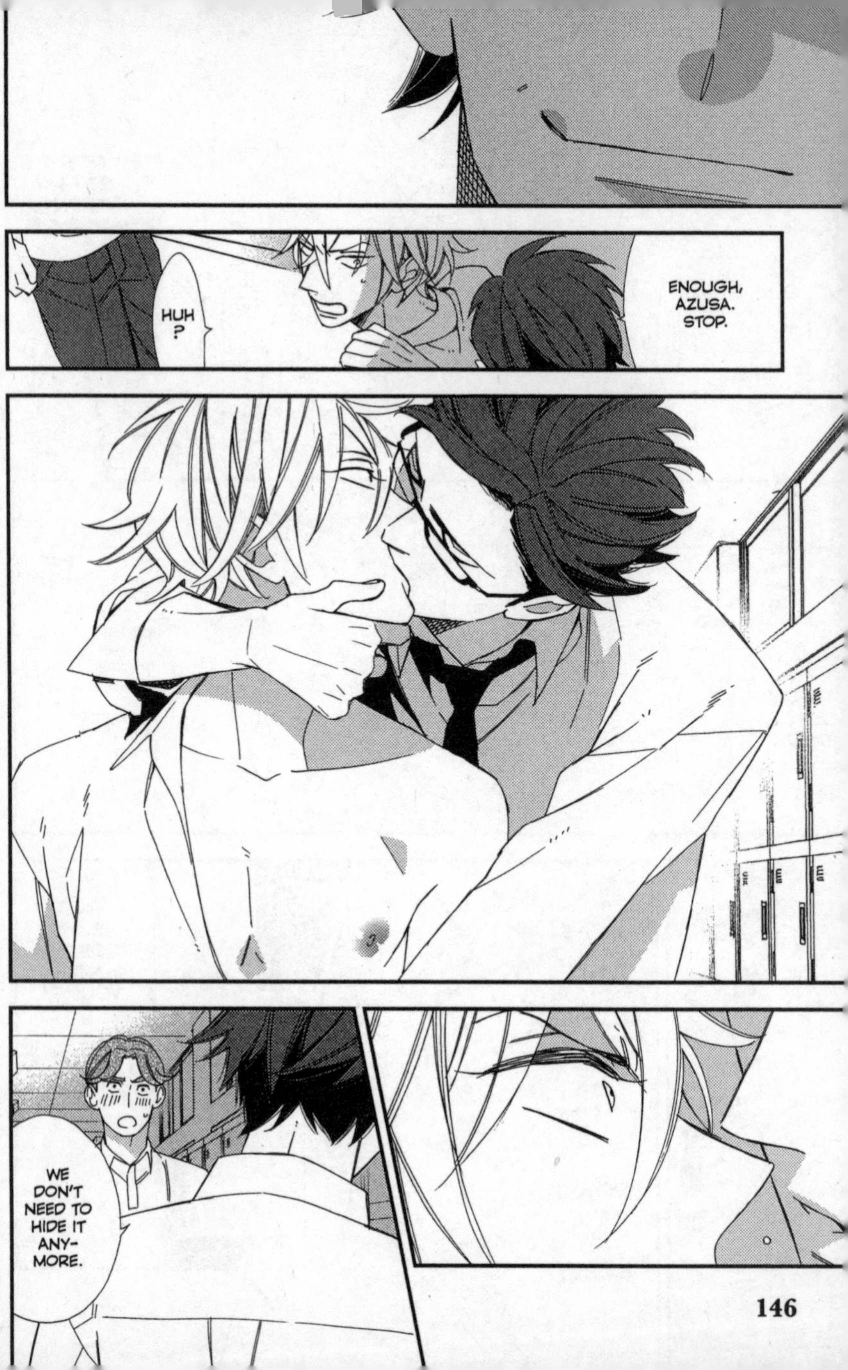
ENOUGH, AZUSA. STOP.
HUH?
WE DON'T NEED TO HIDE IT ANYMORE.

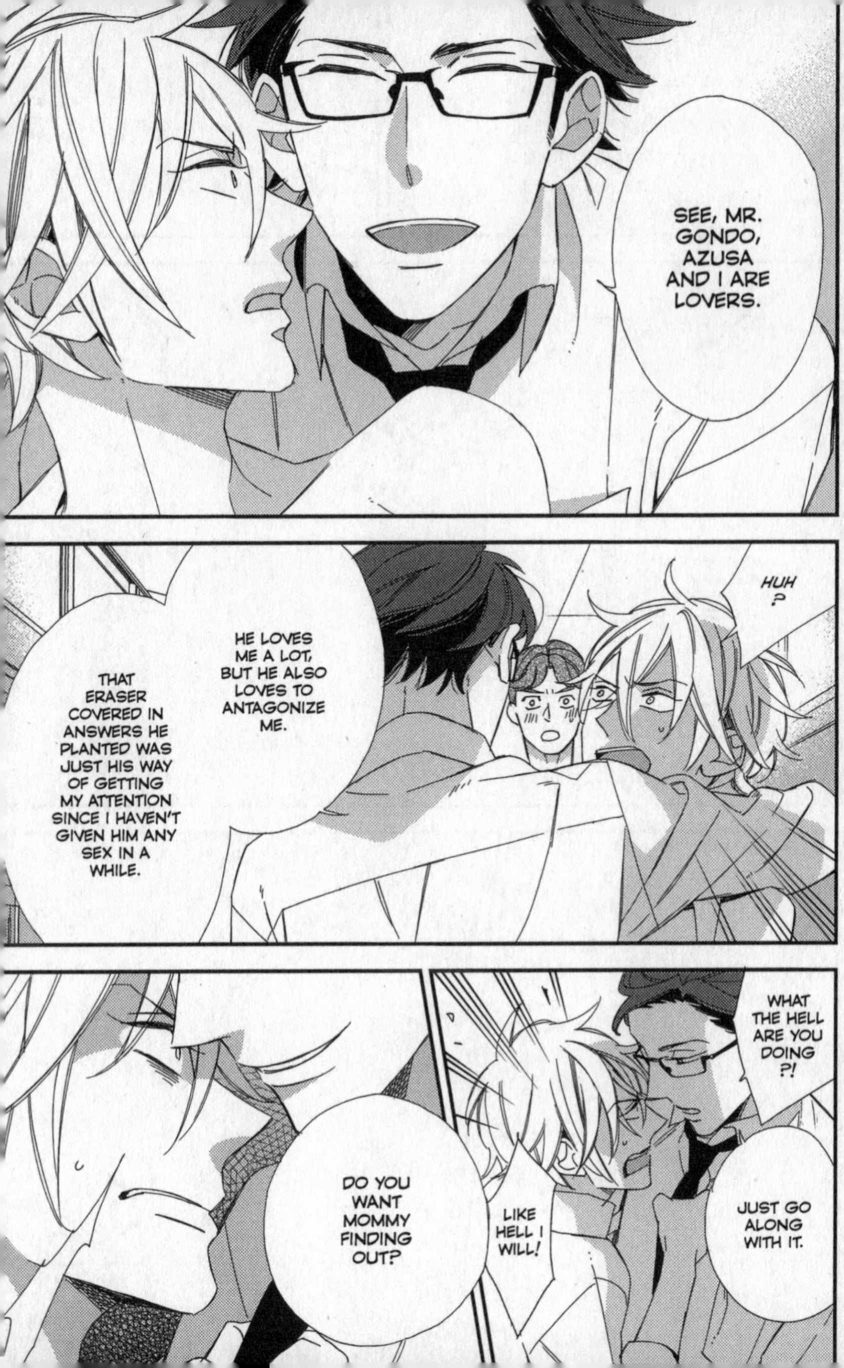
SEE, MR. GONDO, AZUSA AND I ARE LOVERS.
HUH?
HE LOVES ME A LOT, BUT HE ALSO LOVES TO ANTAGONIZE ME.
THAT ERASER COVERED IN ANSWERS HE PLANTED WAS JUST HIS WAY OF GETTING MY ATTENTION SINCE I HAVEN'T GIVEN HIM ANY SEX IN A WHILE.
WHAT THE HELL ARE YOU DOING?!
JUST GO ALONG WITH IT.
LIKE HELL I WILL!
DO YOU WANT MOMMY FINDING OUT?

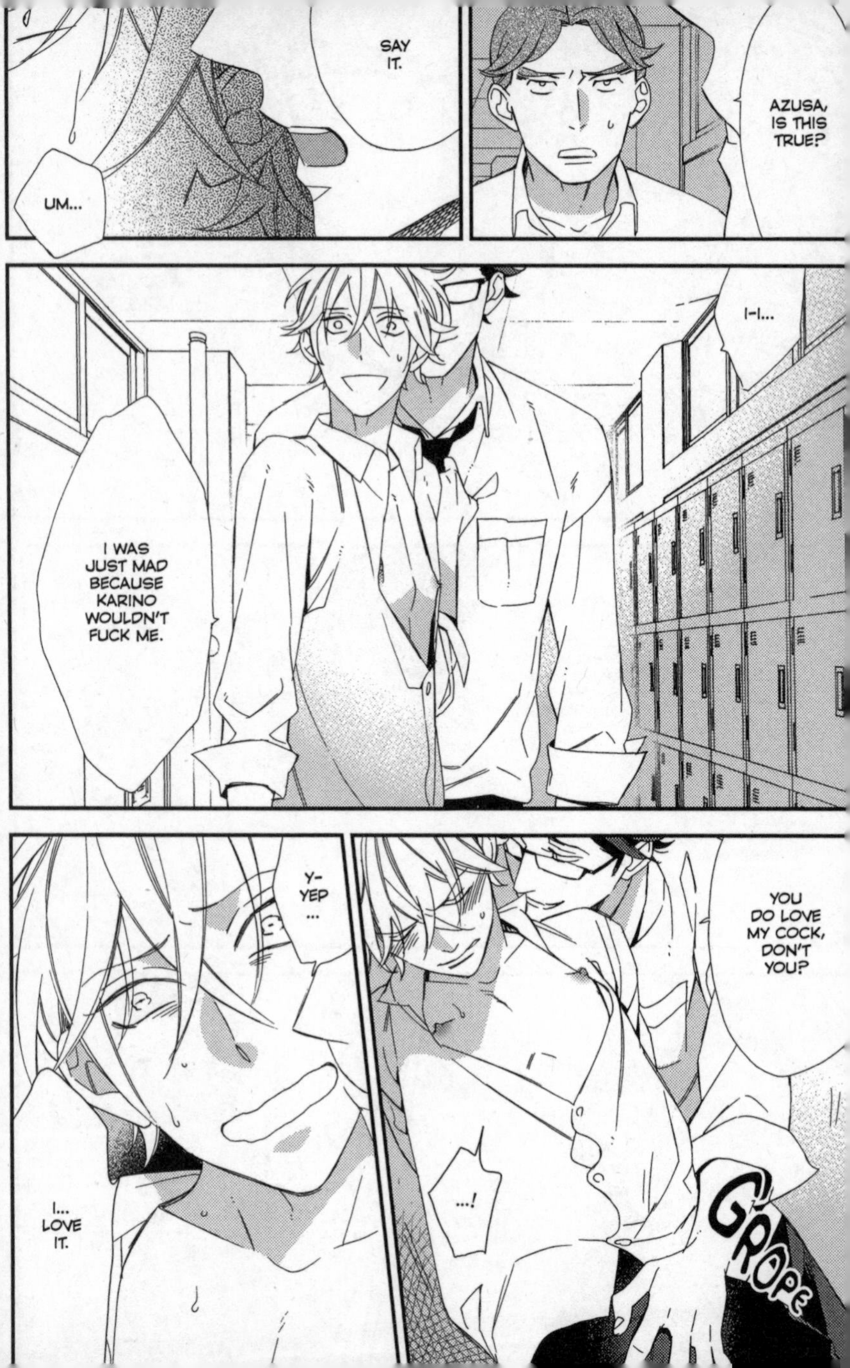
AZUSA, IS THIS TRUE?
SAY IT.
UM...
I-I...
I WAS JUST MAD BECAUSE KARINO WOULDN'T FUCK ME.
YOU DO LOVE MY COCK, DON'T YOU?
GROPE
...!
Y-YEP ...
I... LOVE IT.

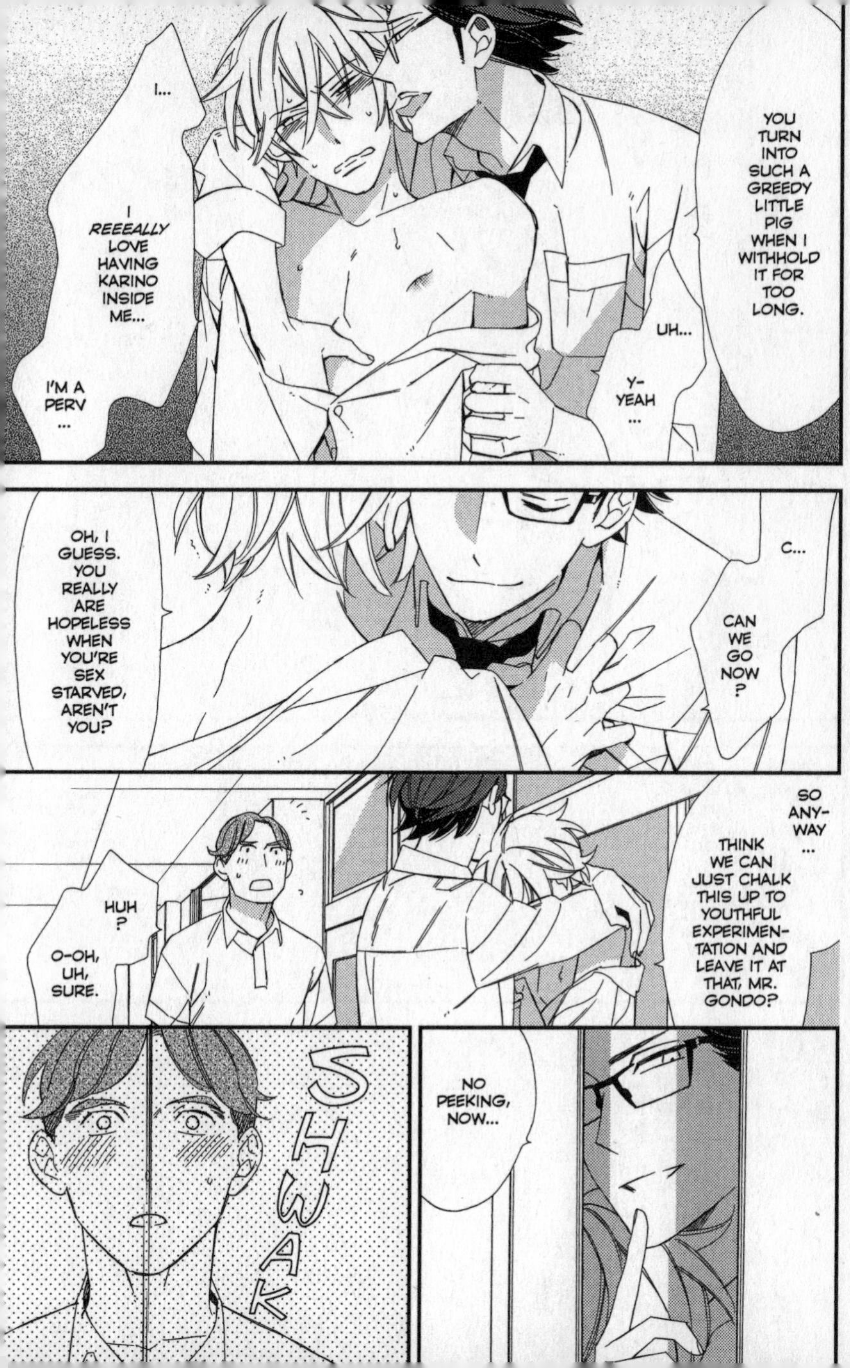
YOU TURN INTO SUCH A GREEDY LITTLE PIG WHEN I WITHHOLD IT FOR TOO LONG.
UH...
Y-YEAH ...
I...
I *REEEALLY* LOVE HAVING KARINO INSIDE ME...
I'M A PERV ...
C...
CAN WE GO NOW?
OH, I GUESS. YOU REALLY ARE HOPELESS WHEN YOU'RE SEX STARVED, AREN'T YOU?
SO ANYWAY ...
THINK WE CAN JUST CHALK THIS UP TO YOUTHFUL EXPERIMENTATION AND LEAVE IT AT THAT, MR. GONDO?
HUH?
O-OH, UH, SURE.
NO PEEKING, NOW...
SHWAK

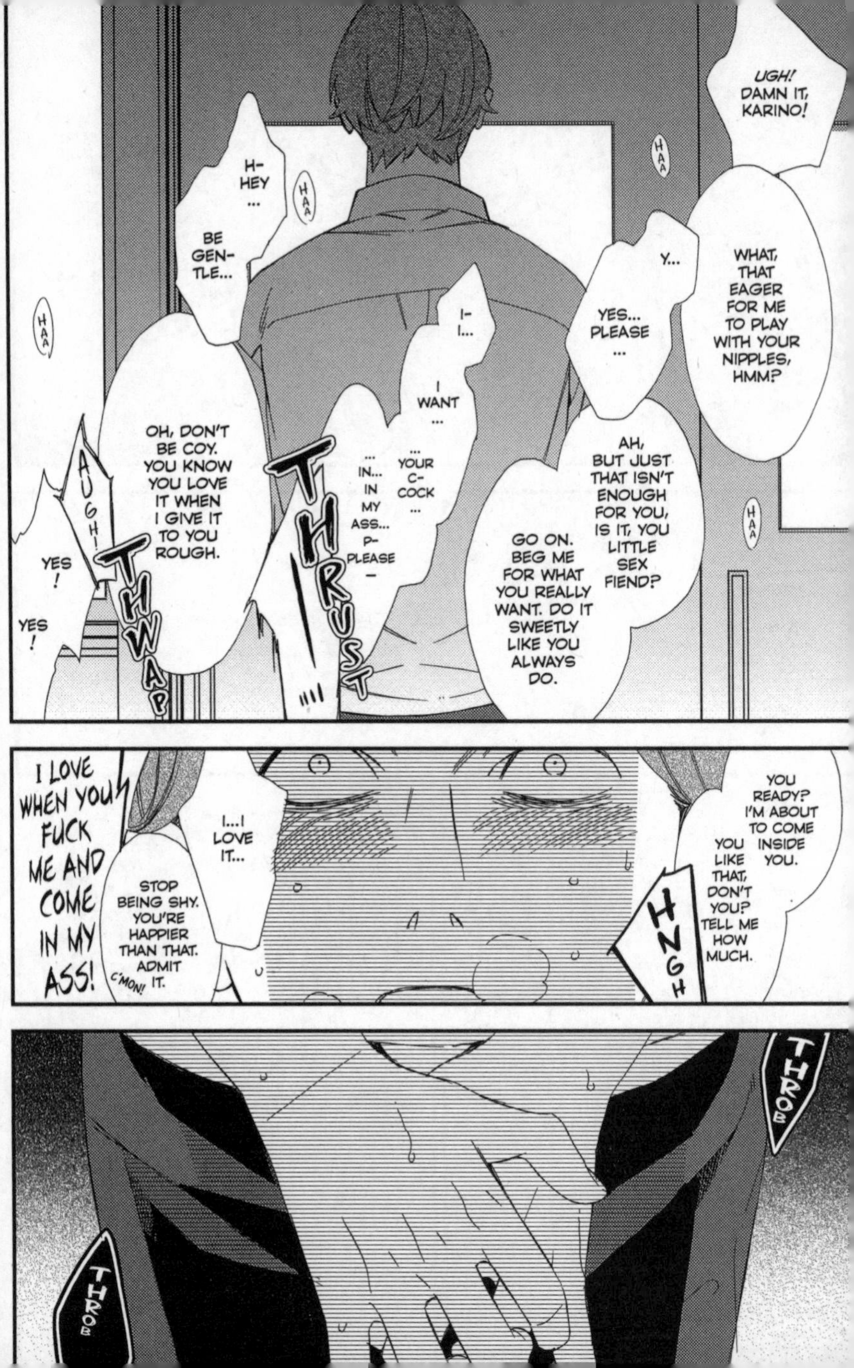
UGH! DAMN IT, KARINO!
HAA
WHAT, THAT EAGER FOR ME TO PLAY WITH YOUR NIPPLES, HMM?
Y...
YES... PLEASE...
AH, BUT JUST THAT ISN'T ENOUGH FOR YOU, IS IT, YOU LITTLE SEX FIEND?
GO ON. BEG ME FOR WHAT YOU REALLY WANT. DO IT SWEETLY LIKE YOU ALWAYS DO.
HAA
I- I...
I WANT...
...YOUR C-COCK...
...IN... IN MY ASS... P-PLEASE—
THRUST
H-HEY...
HAA
BE GENTLE...
OH, DON'T BE COY. YOU KNOW YOU LOVE IT WHEN I GIVE IT TO YOU ROUGH.
THWAP
AUGH!
HAA
YES! YES!
YOU READY? I'M ABOUT TO COME INSIDE YOU.
YOU LIKE THAT, DON'T YOU? TELL ME HOW MUCH.
HNGH
I...I LOVE IT...
STOP BEING SHY. YOU'RE HAPPIER THAN THAT. ADMIT IT.
C'MON!
I LOVE WHEN YOU FUCK ME AND COME IN MY ASS!
THROB
THROB

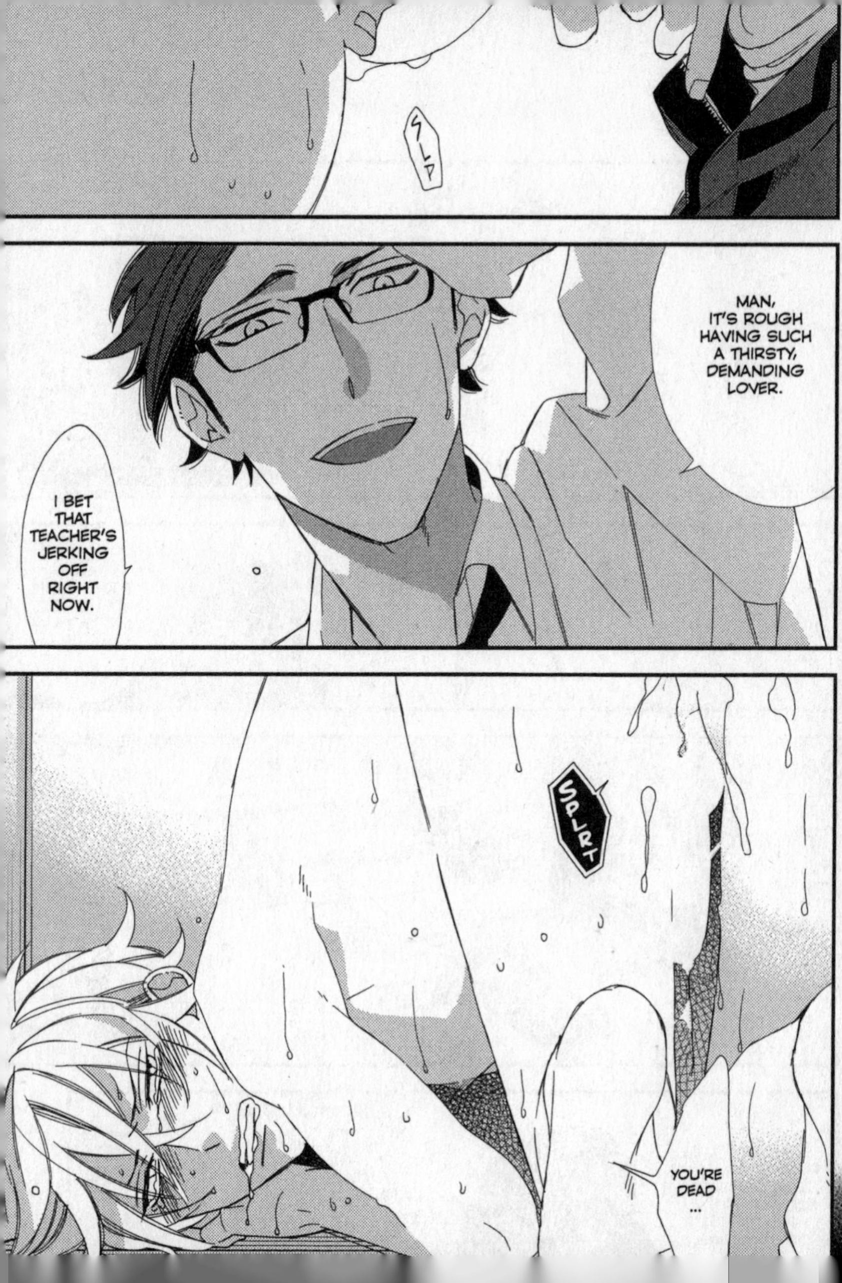
SLP
MAN, IT'S ROUGH HAVING SUCH A THIRSTY, DEMANDING LOVER.
I BET THAT TEACHER'S JERKING OFF RIGHT NOW.
SPLRT
YOU'RE DEAD ...

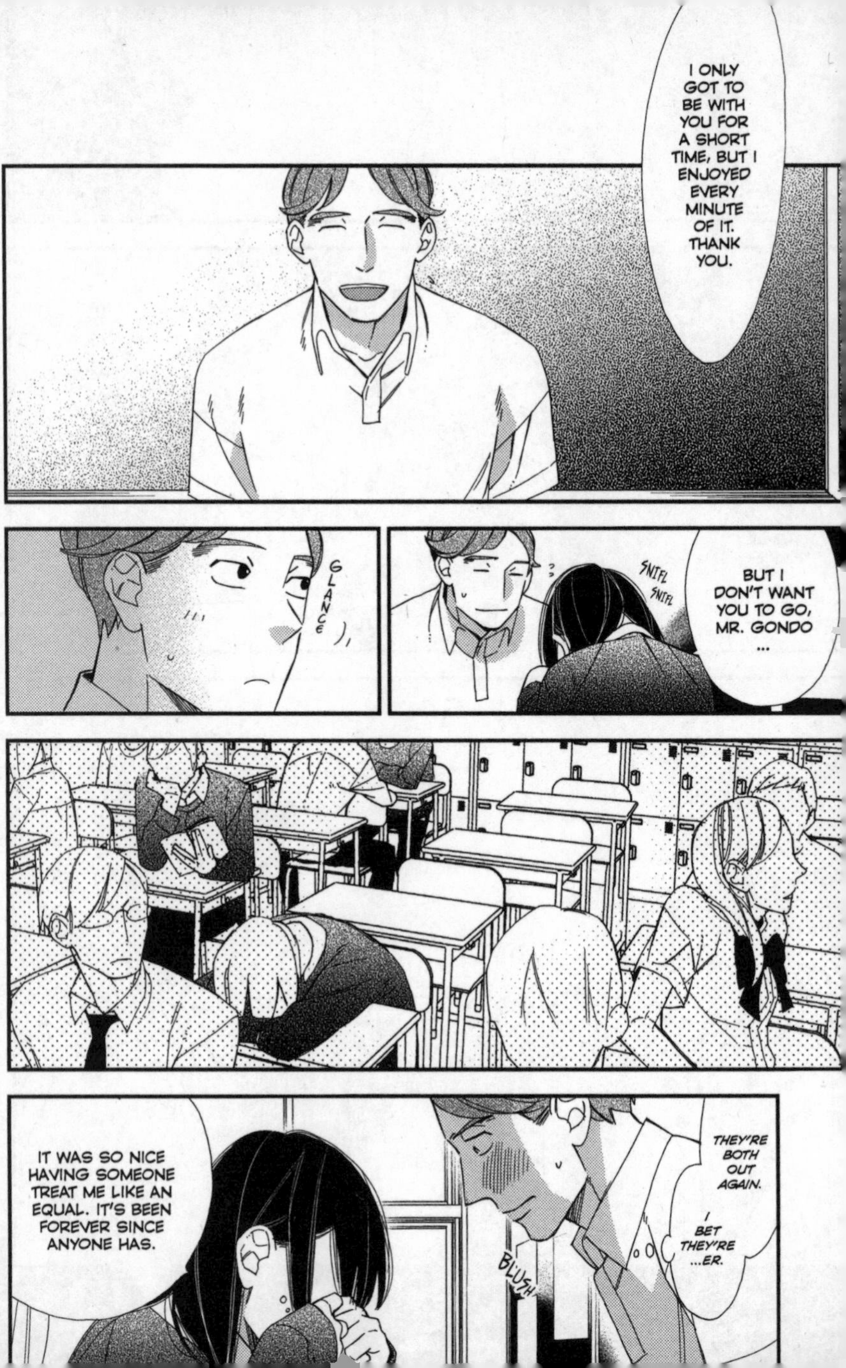
I ONLY GOT TO BE WITH YOU FOR A SHORT TIME, BUT I ENJOYED EVERY MINUTE OF IT. THANK YOU.
BUT I DON'T WANT YOU TO GO, MR. GONDO ...
SNIFL SNIFL
GLANCE
THEY'RE BOTH OUT AGAIN.
I BET THEY'RE ...ER.
BLUSH
IT WAS SO NICE HAVING SOMEONE TREAT ME LIKE AN EQUAL. IT'S BEEN FOREVER SINCE ANYONE HAS.

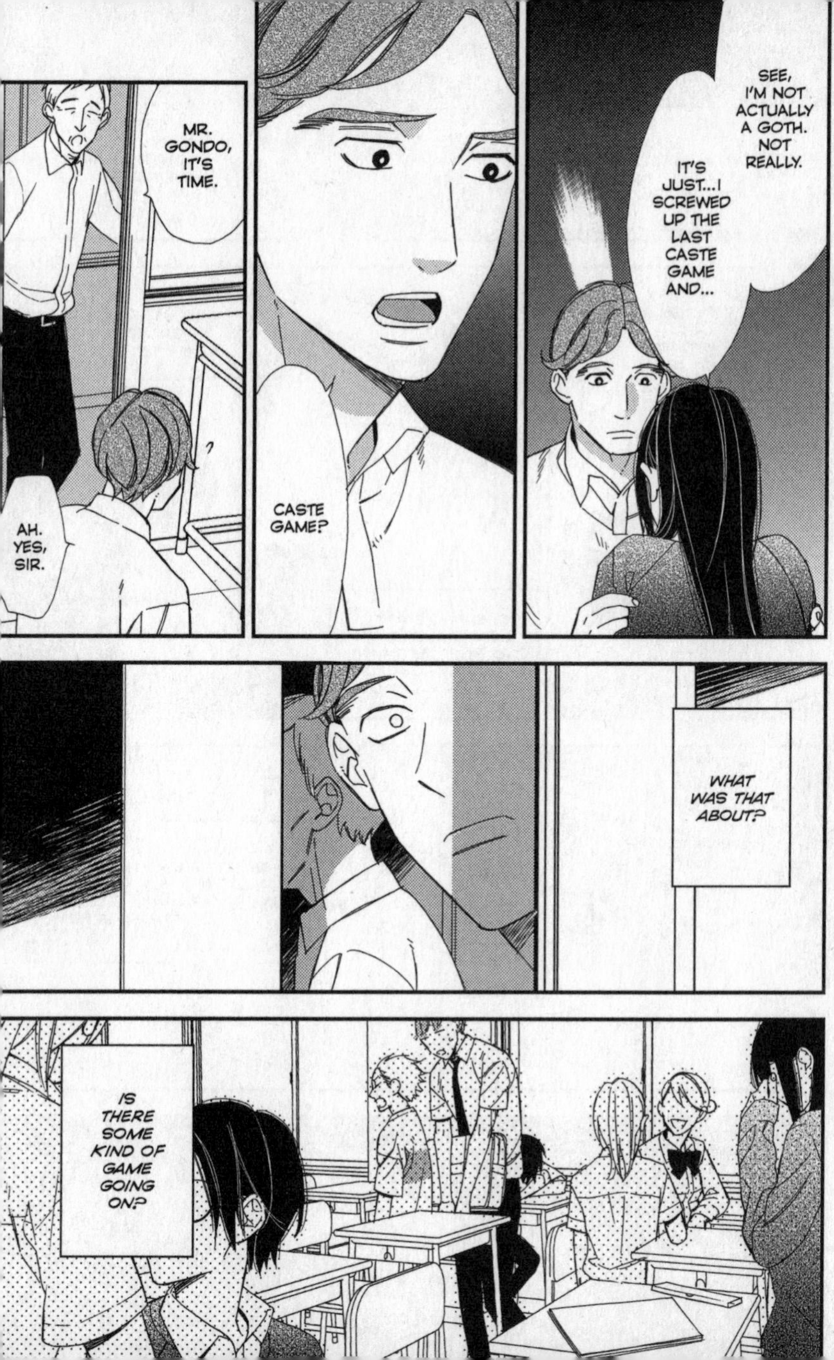
SEE, I'M NOT ACTUALLY A GOTH. NOT REALLY.
IT'S JUST...I SCREWED UP THE LAST CASTE GAME AND...
CASTE GAME?
MR. GONDO, IT'S TIME.
AH. YES, SIR.
WHAT WAS THAT ABOUT?
IS THERE SOME KIND OF GAME GOING ON?

A GOTH, HM?
THAT'S A TYPE OF FASHION MOSTLY FOUND IN AMERICA AND EUROPE...
NOW THAT I THINK ABOUT IT, THERE WAS SOMETHING OFF ABOUT THE NATURAL HIERARCHY OF THAT CLASS.
THE GIRL WHO CALLED HERSELF A GOTH HAD PIERCED EARS BUT NEVER WORE EARRINGS.
KIDS WHO LOOKED LIKE THEY'D BE AT THE BOTTOM OF THE LADDER BOSSED OTHERS AROUND...
...WHILE THE SHY, MOUSY KID SEEMED TO BE GOOD FRIENDS WITH THE CLASS HOT GUY.
THERE WAS AN UNNATURAL AIR ABOUT IT TOO, LIKE EVERY-ONE WAS PLAYING ROLES THEY WERE FORCED INTO.

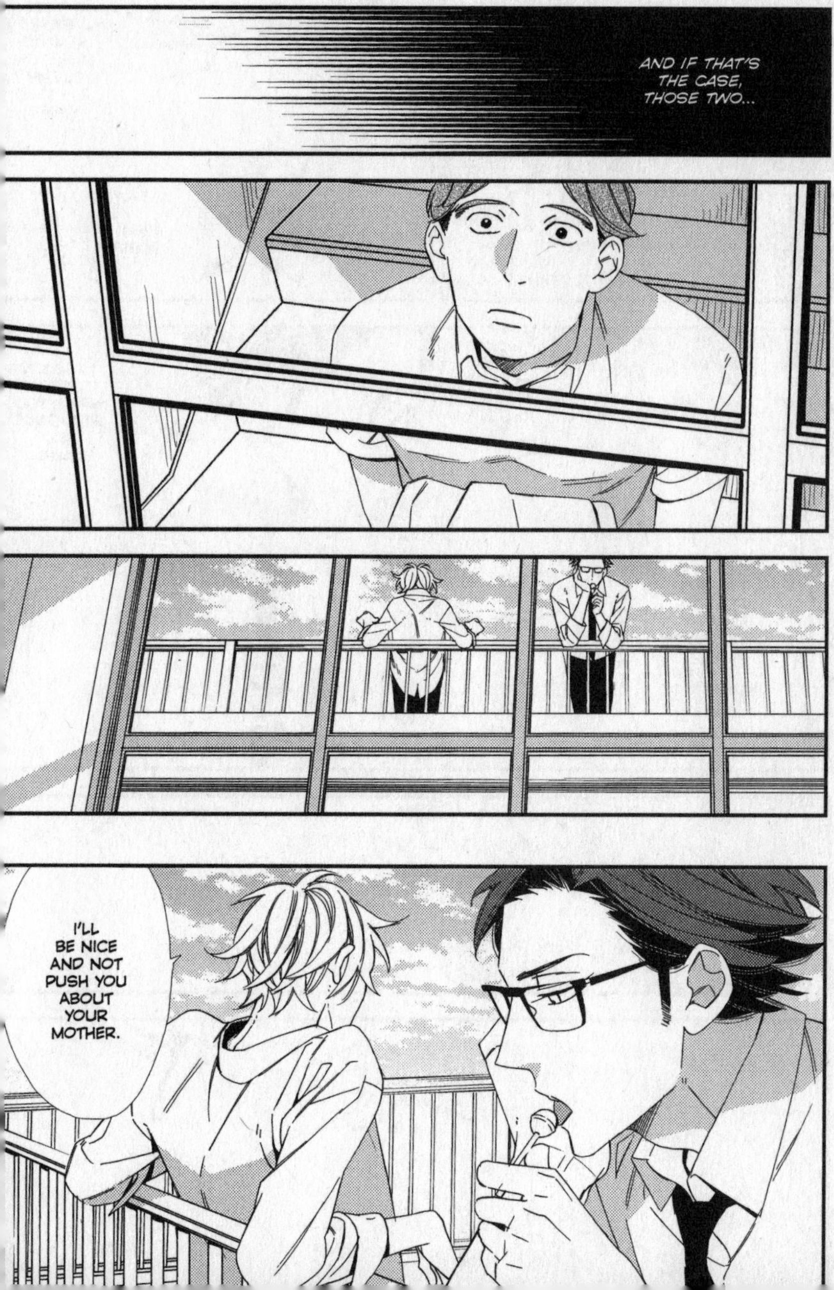
AND IF THAT'S THE CASE, THOSE TWO...
I'LL BE NICE AND NOT PUSH YOU ABOUT YOUR MOTHER.

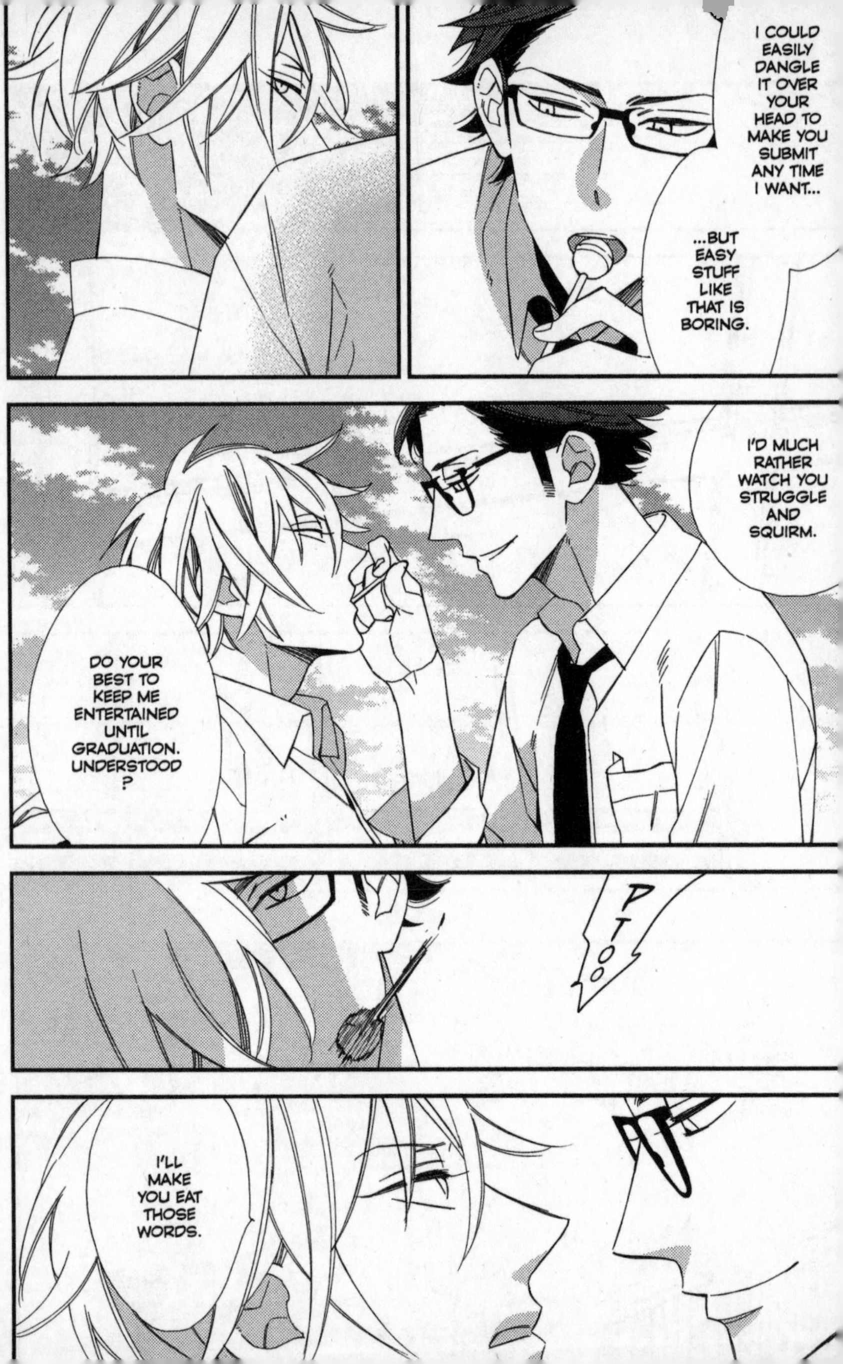
I COULD EASILY DANGLE IT OVER YOUR HEAD TO MAKE YOU SUBMIT ANY TIME I WANT...
...BUT EASY STUFF LIKE THAT IS BORING.
I'D MUCH RATHER WATCH YOU STRUGGLE AND SQUIRM.
DO YOUR BEST TO KEEP ME ENTERTAINED UNTIL GRADUATION. UNDERSTOOD?
PTOO
I'LL MAKE YOU EAT THOSE WORDS.

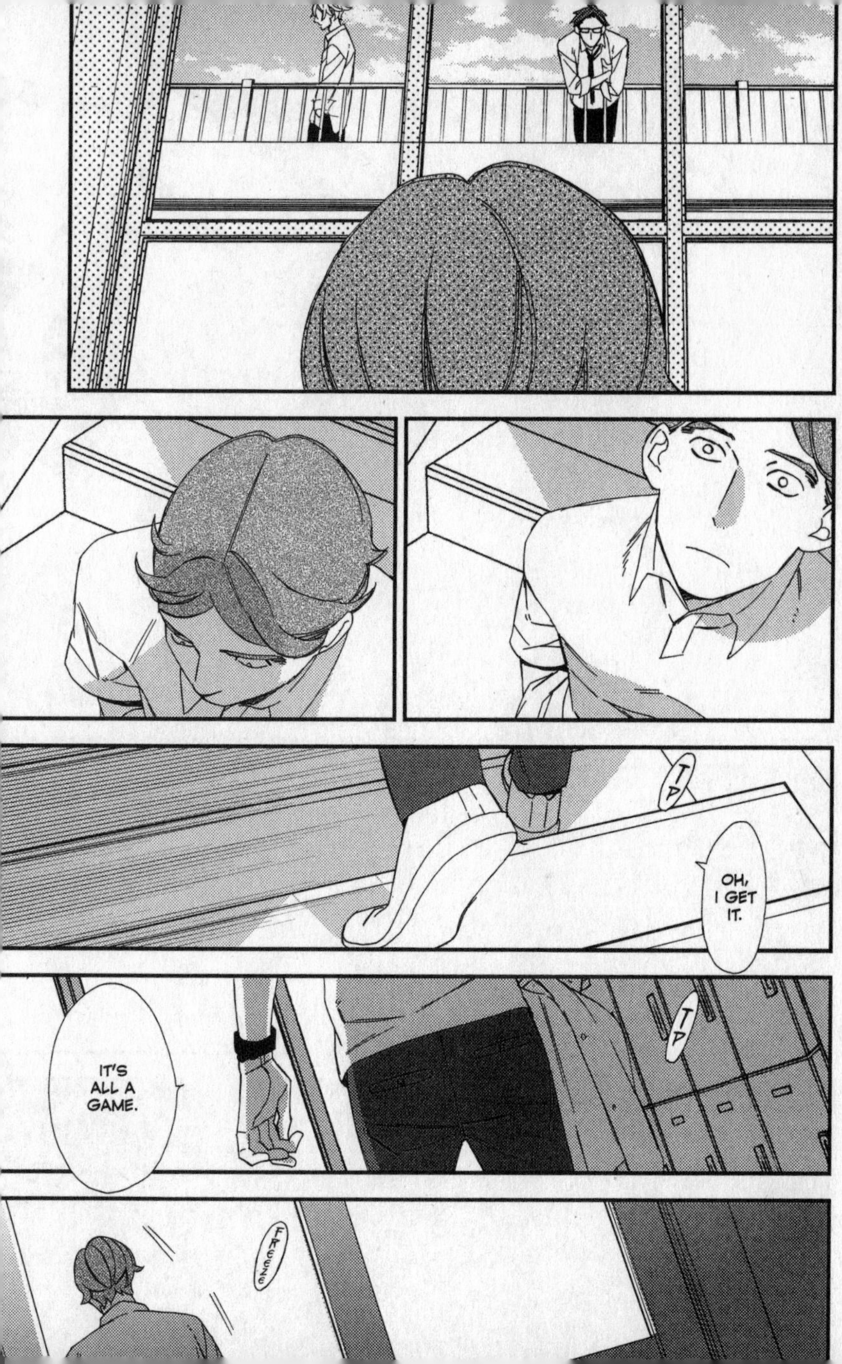
TP
OH, I GET IT.
TP
IT'S ALL A GAME.
FREEZE

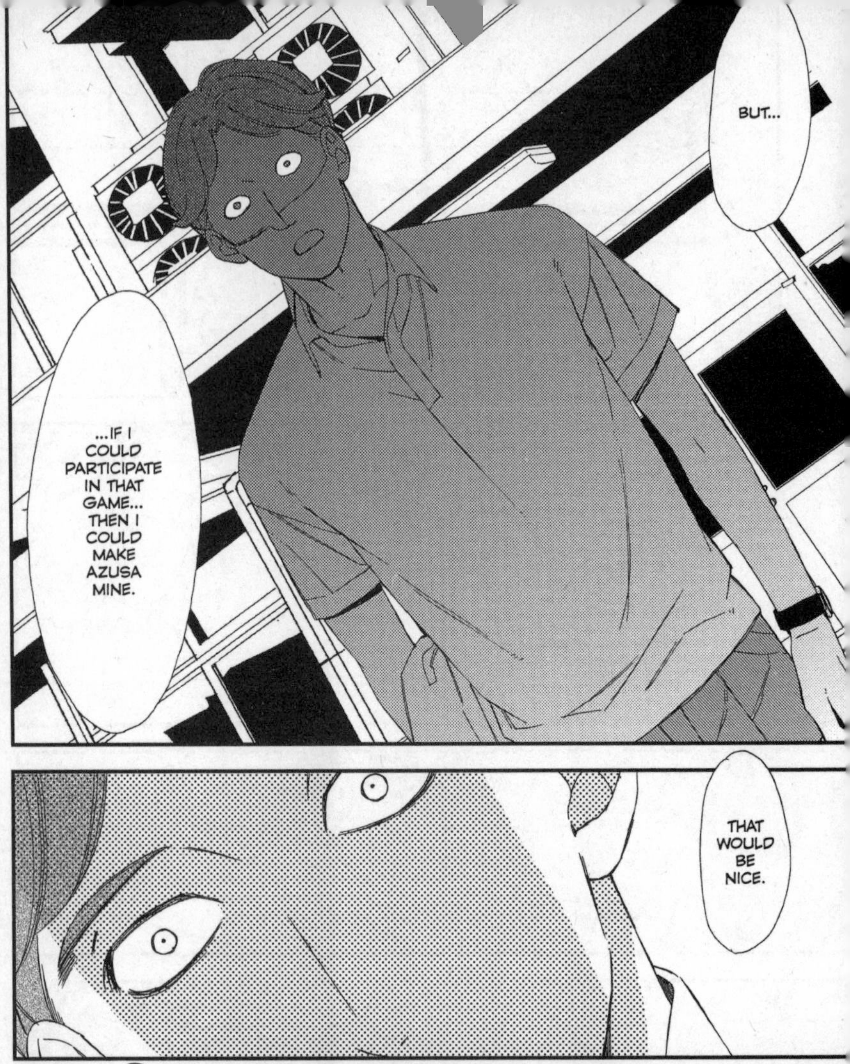
BUT...
...IF I COULD PARTICIPATE IN THAT GAME... THEN I COULD MAKE AZUSA MINE.
THAT WOULD BE NICE.

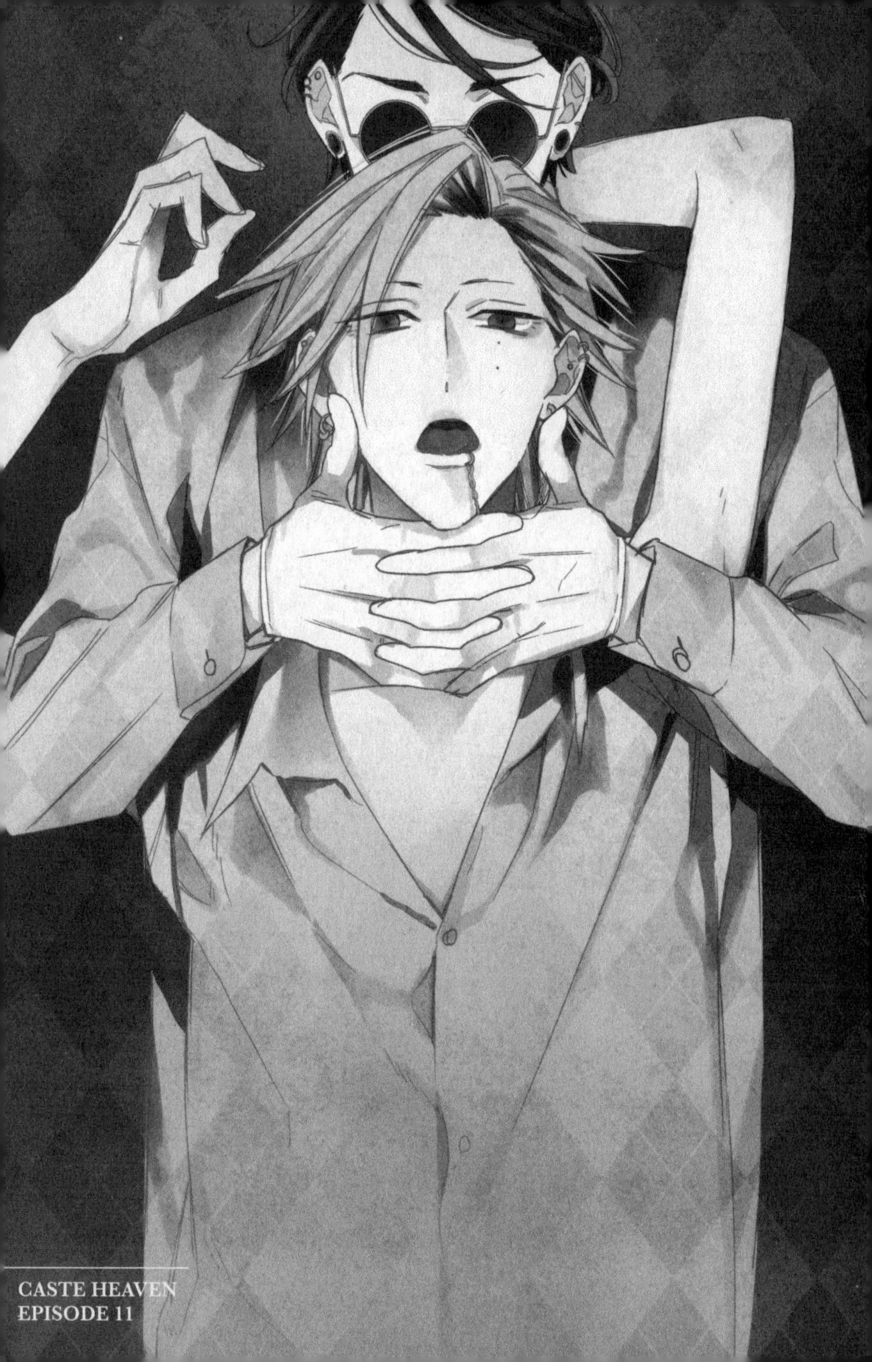

CASTE HEAVEN
EPISODE 11

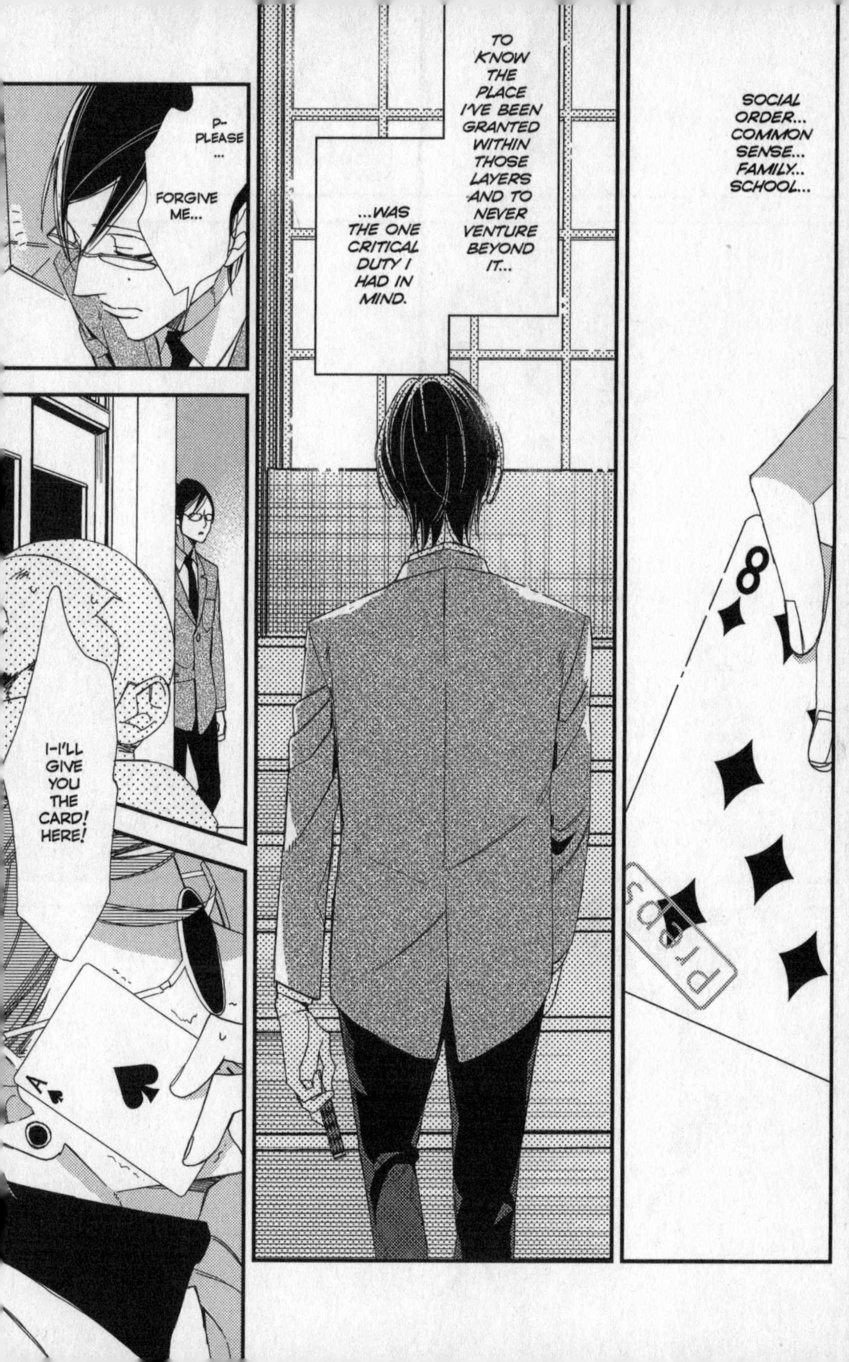
SOCIAL ORDER... COMMON SENSE... FAMILY... SCHOOL...
TO KNOW THE PLACE I'VE BEEN GRANTED WITHIN THOSE LAYERS AND TO NEVER VENTURE BEYOND IT...
...WAS THE ONE CRITICAL DUTY I HAD IN MIND.
P-PLEASE...
FORGIVE ME...
I-I'LL GIVE YOU THE CARD! HERE!

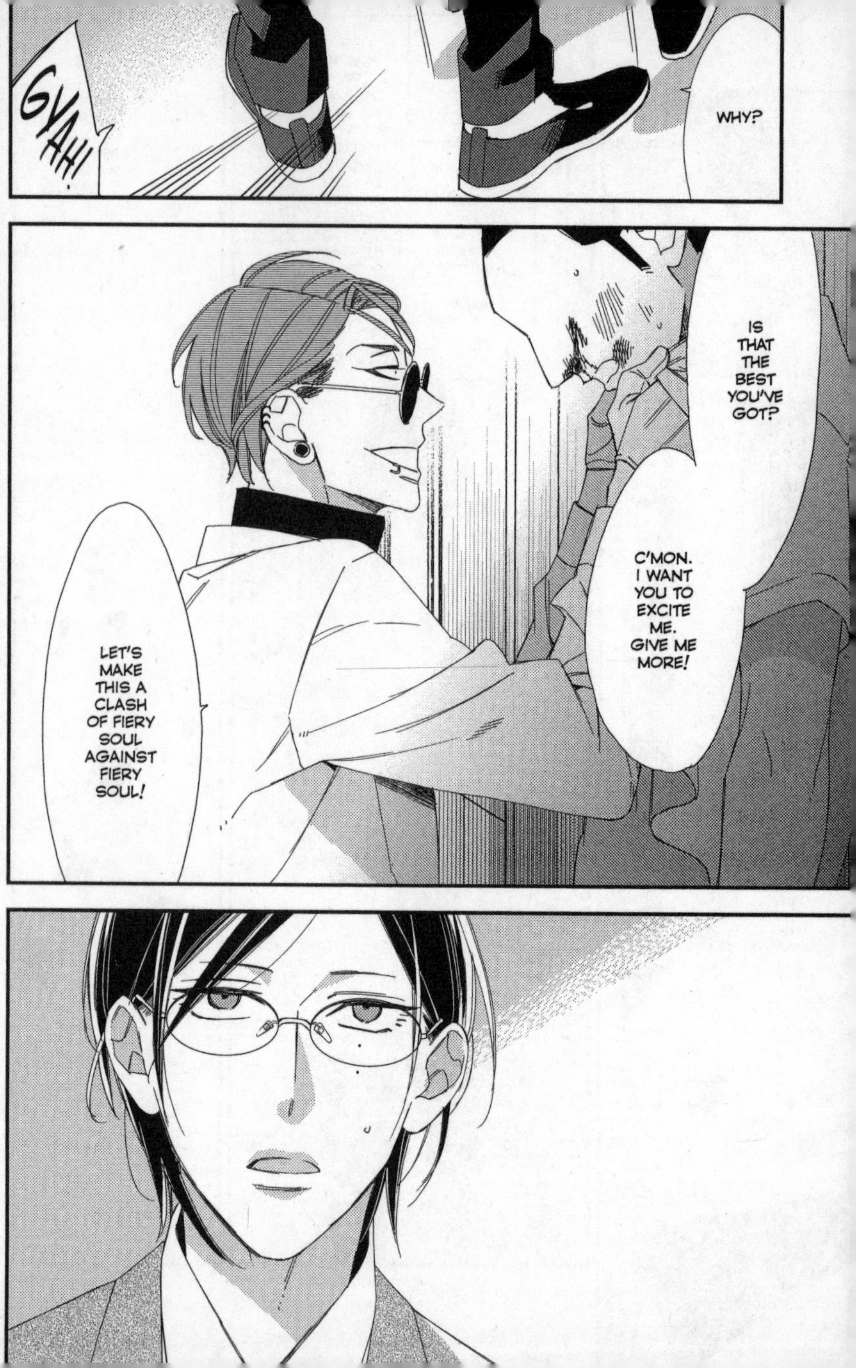
WHY?
GYAH!
IS THAT THE BEST YOU'VE GOT?
C'MON. I WANT YOU TO EXCITE ME. GIVE ME MORE!
LET'S MAKE THIS A CLASH OF FIERY SOUL AGAINST FIERY SOUL!

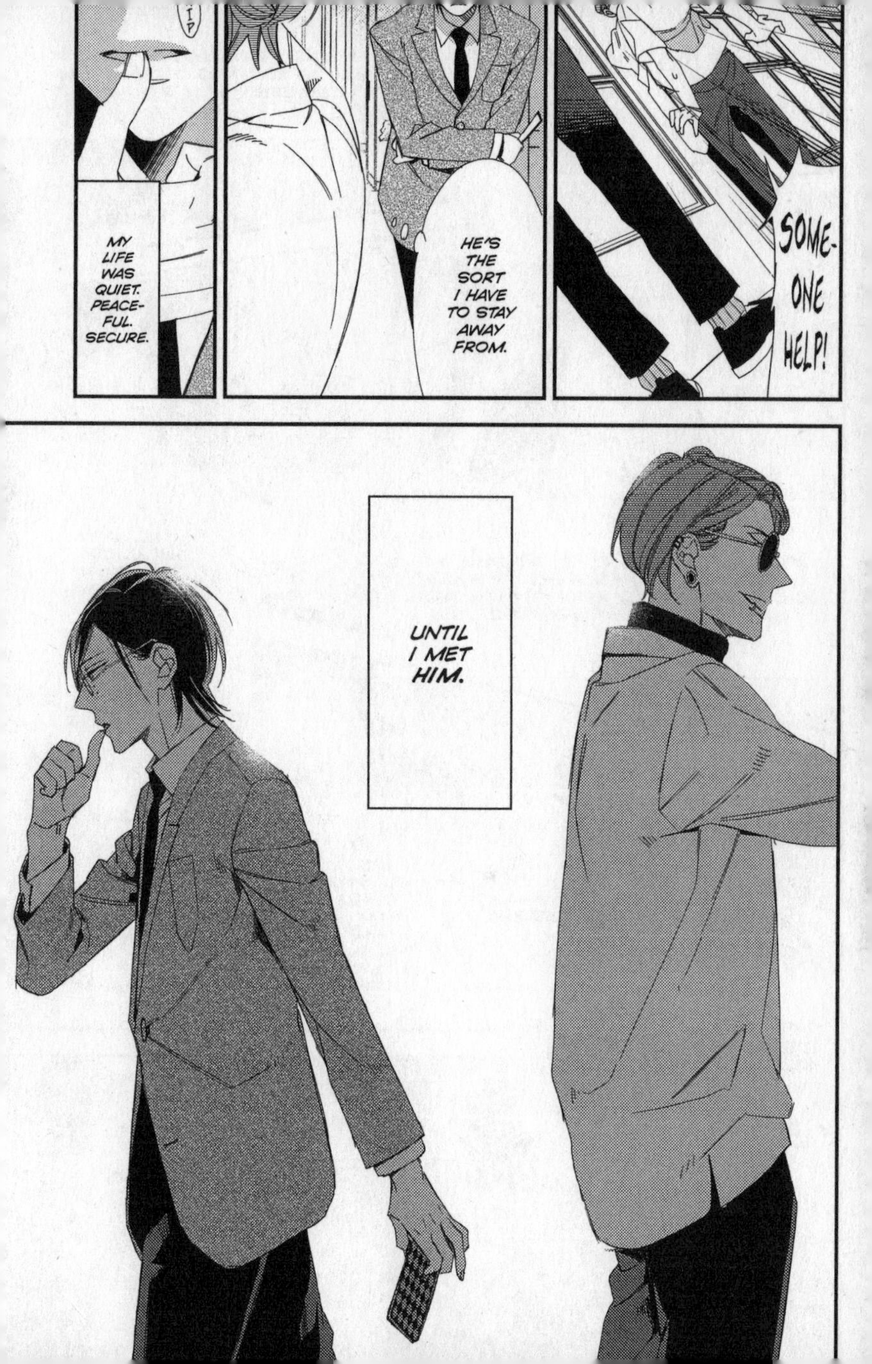
SOME-ONE HELP!
HE'S THE SORT I HAVE TO STAY AWAY FROM.
MY LIFE WAS QUIET. PEACEFUL. SECURE.
UNTIL I MET HIM.

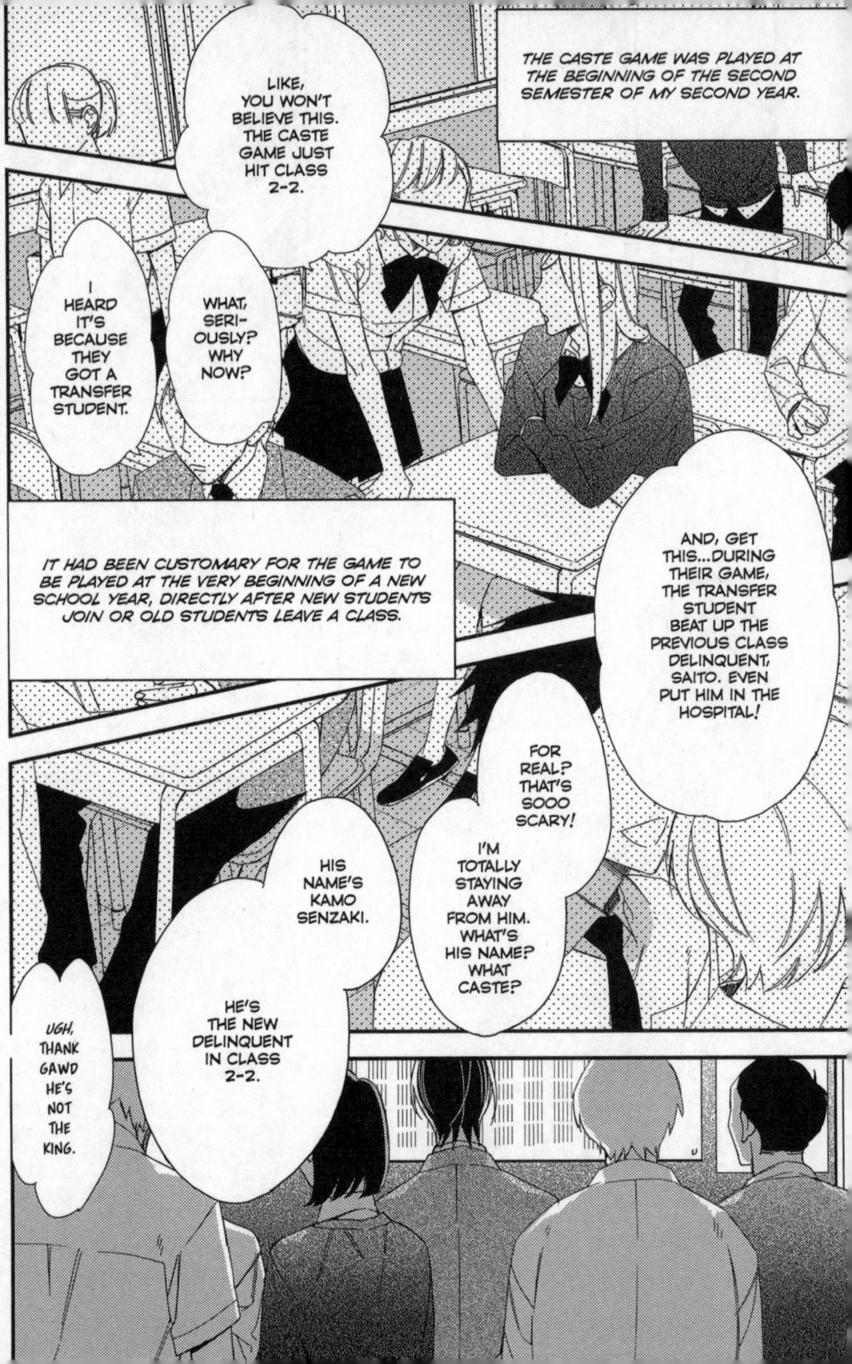
THE CASTE GAME WAS PLAYED AT THE BEGINNING OF THE SECOND SEMESTER OF MY SECOND YEAR.
LIKE, YOU WON'T BELIEVE THIS. THE CASTE GAME JUST HIT CLASS 2-2.
WHAT, SERI-OUSLY? WHY NOW?
I HEARD IT'S BECAUSE THEY GOT A TRANSFER STUDENT.
AND, GET THIS...DURING THEIR GAME, THE TRANSFER STUDENT BEAT UP THE PREVIOUS CLASS DELINQUENT, SAITO. EVEN PUT HIM IN THE HOSPITAL!
IT HAD BEEN CUSTOMARY FOR THE GAME TO BE PLAYED AT THE VERY BEGINNING OF A NEW SCHOOL YEAR, DIRECTLY AFTER NEW STUDENTS JOIN OR OLD STUDENTS LEAVE A CLASS.
FOR REAL? THAT'S SOOO SCARY!
I'M TOTALLY STAYING AWAY FROM HIM. WHAT'S HIS NAME? WHAT CASTE?
HIS NAME'S KAMO SENZAKI.
HE'S THE NEW DELINQUENT IN CLASS 2-2.
UGH, THANK GAWD HE'S NOT THE KING.

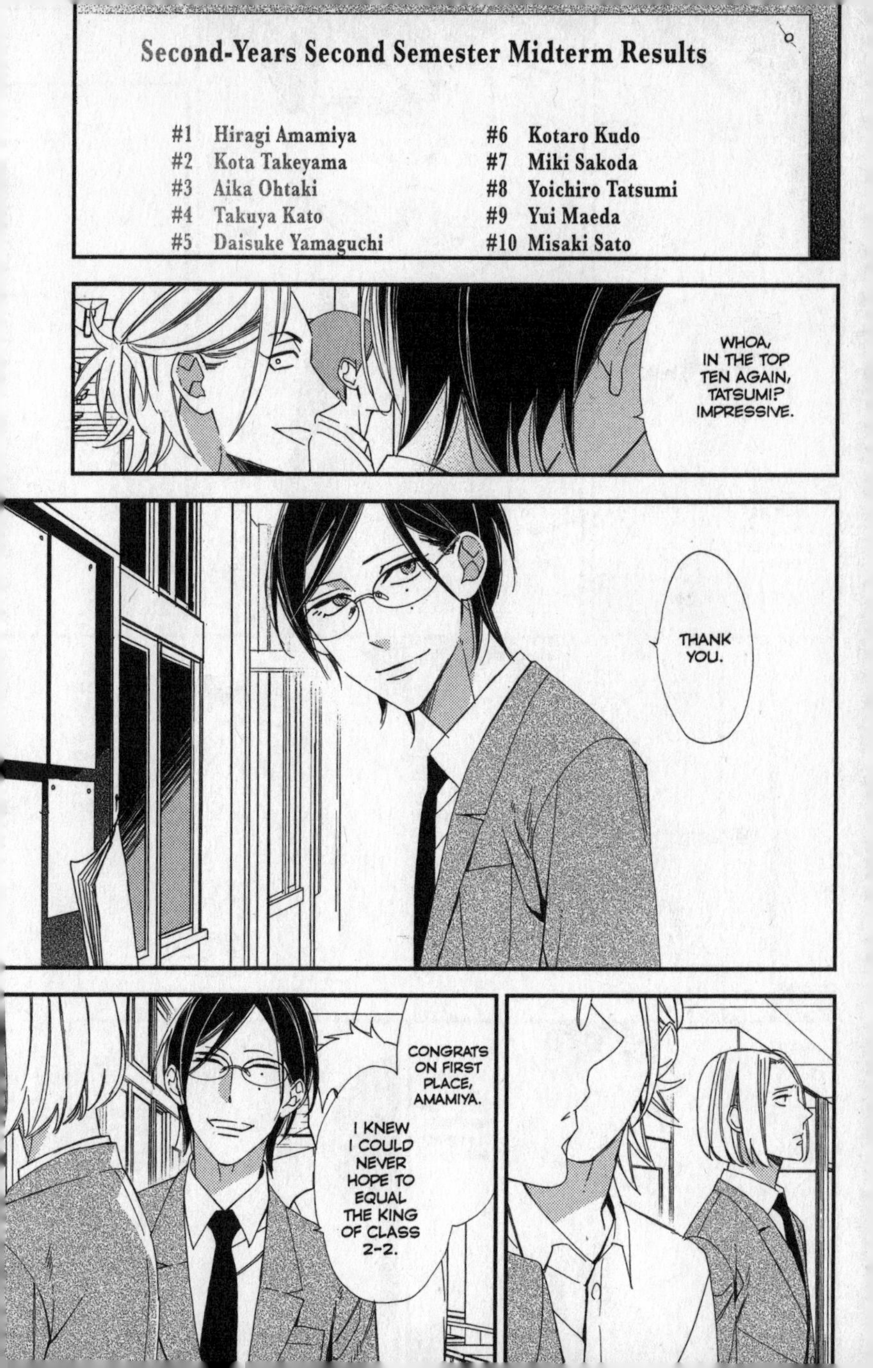
Second-Years Second Semester Midterm Results
#1 Hiragi Amamiya
#2 Kota Takeyama
#3 Aika Ohtaki
#4 Takuya Kato
#5 Daisuke Yamaguchi
#6 Kotaro Kudo
#7 Miki Sakoda
#8 Yoichiro Tatsumi
#9 Yui Maeda
#10 Misaki Sato
WHOA, IN THE TOP TEN AGAIN, TATSUMI? IMPRESSIVE.
THANK YOU.
CONGRATS ON FIRST PLACE, AMAMIYA.
I KNEW I COULD NEVER HOPE TO EQUAL THE KING OF CLASS 2-2.

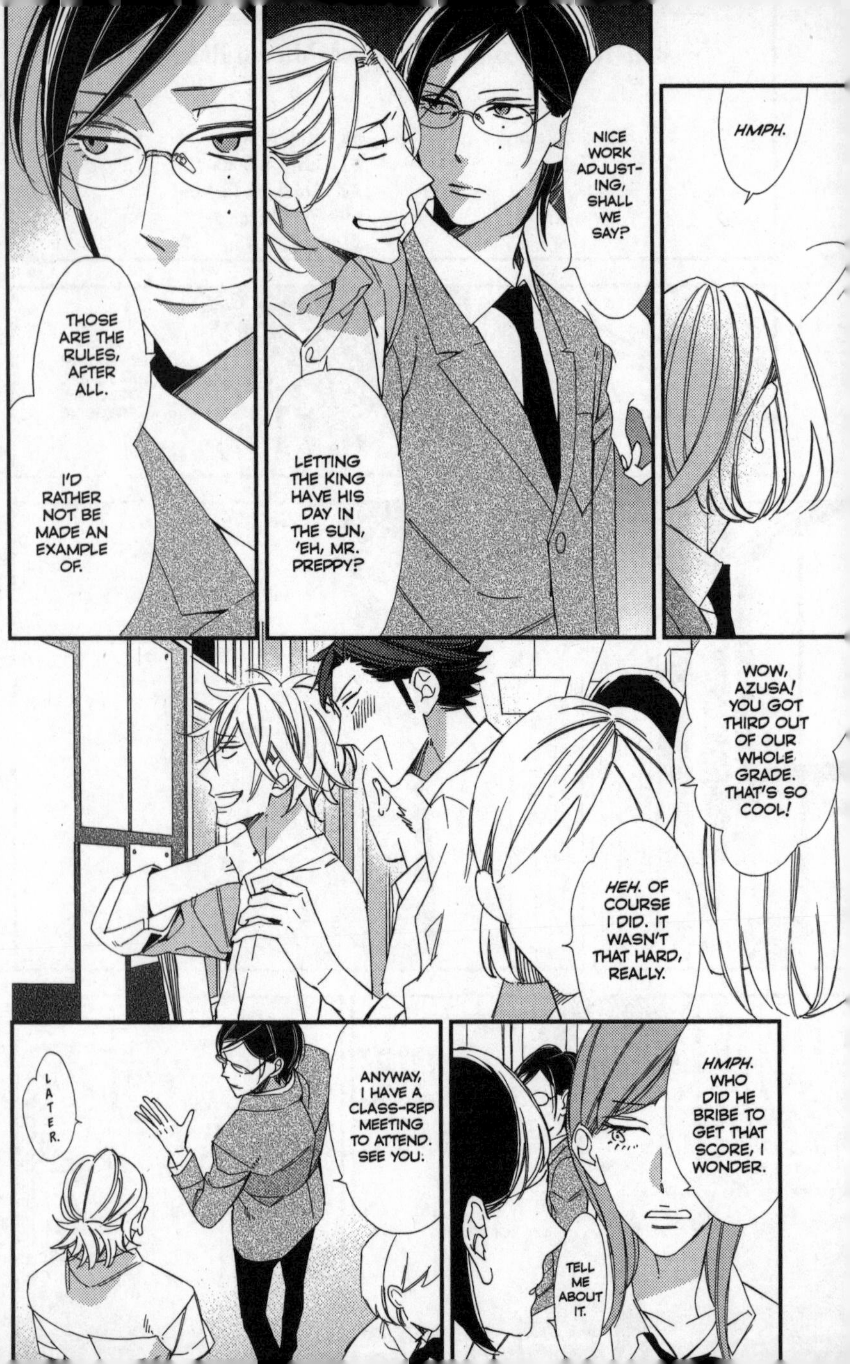
HMPH.
NICE WORK ADJUSTING, SHALL WE SAY?
LETTING THE KING HAVE HIS DAY IN THE SUN, 'EH, MR. PREPPY?
THOSE ARE THE RULES, AFTER ALL.
I'D RATHER NOT BE MADE AN EXAMPLE OF.
WOW, AZUSA! YOU GOT THIRD OUT OF OUR WHOLE GRADE. THAT'S SO COOL!
HEH. OF COURSE I DID. IT WASN'T THAT HARD, REALLY.
HMPH. WHO DID HE BRIBE TO GET THAT SCORE, I WONDER.
TELL ME ABOUT IT.
ANYWAY, I HAVE A CLASS-REP MEETING TO ATTEND. SEE YOU.
LATER.

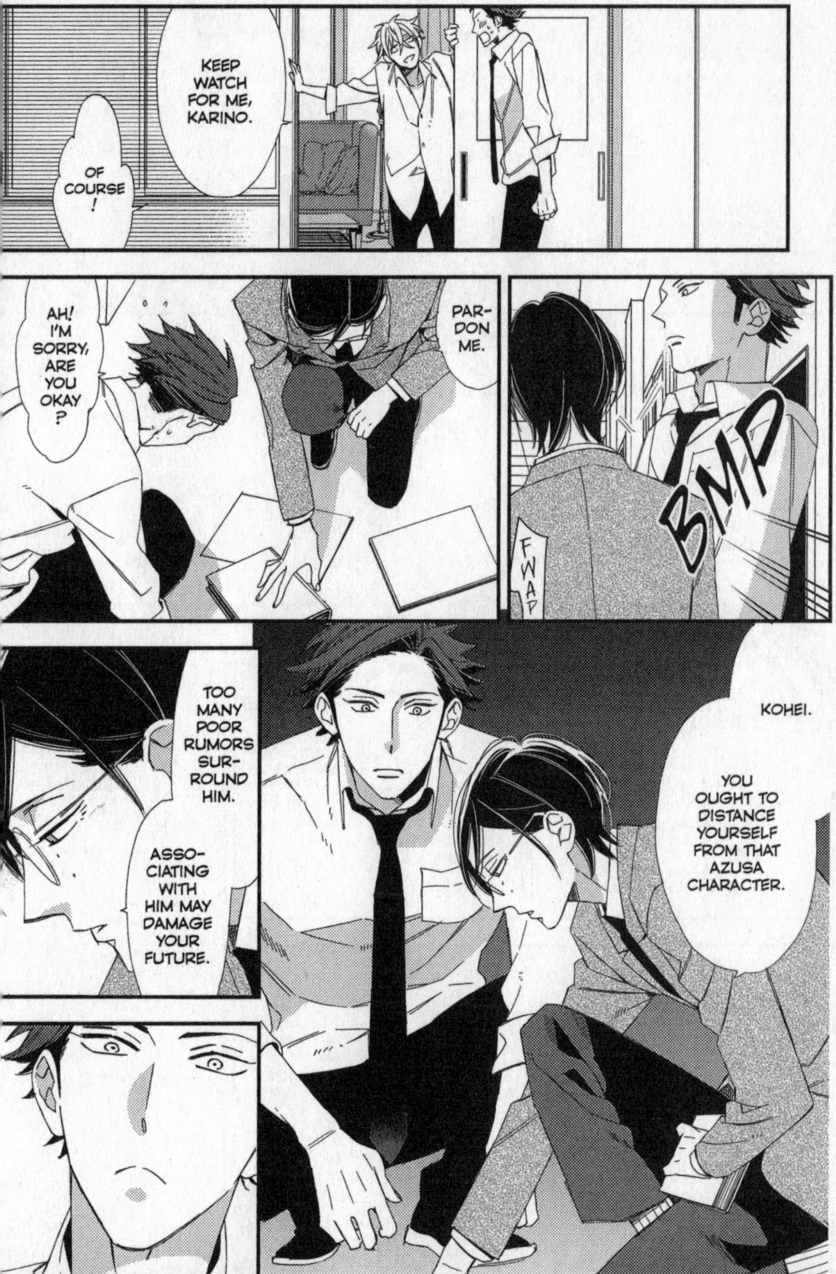
KEEP WATCH FOR ME, KARINO.
OF COURSE!
BMP
FWAP
PARDON ME.
AH! I'M SORRY, ARE YOU OKAY?
KOHEI.
YOU OUGHT TO DISTANCE YOURSELF FROM THAT AZUSA CHARACTER.
TOO MANY POOR RUMORS SURROUND HIM.
ASSOCIATING WITH HIM MAY DAMAGE YOUR FUTURE.

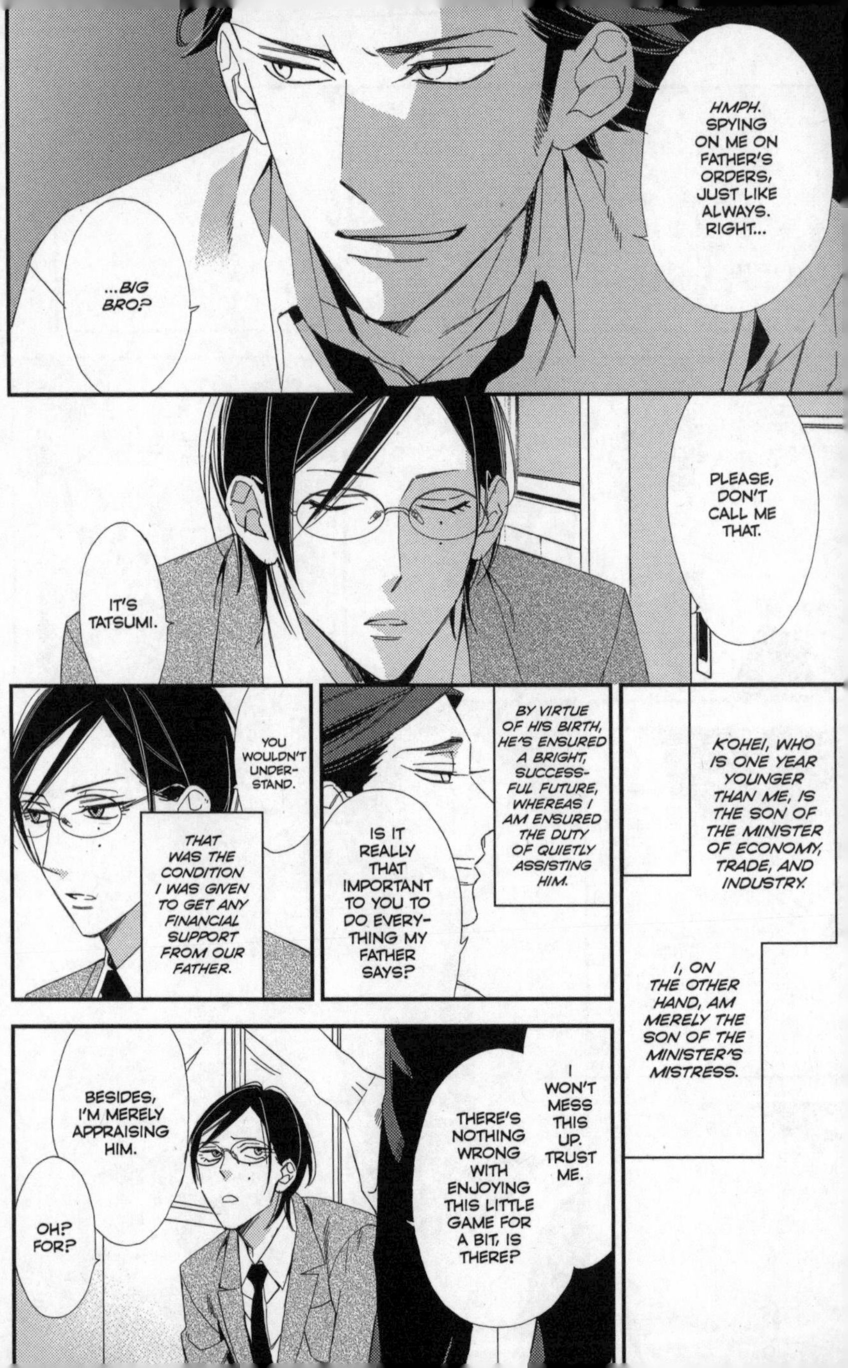
HMPH. SPYING ON ME ON FATHER'S ORDERS, JUST LIKE ALWAYS. RIGHT...
...BIG BRO?
PLEASE, DON'T CALL ME THAT.
IT'S TATSUMI.
KOHEI, WHO IS ONE YEAR YOUNGER THAN ME, IS THE SON OF THE MINISTER OF ECONOMY, TRADE, AND INDUSTRY.
I, ON THE OTHER HAND, AM MERELY THE SON OF THE MINISTER'S MISTRESS.
BY VIRTUE OF HIS BIRTH, HE'S ENSURED A BRIGHT, SUCCESS-FUL FUTURE, WHEREAS I AM ENSURED THE DUTY OF QUIETLY ASSISTING HIM.
IS IT REALLY THAT IMPORTANT TO YOU TO DO EVERY-THING MY FATHER SAYS?
YOU WOULDN'T UNDER-STAND.
THAT WAS THE CONDITION I WAS GIVEN TO GET ANY FINANCIAL SUPPORT FROM OUR FATHER.
I WON'T MESS THIS UP. TRUST ME.
THERE'S NOTHING WRONG WITH ENJOYING THIS LITTLE GAME FOR A BIT, IS THERE?
BESIDES, I'M MERELY APPRAISING HIM.
OH? FOR?

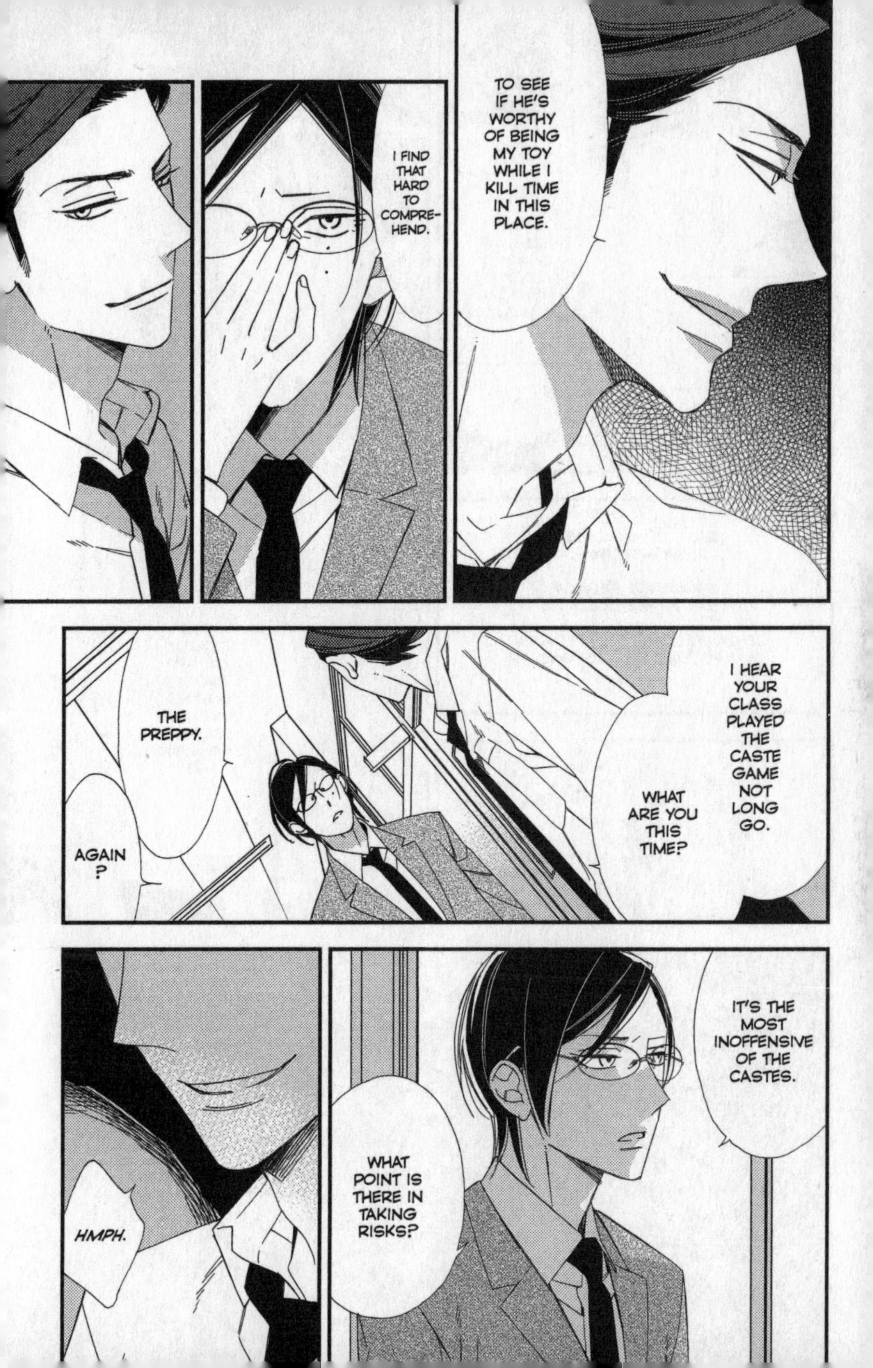
TO SEE IF HE'S WORTHY OF BEING MY TOY WHILE I KILL TIME IN THIS PLACE.
I FIND THAT HARD TO COMPRE-HEND.
I HEAR YOUR CLASS PLAYED THE CASTE GAME NOT LONG GO.
WHAT ARE YOU THIS TIME?
THE PREPPY.
AGAIN?
IT'S THE MOST INOFFENSIVE OF THE CASTES.
WHAT POINT IS THERE IN TAKING RISKS?
HMPH.

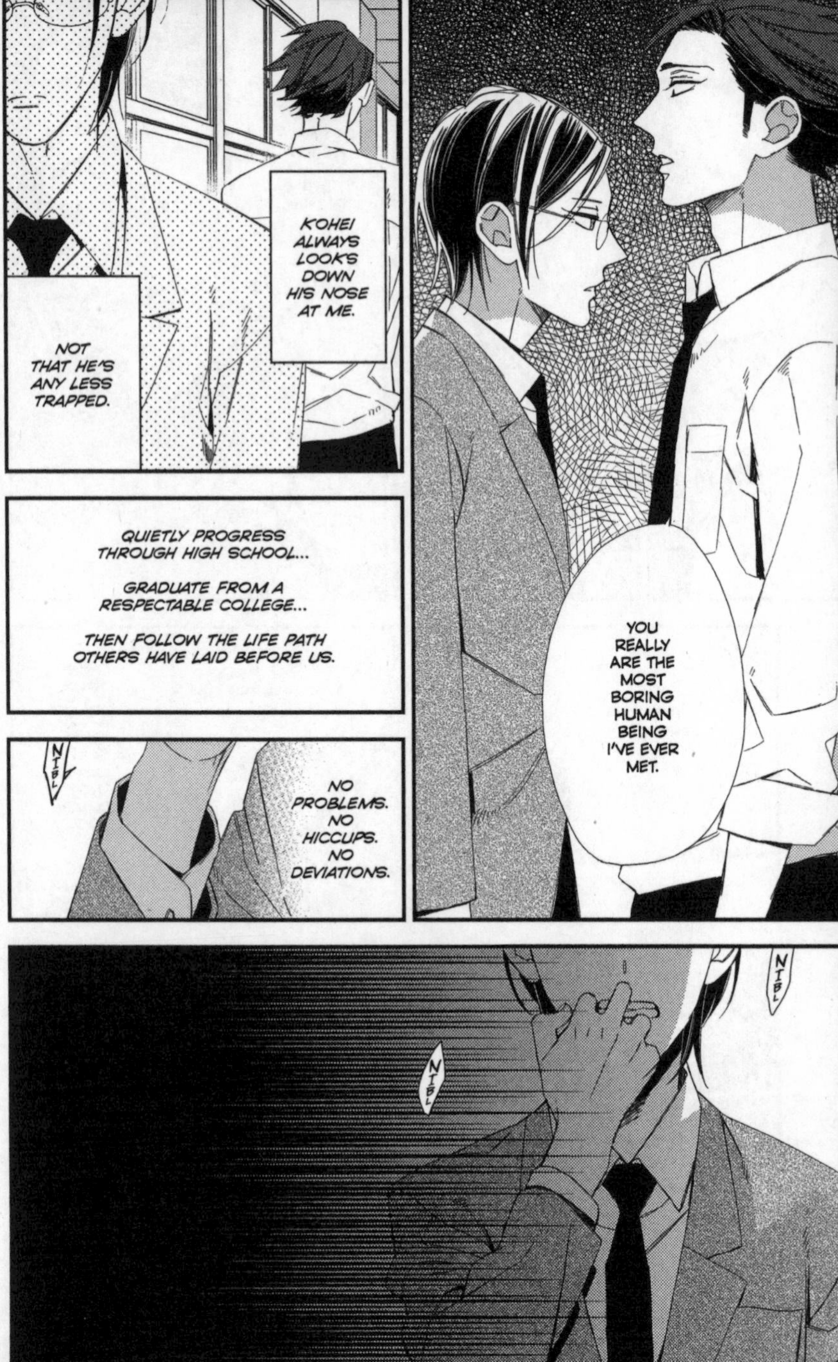
YOU REALLY ARE THE MOST BORING HUMAN BEING I'VE EVER MET.
KOHEI ALWAYS LOOKS DOWN HIS NOSE AT ME.
NOT THAT HE'S ANY LESS TRAPPED.
QUIETLY PROGRESS THROUGH HIGH SCHOOL...
GRADUATE FROM A RESPECTABLE COLLEGE...
THEN FOLLOW THE LIFE PATH OTHERS HAVE LAID BEFORE US.
NIBL
NO PROBLEMS. NO HICCUPS. NO DEVIATIONS.
NIBL
NIBL

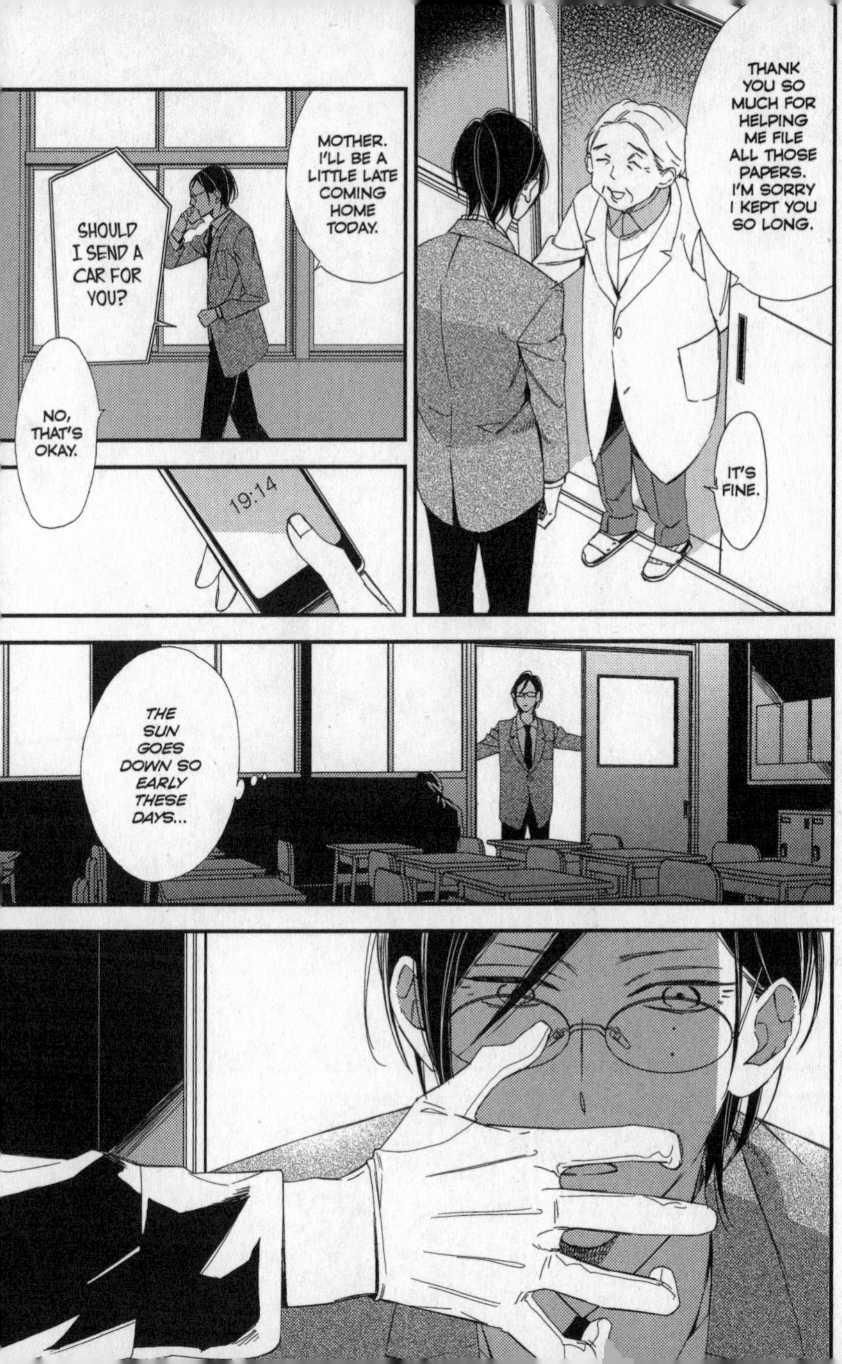
THANK YOU SO MUCH FOR HELPING ME FILE ALL THOSE PAPERS. I'M SORRY I KEPT YOU SO LONG.
IT'S FINE.
MOTHER. I'LL BE A LITTLE LATE COMING HOME TODAY.
SHOULD I SEND A CAR FOR YOU?
NO, THAT'S OKAY.
19:14
THE SUN GOES DOWN SO EARLY THESE DAYS...

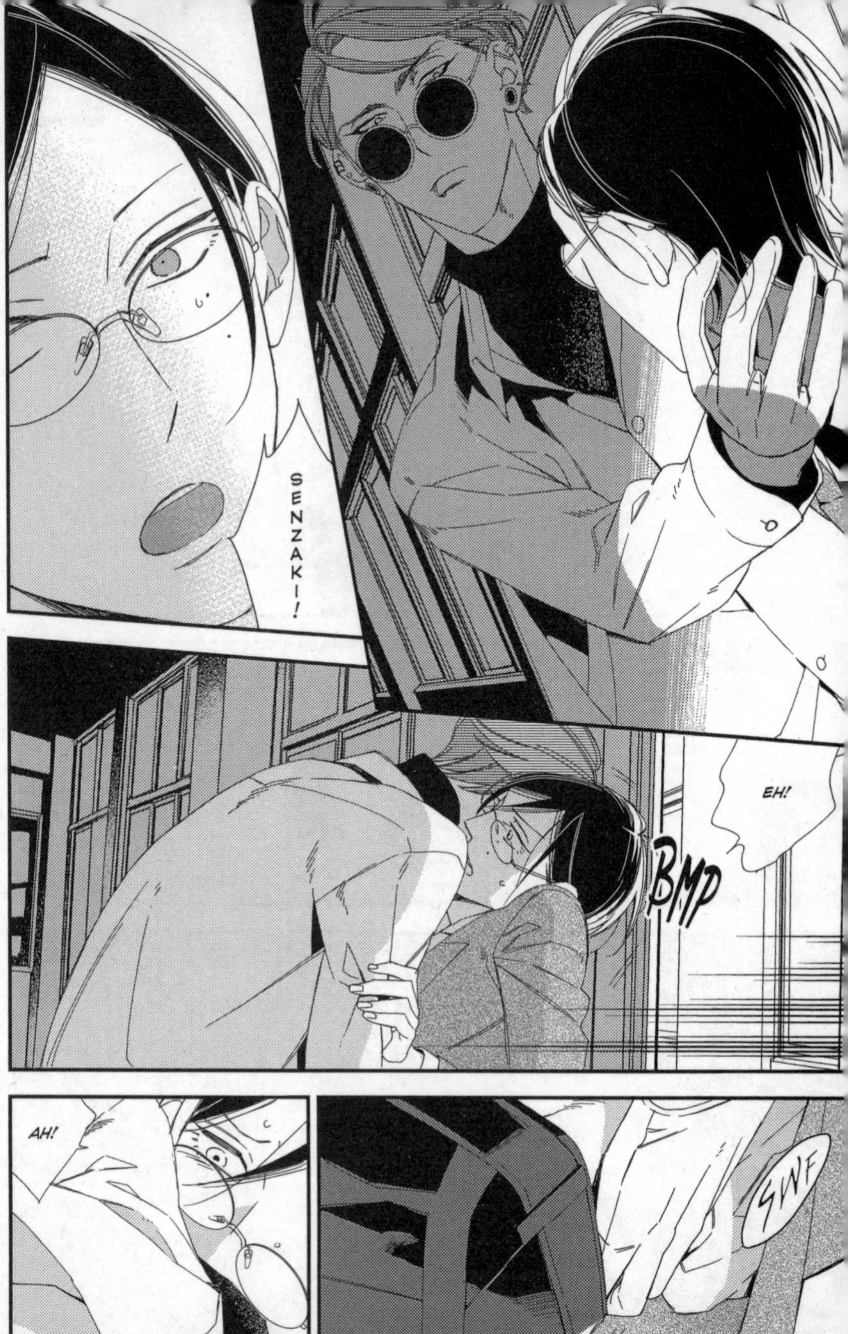
SENZAKI!
EH!
BMP
SWF
AH!

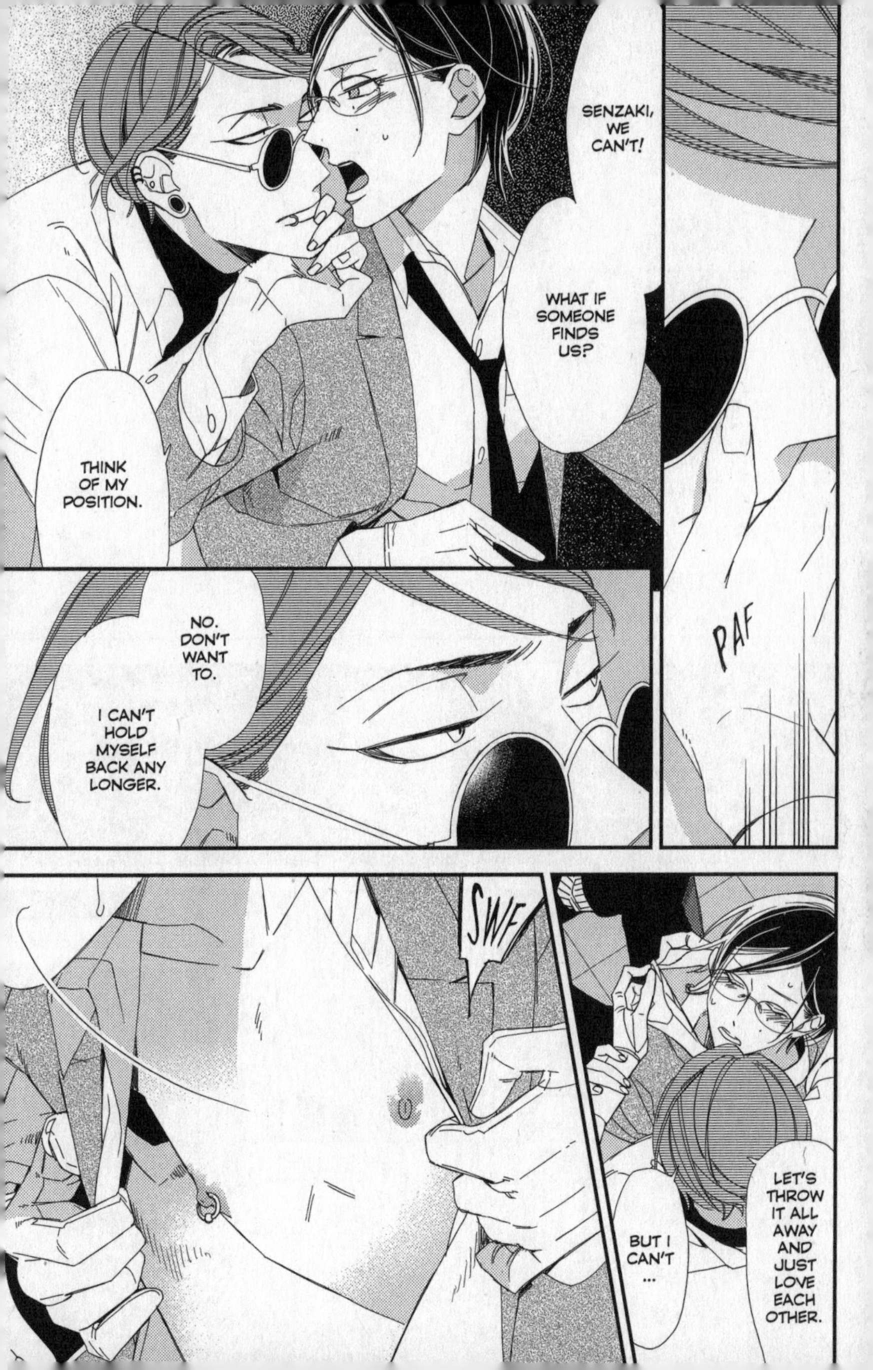
SENZAKI, WE CAN'T!
WHAT IF SOMEONE FINDS US?
THINK OF MY POSITION.
PAF
NO. DON'T WANT TO.
I CAN'T HOLD MYSELF BACK ANY LONGER.
LET'S THROW IT ALL AWAY AND JUST LOVE EACH OTHER.
BUT I CAN'T ...
SWF

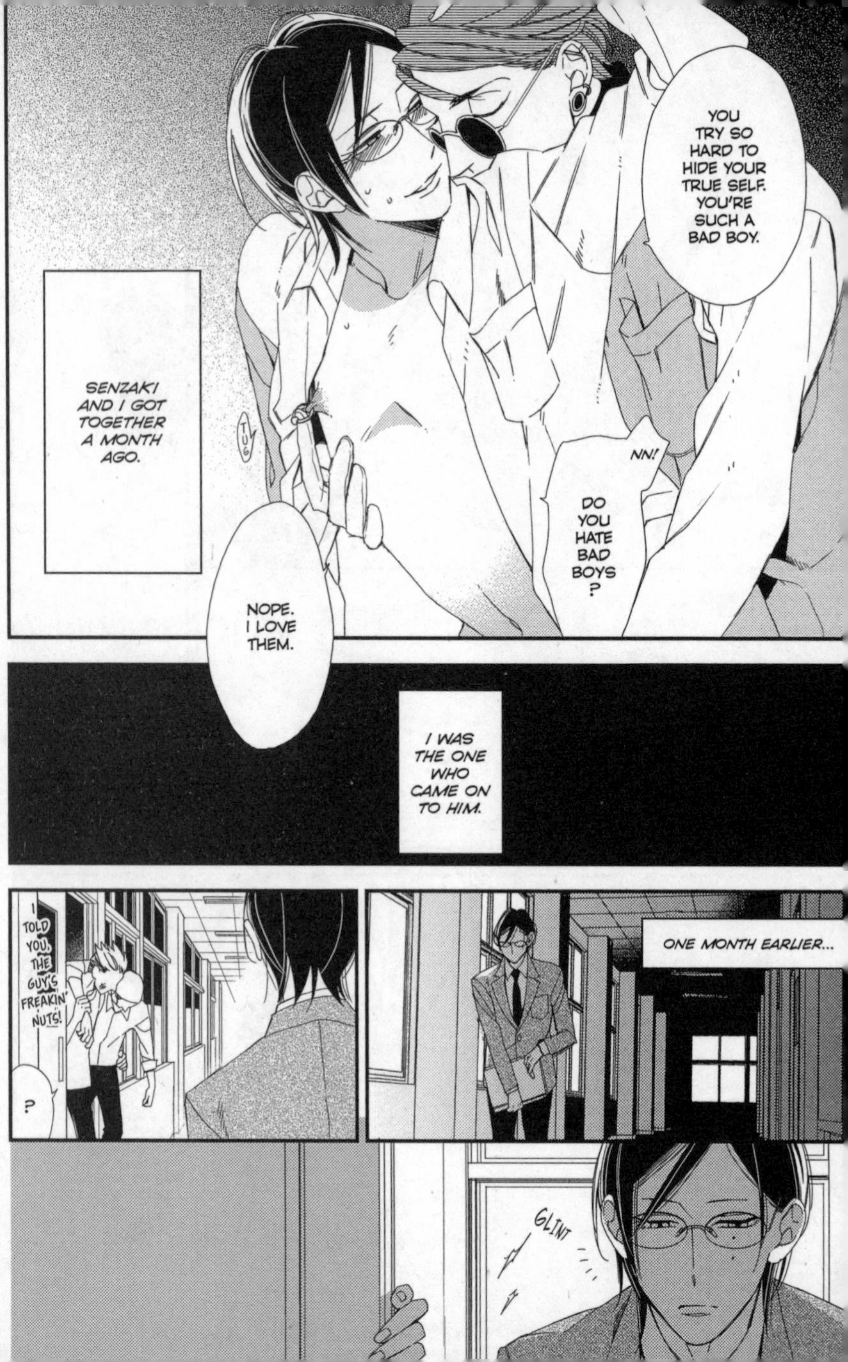
YOU TRY SO HARD TO HIDE YOUR TRUE SELF. YOU'RE SUCH A BAD BOY.
NN!
DO YOU HATE BAD BOYS?
SENZAKI AND I GOT TOGETHER A MONTH AGO.
TUG
NOPE. I LOVE THEM.
I WAS THE ONE WHO CAME ON TO HIM.
ONE MONTH EARLIER...
I TOLD YOU, THE GUY'S FREAKIN' NUTS!
?
GLINT

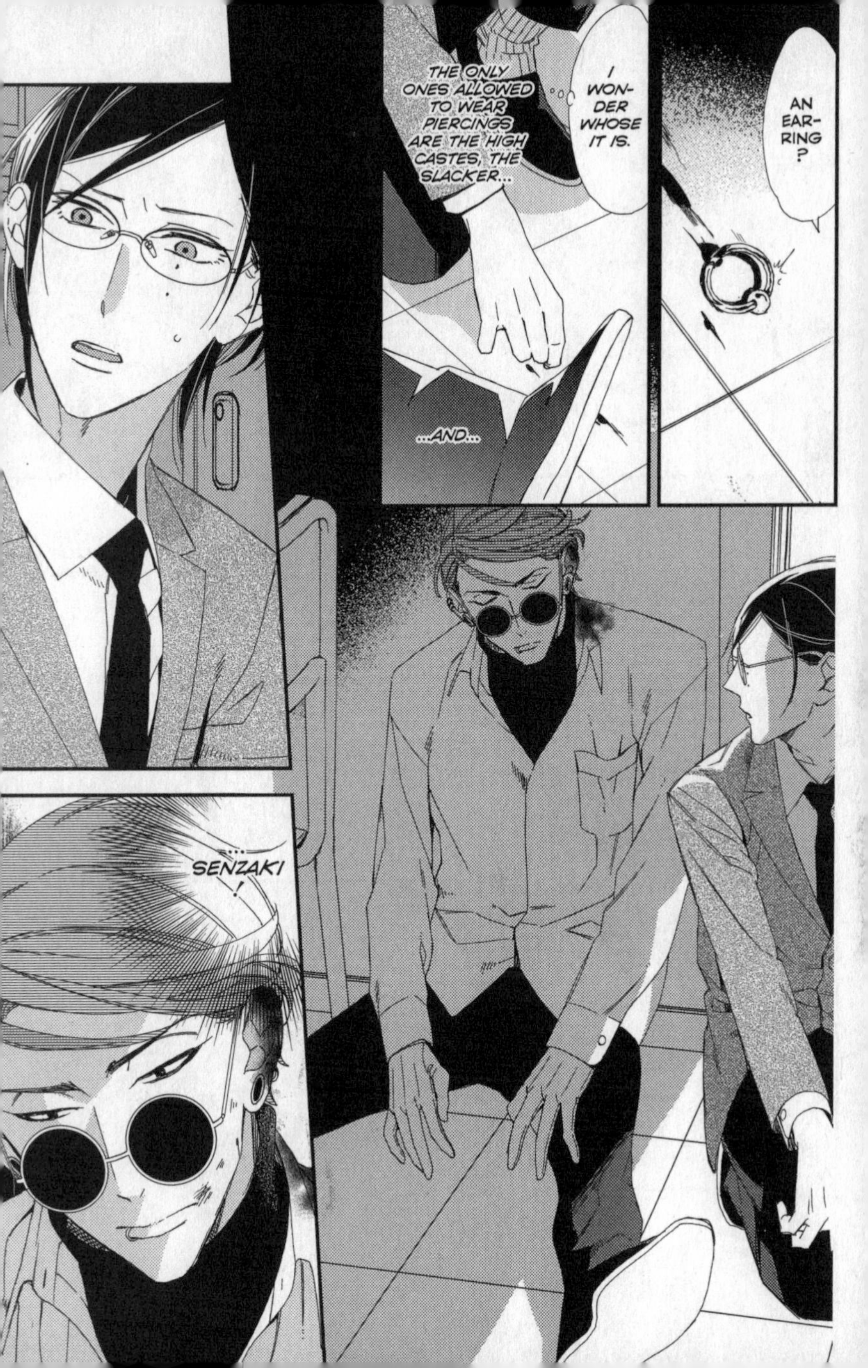
AN EAR-RING?
I WONDER WHOSE IT IS.
THE ONLY ONES ALLOWED TO WEAR PIERCINGS ARE THE HIGH CASTES, THE SLACKER...
...AND...
...SENZAKI!

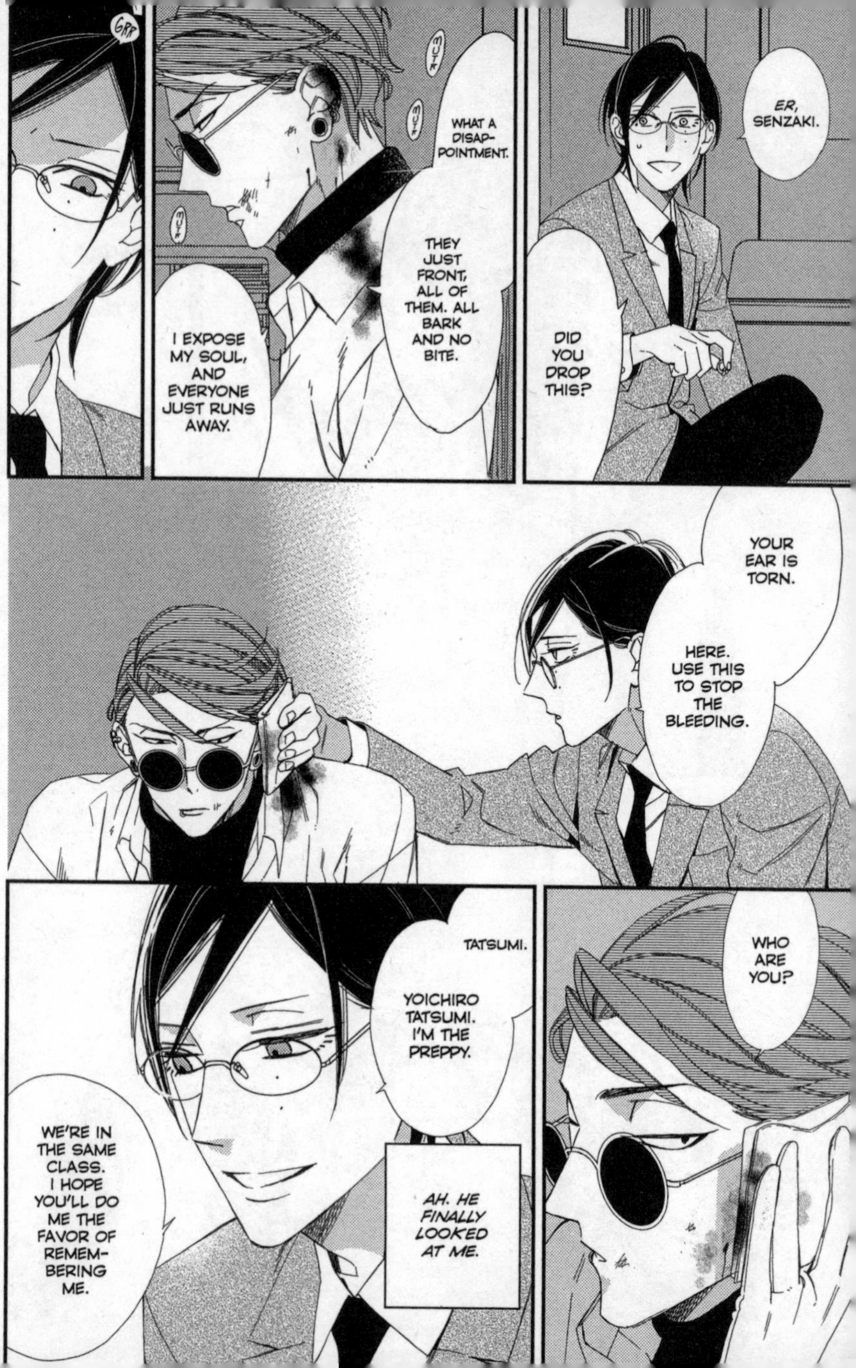
ER, SENZAKI.
DID YOU DROP THIS?
MUTR
MUTR
MUTR
WHAT A DISAP-POINTMENT.
THEY JUST FRONT, ALL OF THEM. ALL BARK AND NO BITE.
I EXPOSE MY SOUL, AND EVERYONE JUST RUNS AWAY.
GRR
YOUR EAR IS TORN.
HERE. USE THIS TO STOP THE BLEEDING.
WHO ARE YOU?
TATSUMI.
YOICHIRO TATSUMI. I'M THE PREPPY.
AH. HE FINALLY LOOKED AT ME.
WE'RE IN THE SAME CLASS. I HOPE YOU'LL DO ME THE FAVOR OF REMEMBERING ME.

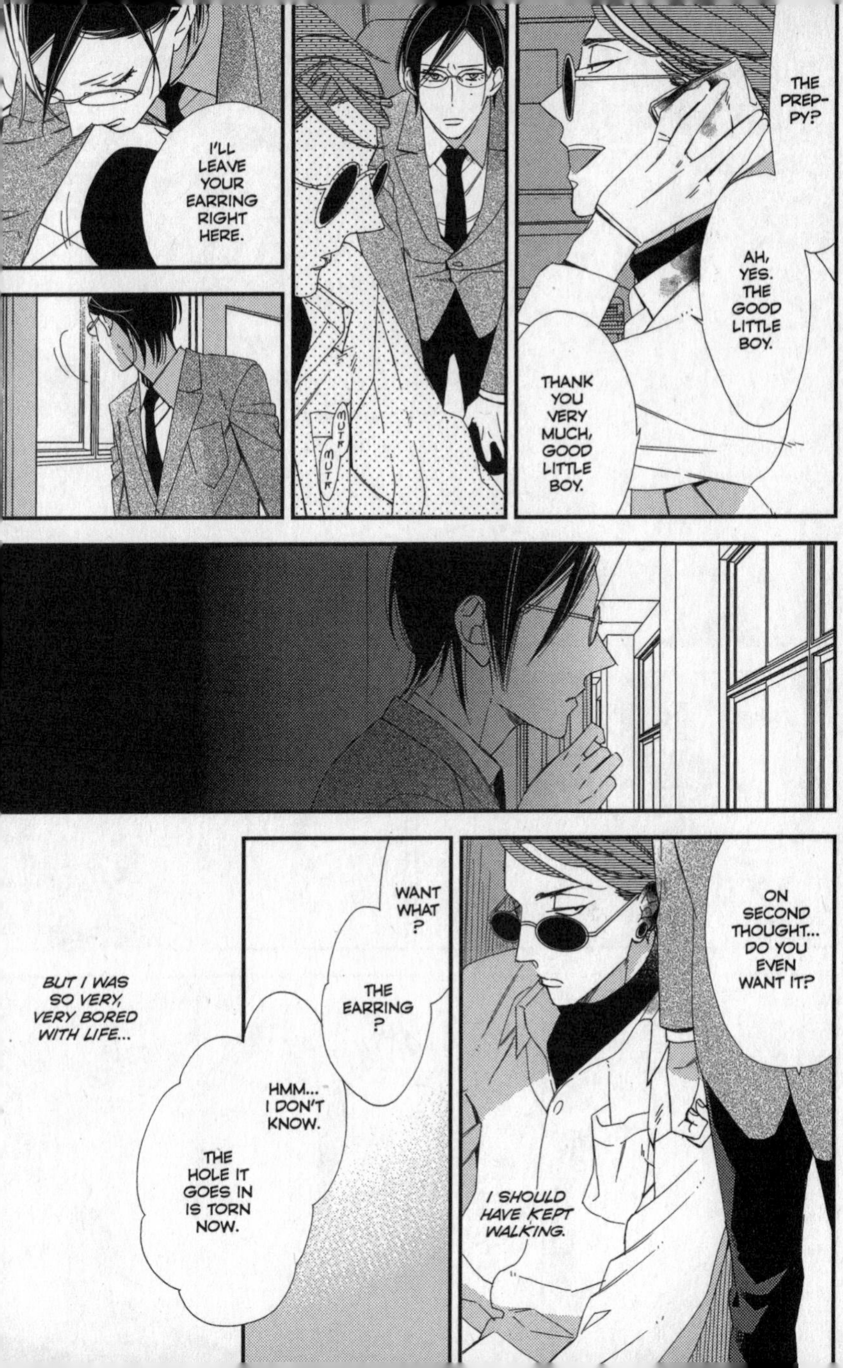
THE PREP-PY?
AH, YES. THE GOOD LITTLE BOY.
THANK YOU VERY MUCH, GOOD LITTLE BOY.
I'LL LEAVE YOUR EARRING RIGHT HERE.
ON SECOND THOUGHT... DO YOU EVEN WANT IT?
I SHOULD HAVE KEPT WALKING.
WANT WHAT?
THE EARRING?
HMM... I DON'T KNOW.
THE HOLE IT GOES IN IS TORN NOW.
BUT I WAS SO VERY, VERY BORED WITH LIFE...

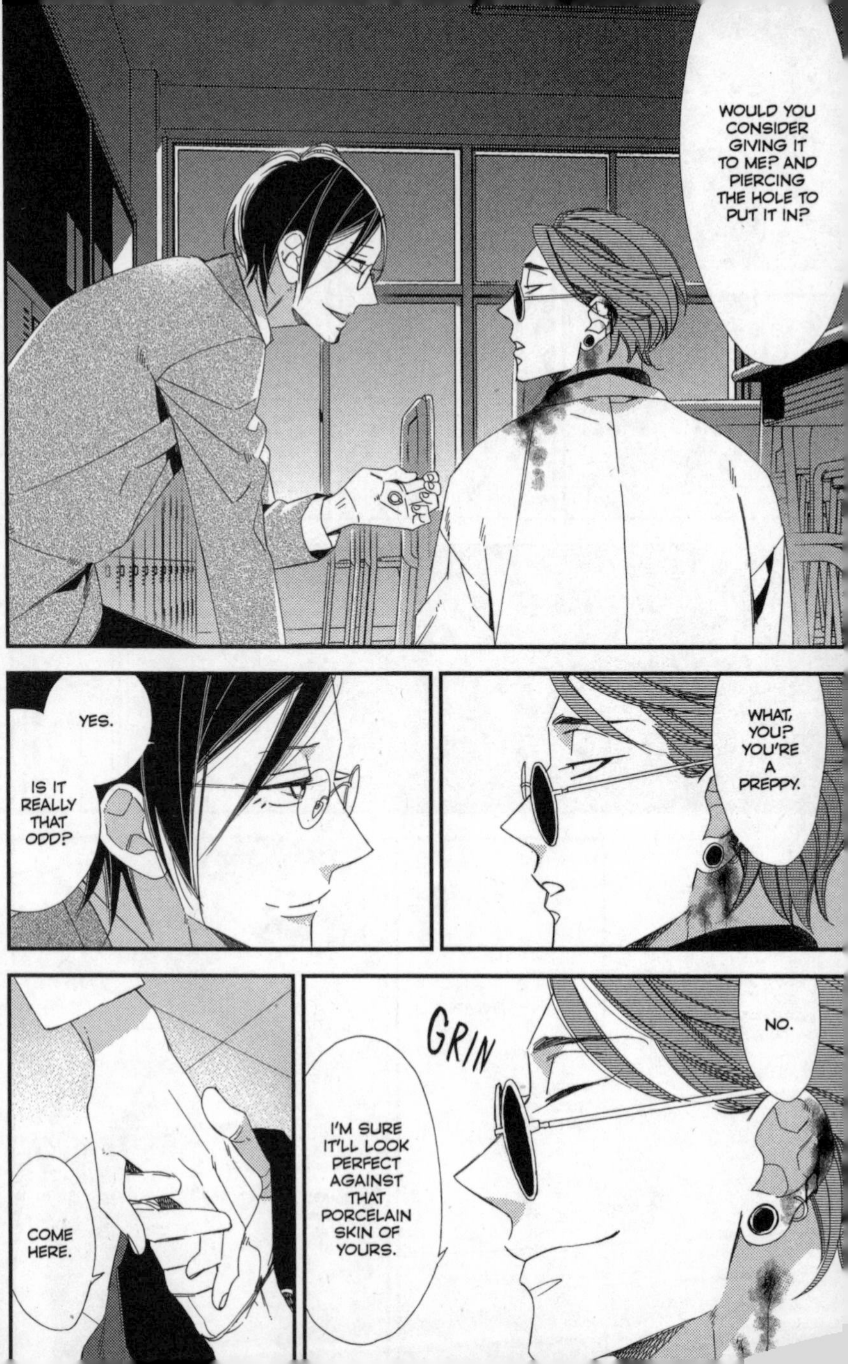
WOULD YOU CONSIDER GIVING IT TO ME? AND PIERCING THE HOLE TO PUT IT IN?
WHAT, YOU? YOU'RE A PREPPY.
YES.
IS IT REALLY THAT ODD?
NO.
GRIN
I'M SURE IT'LL LOOK PERFECT AGAINST THAT PORCELAIN SKIN OF YOURS.
COME HERE.

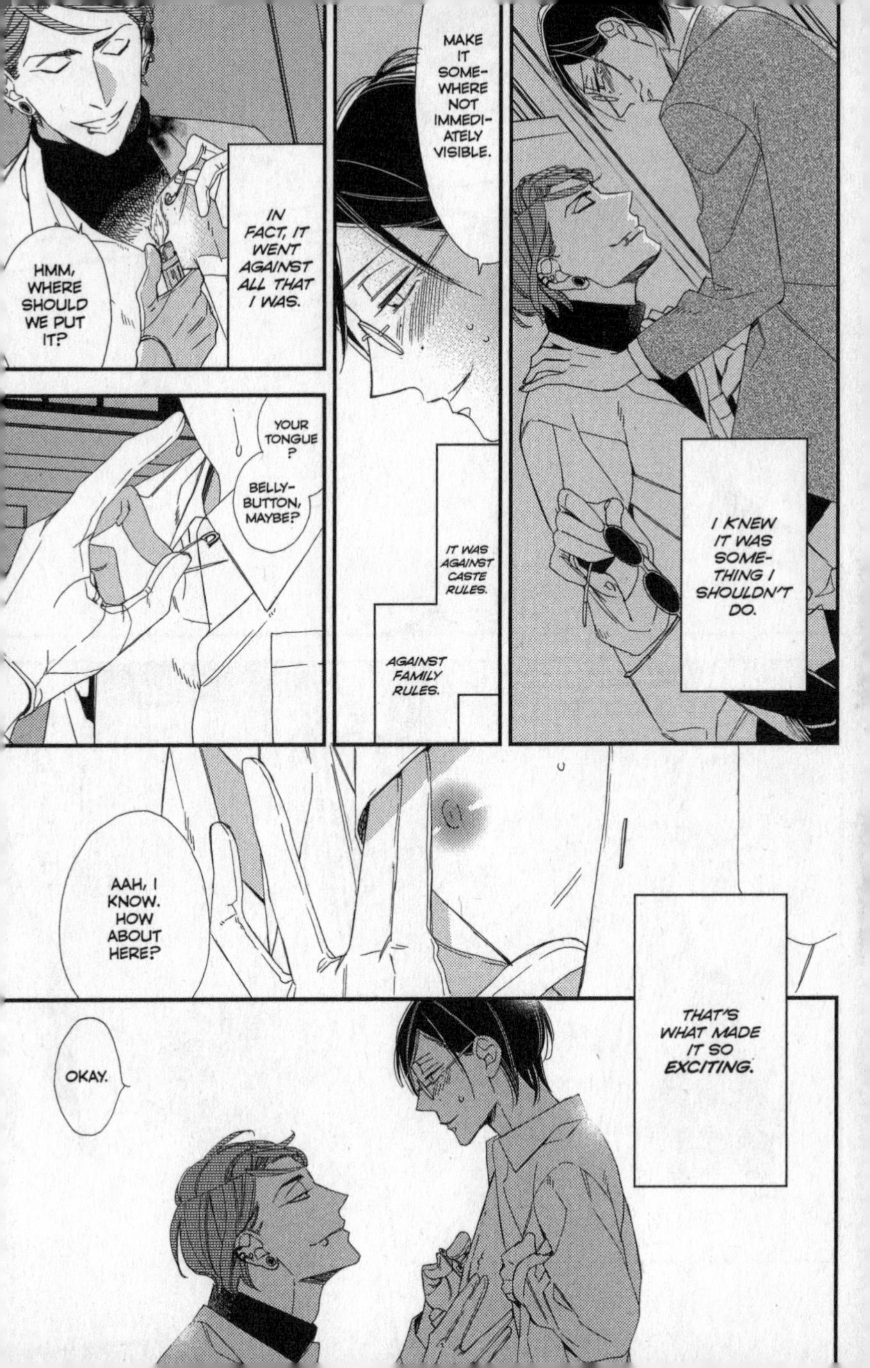
I KNEW IT WAS SOMETHING I SHOULDN'T DO.
MAKE IT SOMEWHERE NOT IMMEDIATELY VISIBLE.
IT WAS AGAINST CASTE RULES.
AGAINST FAMILY RULES.
IN FACT, IT WENT AGAINST ALL THAT I WAS.
HMM, WHERE SHOULD WE PUT IT?
YOUR TONGUE?
BELLY-BUTTON, MAYBE?
THAT'S WHAT MADE IT SO EXCITING.
AAH, I KNOW. HOW ABOUT HERE?
OKAY.

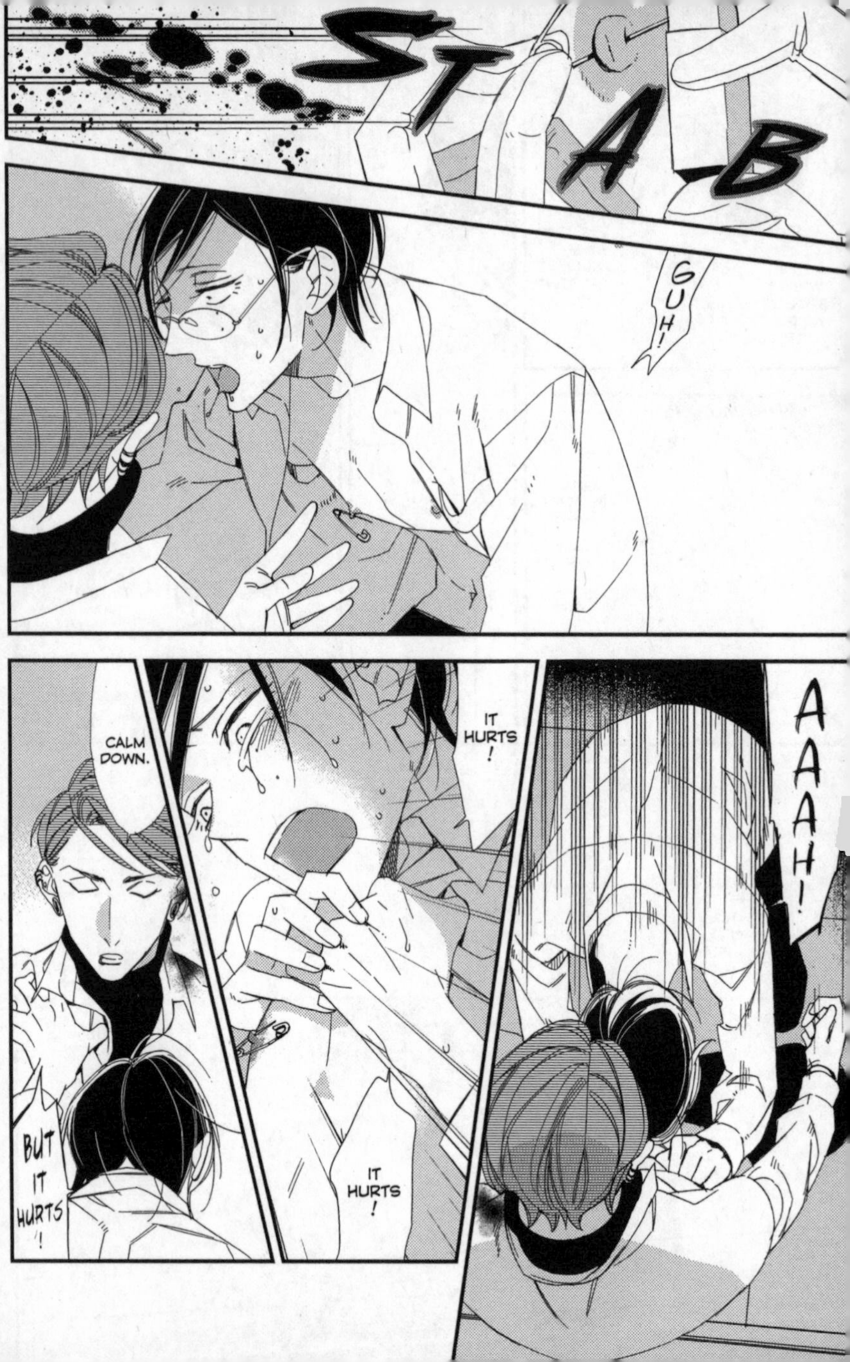
STAB
GUH!
AAAAH!
IT HURTS!
IT HURTS!
CALM DOWN.
BUT IT HURTS!

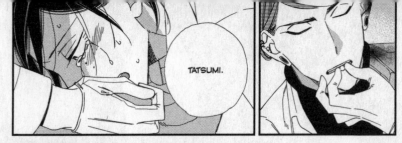

TATSUMI.

GULP

AH?

JUST A PAIN-KILLER.

IT'LL KICK IN SOON.

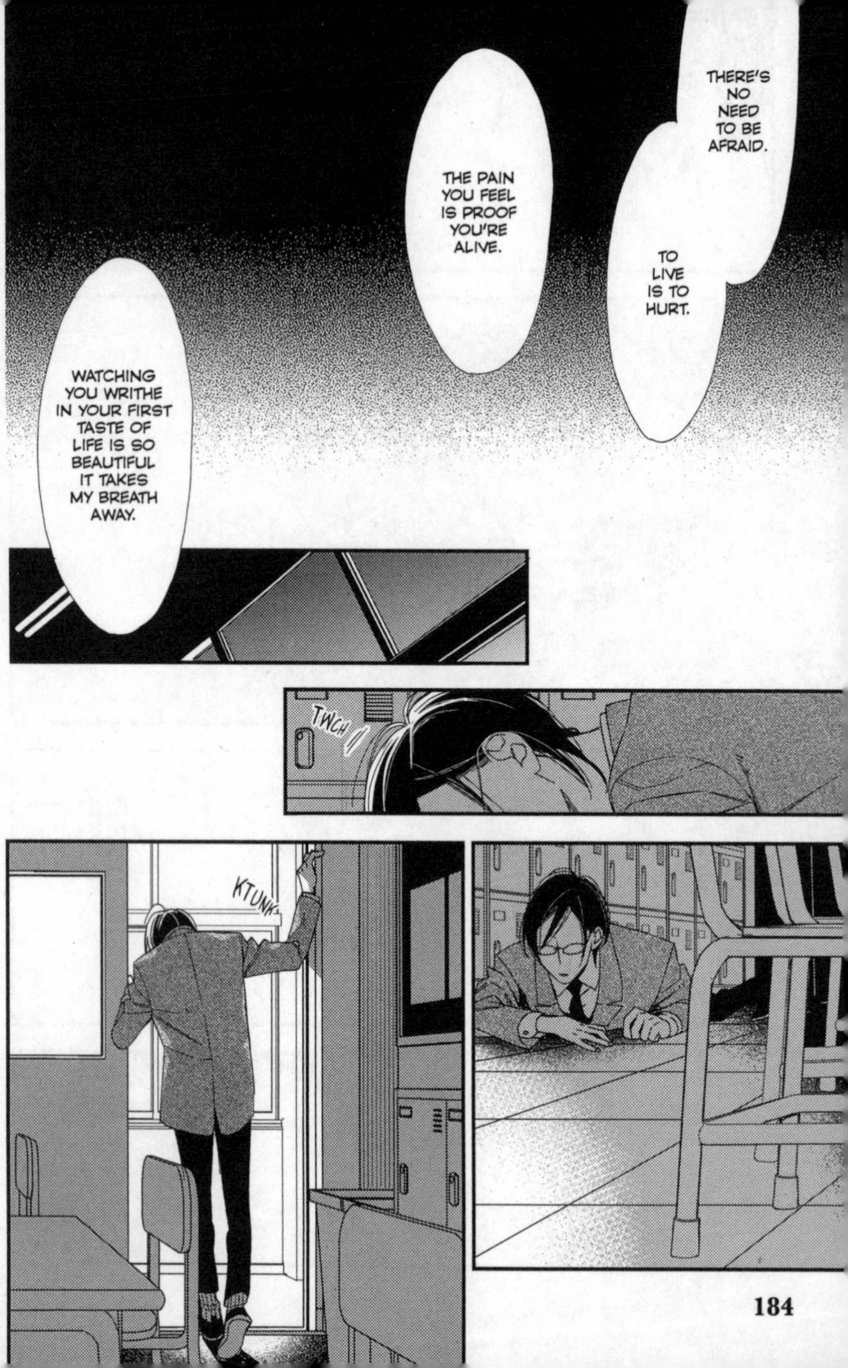
THERE'S NO NEED TO BE AFRAID.
TO LIVE IS TO HURT.
THE PAIN YOU FEEL IS PROOF YOU'RE ALIVE.
WATCHING YOU WRITHE IN YOUR FIRST TASTE OF LIFE IS SO BEAUTIFUL IT TAKES MY BREATH AWAY.
TWCH
KTUNK

YOICHIRO.

YOICHIRO?

BTAM

MY, YOU'RE HOME AWFULLY LATE TODAY.

THROB

THROB

WAS IT A DREAM?

THROB

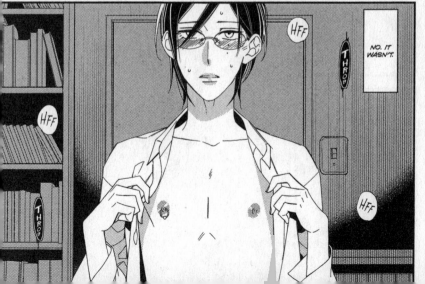

HFF

THROB

NO. IT WASN'T.

HFF

HFF

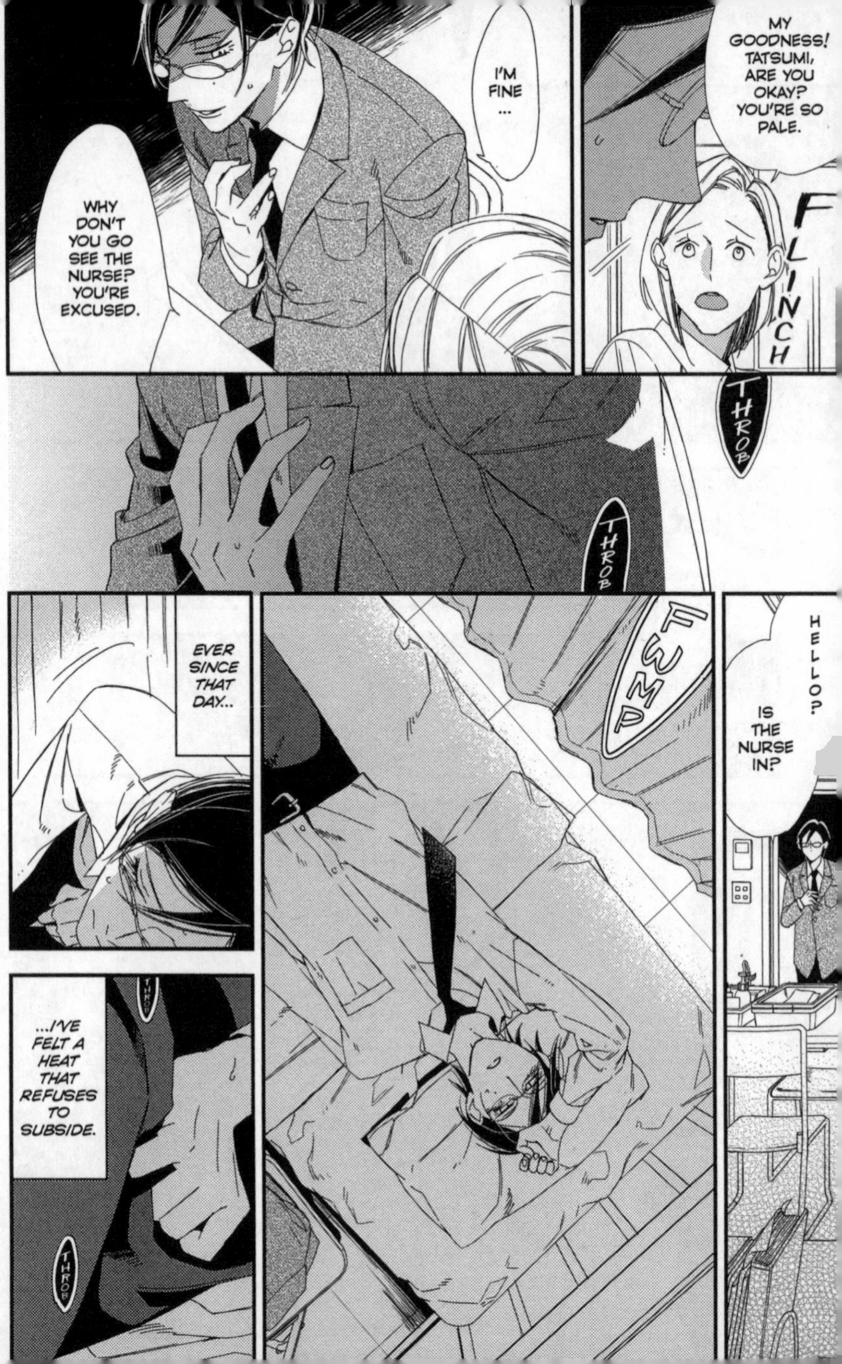
MY GOODNESS! TATSUMI, ARE YOU OKAY? YOU'RE SO PALE.
FLINCH
I'M FINE ...
WHY DON'T YOU GO SEE THE NURSE? YOU'RE EXCUSED.
THROB
THROB
HELLO?
IS THE NURSE IN?
FWMP
EVER SINCE THAT DAY...
...I'VE FELT A HEAT THAT REFUSES TO SUBSIDE.
THROB

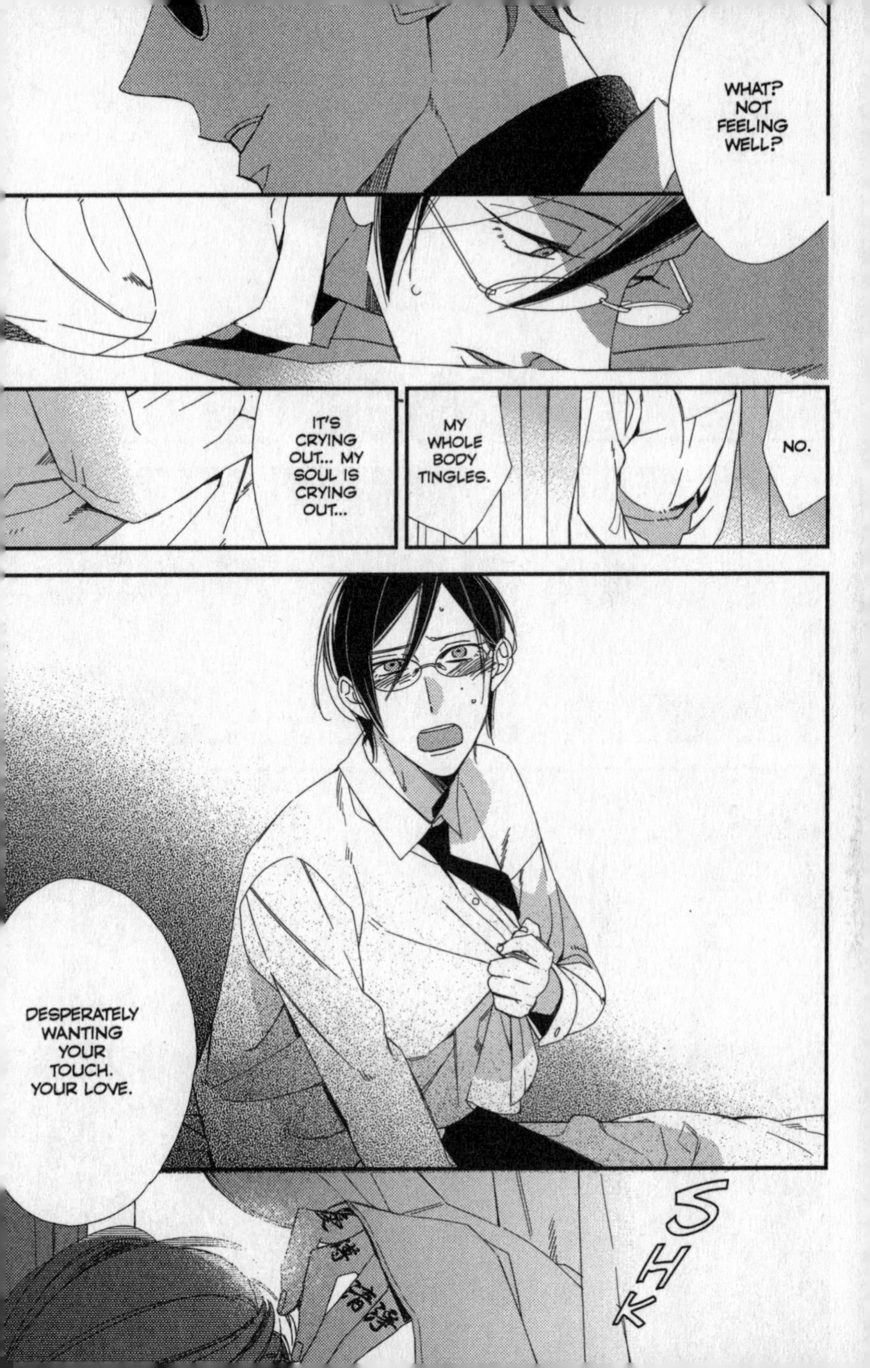
WHAT? NOT FEELING WELL?
NO.
MY WHOLE BODY TINGLES.
IT'S CRYING OUT... MY SOUL IS CRYING OUT...
DESPERATELY WANTING YOUR TOUCH. YOUR LOVE.
SHK

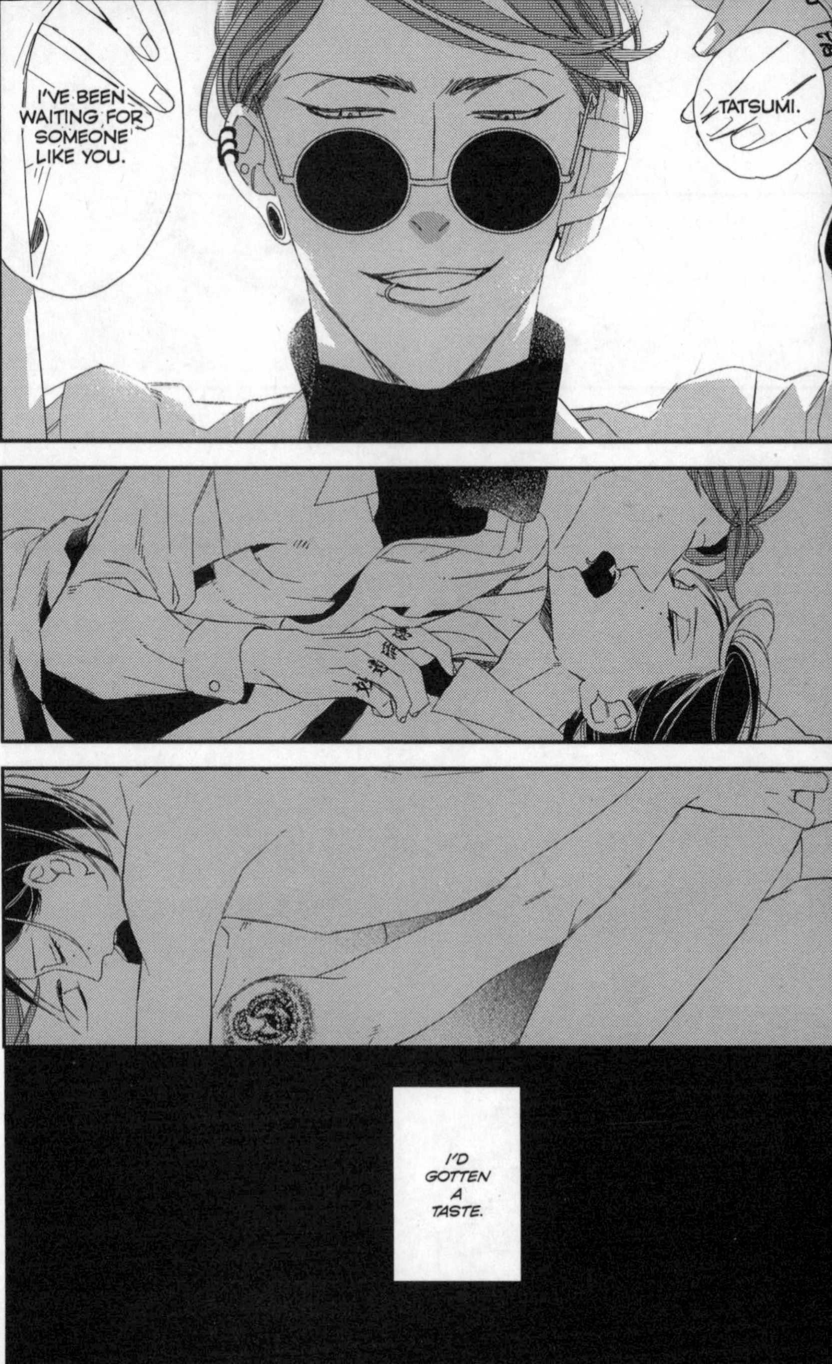
TATSUMI.
I'VE BEEN WAITING FOR SOMEONE LIKE YOU.
I'D GOTTEN A TASTE.

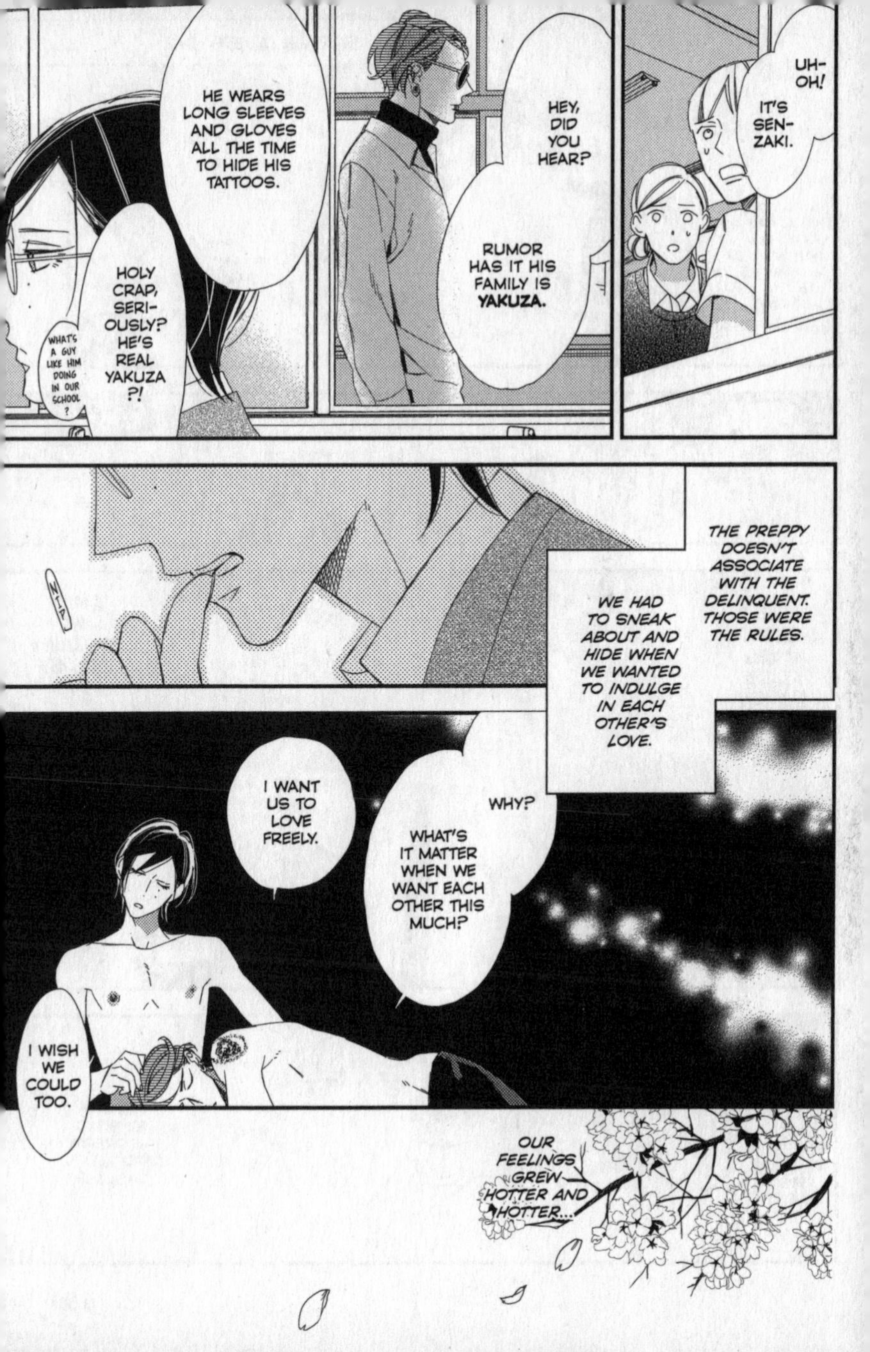
UH-OH!
IT'S SEN-ZAKI.
HEY, DID YOU HEAR?
RUMOR HAS IT HIS FAMILY IS **YAKUZA.**
HE WEARS LONG SLEEVES AND GLOVES ALL THE TIME TO HIDE HIS TATTOOS.
HOLY CRAP, SERIOUSLY? HE'S REAL YAKUZA?!
WHAT'S A GUY LIKE HIM DOING IN OUR SCHOOL?
THE PREPPY DOESN'T ASSOCIATE WITH THE DELINQUENT. THOSE WERE THE RULES.
WE HAD TO SNEAK ABOUT AND HIDE WHEN WE WANTED TO INDULGE IN EACH OTHER'S LOVE.
NIP
WHY?
WHAT'S IT MATTER WHEN WE WANT EACH OTHER THIS MUCH?
I WANT US TO LOVE FREELY.
I WISH WE COULD TOO.
OUR FEELINGS GREW HOTTER AND HOTTER...

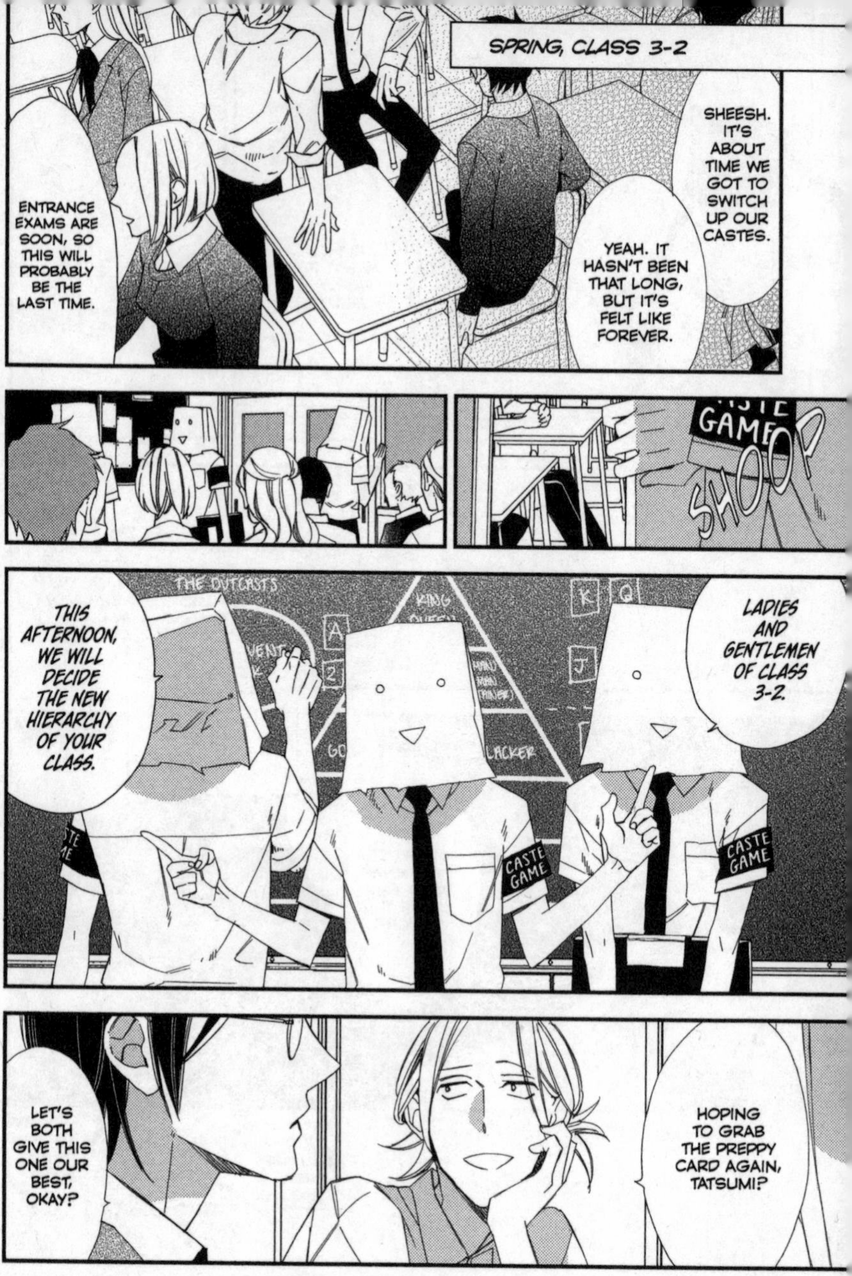
SPRING, CLASS 3-2
SHEESH. IT'S ABOUT TIME WE GOT TO SWITCH UP OUR CASTES.
YEAH. IT HASN'T BEEN THAT LONG, BUT IT'S FELT LIKE FOREVER.
ENTRANCE EXAMS ARE SOON, SO THIS WILL PROBABLY BE THE LAST TIME.
CASTE GAME
SHOOP
LADIES AND GENTLEMEN OF CLASS 3-2.
THIS AFTERNOON, WE WILL DECIDE THE NEW HIERARCHY OF YOUR CLASS.
THE OUTCASTS
KING
SLACKER
CASTE GAME
CASTE GAME
HOPING TO GRAB THE PREPPY CARD AGAIN, TATSUMI?
LET'S BOTH GIVE THIS ONE OUR BEST, OKAY?

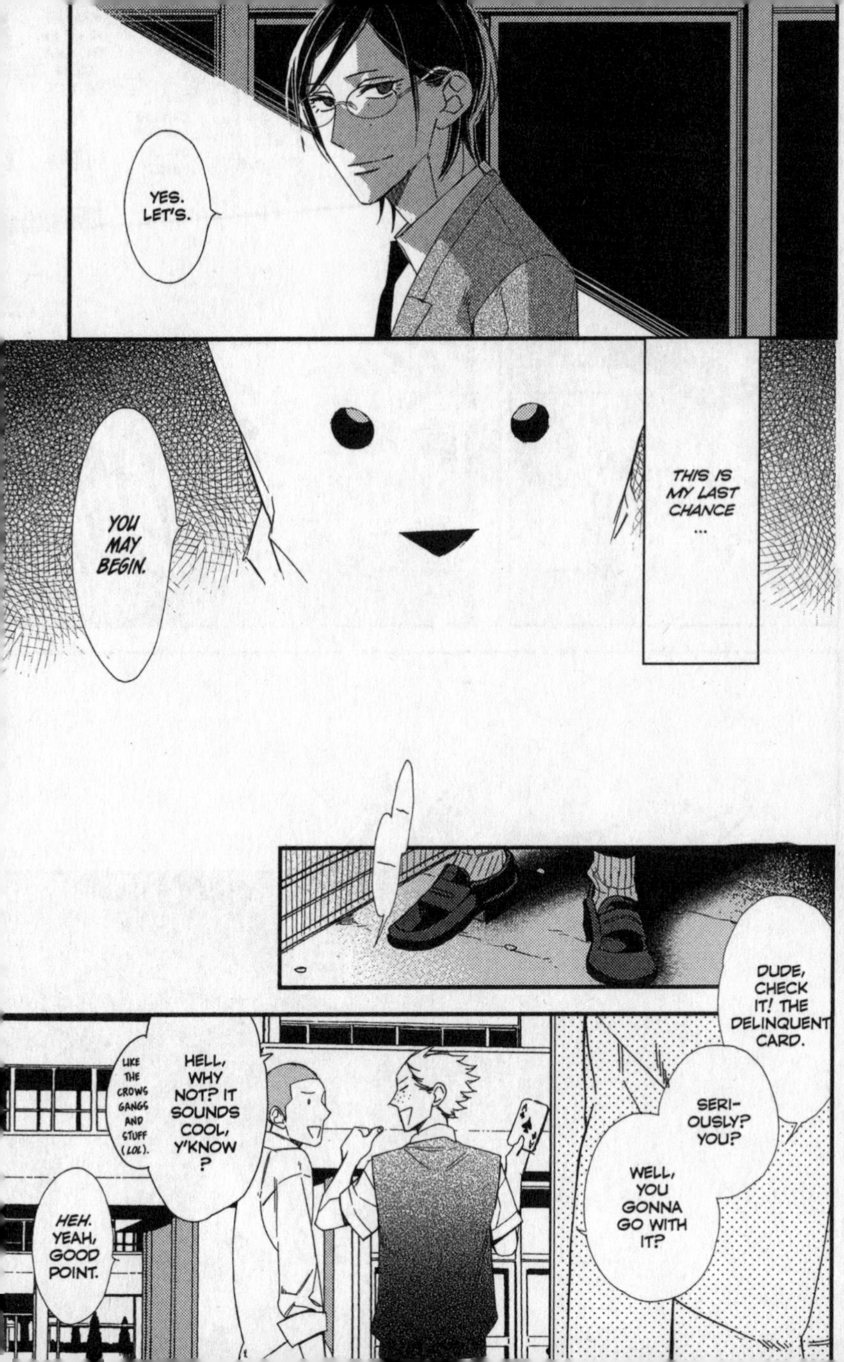
YES. LET'S.
THIS IS MY LAST CHANCE ...
YOU MAY BEGIN.
DUDE, CHECK IT! THE DELINQUENT CARD.
SERI-OUSLY? YOU?
WELL, YOU GONNA GO WITH IT?
HELL, WHY NOT? IT SOUNDS COOL, Y'KNOW?
LIKE THE CROWS GANGS AND STUFF (LOL).
HEH. YEAH, GOOD POINT.

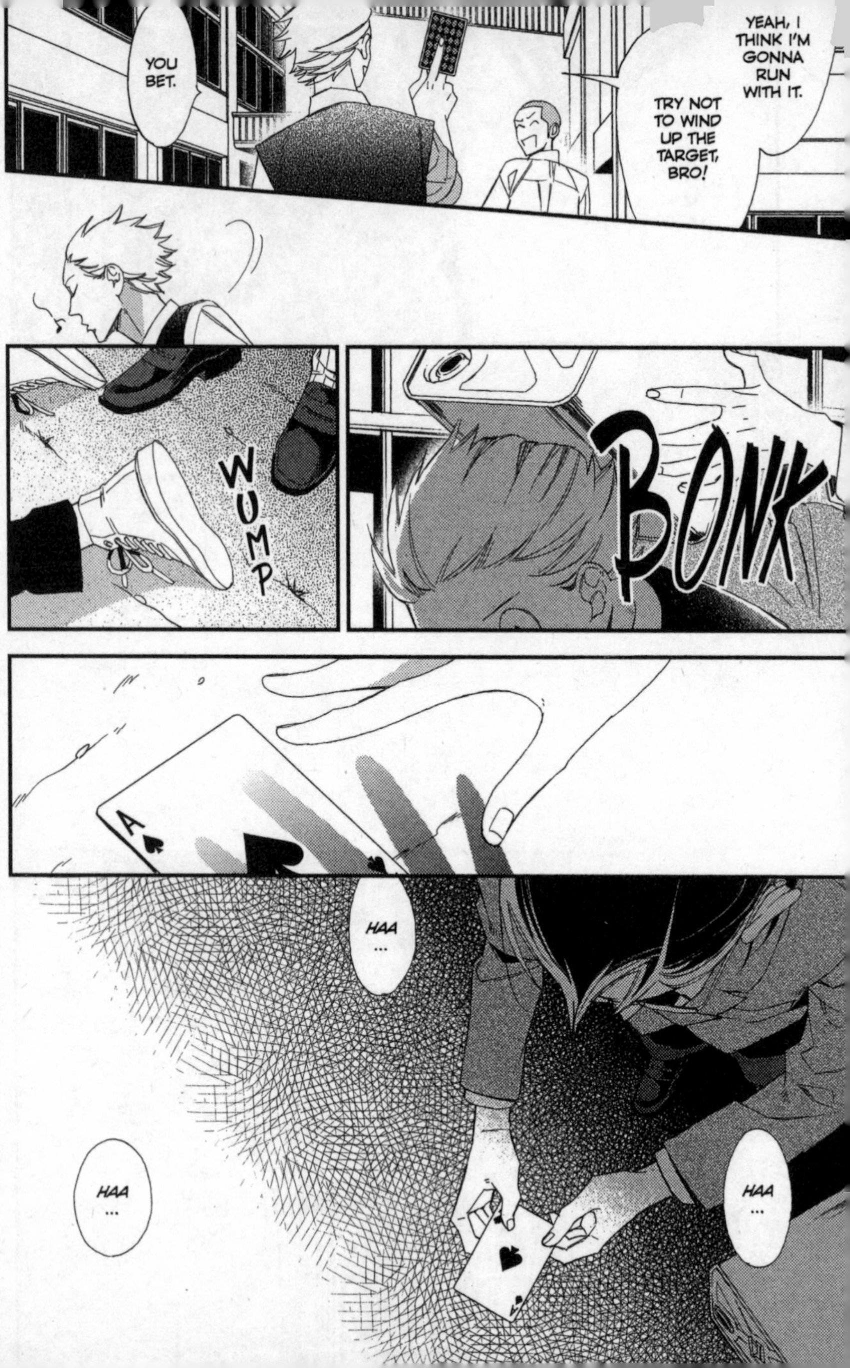
YEAH, I THINK I'M GONNA RUN WITH IT.
TRY NOT TO WIND UP THE TARGET, BRO!
YOU BET.
BONK
WUMP
A
HAA ...
HAA ...
HAA ...

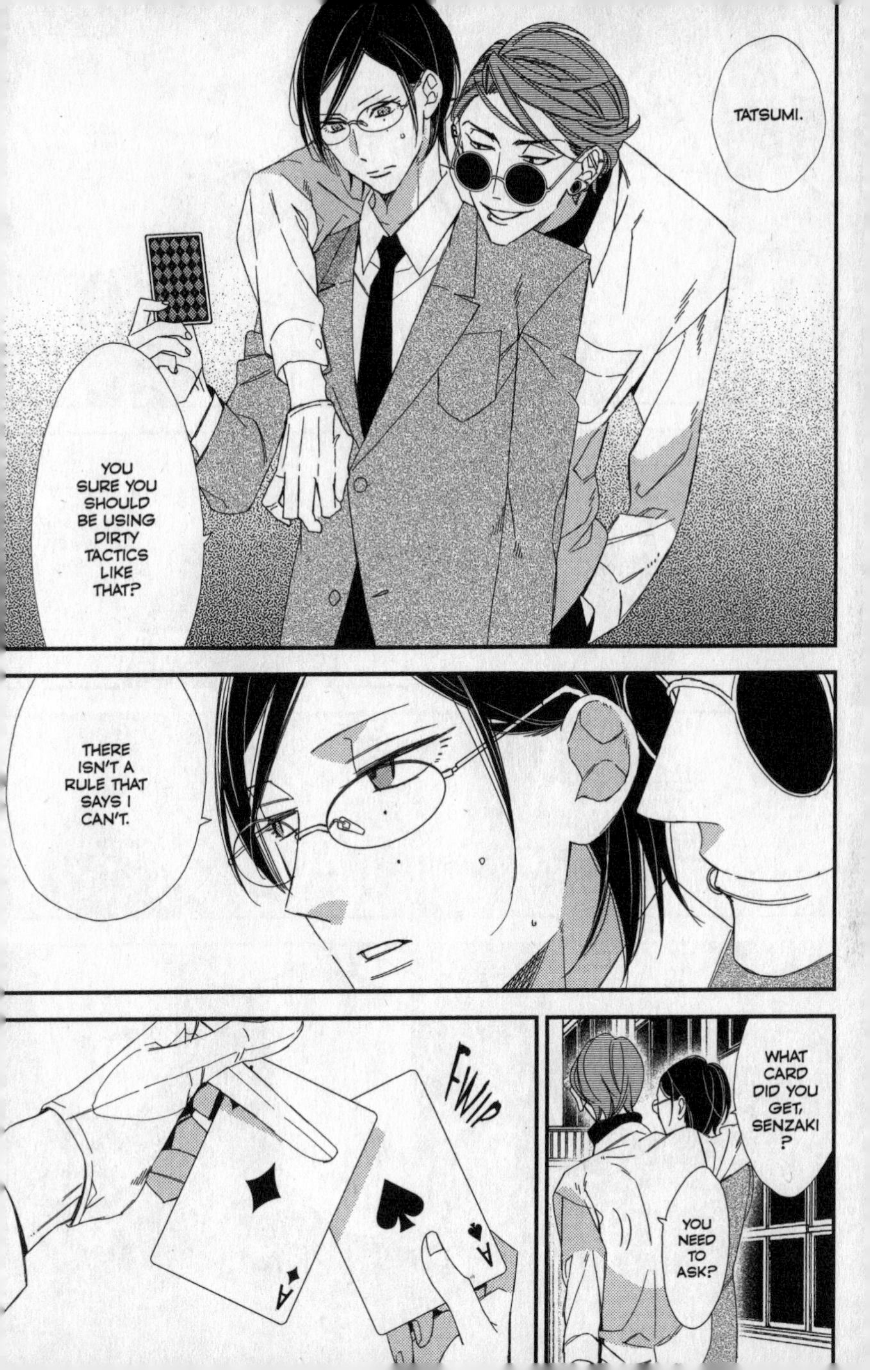
TATSUMI.
YOU SURE YOU SHOULD BE USING DIRTY TACTICS LIKE THAT?
THERE ISN'T A RULE THAT SAYS I CAN'T.
WHAT CARD DID YOU GET, SENZAKI?
YOU NEED TO ASK?
FWIP

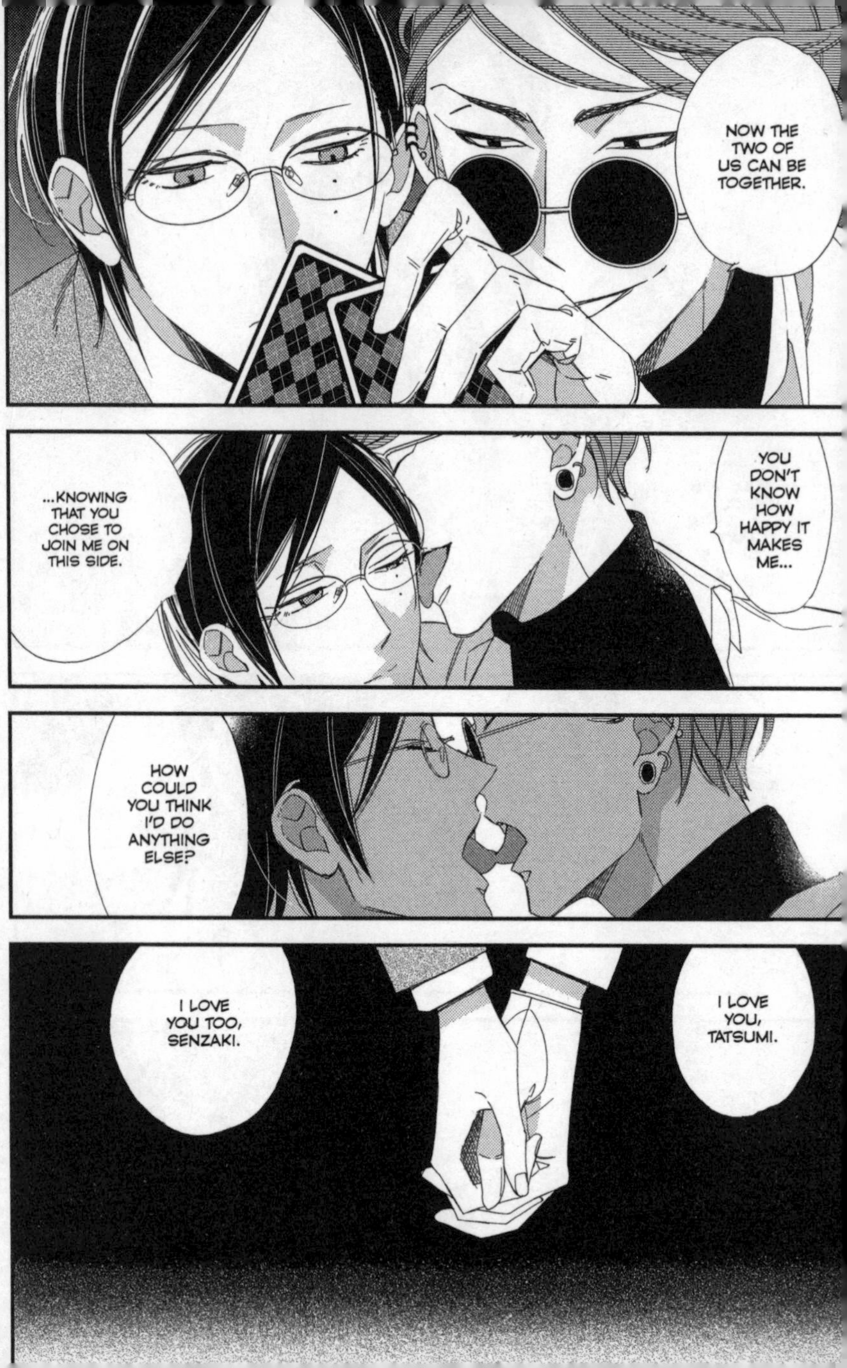
NOW THE TWO OF US CAN BE TOGETHER.
YOU DON'T KNOW HOW HAPPY IT MAKES ME...
...KNOWING THAT YOU CHOSE TO JOIN ME ON THIS SIDE.
HOW COULD YOU THINK I'D DO ANYTHING ELSE?
I LOVE YOU, TATSUMI.
I LOVE YOU TOO, SENZAKI.

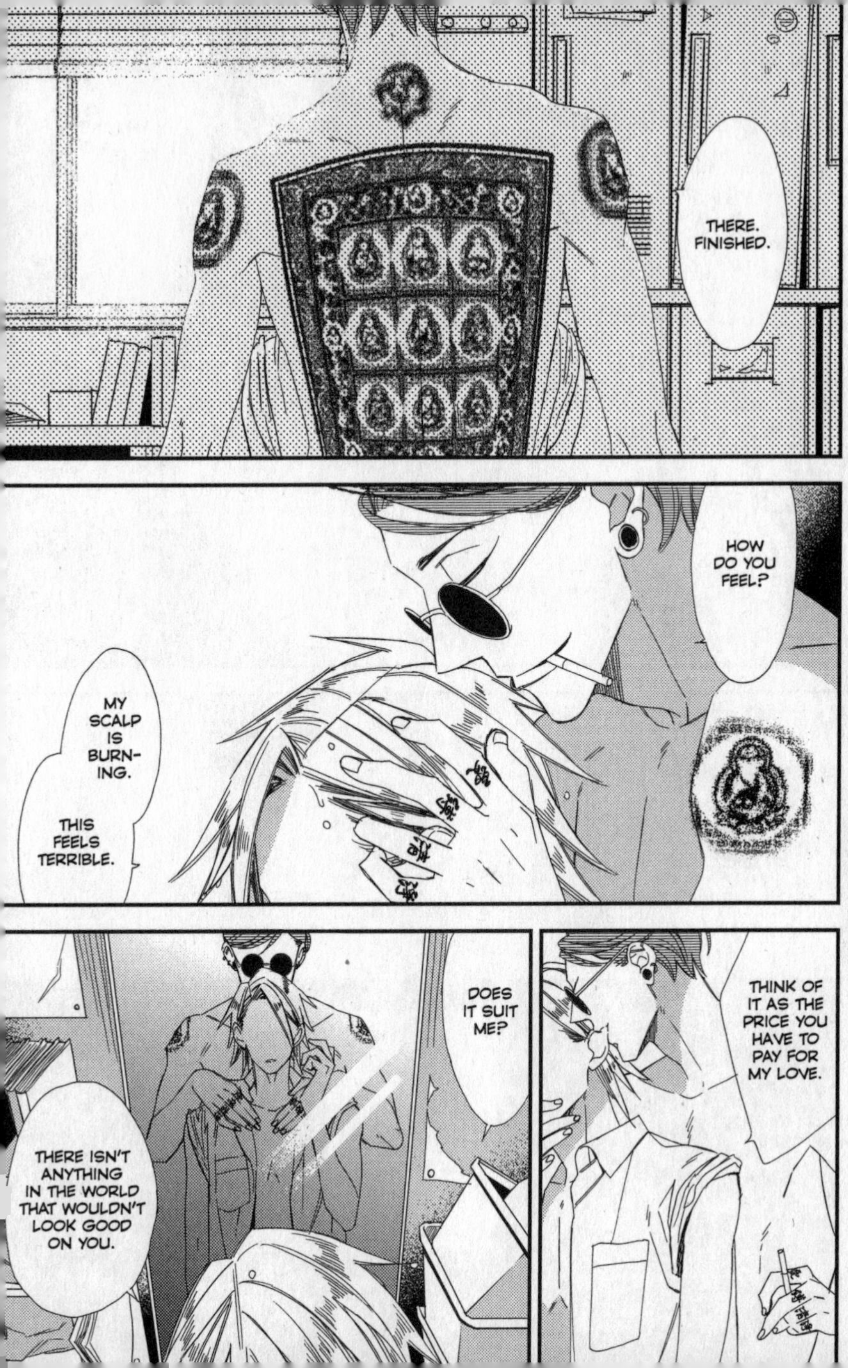
THERE. FINISHED.
HOW DO YOU FEEL?
MY SCALP IS BURN-ING.
THIS FEELS TERRIBLE.
THINK OF IT AS THE PRICE YOU HAVE TO PAY FOR MY LOVE.
DOES IT SUIT ME?
THERE ISN'T ANYTHING IN THE WORLD THAT WOULDN'T LOOK GOOD ON YOU.

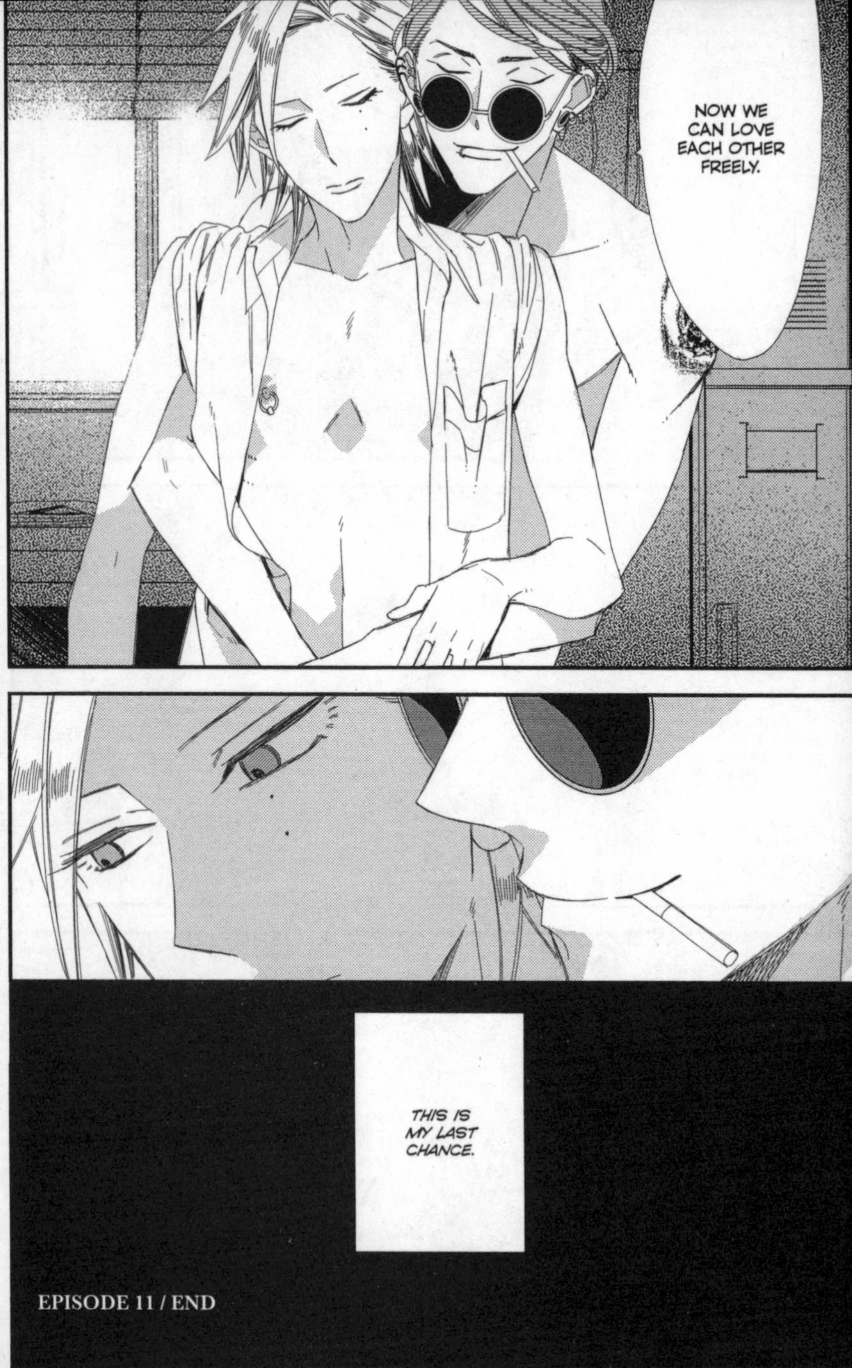
NOW WE CAN LOVE EACH OTHER FREELY.
THIS IS MY LAST CHANCE.
EPISODE 11 / END

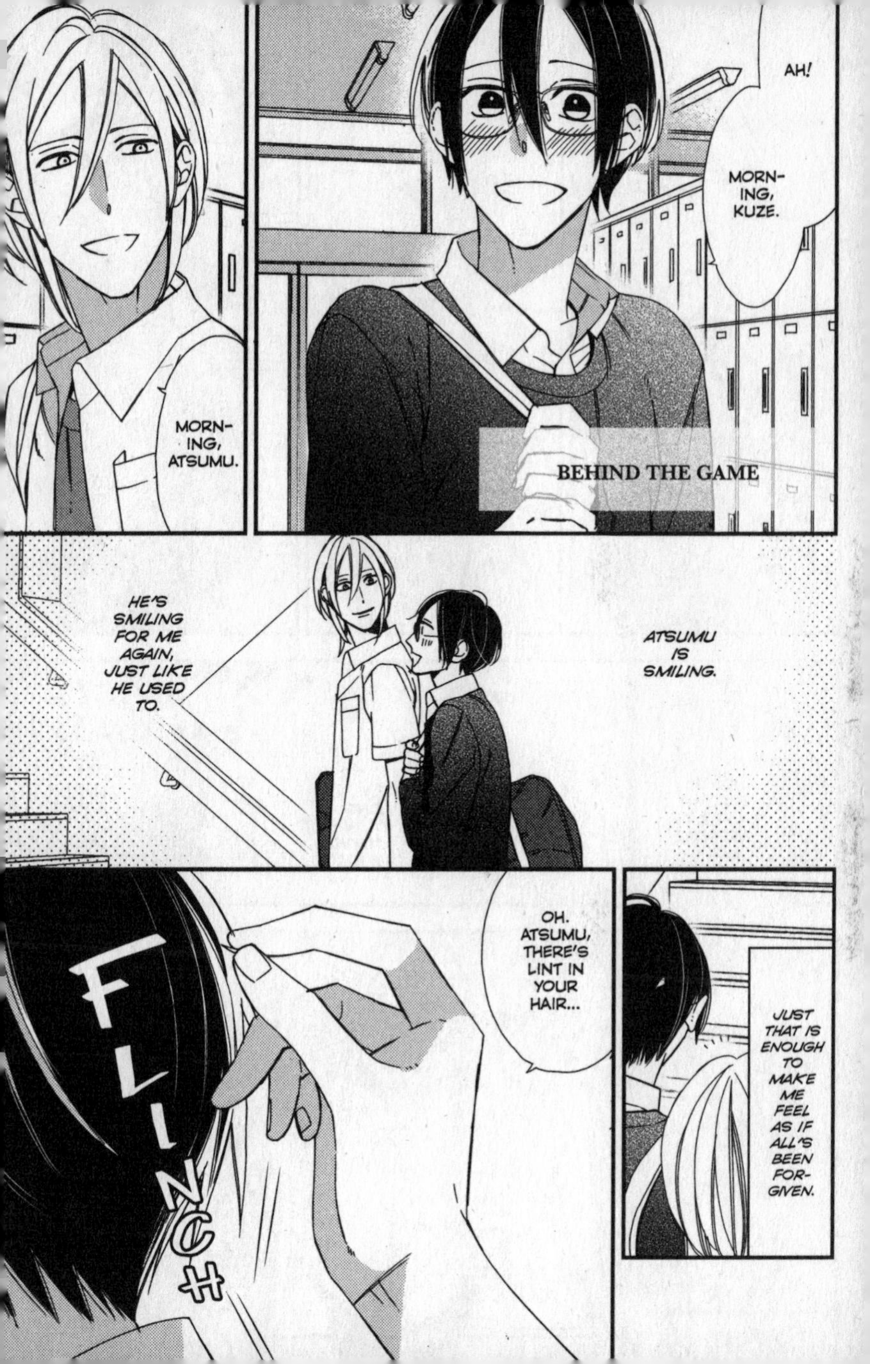
AH!
MORN-ING, KUZE.
BEHIND THE GAME
MORN-ING, ATSUMU.
ATSUMU IS SMILING.
HE'S SMILING FOR ME AGAIN, JUST LIKE HE USED TO.
JUST THAT IS ENOUGH TO MAKE ME FEEL AS IF ALL'S BEEN FOR-GIVEN.
OH. ATSUMU, THERE'S LINT IN YOUR HAIR...
FLINCH

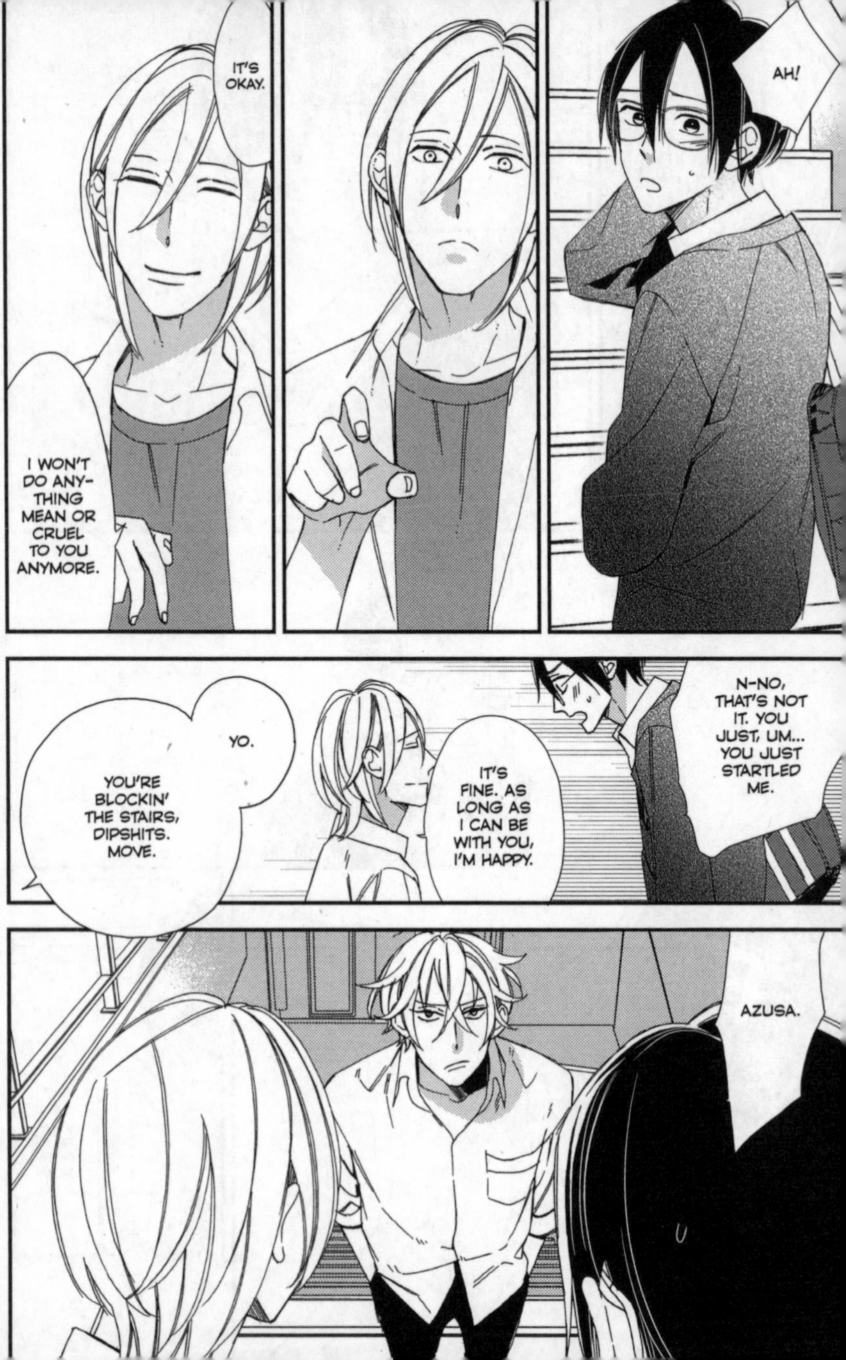
AH!
IT'S OKAY.
I WON'T DO ANY-THING MEAN OR CRUEL TO YOU ANYMORE.
N-NO, THAT'S NOT IT. YOU JUST, UM... YOU JUST STARTLED ME.
IT'S FINE. AS LONG AS I CAN BE WITH YOU, I'M HAPPY.
YO.
YOU'RE BLOCKIN' THE STAIRS, DIPSHITS. MOVE.
AZUSA.

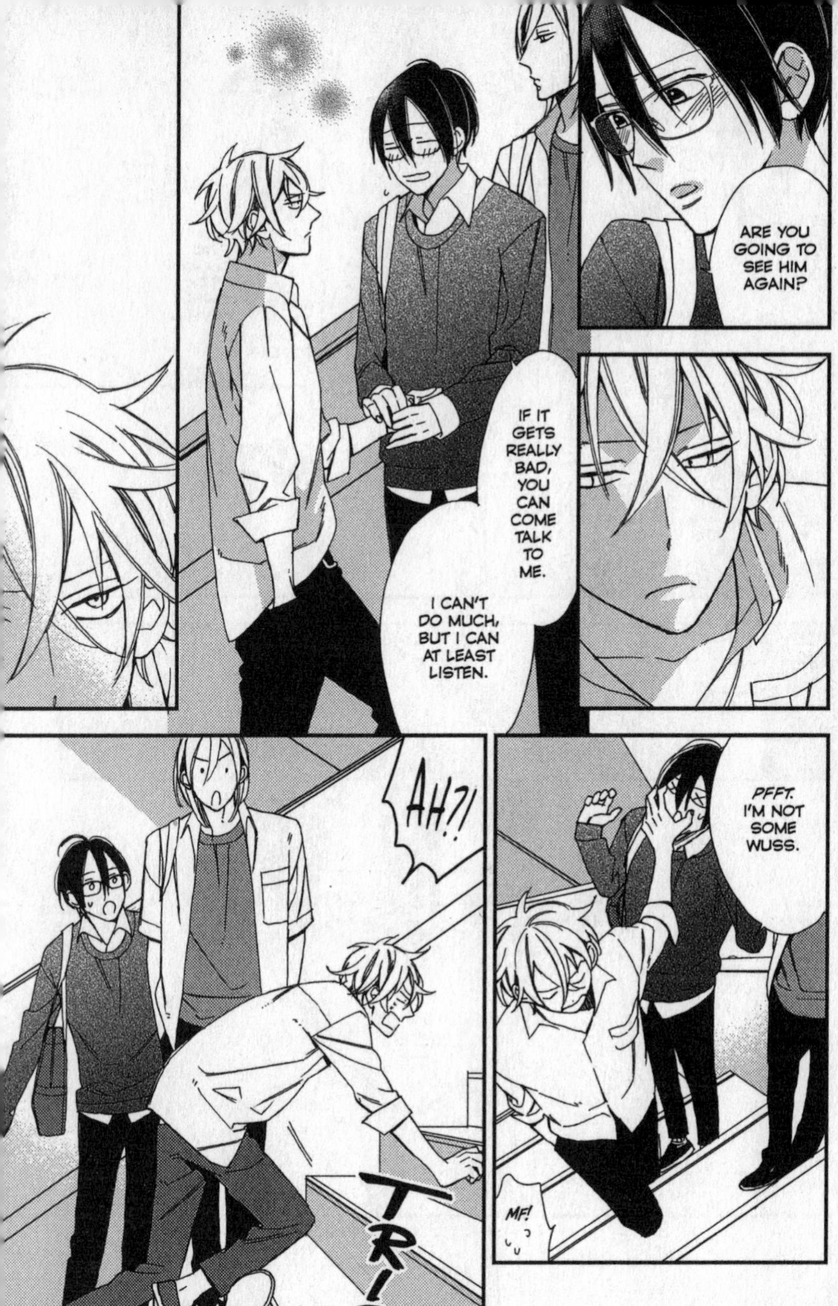
ARE YOU GOING TO SEE HIM AGAIN?
IF IT GETS REALLY BAD, YOU CAN COME TALK TO ME.
I CAN'T DO MUCH, BUT I CAN AT LEAST LISTEN.
PFFT. I'M NOT SOME WUSS.
MF!
AH?!
TRIP

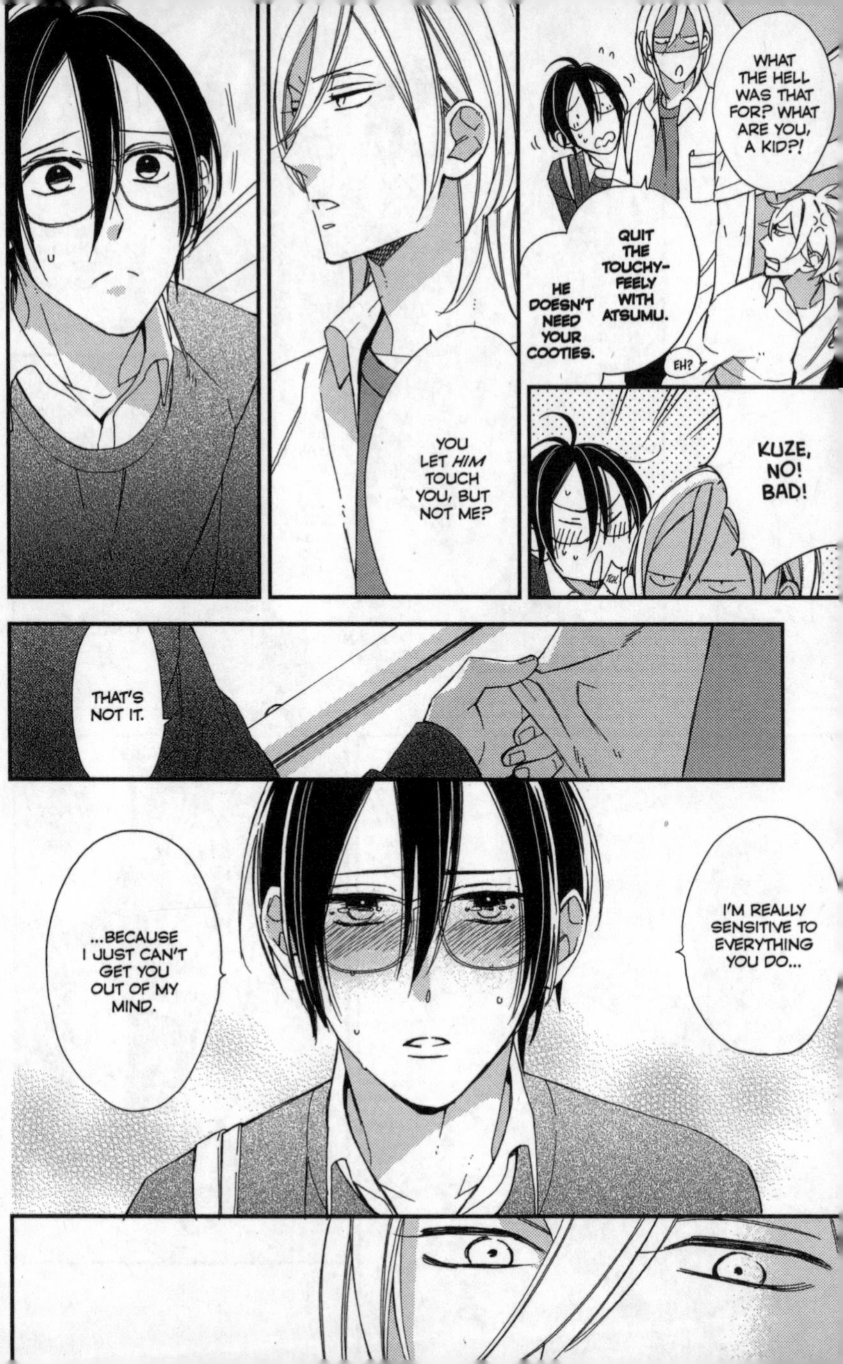
WHAT THE HELL WAS THAT FOR? WHAT ARE YOU, A KID?!
QUIT THE TOUCHY-FEELY WITH ATSUMU.
HE DOESN'T NEED YOUR COOTIES.
EH?
KUZE, NO! BAD!
YOU LET *HIM* TOUCH YOU, BUT NOT ME?
THAT'S NOT IT.
I'M REALLY SENSITIVE TO EVERYTHING YOU DO...
...BECAUSE I JUST CAN'T GET YOU OUT OF MY MIND.

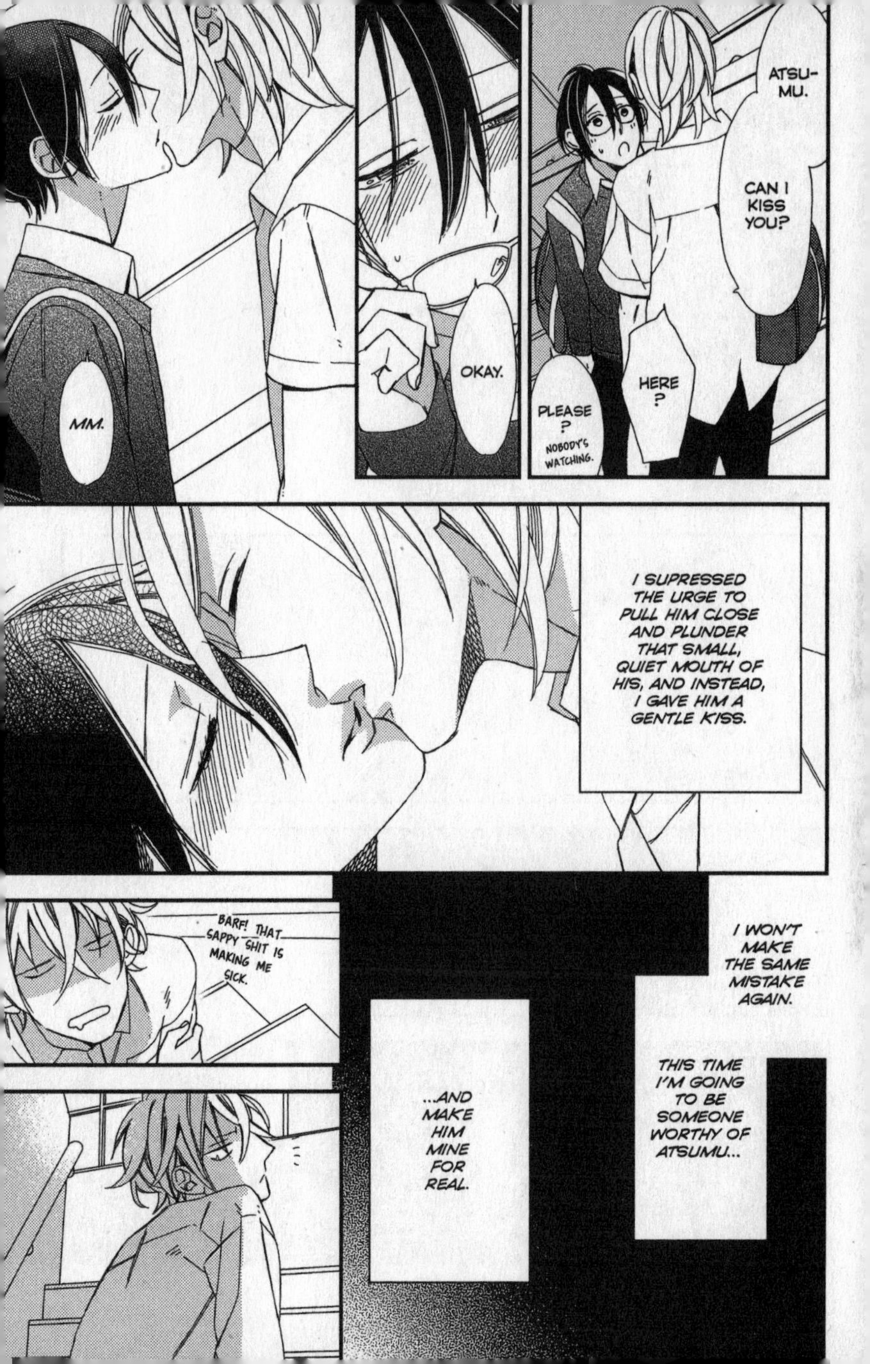
ATSU-MU.
CAN I KISS YOU?
HERE?
PLEASE? NOBODY'S WATCHING.
OKAY.
MM.
I SUPRESSED THE URGE TO PULL HIM CLOSE AND PLUNDER THAT SMALL, QUIET MOUTH OF HIS, AND INSTEAD, I GAVE HIM A GENTLE KISS.
I WON'T MAKE THE SAME MISTAKE AGAIN.
THIS TIME I'M GOING TO BE SOMEONE WORTHY OF ATSUMU...
...AND MAKE HIM MINE FOR REAL.
BARF! THAT SAPPY SHIT IS MAKING ME SICK.

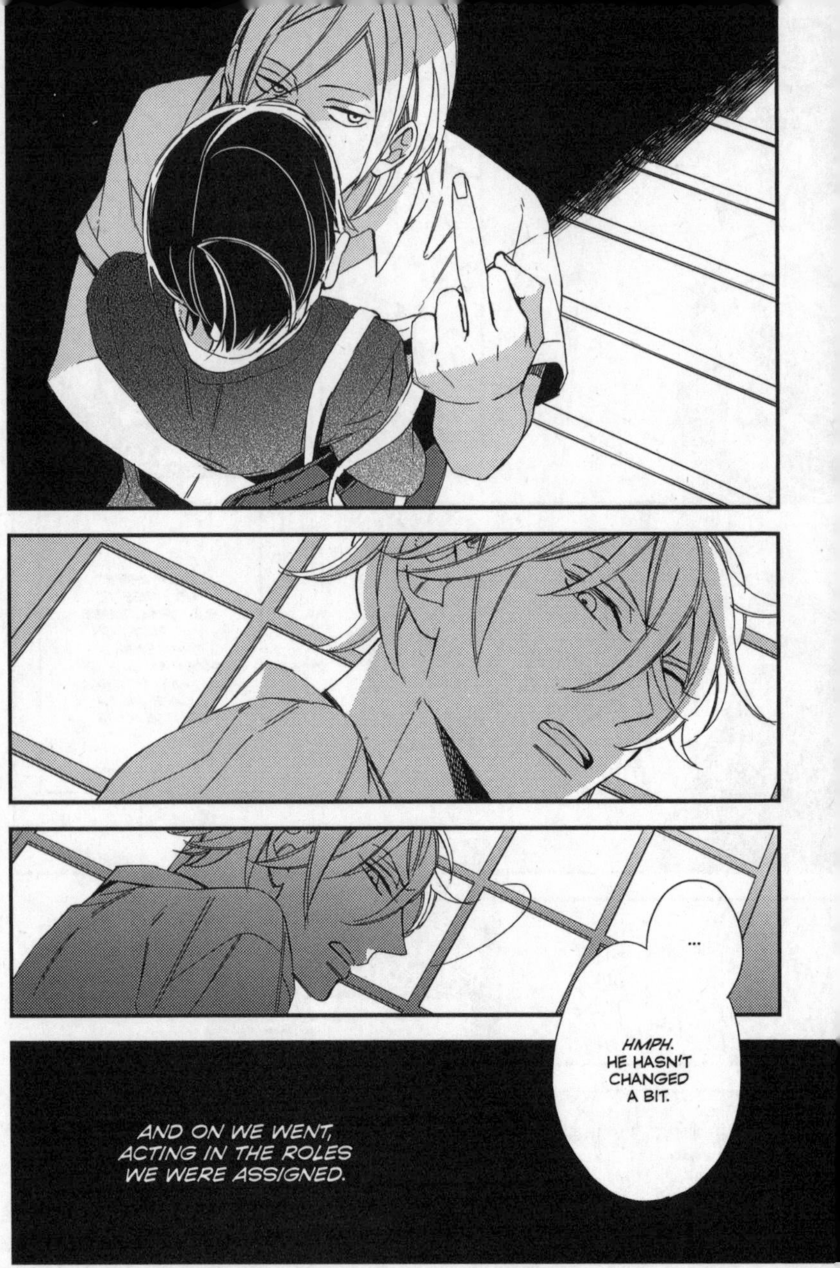
...
HMPH. HE HASN'T CHANGED A BIT.
AND ON WE WENT, ACTING IN THE ROLES WE WERE ASSIGNED.

END

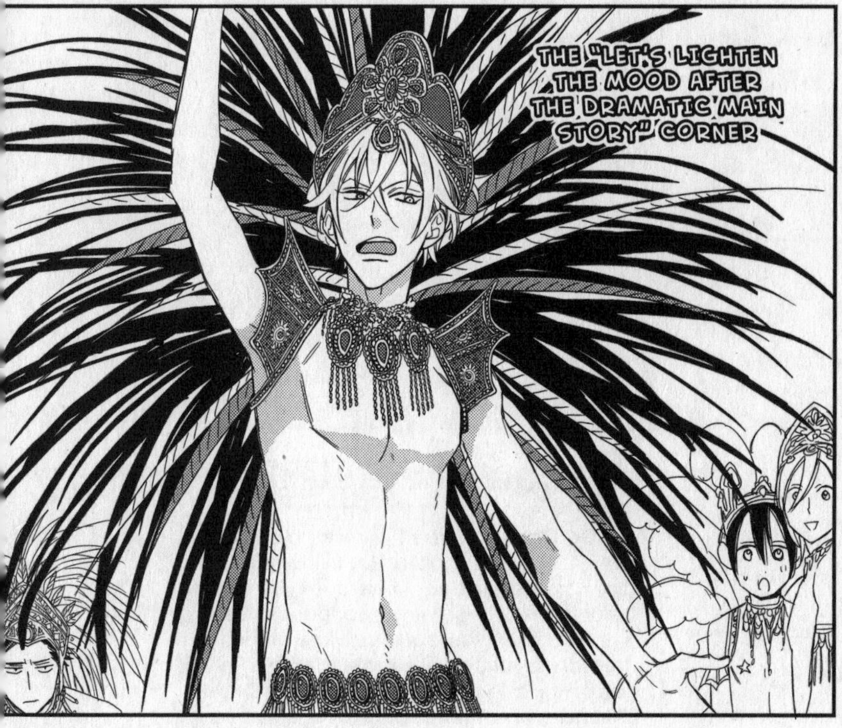
THE "LET'S LIGHTEN THE MOOD AFTER THE DRAMATIC MAIN STORY" CORNER

HELLO. THANK YOU FOR PURCHASING VOLUME 2 OF *CASTE HEAVEN*. DUE TO PAGE CONSTRAINTS, I HAD TO CHANGE SOME THINGS WHEN CHAPTER 8 FIRST RAN IN THE MAGAZINE. I'VE TAKEN THE LIBERTY OF REVISING PARTS OF THAT CHAPTER FOR THIS VOLUME.

I'M AWARE THAT *CASTE HEAVEN* ISN'T A SERIES THAT WILL BE LOVED BY EVERYONE. TO THOSE READERS WHO DO STILL LIKE IT, THOSE WHO SAY THEY AREN'T FOND OF IT BUT STILL READ IT, THOSE WHO SAY THEY DON'T READ IT BUT THEY READ MY OTHER SERIES, AND MANY OTHERS... THANK YOU VERY MUCH. I'D BE HONORED IF YOU ALL CONTINUED TO CONNECT WITH MY HUMBLE WORKS IN WHATEVER WAYS SUIT YOU BEST.

2016.5. 緒川千世

CHISE OGAWA

About the Author

Chise Ogawa made her manga debut with *Ouji no Hakoniwa*. Her beautiful art style captivates readers, as does her wide storytelling range—from serious stories that explore the dark recesses of the human psyche to character-driven rom-coms. You can find out more about Chise Ogawa on her Twitter page, **@ogawaccc**.

Caste Heaven
Volume 2
SuBLime Manga Edition

Story and Art by **Chise Ogawa**

Translation—**Adrienne Beck**
Touch-Up Art and Lettering—**Eve Grandt**
Cover and Graphic Design—**Shawn Carrico**
Editor—**Jennifer LeBlanc**

Caste Heaven 2 © 2016 Chise Ogawa
Original Cover Design: UCHIKAWADESIGN
Originally published in Japan in 2016 by Libre Inc.
English translation rights arranged with Libre Inc.

libre

Printed in the U.S.A.

Published by SuBLime Manga
P.O. Box 77010
San Francisco, CA 94107

10 9 8 7 6 5 4 3 2 1
First printing, June 2020

PARENTAL ADVISORY
CASTE HEAVEN is rated M for Mature and is recommended for mature readers. This volume
MATURE   contains graphic imagery and mature themes.

www.SuBLimeManga.com

For more information

on all our products, along with the most up-to-date news on releases, series announcements, and contests, please visit us at:

 SuBLimeManga.com

 twitter.com/**SuBLimeManga**

 facebook.com/**SuBLimeManga**

 instagram.com/**SuBLimeManga**

 SuBLimeManga.tumblr.com

Finder

DELUXE EDITION

PAIN AND PLEASURE COLLIDE when a sophisticated underworld boss crosses paths with a naive photographer hell-bent on bringing him down!

STORY AND ART BY
AYANO YAMANE

This deluxe edition includes never-before-released material as well as a double-sided color insert and special cover treatment!

Photographer Akihito Takaba takes on a risky assignment trying to document the illegal activities of the Japanese underworld. When he captures its leader—the handsome, enigmatic Ryuichi Asami—in the cross-hairs of his viewfinder, Takaba's world is changed forever.

When a playboy falls for a nerd,
chemistry results in an explosive reaction!

Don't Be Cruel

Story and Art by **Yonezou Nekota**

Playboy Maya catches studious Nemugasa
cheating on a test, and to ensure his silence,
Maya blackmails Nemugasa into doing whatever
he wants! But is this merely just a ruse so Maya
can spend more alone time with him?

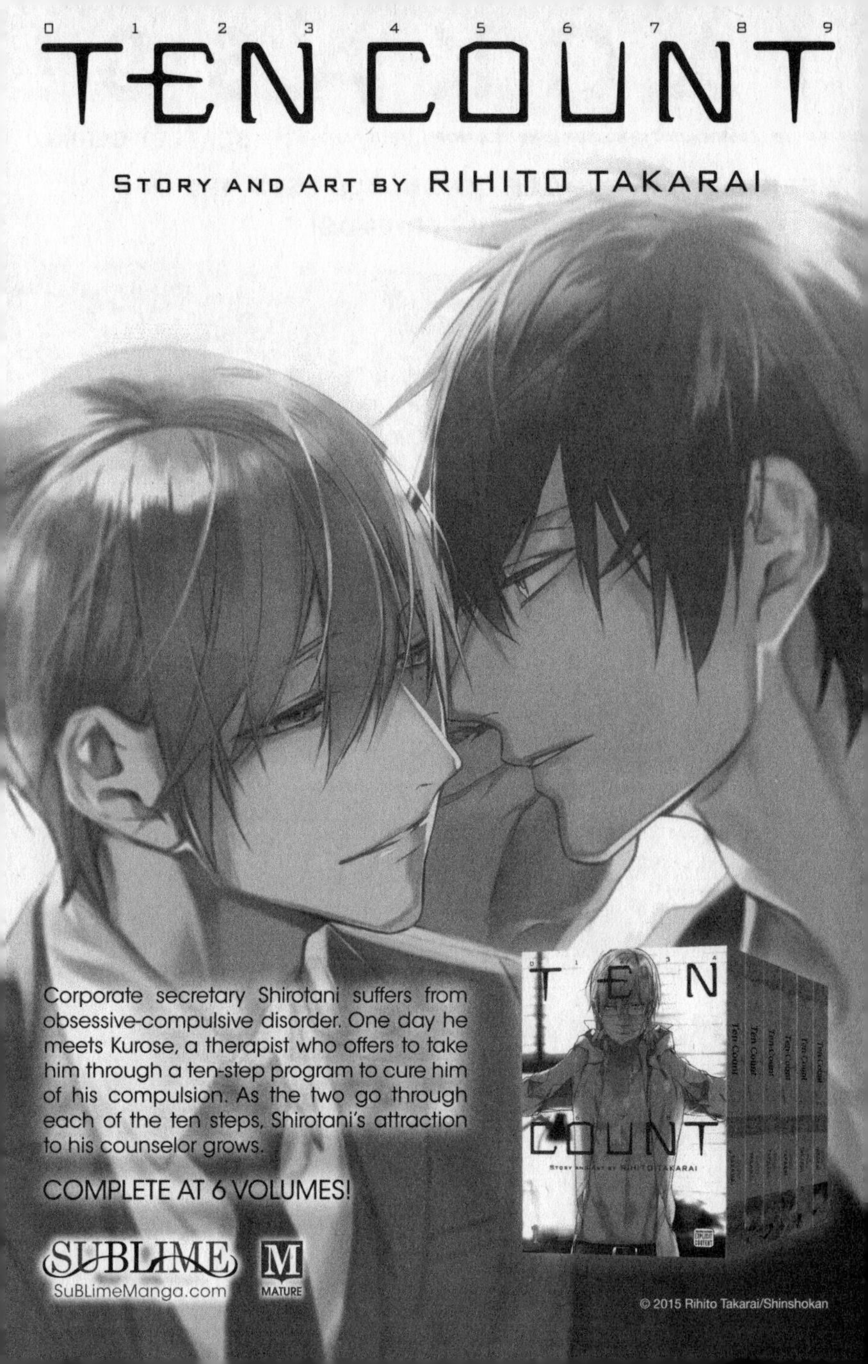
0 1 2 3 4 5 6 7 8 9
TEN COUNT
STORY AND ART BY RIHITO TAKARAI
Corporate secretary Shirotani suffers from obsessive-compulsive disorder. One day he meets Kurose, a therapist who offers to take him through a ten-step program to cure him of his compulsion. As the two go through each of the ten steps, Shirotani's attraction to his counselor grows.
COMPLETE AT 6 VOLUMES!
SUBLIME
SuBLimeManga.com
M
MATURE
© 2015 Rihito Takarai/Shinshokan

J A C K A S S !

STORY AND ART BY **SCARLET BERIKO**

WHEN THE PANTY HOSE GO ON, ALL BETS ARE OFF BETWEEN THESE BEST GUY FRIENDS!

Practical Keisuke's incredibly handsome best friend Masayuki has always rubbed him just a little bit the wrong way. Maybe it's because Masayuki is rich, carefree, and so stunningly handsome that he can, and does, have any girl he wants? But one day, when Keisuke accidentally wears his older sister's panty hose to gym class, it's suddenly his hot friend who's doing the rubbing... on Keisuke's panty hose-clad legs! Has he unwittingly unleashed a secret fetish that will change their relationship forever?